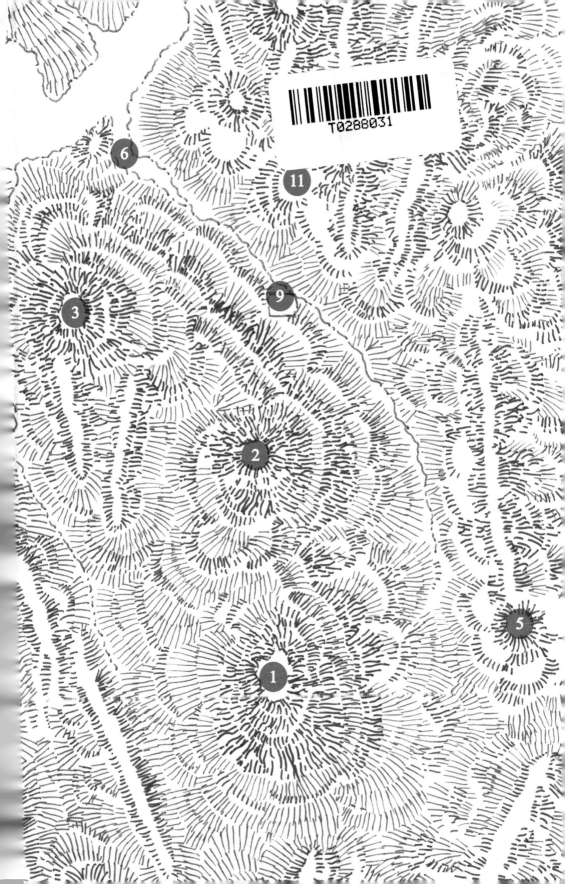

MOUNT SINAI

MOUNT SINAI

A History of Travellers and Pilgrims

George Manginis

First published in 2016 by
HAUS PUBLISHING LTD
70 Cadogan Place
London SW1X 9AH
www.hauspublishing.com

The moral right of the author has been asserted

A CIP catalogue record for this book is available from the British Library

ISBN: 978-1-910376-50-8
eISBN: 978-1-910376-51-5

Maps on endpapers by Fiorella Modolo
www.fiorellamodolo.com

Frontispiece. *Looking East from Râs Sufsâfeh, Sinai. In the small illustration is represented the summit of Jebel Músa, with the chapel and the less conspicuous mosque.* Wood engraving on paper.

Typeset in Times by MacGuru Ltd

Printed in the Czech Republic via Akcent Media Limited

Contents

Acknowledgements

This book would not have existed without the invitation of Sophia Kalopissi-Verti and Maria Panayotidi-Kesisoglou to participate in the Jabal Mūsā excavation and without the offer of Ilse Schwepcke, Barbara Schwepcke and Harry Hall of Haus Publishing to distill fifteen years of research into these pages. Thanks are due to Geoffrey R.D. King for his support and to Robert Hillenbrand and Hugh Kennedy for their advice. My research was supported by the Greek Archaeological Committee, U.K. and especially Matti Egon. The Harold Hyam Wingate Foundation, London, the A.G. Leventis Foundation, Paris, and the Benevolent Fund of the Greek Cathedral of Saint Sophia, London, also contributed through grants.

Fellow excavators Nikolas Fyssas and Zeta Foukaneli and the brotherhood of the Monastery of Saint Catherine made my survival at Jabal Mūsā possible and indeed enjoyable. Particular gratitude should be extended to Fathers Daniel, Porphyrios, Symeon and Ioannis. Petros Koufopoulos introduced me to Sinai and I owe to him my communion with the place.

Emma Henderson edited the manuscript with rare patience and Fiorella Modolo contributed the maps for the endpapers. Friends and colleagues embraced my effort, among them Janet Anderson, Theonas Bakalis, Christos Bitzis-Politis, Inne Broos, Moya Carey, Philip Constantinidi, Hettie Elgood, Babis Floros, Melanie Gibson, Charlotte Horlyck, Nadania Idriss, Ira Kaliabetsos, Michael Lee, David Lilley and Glen Stuart, Mina Moraitou, Dionyssis Mourelatos, Charles Plante, Peggy Ringa, Salam Said, Maria Sardi, Jane Sconce, Nicholas Sikorski, Artemis Symvoulaki, Zetta Theodoropoulou and Antonis Polychroniadis, Tania Tribe, Giorgos Vavouranakis and Georgia Vossou. Finally, words of thanks are due to my mother Scarlata, late father Eustathios, sister Golfo and aunt Phrosso Tsakalaki.

Figure 1. David Roberts (British, 1796–1864), *The Monastery of St. Catherine*. Lithograph on paper. Based on drawings executed in February 1839.

Introduction

'But good heavens, man!' the Colonel suddenly exploded. 'That's all been done before! Every inch of it! Mount Sinai! Everybody's Mount Sinai!'

'Yes, sir!' I hastened. 'That's rather the point of it, in a way.'

'But what original ideas have you on the subject? Don't you see? Mustn't write a book like this without having original ideas!'

Louis Golding, *In the Steps of Moses the Lawgiver*, London 1938, viii–ix.

The 'Mount Sinai' about which a certain 'Colonel Smith' erupted while sitting at the dining room of the Bel Air hotel in Suez is a mountain peak towering above the Monastery of Saint Catherine in Egypt's peninsula of Sinai. The Greek name of the peak is Hagia Koryphē, the 'Holy Summit', and its Arabic name, Jabal Mūsā, 'Summit of Moses', reflects a biblical association. Jabal Mūsā has been known for centuries as the place where the prophet Moses met God and received the Law, as described in the book of Exodus. The identification was first made around the third century AD and this is where the narrative of this book begins, extending to the outbreak of World War I.

In the last years of the last century an excavation was organised at the summit. It brought to light a sixth-century church, dated to the time of the Roman emperor Justinian I (483–565, ruled 527–565). Previously unknown remains of an earlier church, built according to sources between 360 and 367, survived underneath. The agreement between the textual and the archaeological record was remarkable. By the time the excavation was finished in October 1999, the historical succession of building phases at Jabal Mūsā had been established, though few questions as to the importance of the site for the people who visited had either been asked or answered. The nature of the moveable finds, a haphazard accumulation that came to be broken on Jabal Mūsā after long journeys from distant destinations, made the typological variations so diverse that few patterns of traffic or use could be determined. The site seemed like a Noah's Ark of European and Near Eastern material culture: two specimens of each kind – and not much of any. The ways in which Jabal Mūsā has been experienced and transformed can only be grasped through an interdisciplinary study, using textual criticism, archaeological interpretation, historical analysis and art historical appreciation.

This integrated approach to the site's bimillennial history is the aim of the 'biography' at hand which records the 'life' of the place.[1] The pattern of this 'life' is organic: periods of growth were followed by quiet spells, times of commotion preceded peaceful centuries. Jabal Mūsā's 'biography' focuses on its periods of activity: the fourth century, the mid-sixth century, the early seventh century, the early eleventh century, the early sixteenth century and the nineteenth century (Table 1). These are turning points which mark major changes of the site's history and will set a pattern for the discussion in the following pages.

Table 1. 'Ages' of Jabal Mūsā's history

JABAL MŪSĀ	DATES	EGYPTIAN HISTORY
Pre-Christian period	prehistory to third century AD	prehistory to Roman period (until AD 330)
Turning point 1: Coming of anchorites to South Sinai (third to early fourth century)		
Early Christian period	third to mid-sixth century	Early Christian period
Turning point 2: Justinianic building project (mid-sixth century)		
Justinianic/Early Byzantine period	mid-sixth century to 630s	Early Christian and Early Byzantine periods
Turning point 3: Islamic conquest (630s)		
Early Islamic period	630s to eleventh century	patriarchal caliphs, Umayyad, ᶜAbbāsid, Ṭūlūnid and early Fāṭimid periods
Turning point 4: Beginning of Muslim and 'Latin' patronage (1010–1030s)		
'Age of Pilgrimage'	eleventh century to 1517	late Fāṭimid, Ayyūbid and Mamlūk periods
Turning point 5: Ottoman conquest of Egypt (1517)		
Ottoman period	1517 to 1822	Ottoman Egypt (1517–1805)
Turning point 6: J.L. Burckhardt, *Travels in Syria and the Holy Land* (published 1822)		
'Age of Enquiry'	1822 to early twentieth century	Modern Egypt (after 1805)

Figure 2. Léon, marquis de Laborde (French, 1807–1869, painter) and
Godefroy Engelmann (French, 1788–1839, engraver), *Vue du somet du
Sinaï.* Lithograph on paper. Based on drawings executed in 1828.

Geography

Place names

Most of the sources on Jabal Mūsā are in Greek and the longest-living tradition is preserved by the Greek-speaking monks of the Monastery of Saint Catherine. Accordingly, Greek place names are older than Arabic ones, which largely follow Christian biblical identifications.[1] However, Arabic place names are more widely used today and are therefore preferred in this book. A list of the main place names in their Greek, Arabic and Hebrew versions appears in Table 2; names used in the book appear in bold and most are situated in the *Localities of the Horeb* map on the front endpaper.

Table 2. **Sinaitic place names**

GREEK	ARABIC	HEBREW	NOTES
Hagia Aikaterinē (Ἁγία Αἰκατερίνη)	**Jabal Kathrin** (جبل كاثرين)		The tallest mountain of Sinai, altitude 2,641 m.
Hagia Epistēmē (Ἁγία Ἐπιστήμη)	**Jabal al-Dayr** (جبل الدير)		Mountain to the north of Wādī 'l-Dayr.
Hagia Koryphē (Ἁγία Κορυφή)	**Jabal Mūsā** (جبل موسىٰ)		'Holy Summit'. Summit of Horeb, altitude 2,285 m
Hagia Zōnē (Ἁγία Ζώνη)	**Ra's Ṣafṣāfa** (رأس صفصافة)		The northern 'brow' of Horeb, altitude 2,168 m.
Hagioi Tessarakonta (Ἅγιοι Τεσσαράκοντα)	**Dayr al-Arbaʿīn** (دير الاربعين)		Garden and small priory, *kathisma*, in Wādī al-Lajā'.

Greek	Arabic	Hebrew	Notes
Hagioi Theodōroi (Ἅγιοι Θεόδωροι)	**Jabal Mu´tamr** (جبل مؤتمر)		Conical hill at the foot of Horeb, at the head of Wādī ´l-Dayr, altitude 1,854 m.
		Horeb (חֹרֵב)	Mountain to the south of Wādī ´l-Dayr, including the summits Jabal Mūsā, Jabal Fara´, Prophētēs Helias and Ra's Ṣafṣāfa.
	Jabal Fara´ (جبل فرأ)		Low peak on Horeb, to the west of Jabal Mūsā.
	Jabal Mu´tamr (جبل مؤتمر)		Low hill in the Wādī Fīran oasis area with Nabatean peak sanctuary. Also encountered as 'Jabal Munayjah'.
	Jabal Sirbāl (جبل سربال)		Mountain near the Wādī Fīran oasis, altitude 2,070 m.
Pharan (Φαράν)	**Wādī Fīran** (ودى فيران)		Oasis valley to the west of Horeb.
Prophētēs Hēlias (Προφήτης Ἠλίας)	**Farsh Elias** (فرش إلياس)		Basin at the foot of Jabal Mūsā, on Horeb, where a chapel of the prophet Elijah is located, altitude 1,900 m.
	al-Rāḥa (الراحة)		Plain to the north of Horeb.
Raithō (Ῥαϊθώ)	**Ṭūr** (الطور)		Town and port on the Gulf of Suez with a major Sinaitic priory, *metochion*.
		Sinai (סיני)	The peninsula of Sinai.
	Wādī ´l-Dayr (واى الاير)		Narrow valley in which the Monastery stands, between Horeb and Jabal al-Dayr.

GREEK	ARABIC	HEBREW	NOTES
	Wādī al-Lajā´ (وادى اللجأ)		Narrow valley to the west of Horeb.

Within the book the name 'Sinai' refers to the peninsula of Sinai. 'Mount Sinai' is not used to denote either the summit of Jabal Mūsā or the mountain it crowns (which is called Horeb), but the biblical 'Mount of the Law' in its textual manifestation. Horeb is a mountain cluster which includes the summits of Jabal Mūsā and Ra's Ṣafṣāfa as well as the basin of Farsh Elias, and is bordered by Wādī ´l-Dayr. However, 'Sinai', 'Jabal Mūsā' and 'Mount Sinai' have often been used interchangeably in texts to describe what here is referred to as 'Horeb'.[2] The third–fourth century writer Eusebios identified Horeb in his work *On Placenames* (*Onomastikon*): 'Horeb (Dt 1:2); mount of God in the land of Madian; near mount Sinai over Arabia in the desert.'[3] Interestingly, the Latin translation of his work commented on the confusion between 'Horeb' and 'Sinai' in the Greek original, suggesting that they were two place names used for the same mountain.[4]

When the terms '(Justinianic) fortress' and 'Monastery' are used here, reference is intended to the Monastery of Saint Catherine in Wādī ´l-Dayr, at the foot of Horeb. However, the dedication to Saint Catherine occurred centuries after a fortress with a church (*katholikon*) and other facilities within its walls were built. It soon became an organised monastery. Early in the text it will be referred to as 'the (Justinianic) fortress' while 'the Monastery' will be used in references to it after the late sixth / early seventh century.

Geomorphology

Sinai is a triangular peninsula situated between the continents of Africa and Asia and covering an area of approximately 60,000 km sq. The red crystalline mountains of South Sinai were originally covered with sediments which slowly eroded and exposed the ancient granite core. The main geological deposits of the area within a 20 km radius around Jabal Mūsā include granite, andesite (in Jabal Kathrin), basalt and dolerite, diorite, gneiss, and pebble gravels in the *wādī* (dry watercourse) beds. The nearest limestone deposits are in Wādī ´l-Tarr and near the Gulf of Suez (40 and 60 km northwest of Jabal Mūsā respectively), with small quantities located in Horeb and Wādī Fīran.[5]

Although few deposits have gathered on the barren mountains of South Sinai, their relief has changed considerably through the action of rainwater drainage, frost and snow. The mountain mass of Horeb is approximately 3 km long (NW–SE) and 1.5 km wide (SW–NE). It was once a volcano and is presently a volcanic neck. It borders on the 160 hectares-wide plain of al-Rāha to the north, from which the Wādī ʾl-Dayr branches out around its northern edge. To the east, the low mountain of Jabal Muʿtamr dominates the skyline. From al-Rāha, the Wādī al-Lajāʾ curves round the southern foot of Horeb.[6]

There are two high points on Horeb, the summit of Jabal Mūsā at 2,285 m and the 'brow' of Ra's Ṣafṣāfa to the north. They are separated by the Farsh Elias basin. The Horeb cluster is made up of red young plutonic rock (granite). However, the colour of the volcanic rock (granite) of Jabal Mūsā is grey, making it distinct from nearby peaks.[7] The archbishop of Sinai Nikēphoros Marthalēs (died 1749, on the throne 1729–1749) in his *proskynētarion* (pilgrim guidebook) noted that Jabal Mūsā is 'blackened with smoke all over', alluding to the supernatural phenomena associated with the 'Mount of the Law' in Exodus.[8] In October 1631 the same remark had been made by V. Stochove.[9] A similar reference also appeared in Nektarios's mid-seventeenth-century *Epitome* and in a brief Greek description of Jabal Mūsā surviving in a sixteenth-century Mount Athos manuscript.[10]

The eastern and southern slopes of Jabal Mūsā are very steep, preventing ascent. However, the northern and eastern slopes are relatively accessible and it was from here that visitors approached (and continue to approach) the place. On the summit, three rocky outcrops define its small area, separated by gaps that have more or less been filled in (*Buildings on Jabal Mūsā* map on the back endpaper). The first outcrop is encountered upon reaching the summit. Underneath gapes a cave where tradition reports that Moses hid in the presence of God (cave B). The second outcrop is under the present-day mosque and over another cave thought to have sheltered the prophet for forty days (cave A).[11] This cave is today buried behind a passageway, but it was open to the winds on the southeastern face of the rock until the twentieth century. A third outcrop is located south of the sanctuary of the chapel of Hagia

Triada, relatively lower than the other two. Both incidents connected with caves A and B are mentioned in Exodus (33: 21–2, 24: 18):

> Then the Lord said, 'There is a place near me where you may stand on a rock. When my glory passes by, I will put you in a cleft in the rock and cover you with my hand until I have passed by.' Then Moses entered the cloud as he went on up the mountain. And he stayed on the mountain forty days and forty nights.

The geomorphology of Horeb allows for five ascent routes.[12] The 'Path of Moses' ascended from Wādī ʾl-Dayr (near the Monastery) through a ravine to Farsh Elias and then up the northern side of Jabal Mūsā. The 'Path of the Pasha' commenced from Wādī ʾl-Dayr, past Jabal Muʿtamr and round the southeastern foot of the mountain to Farsh Elias. The 'Path of Egeria' progressed from Dayr al-Arbaʿīn in Wādī al-Lajāʾ round the southern side of (or over) Jabal Faraʾ and up the western slope of Jabal Mūsā. Two further routes were seldom used: from the Wādī ʾl-Dayr to Raʾs Ṣafṣāfa and then on to Farsh Elias and from below Jabal Faraʾ towards Farsh Elias.

The so-called 'Path of Moses' is the traditional pilgrim path from the Monastery to Jabal Mūsā. It is set with approximately 3,000 steps leading up to Farsh Elias whilst another 700 continue up to Jabal Mūsā.[13] On its lower part the path is crowned by two arches built of dressed stone. The first is called the Gateway of Confession and the second the Gateway of Saint Stephen. The second arch bears a sixth- or seventh-century inscription ('+ For the salvation of Abba Iohannes the Abbot and …') which provides a *terminus ante quem* for the path and probably referred to John 'Klimax', a seventh-century abbot and writer.[14] The fact that the pilgrim Egeria did not go up that way in 383 gives a probable *terminus post quem* for its construction, which must be placed in the sixth century.[15]

The 'Path of the Pasha' was created by ʿAbbās Pasha (1812–1854, ruled 1849–1854).[16] It leads up to the Farsh Elias basin and is accessible to camels. The 'Path of Egeria' seems to have been the earliest one in use since it was taken by the Spanish pilgrim on her way to the summit. It probably fell into disuse as an ascent route before the sixth century, when the buildings in Wādī ʾl-Dayr gave a definite orientation to the approach. However, visitors used it when they descended from Jabal Mūsā and continued to climb Jabal Kathrin.

Climate

Although the Horeb area is often described as rough and desolate desert, research has proved it to be a moderately hospitable environment. The average cloud-free time is 70 per cent, making rainfall a welcomed eventuality which appears with considerable variability.[17] There is a tradition among the monks of the Monastery that before the chapel of Hagia Triada was erected on Jabal Mūsā in 1934, a waiting period of three years was necessary for the reservoir at the summit to replenish. However, when rain does come, the impermeable granite soil does not absorb water and floods occur, often with destructive results. Sometimes the mean annual precipitation (between 65 and 100 mm) may occur within a few hours.[18] The Farsh Elias basin, at the foot of Jabal Mūsā, was turned into a lake following rainfall for a few months in October 1999 owing to the impermeability of its red granite, though the grey granite of Jabal Mūsā is penetrated by water. When snowfall occurs, the ground remains covered from a few days to several weeks.

Mean temperatures are moderate, ranging from 15.5°C–24°C in the summer to 0°C– 4°C during winter, while mean monthly relative humidity fluctuates between 33.3 and 57.9 per cent.[19] In 1891, H.C. Hart found the mean annual temperature of Jabal Mūsā to correspond to that of London.[20] The climate of the Horeb area can be classed as 'desert mountains, mild to cool'.[21] In order to understand the habitation patterns in the area, it is essential to realise that there is a lot of water in the form of springs, wells and streams and that temperatures are mild.

Written sources stress the desertic aridity and poor agriculture of the Sinai. Tellingly, the only two anchorites in the Sinaitic tradition who lived on trees had to consecutively use the same tree because no other was available. They were *dendrites*, an arboreal equivalent to the better-known *stylites*, anchorites living on columns.[22] The introduction of goat herding may have contributed to the depletion of the vegetation cover,[23] however, it seems that in earlier periods South Sinai was wetter than today. Archaeological evidence bears testimony to a possible decrease in precipitation after the Early

Christian period. It seems that finding soil to plant in was a greater concern than finding water to irrigate. Research has brought to light irrigation systems in the area.[24] Such water management systems must have helped in retaining rainwater and improving agricultural production, which – albeit on a small scale – was enough to cover the needs of the locals; a 350 m sq orchard sufficed for a single monk.[25] They testify to a deep knowledge of the climate and its possibilities by both the Bedouin and the anchorites and to the self-supporting character of a developed yet closed economy.

Flora and Fauna

Today the vegetation cover remains substantial and flora is rich in xerophytic forms. Jabal Mūsā has an endemic alpine flora that does not appear below the basin of Farsh Elias, where two cypresses, well-known to visitors past and present, are found growing.[26] The earliest photographs of one of these 'funereal' cypresses were published in 1869.[27] The species, which also appears in the garden near the Monastery, is not native to Sinai and must have been imported from the Balkans or Asia Minor, probably in Early Christian times.[28] The scope of agriculture is limited and concentrates on dates, grown in oases, and fruit and vegetable production in gardens, owned by the Monastery or the Bedouin and tended by the latter.[29]

The fauna of South Sinai is rich and diverse due to its position as a land bridge between Asia and Africa. The desiccation of the northern part of the peninsula isolated areas further south and promoted the development of endemics while attracting new species from the Levant and Africa. Although hunting has depleted the faunal diversity, the presence of species like ostriches and leopards was well-documented in previous centuries. Gazelles, ibex, hyaenas, sand cats and wolves (or jackals) are rarely encountered, though foxes, hares and rodents are common. Birds include vultures, eagles, grackles, ravens, owls, wheatears and finches but it is partridges that dominate the landscape (and diet). Vipers, cobras, lizards and chameleons represent the reptiles while scorpions and galeodes stand out among arachnids. This varied and unique fauna was often mentioned in Early Christian anchoretic literature and, later, traveller accounts as accompanying, assisting or threatening humans who braved the 'terrible wilderness' of Sinai.[30]

Figure 3. *Bedawín Encampment, Wâdy Seba'íyeh, Sinai.* Wood engraving on paper.

Chapter 1

[… Elijah] travelled for forty days and forty nights until he reached Horeb, the mountain of God. [...]

The Lord said, 'Go out and stand on the mountain in the presence of the Lord, for the Lord is about to pass by.'

Then a great and powerful wind tore the mountains apart and shattered the rocks before the Lord, but the Lord was not in the wind. After the wind there was an earthquake, but the Lord was not in the earthquake. After the earthquake came a fire, but the Lord was not in the fire.

And after the fire came a gentle whisper.

1 Kings 19: 8–12

The Early Christian period during which the first Christian anchorites came to South Sinai was one of the most decisive moments in the history of Jabal Mūsā. Two places, a textual one ('Mount of the Law') and an actual one (Jabal Mūsā), were brought together and identified with each other. Biblical narratives were projected onto physical entities: the mountain became 'Mount Sinai', the bush 'the Burning Bush', and the caves had sheltered the prophets Moses and Elijah. The landscape of Horeb was invested with divine grace. The superimposition of patterns of human action – mostly cultic but connected to survival as well – created a stratigraphy of meaning. Written sources and finds from archaeological excavations will be combined to address questions on the life of the Bedouin, the anchorites and the pilgrims, and on the way they perceived and used the place they identified with the 'Mount of the Law'.

People of the Desert

Landscape, climate and technology have changed little in the region from the early years of the Christian era. It can be assumed therefore that the modes of thinking of those inhabiting the landscape, experiencing the climate and using the technology have not been drastically altered. The South Sinai Bedouin still resort to ancient revenue sources like herding, agriculture, hunting, charcoal production, smuggling, protection or transportation services for travellers.[1] They also cling onto traditional ways of perceiving themselves and their surroundings:

> There is no reason to think that the Bedouin code of honor was any different in antiquity from what it is now. The Bedouin are as natural in the desert as its oases and its flowers.[2]

There is little information on the prehistoric antecedents of the South Sinai Bedouin. Round structures, *nawamis*, with a secondary burial usage, appear at several locations.[3] Small summer sites, evidently belonging to nomadic pastoral and hunter-gathering populations and dating from the Pre-Pottery Neolithic period (*circa* 8500–5500 BC), have been excavated in Wādī 'l-Dayr.[4] During the same period triangular-shaped installations of low stone-built walls (the so-called 'desert kites'), an ancient means of hunting game with separate 'herding' and 'killing' areas, were being used in the Horeb vicinity.[5]

It seems that Sinai – even its more remote southern portion – was a thoroughfare of communication and population movement between Asia and Egypt in Chalcolithic times (*circa* 4500–3500 BC), when turquoise was already mined there. This activity continued down to the late second millennium BC, but by then Egyptians supervised a local workforce.[6] Traces of copper mining dating back to the Chalcolithic Age have been recognised on the northern slopes of the South Sinai Massif.[7] Mining encouraged sedentarisation. Semi-sedentary populations also engaged in animal husbandry. However, little agriculture appears to have been developed, with the possible exception of some oases.[8]

The material and textual record is smaller and less researched when it comes to the first millennium BC. Although North Sinai was strategically located between Africa and Asia, the Mediterranean and the Red Sea, South Sinai was distant and isolated.[9] High mountains made the passage of caravans difficult and the presence of minerals seems to have been the only attraction to outsiders. Consequently, references to South Sinai in late antique historiography were scarce and invariably brief.[10] It can be assumed – based on circumstantial evidence – that the area was annexed as part of Provincia Arabia by the Roman Empire in AD 106, like the northern part of the peninsula.[11]

Sinai emerges from obscurity sometime in the first or the second century, thanks to the so-called 'Sinaitic' inscriptions. One of the earliest references to them appeared in the *Christian Topography*. The author, a merchant whose name is believed to have been Kosmas, the so-called 'Indikopleustēs' ('he who sailed to India'), narrated that he had actually seen these 'Hebrew' sculpted letters in the Sinai desert, perhaps sometime in the first half of the sixth century:

> Wherefore, in that wilderness of Mount Sinai, one can see, at all their halting-places, all the stones, that have there been broken off from the mountains, inscribed with Hebrew letters, as I myself can testify, having travelled in these places.[12]

Another reference appeared in Petrus Diaconus's (1107–1153) *Book on Holy Places*, which filled the *lacuna* of the missing part of Egeria's itinerary (discussed below):

> All around the mountains caves have been carved out, and, if you just took the trouble to put up some curtains, they would make marvellous bedrooms. Each bedroom is inscribed with Hebrew letters.[13]

The inscriptions have been the object of scholarly debate as to their authorship, date and decipherment. Today they are attributed to either Nabatean copper miners, who arrived in Sinai with the Romans, or to a Nabatean population that began to appear in the area around the late first century BC.[14] They are dispersed all over the peninsula, unlike Greek, Coptic or Armenian inscriptions, which seem to be concentrated along pilgrim routes.[15] An alternative theory attributes them to local shepherd populations, the 'Bedouin of the past'.[16] The Nabateans themselves had adopted Greek by the late second century, whereas their own language continued to be used in Sinai after the annexation of the Nabatean kingdom by Rome in AD 106 and until the late third century (the latest dated Nabatean inscription from the peninsula dates to 268).[17] South Sinai was distant from trade routes in which the Nabateans would be interested and even copper mining was concentrated away from the area during the period.[18]

The wide usage of the term 'Saracens' for the populations of Sinai (instead of 'Arabs' or 'Nabateans') could underline the indigenous nature of the people inhabiting the area during the Early Christian period. However, the term could also have been used to differentiate between tent-dwelling *scenites* or *scenitae* and sedentary Arabs ('Saracens'), thus encompassing a broader area.[19] In any case, by the sixth century the term 'Saracen' was used for all Arab-speaking peoples.

By the mid-to-late fourth century Provincia Arabia had become a marginal part of the province of Palaestina Tertia, a change that betrays an improved understanding on the part of the imperial government of the difficulties, even threats, posed by the nomadic tribes of the desert areas of Negev and Sinai. Arab Bedouin tribes were by now used as *foederati*, confederates of the Romans who guarded frontiers and ensured the protection of the local population in remote areas.[20] Monastic tradition assigns a tower surviving within the present-day Monastery of Saint Catherine to the early fourth century and connects it with the imperial Holy Land programme associated with the creation of Palaestina Tertia.

An account of the customs and way of living of these tribes appeared in a hagiographical 'historical romance', the *Narrations of Nilos the hermit monk of the demise of the Mount Sinai monks and of the captivity of his son Theodoulos*. This work has been variously dated by scholars between the fourth and the seventh century:

> The aforementioned nation [of the Barbarians] lives in the desert that extends from Arabia to Egypt, the Red Sea, and the river Jordan; they never practiced a craft, or commerce, or agriculture,

and they only have the knife to deal with the necessities of feeding. Because they either live by eating the flesh of the desert animals they hunt; or they provide themselves with what they need, in whatever way they can, by robbing people that happen to pass from the roads near which they lurk. When there is a dearth of both of these and they lack in necessities, they use their beasts of burden (which are dromedary camels) as food, conducting a monstrous and flesh-eating life, slaughtering one per family or tent group, and using a little fire to loosen the firmness of the flesh, so as to say that they do not exercise too much pressure on their teeth, they feed themselves like dogs. They are not aware of the spiritual God, or even a handmade one; they worship the morning star and when it rises, they sacrifice to it the appropriate part of their loot, whenever, from a thieving assault, they come across something worth slaughtering.[21]

The text continues with a description of a camel sacrifice and allusions to human sacrifice, involving circumambulation of the victim, blood drinking and omophagia.[22] The barbarians inhabited the desert of Sinai and the Negev. They appear to have been hunters and brigands, bursting from time to time into murderous rampages. They also worshipped and sacrificed to the morning star.[23] The writer (who shall be referred to as 'Nilos') must have had a distorted view of the Bedouin – contrasting them unfavourably with the virtuous anchorites he praised in following paragraphs – but his testimony cannot be altogether rejected.[24]

Nevertheless, archaeological evidence points to a more civilised population, occupied with farming in oases and small orchards and with the husbandry of goats, sheep and camels.[25] It is probable that the Bedouin also serviced the increasing stream of pilgrims to the area by earning their livelihood as guides.[26] The period from the fourth to the seventh century is one of sedentarisation and even urbanisation in arid areas far from commercial thoroughfares. The presence of anchorites and pilgrims must have been the main reason for this change which would be reversed after the Islamic conquest.[27] The benevolent figure of Ammanes, the Bedouin chief in the work by Nilos, is far removed from the feral barbarians. Ammanes was

probably one of the already mentioned *foederati*, confederates of
the Romans who protected the population of the frontier province of
Palaestina Tertia.[28]

Many of the locals (raiders or traders, farmers or guides) were
converted to Christianity through the zealous action of the anchorites. Urban centres like Ṭūr and Wādī Fīran to the west of the peninsula, with several churches and monasteries, were populated with
Christian, probably Greek-speaking Arabs.[29] Researchers of skeletal
material from Early Christian burials in Wādī Fīran claimed that the
population inhabiting the area was very close in terms of physical
characteristics to the modern Bedouin of South Sinai.[30]

Nonetheless, pagan practices continued in the area. If the incidents described in the *Narrations* by Nilos date to the fourth or the
fifth century (but, even more interestingly, if they actually were
sixth-century fabrications), the Horeb Bedouin had remained pagan
and often rebellious and the Piacenza pilgrim who visited Horeb in
the 550s supported this.[31] Thousands of stones for pagan worship in
Negev and Sinai have been dated as late as the sixth century. Furthermore, the presence of a pagan cult connected with large-scale
agricultural projects in the Negev has been suggested for the fifth
and the sixth century.[32] Although economic conditions in South Sinai
were different, paganism may have been tolerated there as well.

It could be argued that two distinct groups shared the area, a
nomadic pagan element in the mountains and a sedentary Christian
one in the fertile oases and busy ports (the *al-Badw* and *al-ᶜArab*
of the Arabic sources respectively). Both groups would be named
Saracens in Greek sources.[33] However, archaeological evidence
from the Wādī Fīran area testifies to a mixture of Christianity and
paganism, as burials were furnished with crosses as well as altars.[34]
It would be safer to suggest a longer survival of paganism in the
interior of the South Sinai Massif.[35]

While discussing the mid-sixth-century building programme of
the emperor Justinian, historians Prokopios of Caesarea (*circa* 500–
circa 565) and Eutychios of Alexandria (Saᶜīd ibn Biṭrīq, 877 – *circa*
940, writing in the early tenth century) mentioned the settlement of
a substantial new population of frontier guards and their families
(Latin: *limitanei*) near Horeb with the aim of protecting the area and

Figure 4. Jan Luyken (Dutch, 1649–1712, draughtsman) and Jeremias Taylor (British?, engraver), *Awful Appearance of Mount Sinai, previous to the Delivery of the Law.* Copper engraving on paper. 1773.

the anchorites. The Bedouin who live around Horeb today belong to the Jabāliyya (Arabic for mountaineers, from *jabal*, mountain), a tribe claiming their descent from Justinian's settlers.[36] They were supposedly brought over from Egypt and from 'Vlah', in Southeast Europe. Although the tradition of a European 'Vlah' derivation was probably concocted in the eighteenth or the nineteenth century, the memory of a distant origin remains strong. However, it seems more probable that their ancestors were actually members of a Christian Arab *foederati* tribe.[37]

Even if they profess to be distinct from the rest of the Sinai Bedouin, the Jabāliyya share their way of life and customs. Other Bedouin refer to them in contempt as 'the servants to the monastery' and avoid intermarriage, so that endogamy is common.[38] Some Jabāliyya work in the Monastery and cultivate its gardens, others continue to practise orchard agriculture, but most of them prefer the profitable tourism industry or lead a 'hand-to-mouth' existence engaged in seasonal employment.[39] Although most of the Jabāliyya were converted to Islam at the time of Caliph ᶜAbd al-Malik ibn Marwān (646–705, ruled 685–705), a few probably clung to the monks' religion and the last practising Christian woman reportedly died in 1750.[40] In 1929, they numbered 420 souls, 1,100 by 1968, but their population has significantly increased in the past twenty years or so.[41]

Anchorites

> There are very many of us; […] and whenever we are hungry, we readily find food; likewise, if we are thirsty, we have water.
>
> Paphnutius, *Life and polity of our saintly father Onuphrius*.[42]

The Early Christian anchoretic and monastic phenomenon has been a source of inspiration for both believers and scholars. It has been immortalised in a series of narratives and saints' lives and has left numerous albeit humble material remains in the form of hermits' abodes, monasteries, workshops and irrigation structures. The reasons why great numbers of urban and peasant populations felt impelled to socially disengage themselves and retreat into the wilderness, into a life of destitution and hardship (either communal or solitary), have been the object of much discussion. Economic and social conditions pushing debt-ridden peasants in the desert, away from servitude and forced labour, were combined with a growing religious awareness, stemming from Judaeo-Christian traditions which placed personal salvation in the centre of individuals' life plans.

These reasons led to a massive movement from the secular, varied, interrelated and productive societies of Late Antique cities into the sacred, celibate, autarkic and scarcely self-sustaining societies of Early Christian deserts, waiting for the coming of a New Age. New role models emerged for believers: the anchorites, people of little or no education, content in their search for God and complete material denial, inhabiting the desert margin of the urban Mediterranean world.[43]

The question to be answered in relation to the Sinaitic anchoretic tradition refers not to the factors which pushed people away from their previous lives but to those which attracted them to such a remote area. They were fascinated by the sanctity of a place associated with the most important theophany, as Theodoret of Cyrrhus (*circa* 393 – *circa* 457) put it in his *History of the Monks of Syria*:

> [...] Not that we think that the Godhead has been circumscribed in place [...] but since to those who love fervently not only are their beloved thrice desired, but lovable too are the places that have been graced by their presence and frequenting.[44]

It was also the practical possibility of survival in a remote and harsh environment through hard work and patient exploitation of the physical resources that allowed a minimum of necessities to be fulfilled.[45]

How did the summit which is now called Jabal Mūsā come to be considered the 'Mount of the Law'? The Bible itself is vague and even contradictory on the location of Mount Sinai.[46] A passage in Galatians (4:25) seems to locate the 'Mount of the Law' in the Arabian Peninsula: 'Hagar stands for Mount Sinai in Arabia.'[47] Jewish tradition did not identify the holiest of mountains with a specific location, although the Septuagint tradition (which is Alexandrian in origin) must have placed it to the northwest of Arabia.[48] There is no tradition of visitation to an Arabian or any other Mount Sinai before the Christian era. The main Jewish pilgrimage destination was the Temple in Jerusalem, although there is evidence for others of lesser importance.[49] The earliest evidence for Jews visiting Jabal Mūsā as the 'Mount of the Law' dates to Early Christian times and evidently followed Christian tradition.[50]

The question of whether Jabal Mūsā is indeed the biblical 'Mount of the Law' has tantalised scholars.[51] Horeb is the neck of a dead volcano and it could be assumed that the phenomena narrated in Exodus were inspired by its activity.[52] However, volcanic activity had ceased millennia before humans appeared. There is no rigorous way to discover if the promulgation of the Law took place on Jabal Mūsā or any other Sinai mountain. In the words of L. Golding '… the Holy Mountain is a spiritual, not a physical experience'.[53] For the believer, going up 'Mount Sinai' is more of a spiritual quest for God than an ascent up a geographically pinpointed mountain. It is this quest that Mount Sinai came to embody for Christians, Jews and Muslims. Through their mediation, Jabal Mūsā became and remains the 'Mount of the Law', one of the most sacred landscapes.

The earliest anchorites in South Sinai must have arrived in the third century and traffic increased by the fourth century.[54] Three Christian centres developed, one in Wādī Fīran (Pharan, the episcopal see of the peninsula), a second in Ṭūr and a third on Horeb.[55] The first two were adjacent to towns and were linked to date agriculture, fishing and perhaps trade.[56] However, the third was exclusively anchoretic in character and the small local population retained a nomadic economy and pagan religious practices. The anchorites themselves must have been engaged in agriculture alongside prayer and reflection and lived in elementary abodes – it is indicative of their attitude to comfort that in most cells it was possible to sit or lie but impossible to stand upright.[57]

The archaeological evidence on the everyday life of anchorites at Horeb was studied predominantly by Israeli archaeologists during the 1967–1979/1982 occupation of the Sinai Peninsula. They surveyed ruins of hermit cells, chapels, auxiliary buildings, dams, water conduits and other structures. Indeed, the whole of Horeb, outside the main 'pilgrim path' of Burning Bush – Farsh Elias – Jabal Mūsā Dayr al Arbaʿīn, was dotted with such foundations. Many of these must be dated before the sixth century, when Justinian's imperial programme introduced buildings of monumental scale to the area. However, the technical sophistication and considerable ambition of the anchoretic projects makes them impressive in their own right and verifies the written sources (briefly examined below) which testify to many ascetics living on Horeb. The possibility of their subsistence had often been doubted because these installations were unknown, but it is now estimated that more than one hundred of them could have inhabited the arid mountain without importing provisions.[58]

In the *Life and polity and martyrdom of the Saint martyrs Galaktiōn and Epistēmē*, written by Symeon Metaphrastes in the tenth century, the third-century saints from Emesa in Syria were said to have set their ascetic abode on a mountain called Pouplion, which tradition identifies with Jabal al-Dayr.[59] They were incorporated into a community of twelve anchorites:

> After having walked for a full ten days, they arrive at mount Pouplion, as the ones living near it call it, situated near mount Sinai. Having met twelve monks there, living in ascetic polity, they announced their intention, and were worthy enough to be accepted and inscribed in their list.[60]

Galaktiōn and Epistēmē suffered martyrdom during the persecution of Decius (*circa* 201–251, ruled 249–251), when a force was dispatched to arrest Christians at South Sinai.[61]

In his *Ecclesiastical History* (mid-fifth century), Sozomenos (first half of fifth century) mentioned a Palestinian monk, Silvanos, who spent a little time in 'Mount Sinai' in the early fourth century, before creating an anchoretic community at Gerara:

> I think that Silvanus, a native of Palestine, to whom, on account of his high virtue, an angel was once seen to minister, practiced philosophy about the same time in Egypt. Then he lived [for a while] at Mount Sinai […][62]

By 376–378, the rebellious queen Mavia (or Māwiya) requested Moses, a hermit, to become the bishop of her people. It is probable that he was one of the Horeb solitaries, although he could also have come from Wādī Fīran or North Sinai.[63]

In the early fourth century the concentration of anchorites in the area attracted imperial attention anew, this time for protection. A tower, known from the work by Eutychios and identified archaeologically within the confines of the Monastery of Saint Catherine, was built at the place of the Burning Bush (Exodus 3:2):

> Now Moses was tending the flock of Jethro his father-in-law, the priest of Midian, and he led the flock to the far side of the desert and came to Horeb, the mountain of God. There the angel of the Lord appeared to him in flames of fire from within a bush. Moses saw that though the bush was on fire it did not burn up.

It was used to shelter the solitaries from the frequent Bedouin attacks.[64] Eutychios mentioned a chapel there dedicated to the Virgin Mary:

> Before that time [of Justinian] there was no monastery in which the monks could congregate, but they were scattered in the mountains and wadis around the Bush from which God spoke to Moses. Above the Bush they only had a large tower, which is still standing to this day, and within it is a church dedicated to St Mary, and the monks would flee to this tower to protect themselves whenever anyone whom they feared approached.[65]

The age and importance of the tower chapel was well-known to the monks and it was shown to William Turner in 1815, Francis Arundale in 1833 and Edward Robinson in 1838.[66] It signified imperial concern for South Sinai. Such concern was probably associated with the inclusion of this remote area into a wider Holy Land scheme formed in the fourth century with the creation of Palaestina Tertia. The presence of rebellious pagan Arabs, who had to be kept under control, may also have been a contributing factor.[67]

It is not accidental that monastic tradition connected Helena (*circa* 250/257–*circa* 330/36), mother of Constantine I (272–337, ruled 312–337) and major inspiration for the Holy Land project, with the building of the tower.[68] It is also possible that it was erected before the rule of Constantine I and formed part of the reorganisation of the frontier fortresses (Latin: *limes*) during the years of Diocletian (244–311, ruled 284/5–305). The presence of Egyptian high officials to the northeast of Jabal Mūsā, in 299/300, may be related to a mobilisation of the imperial defence system in South Sinai.[69] In this case, the tower was not only built to protect eremitic communities from the Saracens but to police the local population.

Probably in 451, the emperor Marcian (*circa* 392–457, ruled 450–57) addressed a letter to Makarios, bishop and archimandrite, and the 'monks in Mount Sinai' to warn them against the heretical actions of the Monophysite Theodosios, who was causing disturbance in Palestine and the Sinai.[70] It seems that by the mid-fifth century monastic communitites in the area were thriving. It also appears that they avoided the theological debates of the Early Christian period, clinging to Chalcedonian dogmas.[71]

There was extensive literature on the lives and miracles of the wilderness fathers, and *The Spiritual Meadow* by John Moschos (Syrian, mid-sixth century-*circa* 619 or 634) was probably the best-known collection. Several passages testified to a lively to-ing and fro-ing of anchorites and monks between the various monastic centres of the Balkans, Asia Minor, the Near East (especially Palestine) and Sinai.[72] It was a world of piety and eccentric devotion, invested with humour and lyricism, which provided inspiration for generations of believers.

Uneasy Symbiosis

The cosmopolitan community of anchorites was kept separate from the local Bedouin population, both in origin and way of life. Archaeological remains have been interpreted as manifesting an effort to avoid contact.[73] The coexistence was not always harmonious, although it seems that it was mostly peaceful and there is evidence of Bedouin serving as guides to pilgrims. However, when governments changed or intertribal arrangements collapsed, Bedouin bellicosity emerged.[74]

In the *Synaxarium of the Church of Constantinople* (tenth century and later) two attacks were mentioned, one by Vlemmyes (Africans) against fathers in the western coast of Sinai (Ṭūr) – probably dating

between the late fourth and early fifth century – and another by
Agarenoi in the years of Diocletian (284/5–305):

> These [saints] having envied the devil, he urged the savage nation
> of Vlemmyes to revolt against them; they live by the Red Sea
> from Arabia unto Egypt. And they, hoping to find riches, came to
> plunder the monks; since they found nothing but woven mats and
> the saints themselves wearing animal hair garments, they were
> outraged and slaughtered them, even though they did no harm.
> Many years earlier, in the days of Diocletian, saintly fathers were
> killed by the Agarenoi in Sinai and Raithō on the twenty-second
> day of December [...][75]

Eutychios of Alexandria described sixth-century raids by 'Ishmaelite Arabs' who pillaged the possessions of the hermits, broke into
and desecrated their churches:

> [...] The Ishmaelite Arabs injured them by devouring their provi-
> sions, and destroying their places (of habitation). Entering their
> cells they would pillage them of whatever was there, and breaking
> into churches they would gulp down the Eucharist.[76]

The reasoning behind the attack against the fathers in the *Synaxarium*,
and the looting of their riches, seems formulaic. However, when in
the late twentieth century monks renovated the chapel of Hagios
Geōrgios Arselaitēs (Saint George of Arselas), 'Dayr Rumḥān', near
Wādī Isla, the relatively comfortable Bedouin of the area, tending
cannabis plantations along the Wādī, broke into it and shattered a
marble paving slab in front of the altar in the hope of finding buried
treasure underneath; the monk who had paved the chapel had carved
the slab with a sixteen-point star, which was thought to be a treasure
sign.[77] There are long-running traditions among the Bedouin that the
books in the library at the Monastery of Saint Catherine hold the
answers to all questions.[78] They underline the dynamic nature of the
centuries-old symbiosis between anchorites and desert people.

Despite tensions between the Bedouin and the monks, it seems
that the former respected the latter's ability to survive in the desert

despite not having been born there and 'consider[ed] this monastery to be the only stable foreign agency inside the Sinai'.[79] They also propagated deep-rooted traditions of sanctity and miraculous acts surrounding Jabal Mūsā, the Monastery and the monks. Although most of the rituals and customs described below were recorded in the nineteenth and the twentieth century, they undoubtedly reflect older beliefs and practices.

Every year at the Eid the Bedouin used to sacrifice a sheep or goat on Jabal Mūsā after having sacrificed three camels on three consecutive days at shaykhs' tombs. They painted the lintel and doorjambs of the mosque with the victims' blood. They also used to bring their goats to Jabal Mūsā on the day Saint Catherine was celebrated. The pilgrimage to the summit was recommended by elders to women desirous of more children and sometimes the very conception of the children *in situ* was encouraged.[80]

Alexandre Dumas (French, 1802–1870) narrated a story he based on the notes of his friend, the painter Adrien Dauzats, who visited Sinai in 1830. It came from a Bedouin guide named Bechara:

> Allah created the earth square, and covered it with stones. When this labour was completed, he came down with his angels, and stood upon the peak of Sinai, which, as you know, is the centre of the world. He then traced an immense circle, whose circumference touched the four corners of the square, and ordered his angels to throw the stones into the four corners, which correspond with the four cardinal points. The angels obeyed, and when the circle was cleared, he gave it to the Arabs, who are his favourite children, and he named the four corners, France, Italy, England, and Russia.[81]

Pious Bedouin circumambulated the Monastery with their flocks to get a blessing from the angels who supposedly sit at its four corners. Moses, Aaron, Saint George and Saint Catherine were regularly honoured.[82] Sir Frederick, second Baronet Henniker described the Bedouin slaughtering a sheep and parading it 'with great ceremony' round the walls of the Monastery in 1820.[83] He thought this act was meant to tantalise the fasting monks but it seems much more plausible they meant to honour the sacred enclosure.

Figure 5. Francis Frith (British, 1822–1898), *Mount Horeb, Sinai*. Albumen silver print, 36.4 × 46.5 cm. 1858.

Edward Henry Palmer mentioned that the Bedouin left incense offerings in niches on the Monastery wall to venerate the prophet Khidhr (Elijah), adding that they considered the building itself to have been erected in Moses' time.[84] Another visitor several years later added that, according to the Bedouin, Moses did the work himself 'and his daughter, St. Katarina, completed it'.[85] The Bedouin believed the monks to hold a book capable of controlling rainfall (the 'Book of Moses' or 'Book of Rain'), once hidden on Jabal Mūsā.[86] In the *Perigraphē* (*Description*), a compendium of Sinaitic monastic memory printed in Greek in 1710, a story was told of the Bedouin demolishing the Jabal Mūsā chapel and digging deep in its ruins, vainly searching for the 'Book of Rain'.[87] Johann Ludwig Burckhardt quoted his Bedouin guide ᶜAʿīd as saying:

> […] some years since several men, God knows who they were, came to this country, visited the mountains, wrote down every thing, stones, plants, animals, even serpents and spiders, and since then little rain has fallen, and the game has greatly decreased.[88]

In 1815 William Turner was told the following:

> In a season of extraordinary drought, they [the Bedouin] come
> in crowds to the convent and fire on it till the priests promise
> them to pray for rain. Once, after they had thus forced out these
> prayers, there came by chance such a heavy rain, that two Arabs
> and many camels were drowned in a mountain stream that it had
> swelled; on which a multitude of them came to fire on the convent,
> believing that this misfortune had resulted from the malice of the
> monks, who had denounced a curse on them, instead of involving
> a blessing.[89]

A similar story attributed the deadly flood of 1867 to over-praying
for rain to Moses on Jabal Mūsā by shaykh Mūsā Nassir.[90] When
excavation started on Jabal Mūsā in 1998, some of the Bedouin
assumed that the research was aimed at finding the 'Book of Rain'
– and indeed, a three-year drought was ended with heavy rainfall.

Early Buildings
The material record of human activity predating Justinian's basilica
(560–65) is scanty. Excavation in 1998 and 1999 gave few clues; a
few glass shards from bowls and fragments of a flat-based beaker
datable between the fourth and the mid-fifth century are the only
securely-dated small finds from the period.[91] However, architectural
features can be attributed to buildings earlier than the basilica, their
stratigraphic dating corroborated by textual evidence (*Buildings on
Jabal Mūsā* map on the back endpaper).

The features are concentrated to the north of the 1934 chapel of
Hagia Triada, west of its small *parakella* and belfry.[92] Immediately
to the north of the *parakella*, a natural crevice in the rock is usually
identified as the cave where Moses hid in the presence of God (cave
B). Excavation unearthed the remains of three walls. The largest one,
on an E–W axis, is the northern wall of the sixth-century basilica and
is constructed by well-dressed red granite blocks. A second wall, on
a N–S direction, is made up of grey granite boulders. Finally, a third
wall, on an E–W axis, measures an impressive 1 m in width and it is
built from the same large blocks of grey granite. Both grey granite

walls were consolidated with mortar and founded on the natural bedrock. They evidently formed the northwestern corner of a building that predated the basilica, to which the red granite wall belonged. Grey granite is the local stone of Jabal Mūsā, whereas red granite was quarried from the area of Farsh Elias at its foot, 250 m below.[93] Red granite was used extensively by the sixth-century builders, but the local material and position of the grey granite walls distinguishes them as belonging to a different building project.

The early building was coated with a fine white plaster layer on the exterior. Limestone for the production of plaster was probably from the vicinity, while richer deposits appear within a 100 km radius of Jabal Mūsā and ten lime kilns have been identified near monastic settlements in South Sinai.[94] It seems that plastering was a widespread practice in South Sinai and appears on Early Christian structures on Horeb.[95]

The sixth-century account of the Piacenza pilgrim mentioned a square building 'having six feet, more or less, in length and in breadth'. He probably made his calculations in Roman feet (0.296 m) and could have referred to the interior dimensions of the building, 1.77 m by 1.77 m. Given the substantial thickness of the grey granite walls, it is possible that the interior of this early building was 2 m by 2 m, close to the pilgrim's measurement. Therefore, a building with exterior dimensions up to 4 m by 4 m, built of grey granite and coated with white plaster, was the first structure on Jabal Mūsā. At a yet unspecified date, an extension to the west was added. It cannot be known whether its walls enclosed a roofed space or formed a courtyard. The new space measured approximately 4 m E–W. A final extension to the west appears to have been an open area.

By the time a decision was taken to erect a basilica on the summit of Jabal Mūsā in the mid-sixth century, a complex measuring more than 17 m E–W had been erected in a few building phases. The complex consisted of one or two rooms and a few courtyards to the west. Its function cannot be proven conclusively: was it a Christian chapel or an even earlier building, and of what nature? Two examples of pagan peak sanctuaries in South Sinai can be used in comparison. The Nabatean peak sanctuary at Jabal Muʿtamr, near Wādī Fīrān, consisted of an open-air circular *temenos* (5 m in diameter) with several inscriptions

Figure 6. H. Fenn (painter) and C. Cousen (British, 1803–1889, engraver), *Wâdy Sho'eib – Jethro's Valley*. Steel engraving on paper.

carved on its building blocks.[96] A smaller Nabatean temple stood on the almost inaccessible summit of the nearby Jabal Sirbāl, with two concentric enclosures and a court below.[97]

There is no similarity whatsoever between the early building on Jabal Mūsā and the Wādī Fīran sanctuaries. Furthermore, there is no evidence for Nabatean presence on Jabal Mūsā. Although high places around the Nabatean capital of Petra were approached with well-cut flights of steps, the steps of the 'Path of Moses' at Horeb are less impressive and were built rather than carved out of the rock, a practice that required greater investment of manual labour. No Nabatean pottery was recognised among the excavation finds and no 'Sinaitic' inscriptions have been located on the summit, although there are some at the foot of Horeb.[98] It is possible that the inscriptions were considered 'pagan' and therefore erased, a practice recorded elsewhere in Sinai.[99] Although the Nabatean presence would be a tempting solution to the problem of Jabal Mūsā's biblical identification, it is not supported by evidence.[100]

The ground-plan and orientation of the pre-Justinianic complex resemble a Christian building, a chapel looking east with extensions to the west. Textual evidence supports this assumption. In the early accounts of Egeria, Theodoret and the Piacenza pilgrim discussed below, a chapel was specifically described: *ecclesia* (church) in Egeria, *thysiastērion* (altar) in Theodoret, and *oratorium* (oratory) in the Piacenza pilgrim.[101] Had there been a pagan sanctuary, it would have been cited in these narrations, like the one mentioned by the Piacenza pilgrim. The early building phases at Jabal Mūsā belong to a chapel built, according to Theodoret's *History of the Monks of Syria*, by the Syrian Julian Saba between 360 and 367.

Early Narrations

It is not just material remains but textual evidence that contributes to the understanding of the Jabal Mūsā landscape during the early stages of its formation. Apart from providing further insights into the morphology of structures on the summit, texts also record the experiences of visitors and explain the ways in which the place was perceived and used. These accounts reveal a number of standard themes which will be combined below with the archaeological evidence.

Horeb was included on pilgrim itineraries since the Early Christian period. In *On Holy Land Sites* (*circa* 518–530), attributed to Theodosius, distances to it were given:[102]

> The city of Paran near Mount Sinai is where Saint Moses fought Amalek. It is three staging-posts from Jerusalem to Elusa, and seven from Elusa to Aila, a city constructed by Alexander the Great, the Macedonian. It is eight staging-posts from Aila to Mount Sinai, if you choose the short way across the desert, but twenty-five if you go through Egypt.

'Mount Sinai' appeared as a mass of earth-coloured *tesserae* on the mosaic map of Madaba in Jordan (dated between 560 and 565 – contemporary with the basilica on Jabal Mūsā – and based on Eusebios's *On Placenames*) without an inscription clearly identifying it.[103] It also appeared on the eighth portion of the *Tabula Peutingeriana* (twelfth to thirteenth century, probably reproducing a fourth-century map), with the following caption: 'Mount Sinai where they received

the law in mount Sinai'.[104] The latter work clearly depicted the road
network of the Roman Empire, with some additions of Christian
interest like Mount Sinai, and probably belonged to a series of maps
directly related to textual itineraries which do not survive.[105] It was
on this road network that the first pilgrims to Sinai travelled from as
early as the fourth century.

The earliest and indeed the most extensive surviving account of
a visit to Jabal Mūsā from the early part of its history was given by
Egeria, probably a Spanish nun of noble origin.[106] It seems that it
was not unusual for ladies of high rank to undertake such laborious
and dangerous itineraries. Another pilgrim to Sinai between April
592 and August 594 was the patrician lady Rusticiana, accompanied by her daughter, as testified in a letter addressed to her by Pope
Gregory I in August 594.[107] Egeria visited Horeb between November
383 and January 384 and must have ascended Jabal Mūsā on Sunday
17 December 383. The earlier part of Egeria's journey (the narrative
of which does not survive) can be reconstructed using the *Book of
the Holy Places* of Petrus Diaconus.[108]

Egeria approached Jabal Mūsā from the west. She ascended to it
not from Wādī 'l-Dayr (where she saw a church 'at the place of the
Bush') but from Wādī al-Lajā' and most probably from the hermit-
age of Dayr al-Arbaʿīn. The precipitous ascent, probably on Jabal
Faraʿ at first, was followed by a steep descent, only to be resumed
towards Jabal Mūsā itself.

> From here we were looking at the Mount of God; our way first
> took us up it, since the best ascent is from the direction by which
> we were approaching, and then we would descend again to the
> head of the valley (where the Bush was), since that is the better
> way down.
>
> They are hard to climb. You do not go round and round them,
> spiralling up gently, but straight at each one as if you were going
> up a wall, and then straight down to the foot, till you reach the
> foot of the central mountain, Sinai itself. Here then, impelled by
> Christ our God and assisted by the prayers of the holy men who
> accompanied us, we made the great effort of the climb. It was
> quite impossible to ride up, but though I had to go on foot I was

not conscious of the effort – in fact I hardly noticed it because, by God's will, I was seeing my hopes coming true.

Once on the summit itself, Egeria noticed a church:

[…] which is now there is not impressive for its size (there is too little room on the summit), but it has a grace all of its own.[109]

She was greeted there by an elder (*presbyter*) appointed to the church, who came to meet her group from his cell.

All there is on the actual summit of the central mountain is the church and the cave of holy Moses. No one lives there.
    They [the holy men] showed us the cave where holy Moses was when for the second time he went up into the Mount of God and a second time received the tablets of stone after breaking the first ones when the people sinned. They showed us all the other places […]
    From there we were able to see Egypt and Palestine, the Red Sea and the Parthenian Sea (the part that takes you to Alexandria), as well as the vast lands of the Saracens – all unbelievably far below us.[110]

The information Egeria provided is important for understanding how Jabal Mūsā was approached and perceived at an early date. There was a specific itinerary, taking pilgrims up the summit from a particular path. On their way back, they followed a different path, in all probability the one still in use today, down to Wādī ʾl-Dayr. Franca Mian suggested that, on her descent from Jabal Mūsā, Egeria followed a path to the foot of Raʾs Ṣafṣāfa and that the place of the Burning Bush was not where the Monastery stands today but further north.[111] However, it is improbable that such a venerated place changed location within 150 years. The architect who erected the fortress in the mid-sixth century compromised its defensive ability in order to contain the holy place of the Burning Bush within its walls.[112] Had it been possible for the locality to shift a few hundred metres to the west, the much more protected foot of Raʾs Ṣafṣāfa would have been preferred.

On Jabal Mūsā a *presbyter*, who must have been living nearby, serviced a small chapel. Other holy men lived all over the mountain but not on the summit. However, they probably held their Sunday celebration there. These holy men were willing to accompany visitors and offer them hospitality. They also were able to identify locations mentioned in the Scriptures, for example 'the cave of Moses' (probably cave A) and, later in the text, several others on the foot and around the mountain.[113] It is evident therefore that a 'holy topography' had already been created, centred on Jabal Mūsā.[114]

The *History of the Monks of Syria* by Theodoret, bishop of Cyrrhus, composed in the mid-fifth century, narrated the life of Julian Saba (died 367) and other monks.[115] Julian, who became famous as a holy man in the desert of Osrhoene, found refuge in Horeb from his numerous admirers in the years between 360 and 367.[116] He followed a route as far away as possible from settlements thanks to an ingenious method of collecting water using a sponge on a stick.

To escape [being honoured] – for he became conspicuous to all and drew to himself through fame the lovers of the good – he finally set out for Mount Sinai with a few of those closer to him, entering no city or village but making passable the impassable desert. They carried on their shoulders the necessary food – I mean bread and salt – and also a cup made from wood and a sponge tied to a piece of string, in order (if ever they found the water too deep) to draw it up with the sponge, squeeze it into the cup, and so drink it. Accordingly, after completing a journey of many days, they reached the mountain they longed for, and having worshiped their own Master passed much time there, thinking the deserted character of the place and tranquillity of soul supreme delight. On this rock, under which Moses the leader of the prophets hid when he was counted worthy to see God, in so far as it is possible to see him, Julian built a church and consecrated an altar of God, which has remained to this day, and so returned to his own wrestling-school.[117]

When in South Sinai, Julian encountered a dignitary of the Church (a 'despot', bishop) and spent a long time there. Egeria, visiting

Horeb some years later, did not mention such a dignitary. There
may have been a bishop in Pharan (Wādī Fīran) from the fourth
century onwards, evidently presiding over the whole area. By the
sixth century Mount Sinai was put first in the title of the '*presbyter*
and *apokrisarios* of the Holy Mountain of Sinai and the Desert of
Raithō and the Holy Church in Pharan'.[118]

On the rock under which Moses sheltered in the presence of God,
Julian built a church and dedicated an altar, which survived to The-
odoret's time. The account located Julian's church on top of cave
B and archaeological research corroborated the text. The tradition
of Julian's pilgrimage was also mentioned in two Syriac hymns by
Ephraem the Syrian (*circa* 306 – 373) and remained alive in the
Monastery.[119]

Another Syrian who, according to Theodoret, visited Horeb and
Jabal Mūsā was Symeon the Elder, who died *circa* 390 or perhaps
before 380.[120] His account gave little information, but constituted
the first mention of an individual spending a week on the summit –
albeit as a devotional exercise rather than a proper residence.

> It is related that, when they reached the mountain they desired,
> this wonderful old man, on the very spot where Moses was
> counted worthy to see God and beheld him as far as was possible
> for human nature, knelt down and did not get up until he heard a
> divine voice announcing to him the Master's favor. He had spent
> the whole cycle of a week bent double in this way and taking not
> a scrap of food when the voice sounded and bade him take what
> was offered him and eat it willingly.[121]

The two passages in the *History of the Monks of Syria* refer to
visits pre-dating Egeria's, but add little to the information given by
her. However, they allow for a *terminus ante quem* of 360 to be
set for an already strong tradition of pilgrimage to Jabal Mūsā and
narrow the dates for the first Jabal Mūsā chapel to between 360 and
367.

A narrative attributed to the fourth-century Egyptian monk Ammonios from Canopus near Alexandria mentions two massacres.[122] One
was around Horeb and another at Ṭūr. They were well-known by the

late eighth or the ninth century, when the earliest surviving Byzantine *proskynētarion* (Holy Land itinerary or guidebook) was written by Epiphanios.[123] The historical truth of the narratives has been questioned, although scholars have argued otherwise and proposed a date for the raids in Ammonios's text between 373 and 381 or in the 370s, perhaps connected with Mavia's revolt (375–78).[124] It is possible that the attacks mentioned by Ammonios and Nilos indeed took place in the late fourth or the fifth century, although the texts themselves date from the sixth or the seventh century.[125] Whatever the case may be, they provide useful information on the life of the earliest desert fathers and their relationship with the Bedouin.

While describing a Saracen attack against fathers in the Horeb area, Ammonios referred to Jabal Mūsā as playing a role of protection:

And after a few days suddenly many of the Saracens fell upon us; because at that time the king of the Saracens had died, he who was the guardian of the desert. And they killed those of the fathers who were found in distant cells. But those who were dwelling in places near, when they heard (the commotion) fled to a certain fortress in the neighbourhood, [together] with the Governor of the place, he whose name was Dulos; [...] And they killed in Geth-rabbi all those whom they found there; and in Choreb; and people in Codar; and all those whom they found near to the Holy Mountain. [...] And He [God] commanded and a flame of fire was seen on the summit of the Holy Mount, and it was a wonder; and all the mountain {was smoking, and the fire bursting out up to the sky. All being seized with terror, we became insensible through the fear of the vision. And falling on our faces, we worshipped God, and supplicated that He would carry us over the present necessity, which lay heavy on us, to a prosperous issue. Nay, even the Barbarians also, terrified by this new and unwonted sight, by a sudden impulse took to flight, many [of them] even leaving [their] arms with [their] camels, nor did they brook a moment's delay.}[126]

The description of the mountain is similar to the passage from Exodus (19: 18–9):

Mount Sinai was covered with smoke, because the Lord descended
on it in fire. The smoke billowed up from it like smoke from a
furnace, the whole mountain trembled violently, and the sound of
the trumpet grew louder and louder.

Apart from being inaccessible, the holiest of the Horeb sacred locations was also actively engaged in the protection of its worshippers,
a role it would assume again at difficult instances in later centuries.

In his work *On Buildings*, published *circa* 560, Prokopios of
Caesarea, the secretary of Justinian's general Belisarios (500–565),
wrote on Jabal Mūsā:

> In what was formerly called Arabia and is now known as 'Third
> Palestine', a barren land extends for a great distance, unwatered
> and producing neither crops nor any useful thing. A precipitous
> and terribly wild mountain, Sina by name, rears its height close
> to the Red Sea, as it is called. [...] On this Mt. Sina live monks
> whose life is a kind of careful rehearsal of death, and they enjoy
> without fear the solitude which is very precious to them. [...] For
> it is impossible for a man to pass the night on the summit, since
> constant crashes of thunder and other terrifying manifestations of
> divine power are heard at night, striking terror into man's body
> and soul. It was in that place, they say, that Moses received the
> laws from God and published them.[127]

A slight bewilderment on the part of the well-bred urbanite Prokopios lurks behind the admiration for the monks 'whose life is a kind
of careful rehearsal of death'. This phrase is often quoted to demonstrate how hard the anchorites' life was and has been criticised
as unsubstantiated.[128] However, no scholar seems to have noticed
that it was borrowed from Plato's *Phaedo*, a dialogue well known
to educated people of Prokopios's time and popular with Christian
theologians:

> Suppose it [the soul] is separated in purity, while trailing nothing
> of the body with it, since it had no avoidable commerce with it
> during life, but shunned it, suppose too that it has been gathered

together alone into itself, since it always cultivated this – nothing else but the right practice of philosophy, in fact, the cultivation of dying without complaint – wouldn't that be the cultivation of death?[129]

Therefore, the expression was formulaic (*topos*) and aimed to show the writer's erudition rather than the monks' hardship.[130] A comparison can be made with John Moschos: '[…] let the object of your philosophy be always to contemplate death […]'.[131] Prokopios referred to the fortress and its basilica and went on to stress that the reason for not building it on the summit was the supernatural phenomena which were taking place there 'striking terror into man's body and soul'. Thus, he once more affirmed the inaccessibility of Jabal Mūsā. However, at approximately the same time that his book was published, the summit basilica foundations must have been laid and either the phenomena were ignored or the need to honour the place surpassed fear.

Although the Piacenza pilgrim (in older editions named Antoninus – sometimes 'of Cremona') visited Jabal Mūsā after the fortress had been built (after 557 and before 560–65), his account (*circa* 570) will be examined alongside pre-Justinianic texts, since it is pertinent to details of the architecture of the pre-basilical structures and discusses pagan cult practices:

> Thence we ascend unceasingly for three miles farther, to the topmost peak of the mountain, upon which is a small chapel [*oratorium*], having six feet, more or less, in length and in breadth. In this no one is permitted to pass the night; but after the sun has risen, the monks [*monachi*] ascend thither and perform the Divine Office. In this place many, out of devotion, cut off their hair and beard, and throw them away; and there I also trimmed and cut my beard.
>
> Mount Sinai is stony, with earth only in a few places. Round about it are the cells [*cellulae*] of many servants of God, and likewise in Horeb. They say that Horeb means 'clean earth'. At one place upon the mountain, the Saracens have placed a marble idol of their own, as white as snow. There, also, dwells a priest of theirs, dressed in a dalmatic and pallium of linen. When the

time of their festival arrives, as soon as the moon is up (before its rays have departed from the festival) that marble begins to change colour; as soon as the moon's rays have entered in, when they begin to worship the idol, the marble becomes black as pitch. When the time of the feast is over, it returns to its original colour – a great object of wonder to us all.[132]

The Piacenza pilgrim added to Egeria's information an alternative itinerary (he went up the 'Path of Moses') and the actual dimensions of the church on the summit, six by six feet. Even in the sixth century, and while the community of anchorites at the foot of Jabal Mūsā had considerably increased, no one was allowed to reside on the summit. He added that, 'out of devotion', many used to shave both hair and beard (a tradition unrecorded elsewhere). He then went on to describe at length pagan ceremonies (stone-worship) of the 'Saracens' at an unspecified location on 'Horeb', which he probably identified with Jabal al-Dayr to the north of Wādī 'l-Dayr and not with Horeb.[133] He thus gave evidence for the survival of paganism into the sixth century, two centuries after the coming of the first anchorites and only seven decades before the Muslim conquest.

Some of the *Various narrations of the humble monk Anastasios on the holy fathers of Sinai*, written around the third quarter of the seventh century, relate to the inaccessibility of Jabal Mūsā and the supernatural phenomena associated with it.[134] Anastasios, a monk at the Monastery who must have had John Klimax as abbot, is a valuable source, since he wrote out of personal experience in charming and unpretentious Greek and gave reliable and lively details of the lives of the Sinai brethren and of the way they viewed and experienced Jabal Mūsā.[135]

In the second narration, Anastasios told the story of a young monk, apprentice to the *paramonarios* (the overseer or 'concierge' of the church) of the Jabal Mūsā basilica, who spent the night on the place and was punished with something closely resembling partial paralysis after a stroke:[136]

[…] A brother, apprentice [*diakonētēs*] to the *paramonarios*, having neglected [the prohibition], hid inside the church saying that no harm [could] come on the person that would sleep there. The *paramonarios*, thinking that his disciple had already descended before him, having burned incense on the holy place and shut the doors, departed. During the night, the disciple that had hidden in the church woke up to tend the oil lamps; and when he arrived at the first lamp, the very flame he tended, by God's command, hurt his one side, and his entire half was paralysed from this time on, and one of his hands and one of his legs, and he remained half paralysed until he died.[137]

Much better was the luck of a *paramonarios* who was forced to spend the night on Jabal Mūsā. He was miraculously transported to Rome and woke up in the Basilica of Saint Peter. The pope (probably Gregory I, served 590–604) kept him in Rome, ordained him bishop and offered to Sinai furnishings for a 'hospital', a hostel for pilgrims flocking to South Sinai, in which Anastasios himself had served:

[…] In the evening, it suddenly snowed heavily, so that the mountain of Hagia Koryphē was covered with three or four *pēcheis* (six or eight feet). And he [the *paramonarios*] was marooned on the summit and could not descend. In these years, no one dared sleep on Hagia Koryphē. While the *paramonarios* was praying, round about dawn, he fell asleep and transported by God he found himself in Rome in Saint Peter's. […] By divine economy, he was found having in his belt the keys of the doors inscribed as 'of the Hagia Koryphē [holy summit] of Sinai'.[138]

In this passage it is specified that nobody dared sleep on Jabal Mūsā 'in these years', allowing the assumption that the prohibition was not as strictly adhered to in later years, when Anastasios was writing.

Supernatural phenomena, like the one described in the narrative by Ammonios, seem to have been common, not only in relation to hostile attacks against the monks but in the presence of pilgrims and the fathers themselves, too:

[…] A *diakonētēs* at Hagia Koryphē named Elissaios, Armenian in origin, not once or twice but as if to say every night, because he

Figure 7. Horeb. Prayer niche.

was pure and worthy, he reported seeing fire on the holy church of
the Godly lawgiving.[139]

A pilgrim group of eight hundred Armenians witnessed an even
more impressive manifestation of divine power:[140]

> [...] When they arrived at the outer holy rock where Moses
> received the law, a vision of God and terrible miracle happened in
> the holy place, and to all the people – just as in the ancient times of
> the giving of the law, the whole of Hagia Koryphē [holy summit]
> and these people seemed to be in the middle of fire [...] After
> these people were surprised and chanted the 'Kyrie Eleison' for up
> to one hour, the fire subsided, and not even an eyelash of one of
> them was damaged nor a garment, but only their sticks like candles
> were lit during the vision, and then they were extinguished.[141]

Fires appearing on the summit relate to the descriptions of Exodus
and were often interpreted by witnesses as of divine origin. However,
there is a series of meteorological phenomena which occur on a

regular basis on the Sinai mountaintops: magnetic storms produc-
ing strong vibrations and flashes of light were experienced by the
members of the archaeological team who lived for several weeks
on Jabal Mūsā in 1998 and 1999. Scientific knowledge allowed for
their disassociation with the supernatural, but such phenomena fit
well into the frame of thought surrounding the place in the minds
of believers of all periods.[142] A pilgrim in 1999 insisted on having
experienced a wonderful, other-wordly scent on her way up to Jabal
Mūsā, just like the fathers in Anastasios's first narration. The abundant fragrant herbs (lavender, sage, mint and others) growing on
Horeb could be the reason for such olfactory sensations.[143]

Holy Wilderness
The first question usually asked about the site – the possible reasons
for its identification with the 'Mount of the Law' – lies beside the
point of research into how Jabal Mūsā was regarded and experienced
during the early centuries of its history. An apocalyptic explanation
would be more in accordance with the character of the site and the
beliefs of the third-century anchorites who brought the biblical and
the actual places together. What is more historically interesting are
the ways in which the summit was perceived and used after this
identification. This can be examined through scholarly examination
of texts that, as will become apparent, agree on a series of perceptions and practices.

The summit was the *raison d'être* of the anchoretic community
and the focal point of Sinaitic eremitic life. There is a remarkable
archaeological clue as to the centrality of the site. Fourteen prayer
niches, low semicircular or rectangular apses (average dimensions
2 m by 2.5 m, original height 0.75 m to 1 m) built of rough stone,
are scattered around Horeb and most share the same characteristics
(figure 7). There are nine further niches on nearby mountains, most
connected with a view of Horeb.[144] Jabal Mūsā is readily visible from
them and they are oriented towards it. They must have been used by
anchorites and pilgrims for devotions and they have been circum-
stantially but convincingly dated to the Early Christian period. More
prayer niches have been identified in the vicinity of Jabal Umm
Shūmar, not far from Horeb. They are different in construction and

orientated towards the southeast (facing Mecca), and are therefore probably *mihrabs* rather than Early Christian prayer niches.[145] The Jabal Mūsā prayer niches could also have been used as *mihrabs* at a later date.

These niches bear witness to the pre-eminence of Jabal Mūsā among the other holy places of the Horeb sacred landscape which was already well-structured when Egeria visited in 383. This is hardly surprising, since the 'Mount of the Law' was the site of one of the most important theophanies in the Bible, the God-trodden spot where a human, Moses, cast his eyes not on a manifestation of God but on His actual figure. He later received there the Decalogue from Him.

Jabal Mūsā participated in the polemical aspects of the anchorite-Bedouin coexistence. The summit protected its worshippers and averted evil from them. To the Early Christian anchorite sacred locations were safe shelters in a basically hostile landscape of pagans and barbarians – and there were plenty of those around Horeb. Tellingly, in the work of Nilos, mention was made of anchorites seeking refuge on Jabal Mūsā – a place which even the lawless and murderous Bedouin would not approach.[146] However, from the fourth century onwards the task of protecting the holy fathers seems to have gradually fallen on human shoulders and defensive structures were erected to this end like the tower near the Burning Bush.[147]

During the first centuries of its history, Jabal Mūsā was accessible to visitors but there was a restriction on spending the night there. A fourth-century anchorite was reluctant even to ascend it: 'I climbed the height of Mount Sinai, the summit of which almost touches heaven and cannot be reached by human effort.'[148] This was relevant to the extensive prohibitions of access to the mountain in Exodus and to the sanctity of a place touched by God.[149] Many anchorites (perhaps numbering as many as one hundred) gathered around it throughout Horeb but avoided the sacred summit itself.[150] One of them, living close to Jabal Mūsā but not on it, was Stephen. According to the seventh 'word' of the *Heavenly Ladder* (Klimax, early seventh century) by John Klimax, he lived '[…] in his own cell on Hagia Koryphē [holy summit] […]'[151] The location of his cell is still venerated near Farsh Elias and the eighteenth-century chapel standing there seems to have been preceded by a much earlier structure.[152] Several other chapels, small monasteries, cells, paths, prayer niches but also water systems and fences around agricultural plots have been located on Horeb, but not on Jabal Mūsā.[153]

The inaccessibility of holy places, the *avaton*, was common in cultic institutions since antiquity. Parts of church buildings were inaccessible to various groups of people or to all but the clergy on some occasions or at any time. It is hardly surprising that a similar limitation would be set up for Jabal Mūsā, associated as it was with supernatural phenomena, to further discourage trespassers. In the exceptional circumstances when these rules were broken, the consequences ranged from the extraordinary (overnight transportation to Rome) to the detrimental (partial paralysis) for transgressors.

The early hermits dedicated a chapel to the holiest of their places, appropriately the only building on the place. Egeria mentioned Sunday celebration taking place there. If indeed the earliest building on Jabal Mūsā was the one erected by Julian Saba and mentioned in Theodoret's history, it seems that it was well taken care of and was extended in later years. The modest character of these building projects was in accordance with the realities of the anchoretic community that created them, keeping their distance from the attention of the imperial government and the official Church leadership. The liminal character of these humble buildings would be altered with the Justinianic project of large-scale edifices.

Another sign of respect for the site, mentioned only in the sixth-century account of the Piacenza pilgrim, was the tonsuring of both beard and hair for every male who visited the site. It could be a further devotional exercise stressing the sanctity of the place. When John Klimax was to receive his monastic tonsure in the late sixth century, he was taken up to Jabal Mūsā.

The emergence of the pilgrimage phenomenon from the fourth century encouraged the transformation of Horeb from a distant refuge inspired by a biblical identification (third century) to a major monastic centre, important for both imperial and ecclesiastical politics (mid-sixth to early seventh century). Brief references in early itineraries illustrated Jabal Mūsā as if it were surrounded by wilderness and Egeria's account reflected the same saintly simplicity. In the fifth century, the emperor Marcian addressed a letter to the Sinai anchorites. By the mid-sixth century the Piacenza pilgrim mentioned monks speaking three languages and in the early seventh century Pope Gregory I made a substantial donation to the Monastery. Even though sixth-century texts were less focused on Jabal Mūsā than in earlier centuries and mainly referred to monastic life, its importance had not diminished, as the seventh-century *Narrations* of Anastasios demonstrated.

Most importantly, what pilgrim accounts showed was the change in the way Jabal Mūsā was approached. Egeria climbed to it from the west, following a trail which is still there but rarely taken. On her way down she actually took the path later pilgrims (like the Piacenza pilgrim) would follow on their way up. The approach to Jabal Mūsā had obviously changed between 383 and 560–65 and the popularity of the latter choice in following centuries shows that it was not accidental. A prescribed way of experiencing the sacred landscape of Horeb crystallised in these two centuries and a set ascent route, complete with stepped pathway and arched gateways, was put in place. It featured the most interesting visitation spots in the sacred landscape: the Burning Bush, the cave of Elijah and the summit itself.

Although Jabal Mūsā changed after the Justinianic building programme, the approach to it remained the same for the rest of its history. Access to it was gained through a physical and spiritual ascent from the site of the first divine manifestation to Moses (conveniently within a fortified enclosure) and through two gateways. One of them was named 'of Confession', probably at a later date, because pilgrims had to undergo this sacred mystery before crossing it.[154] This 'purification ritual' must have been inspired by Psalm 24:3–4:

Who may ascend the hill of the Lord, who may stand in his holy place?
He who has clean hands and a pure heart, who does not lift up his soul to an idol or swear by what is false.[155]

Several prayer niches aiming at Jabal Mūsā were dispersed around the abode of the second most important prophet, Elijah, also available for visitation. Finally, the cleansed and illuminated pilgrim reached the place of the ultimate theophany. The 'Path of Moses' was more than an ascent route. It was the prescribed initiation process for experiencing the 'Mount of the Law' in its fullness.

Thus, some of the major qualities of the place were already established by the mid-sixth century: sacredness, preeminence over other places within a hallowed landscape, a protective role for worshippers, non-residential character further enhanced by devotional exercises and the erection of cultic structures, pilgrimage and a prescribed, almost processional itinerary of visitation.

Figure 8. *Interior of the Church of the Convent of St. Catherine*. Wood engraving on paper.

Chapter 2

The erection of a fortress protecting the site of the Burning Bush, of a basilica church within its walls, of several adjacent structures of military, residential and industrial character and, finally, of a second basilica on the summit of Jabal Mūsā during the rule of the Roman emperor Justinian I (527–65), remains to this day the most ambitious and formative human intervention in the Horeb landscape. In true imperial fashion, the investment of human and material resources supported a multifaceted construct of religious devotion and political ideology and altered the ways the place was perceived and experienced ever after. The 1998–1999 excavation on Jabal Mūsā revealed the full extent of the sixth-century edifices and no future discussion of Justinianic Sinai can exclude them. Ongoing work outside the walls of the Monastery of Saint Catherine brings to light more units of the mid-to-late sixth century every year. They expand the scale of the scheme further and should be viewed as parts of the same imperial project.

Justinian's Project

The era of Justinian was one of extensive building works throughout the empire, documented in detail by Prokopios in his *On Buildings*. Much of what was being erected was of religious nature (churches, monasteries, pilgrim facilities), often combined with military and wider political agenda. The emperor's Holy Land programme, the most ambitious since the era of Constantine I, included both the erection of new structures and the restoration of older, damaged buildings.[1] The programme was initiated after the destructions of the 529 Samaritan revolt as an affirmation of imperial control in a land plagued by religious conflict.[2] Similarly, a few years later, the crushing of the 532 'Nika' revolt in Constantinople would be sealed with the rebuilding at an unsurpassed scale of Hagia Sophia (532–7).

The interweaving of religious, military and political agenda in Justinian's building programmes was typical of Roman imperial policy. However, it was rarely as well-documented (and as fiercely debated) as in the case of the fortress he erected at the foot of Horeb. Out of the plethora of references to the Horeb project most stressed the direct involvement of the emperor. Some of the earlier Greek sources (contemporary in the case of Prokopios) and a couple of later ones in Arabic are consolidated by the evidence of inscriptions.

Interwoven with Prokopios's already analysed text from *On Buildings*, published *circa* 560, were the following lines on the erection of the fortress, the basilica and the *phylaktērion* at the foot of Horeb:

> Since these monks had nothing to crave – for they are superior to all human desires and have no interest in possessing anything or in caring for their bodies, nor do they seek pleasure in any other thing whatever – the Emperor Justinian built them a church which he dedicated to the Mother of God, so that they might be enabled to pass their lives therein praying and holding services. He built this church, not on the mountain's summit, but much lower down. [...] And at the base of the mountain [the summit] this Emperor built a very strong fortress and established there a considerable garrison [station] of troops, in order that the barbarian Saracens might not be able from that region, which, as I have said, is uninhabited, to make inroads with complete secrecy into the lands of Palestine proper.[3]

The passage has caused controversy, mainly because of its unclear meaning. The statement that the area was uninhabited was incorrect. The fortress and the basilica were mentioned separately although the latter was contained within the former. The strategic reasons behind the construction of the fortress (and the garrison station) were separated from the religious motivation for the erection of the basilica. And the translation quoted above (and all others published so far) missed a point made clear in the Greek original. the word *phylaktērion* (translated as 'garrison' by most editors) did not refer to people but to a building, a 'garrison station'.

It was this last misunderstanding that prompted Philip Mayerson to strongly doubt the historical value of Prokopios's account.[4] He claimed that the garrison could not have been stationed in the surviving fortress, the present-day Monastery of Saint Catherine, and therefore, he concluded, it had not been positioned there at all. However, excavations since 2001 have brought to light one more fortified structure to the east of the Monastery (discussed below). This could be what Prokopios meant by '*phylaktērion*', the garrison's abode.

As far as Justinian's dual motivation and the area's lack of occupants is concerned, perhaps Prokopios's sources were inadequate or contradictory. It is also possible that he was not interested in accurate description but in celebrating and glorifying 'the sensational and the dramatic'.[5] As mentioned before, he was fairly unaccustomed to the realities of the desert and held its ways in disdain. However, it seems that the imperial agenda was indeed twofold, aiming to protect the anchorites and pilgrims and to police the Bedouin.

Between the two objectives, the religious one seems to have been more important, since there could not have been a strategically worse position for the fortress and the *phylaktērion* than the one chosen. Situated at the foot of the mountain, they were open to attacks from adjacent heights.[6] However, the fortress protected the Burning Bush and the *katholikon*, which was aptly dedicated to the Mother of God; just as her virginity was not consumed by giving birth to Christ, so the Bush was not consumed by the fire of God's presence within it.[7] A Saracen raid in *circa* 570 was successfully fended off thanks to the walls.[8] Their volume inspired awe and performed a diplomatic role by consolidating imperial authority in a hard-to-control area.[9]

Eutychios (Saʿīd ibn Biṭrīq, 877–940, patriarch of Alexandria between 933 and 940, writing in the early tenth century) gave the longest and most detailed account for the building of the fortress and the two churches:

> When the monks of Mount Sinai heard of the receptive disposition
> of Emperor Justinian and that he delighted in building churches
> and monasteries, they came to him and complained that the

Ishmaelite Arabs injured them by devouring their provisions, and destroying their places [of habitation] [...] When the Emperor asked them what they wanted, they said: 'Oh king, that you build us a monastery in which we may be protected.' [...] The Emperor consequently sent a legate with full authority and with written instructions to the prefect of Egypt that he supply him [the legate] with as much money as needed, and that he provide men and provisions from Egypt. The legate was also ordered to build a church at Clysma, and a monastery at Raya; and to build a monastery on Mount Sinai and to fortify it so that no better could be found in the entire world, and to make it so strong that the monks or the monastery would not fear or suffer from any quarter. The legate built the church of St. Athanasius at Clysma and the monastery at Raya; and then going to Mount Sinai he found the Bush located in a narrow place between two mountains, and in the same spot he found a tower built near the Bush and some running springs of water near it, and monks scattered about the wadis. It was his intention to build the monastery high up on the mountain and to leave the Bush and the tower (where they were). However, he rejected the plan because of the water, since there was no adequate supply of water on the mountain. He therefore built the monastery close to the Bush and enclosed the tower within the monastery. The monastery was situated between two mountains and in a narrow spot, so much that if anyone climbed the northern slope of the mountain and threw a stone, it would land in the middle of the monastery and injure the monks. Hence he built the monastery in this narrow spot, close by the Bush and the famous [biblical] monuments and a supply of water. On the mountain top, above the spot where Moses received the law, he built a chapel. The name of the abbot of the monastery was Doulas. The legate returned to Emperor Justinian and informed him of the churches and monasteries that he had built. He also described how he built the monastery of Mount Sinai. The emperor answered and said: 'You made a mistake and you have harmed the monks and placed them in the hands of the enemy. Why did you not build the monastery on top of the mountain?' The legate answered: 'I placed it near the Bush and close to the water supply; but if it had been built on the mountain top, the monks would lack water so much so that if they were at any time besieged, their water supply would be shut off and they would die of thirst. Moreover the Bush would be too far away from them.' The emperor said: 'You must reduce the mountain, which dominates the monastery on the north, to ground level.' The legate answered him: 'If we applied to that task all the resources of Rome, Egypt and Syria, we still could not level that mountain to the ground.' At this the emperor was enraged, and had him beheaded. Then he dispatched another legate, and with him a party consisting of domestic slaves of the Romans with their wives and children, to the number of a hundred persons, and he ordered him to take from Egypt another hundred, including wives and children. He was to build houses outside the monastery for them to live in, so that they might protect the monastery and the monks. He further bade him provide them with sustenance, and to cause a sufficient supply of grain to be procured from Egypt for them and for the monastery. When the legate reached Mount Sinai, he built the required number of dwellings outside the monastery on the east, and fortified them with a castle. He caused the above-mentioned slaves to settle in these dwellings, so that they could guard the monastery and protect it. This place is called to this day Deir el Abid, or 'Serfminster'.[10]

The strategic concerns of Prokopios's account are better explained in this passage by an author closely acquainted with the topography and realities of Sinaitic life. The dilemma faced by the legate was a real one. The surrender of Christian refugees at Jabal Mūsā to Muslim besiegers a century and a half later was due to the lack of water and the corruption of fortress defences by human and natural agents.

Eutychios's sources were probably local, different from the official sources Prokopios had used. Yet, both authors referred to a delegation (or petition) of anchorites to the imperial court and to the subsequent building of the fortress and basilica at the foot of the mountain.[11] Whether the legate story was true or not, it illustrates the importance of both the metaphysical element and the practical considerations in the imperial decision-making process. It also explains the mechanism through which orders were implemented. An order was carried out through the dispatch of an official from the capital who raised funds, mobilised a local workforce and was allowed considerable freedom in making choices and interpreting instructions. After work was finished, a report was presented to the imperial authority and necessary amendments were made.

Eutychios also briefly mentioned the 'chapel' at the summit, clearly a part of the same Justinianic project, and described the 'serfminster', which can be safely identified with the *phylaktērion* of Prokopios. The dwellings and fortress commissioned by the emperor were demolished in the eighth century by the monks to prevent the lay population latterly converted to Islam from disturbing their ascetic lives. The ruins were still visible at the time Eutychios wrote and indeed remained visible (and ignored) until excavations brought to light a large fortified enclosure and a workshop complex. Both Prokopios and Eutychios were aware of the full scale of the project and discussions about their presumed mistakes and inconsistencies were simply due to partial knowledge of the archaeological record.

Information in Anastasios's mid-seventh-century *Narrations* complements the picture created by Prokopios and Eutychios and relates to the way the Jabal Mūsā basilica functioned by the seventh century.[12] In the second, thirty-seventh and thirty-ninth narrations, the post of *paramonarios*, overseer, was mentioned for the summit church. He was obviously occupied with the care of the structure, carried the keys to it and was important enough within the monastic hierarchy to be deemed worthy of an apprentice (*diakonētēs*). The *paramonarios* would not spend the night on Jabal Mūsā thanks to the prohibition already discussed, although he was there early enough to welcome two fathers visiting the place (first narration). Probably he was stationed at a nearby cell, at Farsh Elias or further up the stepped path. Such a cell was identified by Uzi Dahari on the extremely steep southern slope of Jabal Mūsā some 250 m below the summit.[13]

Finally, in the third narration, Pentecost was mentioned as being celebrated at Jabal Mūsā:

Once as the *anaphora* was performed during the celebration for the holy Pentecost, and the priest having recited the *epinikios* hymn of the magnificent glory, all the mountains responded by saying three times with terrible thunder: Holy, Holy, Holy; and the reverberating sound and the thunder continued up to half an hour.[14]

In the *Synaxarium of the Church of Constantinople*, dated to the tenth century or later, another mention was made to the Justinianic programme:

> This king, blessed be his memory, built the magnificent fortress on the sacred Sinai mountain and glorified the holy churches within it having built them with honour; and he erected the admirable church of the sacred summit of the sacred mountain; and he plentifully provided monetary resources to the monasteries living in prudency and celibacy in the Sinai, and the whole of Egypt and Palestine.[15]

A number of churches were mentioned within the fortress, but they were probably chapels (several of them were built along the aisles of the basilica and in other places within the enclosure). The Jabal Mūsā basilica was clearly considered as part of the same project and its mountaintop location was carefully separated from the fortress and its churches.

In a 1338 manuscript of a text composed in the late twelfth or early thirteenth century (before 1208) and attributed to a Coptic writer probably named Abu'l-Makārim, a detailed description of the Monastery of Saint Catherine and its environs was given. The Horeb description probably dated from after 1180.[16] The possibility of first-hand familiarity with the place makes this description valuable:

> [Paragraph 4] There [on al-Ṭūr, Mount Sinai] is a church on the summit of the mountain, over the place where the prophet Moses received the Law. There is also the church of Saint George, the church of Saint Stephanos, the church of Aaron the priest, a church dedicated to Saint Basil. And there was constructed a church dedicated to the prophet Elijah. [...]
> [Paragraph 6] On this mountain God spoke to the prophet Elijah at a place different from the one where God spoke to Moses. There one finds traces of his ascension: the imprints of his hands, of his

elbows and of his legs. The place of his removal is under a dome.
[…]
[Paragraph 15c] It is mentioned that there were in this valley at the
time of the Byzantine Empire twelve thousand monasteries and
churches filled with monks. There also was a hospital the traces of
which survive to this day.
[Paragraph 16a] The church that is on the summit of the mountain
is built of black stones. The width of its enclosure is seven cubits.
It comprises three iron doors and a small door on its western side,
in front of which rests a small moveable stone. If the monks wish
to lift it, they do it. When a visitor approaches, they make it glide
in such fashion that it obstructs and obscures the position of the
door. In the interior, a spring is found and another on the exterior.
The Christians allege that there is a sacred flame of the same sort
with the flame that revives itself in Jerusalem. They use it for illumination every evening. Its light is white and of a weak heat that
does not burn. It becomes stronger when it is used to light a lamp.
It is populated by monks and people that come to visit them. It is
one of the monasteries that are known for their miracles.
[Paragraph 16b] It is mentioned that the number of steps taken to
ascend [to the summit] amounts to seven thousand five hundred
and sixty. The ascent requires a whole day, like the descent.[17]

The editors of Abu'l-Makārim's text proposed that the description in paragraph 16a did not refer to the Jabal Mūsā basilica but to
the Monastery, and suggested he misunderstood a confusing earlier
source.[18] It is more probable that the description was a *mélange* of
details from both buildings, since the reference to 'black stones' was
accurate as far as the grey granite foundations of the summit basilica
were concerned but did not apply to the fortress. The three 'iron'
doors and the sliding rock appeared in several descriptions of the
Monastery.[19] The two springs could refer either to the Monastery
(with the two wells) or to Jabal Mūsā (with the cisterns) and the
seven-cubit-wide enclosure (whichever of the many possible cubit
lengths was meant) applied to neither.
    Abu'l-Makārim mentioned the 'serfminster' or *phylaktērion* in
paragraphs 3 and 5, a 'hospital' and the conversion of the laymen to

Islam in paragraph 5, probably quoting Eutychios.[20] He also listed
churches of Saints George, Stephanos, Basil, the prophet Elijah and
the priest Aaron, obviously referring to chapels within and around
the Monastery.[21]

The Cairene historian al-Maqrīzī's (1364–1442) text on Mount
Sinai, although written at a later age, also contained a description of
the Jabal Musa basilica:

> To ascend to Sinai, one has to climb 6,666 steps. Half way up there
> is a church dedicated to the prophet Elijah. On the summit there
> is another church dedicated to Moses (blessed be his name) with
> columns of marble and doors of bronze. It is the place where God,
> the most High, talked to Moses and it is from there that the latter
> took the rock with the Tablets of the Law. There is but one monk
> in the service of the church. They claim that no one can spend the
> night there, but there is outside a shelter for the guardian, where he
> can spend the night. There is now nothing left of these churches.[22]

Al-Maqrīzī's description was accurate (only the number of steps
was overstated) and so were the references to a *paramonarios* and
the prohibition to spend the night on the summit. He reported the
church as being dedicated to Moses. The source al-Maqrīzī used for
the description was obviously an earlier one, but he was informed
enough to specify that at the time of writing the basilica had been
destroyed. He also mentioned a church at Farsh Elias, of which no
trace exists. Abu'l-Makārim had added that this church was crowned
by a dome.[23]

Both Abu'l-Makārim and al-Maqrīzī probably got their information from a pool of references which included Eutychios and other
Coptic and Melkite (Orthodox Christian of the Chalcedonian rite)
sources in Arabic.[24] However, each added interesting details that
were sourced from first-hand experience, either personal or derived
by others who had recently visited Horeb.

The fortress and other buildings in Wādī 'l-Dayr
The Monastery as it stands today is a labyrinthine complex of dozens
of buildings dating from the fourth to the twentieth century. Within

Figure 9. David Roberts (British, 1796–1864), *Chapel of the Convent of St. Catherine on Mount Sinai*. Lithograph on paper. Based on drawings executed in February 1839.

the same room, walls from different periods often coexist under a later roof. The dry climate prevents materials from decomposing and dating is a process of trial and error.[25]

The fortress measures approximately 76 m N–S by 87 m E–W and its walls vary in height between 12 m and 15 m. Today it has two main entrances on the western and on the northern wall and a few lesser-known ones. The western entrance has had its iron-clad cypress wood door dated to the twelfth century and lies to the left of the original sixth-century gateway, which is now walled up.[26] Above the latter a *machicoulis* bears a *tabula ansata* carved into the granite wall with the following inscription:

> This is the gate of the Lord through which the righteous may enter
> + of Justinian the emperor the friend of buildings [or 'of Christ'][27]

The northern portion of the fortress was founded on a crevice in the *wādī* bed, whilst the southern half was erected on solid granite. All structures within and around were built of large blocks of relatively friable local red granite. A series of buildings and facilities dating from the sixth century are arranged inside the enclosure, in casemate fashion, like the mill on the northeastern corner and the painted chapel within the southern wall. However, the best-known early features of the complex are the present-day mosque, originally used as the refectory, and the basilical church (*katholikon*) opposite.

The mosque is roughly square with two cross-sectioned pillars supporting a flat roof and it has been extensively plastered and remodelled in recent years, thus rendering research into its various phases very difficult. According to H.L. Rabino, a Byzantine marble altar cover with sixteenth- and seventeenth-century Muslim pilgrim inscriptions in ink was originally incorporated into the *mihrab* niche.[28] The Russian pilgrim and envoy of the tsar Vasiliĭ Posniakov (travelled 1558–1561) mentioned that the building was originally a chapel dedicated to Saint Basil of Caesarea (Basil the Great, 330–379).[29] George H. Forsyth identified it with the fortress's original guest house.[30] Both these views do not agree with similar examples of monastic architecture, in which buildings axially situated to the west of *katholikon* churches are used as refectories.[31] Probably in the

Figure 10. Léon, marquis de Laborde (French, 1807–1869, painter) and Godefroy Engelmann (French, 1788–1839, engraver), *Grande mosaique de l'église du Couvent de Ste. Catherine. (Mont Sinaï.)* Lithograph on paper. Based on drawings executed in 1828.

early twelfth century a minaret was added to the northeastern corner of the mosque. The minaret retains its original roof of date palm, black poplar and cypress timber.[32]

The church (*katholikon*) contains a unique collection of original fittings and icons. Its first dedication was to the Virgin Mary (*Theotokos*), according to Prokopios, and now it is to the Transfiguration. The *katholikon* was orientated off-axis within the fortress and its floor was sunken four metres below the level of the western entrance, solutions probably dictated by the geomorphology of the site and the need to place the Burning Bush to the east of the sanctuary arch.[33] A three-aisled nucleus terminates with a semicircular apse which is inscribed within a rectangle and surrounded by two (slightly later) chapels with three apses each. Three chapels flank each of the aisles. A slightly later narthex stands to the west with its entrance opposite the former refectory (present-day mosque).

The chapel of the Burning Bush is a later addition and the botanical attraction for pilgrims visiting the fortress was originally growing within an open-air enclosure, or small courtyard.[34] The semidome of the small apse in the chapel is decorated with a cross in mosaic probably dating from the eleventh century, whilst the rest of the interior was clad in glazed tiles in 1680, restored and possibly added to in 1770.[35] The chapel was accessible via the northern aisle of the basilica through the chapel to the left of the apse. The return route passed through the corresponding chapel to the right and along the southern aisle.[36] The focus of interest of the entire complex, the Burning Bush, originally lay outside the main structure of the *katholikon* rather than being placed at its centre, a practice connected to the Constantinian tradition of Palestinian Holy Land pilgrimage buildings.[37] It could also be argued that the 'Burning Bush' was (and remains) a living organism much in need of fresh air and light; the open-air court was necessary for its survival and today it grows outside the chapel.

The nave of the basilica is separated from the aisles by plastered granite colonnades supporting arches. Their granite capitals were carved with a variety of devices.[38] The building is covered by a roof retaining a large part of its original sixth-century timber. It was restored and boards were added between the beams to create a ceiling in 1732 46. The lead sheet sheathing survived until 1911.[39]

On the beautifully carved ceiling beams, pinewood boards facing east (the first one) and west (the two others) bear carved inscriptions:

> + Lord God who appeared in this place, save and have mercy on your servant Stephanos Martyriou, deacon and architect from Aila, and rest in peace the souls of his children Georgios and Nonna +

> + To the memory and for the repose of our departed queen Theodora +

> + For the salvation of our most pious king Justinian +[40]

Since the church originally had no ceiling, the beams were exposed and the inscriptions were visible from below.[41] In this way, people in the nave could read the imperial names whereas those of the architect and his children would be seen by officiating priests. The builder of the edifice was Stephanos from Aila in the Gulf of Aqaba. Thus Eutychios's claim that local forces were used for the project is verified.[42] The two other inscriptions are the best testimony for the dating of the building, since Theodora died in 548 and Justinian in 565. Therefore, the roof was constructed sometime after the empress's death and before Prokopios's *On Buildings* was published *circa* 560.[43]

The wooden doors separating the narthex from the nave are of the sixth century, whilst the exterior narthex doors are of Fāṭimid date (eleventh or twelfth century).[44] In the Early Christian period, pilgrims and lay visitors would enter the church through the side doorways into the aisles rather than through the main entrance into the nave, a way in reserved for clerics and important visitors.[45]

The original floor was destroyed in 1401 during an attack by the Mamlūk army and the present one in the nave, the work of a Damascene artisan, dates from 1583–1592 (restored in 1714–5).[46] The aisles and narthex were paved anew in 1766 by the Sinai *skeuophylax* (sacristan) Prokopios, a marble carver formerly in the Ottoman sultan's court.[47] However, the apse retains its original marble cladding. The semidome above was decorated with a mosaic of the Transfiguration surrounded by bands of protomes of the apostles and prophets within medallions.[48] A long mosaic inscription underneath is the only one in the fortress which is free of errors. It reads:

> + In the name of the father and the son and the holy ghost the whole of this work was executed for the salvation of those who contributed towards it in the time of Longinos, most holy priest and superior + + By the effort of Theodōros, priest and second in command, indiction fourteen.[49]

The keystone of the arch is flanked by two globe-bearing angels flying towards the Lamb of the Eucharist, with protomes of John the Baptist and the Virgin Mary on either side. The window on top is surrounded by two panels depicting Moses removing his sandals before the Burning Bush and Moses receiving the Law.[50]

The sophisticated iconographic programme of the apse alluded to all the elements of the Sinaitic narrative bringing together Old and New Testament. Elijah and Moses, the prophets associated with Horeb and commemorated at Jabal Mūsā and Farsh Elias, are flanking Christ, hovering between His human and divine natures (a reference to the Christological controversy raging in the sixth-century Near East).[51] At His feet three New Testament figures, the apostles Peter, John and James, squirm and marvel at the miracle. The Sinaitic moments of Moses are illustrated over the Transfiguration and below them the faces of the Baptist and the Virgin Mary create the earliest Deesis arrangement with the medallion of the Eucharistic Lamb at the keystone of the arch.[52]

A marble altar (covered in 1675 with a mother-of-pearl and ivory-inlaid wooden canopy by Stamatios from Athens), a marble altar screen (partly reused in various parts of the church) and a few icons which have been stylistically dated to the period survive from the original furnishings of the church.[53] They were imported into South Sinai and, at least as far as the monumental encaustic icons are concerned, they originated in Constantinople.[54] Although the mosaic decoration is obscured today by the altar screen erected in 1612, it would originally have been visible from the nave's entrance.[55] The semidome would look from a distance like an enormous eye with the mandorla around the figure of Christ as its pupil.[56] The interior of the basilica was magnificent in scale and rich in detail, in keeping with developments in Constantinopolitan church decoration.

Outside the fortress walls, further structures date from the same period (mid-to-late sixth century). Their ruins were mentioned by Eutychios in the early tenth century and Abu'l-Makārim in the late twelfth or the early thirteenth century, and remained visible but ignored. A brief excavation of the rubbish heaps outside the Monastery, probably in spring 1906, under C.T. Currelly proved fruitless.[57] In 2000 an article including a simple ground-plan was published.[58] In the spring of that year, archaeological research started to the east of the Monastery of Saint Catherine and at a distance of approximately 30 m from its wall. It brought to light two enclosures, one approximately 60 m sq and the other smaller and of irregular shape. The former has been only partially excavated but the latter has been investigated completely and is thought to be a cluster of workshops, servicing both the adjacent enclosure and the fortress.[59]

The nature of the larger structure is as yet unclear, but there is reason to believe it is the *phylaktērion* mentioned by Prokopios or 'serfminster' described by Eutychios. It consists of a series of rooms arranged along a strongly-built outer wall and opening into corridors. A tower appears to be projecting from the middle of the eastern wall, which dominates a slope overlooking the eastern approach to Wādī 'l-Dayr. Inside the eastern half of the southern wall is an impressive room with buttresses. The character of the building is defensive and the architecture of Early Christian frontier fortresses, *limes*, provides similar examples.[60]

An alternative interpretation could also be proposed. A 'hospital' existed in the early seventh century and was mentioned by Anastasios and Abu'l-Makārim. A miracle witnessed by John Klimax in the early seventh century happened during a meal served to six hundred people, presumably in a very large room.[61] The southeastern buttressed room could very well have been the one. A similar structure with a large buttressed room has been excavated at Mount Nebo in Jordan and has been interpreted as a 'hospital'. This mountaintop pilgrimage facility, associated with Moses as well, was also of Justinianic date and could be paralleled with the Horeb buildings. In any case, the *phylaktērion* could accommodate multiple functions. Similar sharing of a fortified building's area for military purposes and for hospitality appears in the *castrum* and *xenodochium* 'of Saint George' 30 km outside Elusa in the Negev desert, built during the later sixth century.[62]

These previously unknown buildings change our understanding of Justinian's building programme. Scholars so far have assumed that the Sinai project was relatively small in scope, a basilica protected by a fortress. The investment was modest when compared with costly undertakings in Palestine and Egypt. However, the fortress and basilica ought to be included now within a larger scheme, encompassing another fortified structure and organised workshops.

Furthermore, the ground-plan of the recently excavated sixth-century monastery at Wādī al-Ṭūr near the coastal town of Ṭūr reflects the defensive arrangement of the Horeb structures, especially the *phylaktērion*.[63] Although no textual confirmation exists, this coastal complex may perhaps be included into a wider project aimed at channelling pilgrim traffic from the Red Sea port to Horeb and protecting the area from threats. The route connecting the sea with the mountain sites has been well-documented and surveyed.[64] The ultimate destination of this traffic was another church, built with even greater effort and expense 700 m above Wādī 'l-Dayr.

The basilica on Jabal Mūsā
Although the antiquity and scale of the Jabal Mūsā ruins were well-known since the medieval period, research during the nineteenth century was limited,[65] and scholars in the twentieth century were preoccupied with the Monastery and its treasures.[66] The discussion below draws on the excavations conducted by the Hellenic Archaeological Mission at South Sinai since 1998.[67]

By the time the erection of a basilica started at Jabal Mūsā, a series of small-scale building projects had already been completed on site (discussed above). To allow for the monumental three-aisled structure to be founded, retaining walls supporting terraces were built, encasing previous architecture and creating a platform of sufficient length and width. The foundation of the lowest westernmost of these retaining walls was 7 m below the level of the natural bedrock to the east. Bridging this chasm required imaginative planning of transitional levels between the two extremes and a large volume of filling material. The effort to transport this filling material must have rivalled the manpower necessary to raise the blocks of friable red granite from hundreds of metres below. The transportation of lighter items must have been effected by means of beasts of burden. However, granite boulders weighing up to 300 kg could only have been hoisted up the vertical eastern drop of Jabal Mūsā with cranes.[68]

Building materials also included wood, a rarity in Sinai. The roof was made of long beams and rafters, similar to the ones in the fortress basilica. Materials also included lead for roof covering (a few traces were unearthed), marble and sandstone cut in geometric shapes for paving (*opus sectile*), stone and glass *tesserae* for mosaic work, and lime for wall plastering. The marble was of the 'Proconnesian' variety, white veined with grey and quarried at the island of Proconnesos (present-day Marmara) near Constantinople.[69] The use of heavy, bulky and expensive materials transported from afar testifies to the scale and cost of the undertaking.

The structures erected with these materials included a three-aisled basilica church with a narthex, a vaulted cistern below the southern aisle and two more underground cisterns about 70 m to the west (*Buildings on Jabal Mūsā* map on the back endpaper). The exterior dimensions of the church and narthex complex were approximately 28.35 m E–W by 11.85/12.10 m N–S, with an estimated height of 11 m.[70] The northern and southern walls of the basilica were founded on the natural bedrock to the east and on the earth fill to the west. There is no evidence to support the use of columns in the Jabal Mūsā basilica, this being one of its main differences from the fortress church.[71]

The narthex seems to have been added shortly after the main church was completed. There is a masonry seam between them but the building method was identical. It may be assumed that the work was not finished in one season and the narthex was added in the next term. An entrance survives up to the lintel on the southern wall of the narthex. It corresponds to an external stone staircase ascending from west to east; another staircase leads up to this southern entrance. In this way, the steep difference in altitude between the western and eastern ends of the complex was cleverly bridged.

The interior of the vaulted southern cistern was plastered on a foundation consisting of rubble walls and the natural bedrock floor.[72]

On this plasterwork several pilgrims' inscriptions were unearthed, some perhaps dating from the first millennium. The flat roof of the cistern must have served as the southern terrace of the basilica. Along with the underground cisterns at the foot of the summit, which collected rainwater through a water channel, it would have met the needs of visitors to Jabal Mūsā and strengthened the defensive ability of the place.

Opposite the southern cistern, the opening of cave A was exposed on the face of the rock which today supports the mosque; it is now buried behind a modern terrace. The cave had been identified since the time of Egeria with the place where Moses spent forty days and nights and the inscriptions carved on its face testify to its importance. It lay outside the main basilica building and probably had no roof. The subsidiary situation of this visitation spot can be compared with the exposed position of the Burning Bush to the east of the *katholikon*. However, cave B was included within the church and could be visited at the far end of its northern aisle.

After having suffered the arduous climb, the pilgrim was rewarded with much to marvel at. Although there is no way to reconstruct the interior decoration scheme of the building, *crustae* of white marble and sandstone must have adorned the floor, creating a geometric *opus sectile*, while parts of the walls must have been covered with mosaics. The quantity of *tesserae* that was collected is small and it is likely that walls were selectively decorated, as in the *katholikon*. There is no evidence on the subject matter of the mosaic. Architectural decoration was similar to that of the *katholikon*, with twisted shaft and plain colonettes and carved pilaster capitals. The excavation brought back to light an inscribed red granite keystone, first recorded in 1966 and since considered missing. It reads: 'God having been seen in this / place / remember Hēsychios.'[73] The connection of Hēsychios to the church is unclear. Architectural members with traces of lime plaster came to light during the excavation and testify to the building's original plaster coating.

Small finds from the Justinianic and pre-Islamic periods include sherds that belonged predominantly to the Late Roman Amphora I type (early sixth to late seventh century), produced in Cilicia, Antioch and Cyprus. They were mainly used for the transportation

Figure 11. Elijah Walton (British, 1832–1880, painter) and William Forest (British, 1805–1889, engraver), *Mount Sinai. [Jebel Musa as seen from Jebel Katharina]*. Engraving on paper.

of liquids like oil and wine, necessary for the running of the church (illumination with lamps and preparation of the Eucharist) and probably offered by pilgrims and visitors as well as produced on Horeb. The Aegean origin Late Roman Amphora II type (fifth to seventh century) was seldom encountered. Finally, fragments of window panes made with the 'bull's eye' or 'crown' technique testified to the screening material of the basilica's windows.[74]

Uzi Dahari's suggestion that the summit basilica was dedicated to the Virgin Mary (*Theotokos*, Mother of God) begs for revision.[75] The parallelism of Mary with the Burning Bush was only meaningful at the *katholikon* and made no sense for Jabal Mūsā. The notion that writers like Anastasios would not mention the supposed Marian consecration because they did not agree with Justinian's choice ignores the respect commanded by an imperial donor.[76] The identification of the Greek letters *ΘΚ* carved on architectural members with monograms of the *Theotokos* is also problematic as other letter combinations also appear.[77]

The date of the building can be established between 560 (when Prokopios's *On Buildings*, which ignores it, was published) and 565 (when Justinian died) and finds support this date.[78] It is possible that the interior decoration, especially the mosaics, was finished later in the century, as has been proposed for the mosaics at the *katholikon*.[79] However, the scale of the Jabal Mūsā project can only be attributed to the great era of imperial building that was the rule of Justinian.

The Monastic Ultimate

Apart from protection against aggressors, the sixth-century imperial building project consolidated Sinaitic status in the ecclesiastical hierarchy. The area's inclusion into the Holy Land programme by Justinian placed it alongside the Palestinian pilgrimage destinations of Jerusalem, Bethlehem and Nazareth. From the second half of the sixth century onwards, 'Mount Sinai' would be a station in most Holy Land itineraries despite its considerable distance from the other sites and the difficulties associated with its visitation.

The flow of pilgrims must have had a positive impact on the economy of the area and ensured plentiful resources for the community of frugal ascetics. In a sixth- or seventh-century caravan account list, a Father Martyrios from Sinai is mentioned as entrusting the sum of 270½ *solidi* to a small company of traders, supposedly to transfer them to a larger episcopal see for safety. This remarkable sum, the equivalent of fifty-two years' wages for a labourer or 1.23 kg of solid gold, must have been gathered from the contributions of pilgrims adhering to various dogmatic groups, Monophysite and Chalcedonian, Coptic, Syriac and Armenian, travelling from all over Christendom.[80]

The cosmopolitan anchoretic and later coenobitic community of Horeb attracted the entire *Orbis Christianus*. Christian Arabs, Georgians, Slavs, Monophysite Coptics, Syrians, Armenians and even Roman Catholics (deemed schismatic after 1054 but disliked by eastern Christians before that) coexisted within the Monastery walls. Icons and manuscripts of various origins and styles must have once furnished chapels dedicated to these heterodox rites.[81] It was this distance from theological debates, coupled with the inclusion of Sinai within the Islamic world, which prevented iconoclasts from eliminating works of representational religious art during their heyday (730–842).

Although the attraction of 'Mount Sinai' emanated from Jabal Mūsā, from the late sixth century to the early years of Muslim rule the reputation of Sinaitic saintly figures added an extra appeal for pious visitors.[82] Preeminent among them was John Klimax (early seventh century), an abbot of the coenobium at the fortress, later to be canonised as a saint. John received his monastic tonsure at Jabal Mūsā at the age of twenty and was probably commemorated with an inscription on an arch above the steps leading to the summit itself.[83] His best-known work, *The Heavenly Ladder* (*Klimax*), remains the most important book of Orthodox monasticism.[84] In it, he described the thirty spiritual steps which ascetics had to climb to reach the love of God, the ultimate step of the 'Heavenly Ladder'. John himself had lived in a cell for twenty years prior to becoming abbot and he returned to it before dying.[85]

The Heavenly Ladder was translated into Latin and was read across Christianity.[86] A letter by Pope Gregory I (on the throne 590–604), dated 1 September 600, to a certain John, abbot of Sinai, could have been addressed to John Klimax. It mentioned the pope's donation of apparel for a 'hospital' (perhaps the *phylaktērion*) and clothes to the Monastery.[87] John's reputation enhanced the status of Horeb and attracted monks, solitaries and pilgrims.

The first volumes of the library of the Monastery of Saint Catherine must have arrived at this period. The earliest ones could have been offered by the emperor alongside icons and other furnishings. Many ascetics were literate and carried with them theological works, in addition to liturgical books necessary for the ecclesiastical life of the community. However, no evidence of a scriptorium appears to exist from such an early date – although it was a feature of the Monastery's life in later centuries.[88]

The erection of the fortress around the church of the Virgin Mary at the foot of Horeb offered the anchorites safe shelter and a place to practise communal veneration. In earlier times the only form of organised life was *laurai*, small monasteries of five to ten anchorites around a master. It seems that the process of the anchoretic community's transformation into a coenobitic one started in the later sixth century, although the paradigm of eremitic life remained strong in the Sinaitic psyche and continues to this day, inspired by the stories and exhortations of the *Heavenly Ladder*.[89]

The archaeological remains from this sizeable community extended beyond the imperially-funded structures (the fortress and its great church, the *phylaktērion* and workshops and the summit basilical complex). Although their exact dates are impossible to determine, up to forty-one building complexes from the Early Christian period survive on the slopes and valleys of the mountain and allow the reconstruction of an everyday life devoted to agriculture as well as prayer.

The complexes include isolated chapels, fourteen small 'monasteries' (*laurai* is the correct term, due to their diminutive size), dams, water conduits, natural pools and built reservoirs (to collect, channel and store rainwater) and wells. A Horeb *laura* consisted of a central building with a chapel, orchards and adjacent gardens, usually around a well, and at least one cell. The gardens supported both nearby solitaries and *laurai* inhabitants. Their abodes were connected with paths, sometimes stepped and resembling the 'Path of Moses'.[90]

By the early seventh century Horeb, once a remote wilderness, was pullulating with holy men busy leading devout lives which revolved around Jabal Mūsā. Together with the hundreds of families living near the *phylaktērion* at the foot of the mountain, the large groups of pilgrims and their escorts, the local Bedouin and the monks resident in the fortress coenobium, had turned the desert into a city, an economically sound, socially diverse and spiritually important community.

A few decades later the Sinai Peninsula was incorporated into the Islamic empire, but Horeb remained an important religious centre. By the eighth or mid-ninth century it became an independent bishopric and its first bishop was a certain Constantinos. He appeared at the list of participants in the Eighth Catholic Ecumenical (or Fourth Roman Catholic) Synod of Constantinople (869–870). He signed himself as '*misericordia Dei episcopus Synai*'.[91] It was not only the holy sites like Jabal Mūsā which helped sustain Sinaitic prestige among eastern Christianity, the ancient anchoretic and monastic tradition proved to be an added motivation for those aspiring to attain sainthood. Horeb, 'Mount Sinai', became the definitive destination for ascetics through the ages, the 'monastic ultimate'.

Imperial Landscape

During a brief period from the mid-sixth to the early seventh century the Horeb landscape was indelibly marked by the gifts and fruits of an imperial project. Up to this point Horeb had been an important albeit liminal destination. Anchorites and pilgrims visited it but their numbers did not compare with those flocking to the easily reachable and, since the fourth century, splendidly housed Palestinian holy places. If Mount Sinai was to be incorporated in the Holy Land circuit, it had to provide security, accessibility and splendour. Justinian's project ensured all three.

The changes envisaged by the emperor for Sinai served ecclesiastical, military and political agenda. He 'invented' a major pilgrimage destination by extending its reception facilities (fortress, *phylaktērion* / 'hospital', workshops, probably Ṭūr seafront monastery and associated road stations) and by ensuring the safety of both resident clergy and travellers. Impressive new buildings like the *katholikon* (548–560) and the Jabal Mūsā basilica (560–565) were decorated with mosaics and icons of the highest quality. The nuanced iconographic programme of the *katholikon* mosaics communicated the message of Christian orthodoxy against the Monophysite tide sweeping Egypt and Palestine. A library, possibly inaugurated through imperial munificence, provided the impetus for the intellectual production of John Klimax, among others. His work brought kudos from across Christianity to Horeb. A new life had been injected into the remote anchoretic abode.

Beyond their religious significance, Justinian's buildings had a military character. The fortress incorporated storage and manufacture facilities whilst functioning as a centre of cult for anchoretic communities and solitaries dispersed in the wider area. The total estimated number of ecclesiastics inhabiting Horeb and its surrounding mountains and valleys in the sixth century was approximately 414.[92] The synoecism which resulted in a densely populated coenobium within the walls of the fortress happened only gradually from the later sixth century. The fact that these walls endured several attacks by humans and natural elements for fifteen centuries further testifies to their defensive character.

The threats which dwellers and visitors had to face were most probably Bedouin raids rather than organised attacks by trained armies. The gradual relaxation of imperial control, or rather the nervous effort required to sustain it in areas increasingly remote from Constantinople, may be the explanation behind such fortified structures. The Horeb buildings can be compared to the contemporaneous walls of the Wādī Fīran settlement and demonstrate a shift of self-governed populations towards guarding themselves against occasional hazards rather than relying on troops sent from larger administrative and military centres. The transfer of families of soldiers instead of a military unit to the *phylaktērion* further testifies to such a policy.[93]

Justinian's building programme made an orthodox religious statement within a heterodox milieu, protected and promoted a community of anchorites, gradually altered the character of their society into a coenobitic one, managed a newly created wave of pilgrims, held the ever-threatening Bedouin at bay and consolidated imperial prestige among all these populations by planting a deep footing of centralised authority into a distant and liminal site. However, the buildings did not alter the Sinaitic topography in essence. The main landmarks were set since at least the fourth century and subsequent structures, impressive as they were, did not change their locations or configuration but rather respected them and were built around them 'setting them in stone'.

Recent archaeological work has allowed the full appreciation of this programme. Prokopios's account, often discredited because of supposed inconsistencies, has been proven accurate. Excavation finds complemented his evidence, as did later accounts by Eutychios, the *Synaxarium*, Abu'l-Makārim and al-Maqrīzī and also the reliable and detailed tradition preserved by the Sinaitic community.

In the years following the death of Justinian and especially in the early part of the seventh century, the fragile system of the *foederati* – the confederates of the Romans who guarded on their behalf frontier populations – became redundant and insecurity prevailed.[94] This did not deter a sizeable and cosmopolitan anchoretic and later monastic community from gathering on the mountains of South Sinai. They used natural resources and biblical associations to anchor their presence in this inhospitable land and negotiated a delicate coexistence with the bellicose locals, sometimes with the help of the armed laymen dispatched by Justinian.

Jabal Mūsā remained the focal point of this community. It was now endowed with a magnificent church and serviced by cisterns which ensured its self-sufficiency – further proof of the programme's defensive character. The basilica incorporated earlier structures without obliterating them. The reason for such respect towards the humble fourth-century chapel could have been the divine inspiration of its creator, Julian Saba, as mentioned in Ephraem's *Hymn* 20:

> And Saba stood in prayer / In the holy cave on Mount Sinai
> When suddenly he envisioned / The church's plan and
> dimensions.[95]

By demonstrating such respect, the architect of the basilica struck a balance between his need to create something befitting the majesty of the celebrated event (the theophany and delivery of the Law) and the anchorites' wish to preserve their tradition. A survival of the liminal within the imperial could be read in this act of symbolic enshrinement. It was the first appearance of the Horeb community's ability to negotiate the will of central authority while clinging onto its Sinaitic identity. As will be examined in the following chapter, this idiosyncrasy ensured the community's continued existence through adversities and into the modern era.

The ancient prohibition to spend the night on the summit continued to be observed. Even the basilica's overseer, the *paramonarios*, lived nearby rather than inside it. The fact that the *avaton* persisted at a time when as many as a hundred anchorites inhabited Horeb (outside the fortress) testifies to the awe Jabal Mūsā inspired. Crowned by a granite church covered in white plaster and visible from afar, and adorned with *opus sectile*, mosaics, glass lamps and probably icons and church furniture imported from Constantinople, the centrepiece of the Horeb landscape incorporated the main holy locales of the Old Testament narrative and looked as beautiful as it was sacred.

Figure 12. James M. MacDonald (British, 1822–1885), *Wády Ed Deir and the Plain of Er Ráhah from Jebel Muneijáh.* Albumen silver print, 16.8 × 21.6 cm. 1869.

Chapter 3

The period between the crossing of the Sinai Peninsula by the warriors of Islam in the 630s on their way to conquer Egypt and spread the kerygma of Muḥammad and the first doubting of the identification of Jabal Mūsā with the biblical 'Mount of the Law' in 1822 seems excessively long to cover within a single chapter.[1] However, the metaphysical importance, ritual significance and landscape configuration of the area changed little. Monks and anchorites carried on inhabiting the holy wilderness in symbiosis with a nomadic lay population even after the latter's conversion to Islam. Christian pilgrims continued to visit the sacred places glorified through the Justinianic building programme. The discovery (*inventio*) of the relics of Saint Catherine on the summit of Jabal Kathrin and the establishment of the Palestine Crusader states in the late eleventh century simply increased their numbers. Pious Muslims followed in their footsteps from as early as the seventh century and inaugurated a tradition of patronage. Even the mosque which was erected on the summit stood on the ruins of the basilica, merely adding an extra layer of veneration. The main characteristics of the Horeb landscape had already crystallised and additions rather than changes were effected to them.

Three phases can be separated within this long period. The Early Islamic period stretches from the 630s to the Fāṭimid era, when Horeb witnessed a wave of Muslim interest. The political link of the Sinai Peninsula to the Empire of Constantinople had been severed but religious and cultural ties remained. Although the coming of Islam affected the Sinai clerics, the discovery of the relics of Saint Catherine and the interest of Christians and Muslims kept pilgrim revenue and pious donations coming in, thus ensuring the survival of the community.

The Age of Pilgrimage roughly corresponds to the Fāṭimid (969–1171), Ayyūbid (1171–1250) and Mamlūk (1250–1517) periods. The geographic proximity of 'Latin' Christians to Sinai was due to the foundation of Crusader states (from 1099) and the positive attitude of the Fāṭimid and Mamlūk elites towards pilgrim travel in general and 'Mount Sinai' in particular. Horeb became a favourite destination and a Christian landmark from the Middle East to the British Isles. Travel accounts, combined with artefacts preserved within the Monastery walls or excavated at Jabal Mūsā, reveal a period of cosmopolitanism and growth.

The year 1517 marks the beginning of the Ottoman period and was a turning point in Sinaitic history. It witnessed both the Ottoman conquest of Egypt and the publication of the *Disputation of Martin Luther on the Power and Efficacy of Indulgences* in Germany. These unrelated events did much to slow the influx of pilgrims from West and Central Europe. The Ottomans were suspicious of pilgrims and the Protestant followers of Martin Luther (German, 1483–1546) rejected the tradition of Holy Land visitation. The collapse of the Byzantine Empire in 1453 and the opening of new trade routes to the Far East had already affected the monastic community. Nevertheless, Greek-language material demonstrates the active intellectual life of the Monastery throughout the period.

The Early Islamic Period
Sinai and Islam
By the late sixth century the importance of Horeb had made this remote spot a popular destination. Legend reports that about that time a young Arab from Mecca on a caravan trip stopped outside the walls of the fortress. Frederick Henniker, visiting twelve centuries later, gave the following version of the story:

> It happened that Mohammed, when an unknown youth, was encamped in this neighbourhood, an eagle was observed to hover over him, and one of the monks predicted his future greatness. Mohammed, well pleased with the gipsy tale, made liberal promises to the convent; a piece of paper was produced, but Mohammed, being unable to write, smeared his hand all over with ink, and made

his mark. In about fifteen years afterwards the augury was fulfilled; the soothsayer hastened to Mecca, and claimed performance of the note of hand. Mohammed kept his promise, and swore by the token that the convent should remain for ever sacred; that the country, as far as the eye can scan, should belong to it; and all the inhabitants thereon its slaves. The country produces nothing but rocks and Arabs, and the Arabs are less desirable than the rocks.[2]

Despite the charm of such an anecdote, it is improbable that a caravan, such as the young Muḥammad may have followed, would have strayed as far south as Horeb, which, despite its prominent position in pilgrimage itineraries, was far from important trade routes. The story was obviously concocted to justify the so-called *ahtname*, a declaration or decree in writing which protected the Monastery and its inhabitants and was supposedly written by ᶜAlī ibn Abī Ṭālib on 7 July 623 and signed with the imprint of Muḥammad's own hand. A late Ottoman copy of the declaration survives in the Monastery, purportedly replacing an early sixteenth-century copy granted by the Ottoman sultan Selim I (1465–1520, ruled 1512–1520) upon removal to Constantinople of the seventh-century original after the 1517 conquest. The earliest references to the document date from the beginning of the sixteenth century and it seems that this was the actual date of its production.[3] Despite the obviously fictitious character of the story and the associated article, it was not unusual for Christian communities in Islamic lands to claim special protection status granted to them by the Prophet or one of his followers. Such 'titles' betray the insecurity of non-Muslim communities resisting conversion but also testify to the power of such 'official' documents and the respect emanating from them.[4]

'Mount Sinai' features several times in the Qur'ān.[5] It is the site of God's meeting with Moses and of the delivery of His covenant in *Sūrat al-Baqara* (The Cow), II:63 and II:93, in *Sūrat al-Nisā'* (The Women), IV:154, in *Sūrat al-Aᶜrāf* (The Heights), VII:143–146 and VII:171, in *Sūrat Maryam*, XIX:52, in *Sūrat Ṭā' Hā'*, XX:80, and in *Sūrat al-Qaṣaṣ* (The Story), XXVIII:44. In *Sūrat al-Mu'minūn* (The Believers), XXIII:20, Mount Sinai is the place where the olive tree grows: 'The tree which grows on Mount Sinai gives oil and a condiment for all to eat.' In *Sūrat al-Tīn* (The Fig), XCV:2,

'Mount Sinai' is mentioned in the same verse and next to Mecca as a place of prophetic law handed to Moses. Finally, *Sūrat al-Ṭūr* (The Mountain), LII, is named after the biblical 'Mount of the Law'.

It is evident that references to Mount Sinai in the Holy Book are related to the biblical 'Mount of the Law' and not to Jabal Mūsā and are inspired by the text of Exodus rather than by experience of the place. The prophetic figure of Moses seems to be the reason behind these repeated references since the Decalogue is the pillar of the Abrahamic–Mosaic tradition which both Christianity and Islam inherited.[6] Thus, 'the mountain' symbolises the contact between God and His prophet and the Law which preceded Muḥammad's revelation.

Only the brief mention of Mount Sinai as an olive-bearing mountain strikes a non-biblical note. The association was probably made in order to enhance the blessed status of the olive tree, as designated in *Sūrat al-Nūr* (The Light), XXIV:35. However, the cultivation of olive trees around the fortress and the production of olive oil within the enclosure are attested by the survival of the sixth-century oil press at its northwestern corner. Probably some of the realities of Horeb life were widely known within the trading and caravan communities of the Ḥijāz, to which the Prophet belonged. The Qurʾānic reference to olive-growing is the focus of al-Muqaddasī's (945/6–1000) mention of Mount Sinai (*circa* 985), which was vague and not based on personal experience.[7]

Mount Sinai's prominence in the Qurʾān resulted in the respect Jabal Mūsā commanded from followers of the new faith. By the mid-seventh century a tradition of Muslim veneration had already been generated since Anastasios deplored the 'pollution' ('defilement') of the summit by 'the present nation' (the Muslims).[8] A valuable direct source is the reference in some papyri found in Nessana (present-day town of Nitzana in the Negev) to a certain Abū Rashīd, a provincial governor or *symvoulos* of the town, asking twice for guides for a trip to the Holy Mount (*toursina*, from the Arabic *Ṭūr Sīnāʾ* for 'Mount Sinai') to be paid for by the town in March 684 (or perhaps 669 or 699) and December 683:

In the name of Almighty God! Abū Rashīd, Governor, to George of Nessana. Thanks be to God, etc. etc. When Abu l-Mughīra,

mawla of ᶜUrwa ibn Abū Sufyān, comes to you, be kind enough
to furnish him [with] a man from Nessana bound to guide him on
the trip to the Holy Mount. Also furnish the man's pay. Written in
the month of March, twelfth indiction, by the hand of Theodore.[9]

In 683, the person making the pilgrimage was Abū Rashīd's wife,
Ubayya:

In the name of Almighty God! Abū Rashīd, Governor, to the
people of Nessana. Thanks be to God, etc. etc. When my wife
Ubayya comes to you, furnish her a man bound to direct her on the
road to Mount Sinai. Also furnish the man's pay. Written December 5, twelfth indiction.[10]

The cost of travel appears to have been substantial (a sixth-century
Nessana papyrus mentions 3½ *solidi*), therefore it was made clear in
both notes that the town of Nessana had to cover it.[11]

When al-Maqrīzī (1364–1442), the Egyptian historian of the
Mamlūk period, examined the Sinai Monastery among the other
Christian monasteries of Egypt, he repeated some imaginary descriptions by Yāqūt 'al-Rūmī' (1179–1229) but also gave new information regarding pilgrimage to Jabal Mūsā. He mentioned a saying by
ᶜAbdallāh ibn ᶜUmar (circa 614–693):

Only go on pilgrimage to three mosques. The mosque of the
Prophet of God, the mosque of Al-Ḥaram and the mosque of
Al-Aqsa, but renounce [the one on] Sinai and do not go there.[12]

If this chrestomathy actually dates from the seventh century, it is
practically contemporary with the Nessana papyri and testifies not
only to a tradition of visitation to Jabal Mūsā but also to its importance. Even if the advice is negative, Sinai appears in the same sentence as Medina, Mecca and Jerusalem.

A similar place was reserved for Mount Sinai in the words of the
qāḍi Abū Ishāq al-Buhturi (a member of the Quraysh tribe), quoted
in *The Book of Arousing Souls to Visit Jerusalem's Holy Walls* by
the Damascene Burhān al-Dīn ibn al-Firkāh al-Fazāri (1262–1329).

It was stated that prayer was unacceptable at seven places, among them the Kaʿaba, the Rock of Jerusalem, the Mount of Olives, Mount Arafat and Mount Sinai, for fear of some violation occurring when standing on them.[13] In his 1351 *Book of Inciting Desire*, Abu'l-Fida' of Hebron (died 1429) quoted Ibn ʿAbbās (618/9–687) as saying that the Kaʿaba was built by Abraham with Ishmael's help with materials from five mountains, one of them being Mount Sinai.[14] Both texts were influenced by Qurʾānic references to the biblical mountain. However, combined with the aphorism in al-Maqrīzī, they confirm the respect which lay at the beginning of the Muslim tradition of Jabal Mūsā visitation.

It is possible that the mosque on the summit, mentioned in epigraphic sources from the Fāṭimid period onwards, or at least a prayer place, was actually created in the first decades of Muslim rule. The small niche of cave A, under the present mosque of Jabal Mūsā, faces south and could have been the *mihrab* of this early prayer place, the cave of Moses itself. However, these hypotheses cannot be verified by archaeological methods. By the early eighth century the local lay population was already following Islam and it is likely that the collapse of the basilica on the summit gave further opportunities to lay a claim on the venerated site. Jabal Mūsā became a destination of *ziyāra(t)* (visitation), a tradition which continues to this day.

Another interesting story, preserved in a work compiled in the fifteenth century from an eleventh-century manuscript, can be attributed to the early Islamic period. When ʿAmr ibn al-ʿĀṣ (*circa* 583/9–664), the conqueror of Egypt, asked the Coptic chief of the natives of Upper Egypt for his treasure in the year 641, the chief claimed he had none. Enquiries revealed that he was in contact with a monk in Mount Sinai, to whom ʿAmr wrote in Greek and in the Coptic's name. The monk brought back a bronze jar containing a letter which indicated the location of the chief's treasure. ʿAmr had the Coptic executed and kept the gold; no trouble seems to have befallen the Greek monk.[15] The story is probably a combination of formulaic narrations preserving the tradition of treasure-hiding related with Sinai and its monks.

All sources and evidence therefore suggest that few tribulations were experienced in Horeb as a result of the coming of Islam. Apart from the sanctity of Jabal Mūsā, it was the absence of anything strategically or economically attractive (rather than the Prophet's declaration) that achieved this. Even the Mecca pilgrimage route from Spain, North Africa and Egypt (*darb al-ḥajj*) went through the central rather than the southern part of the Sinai Peninsula.[16]

By the early eighth century the major urban centre of South Sinai, Wādī Fīran, had deteriorated and was eventually abandoned. The local bishopric was transferred to Horeb. Only the small settlement at Ṭūr remained in the wider area.[17] As urban populations diminished and the economy reverted to nomadism, the imperial foundation of the Monastery gradually assumed an additional role as the strongest agent of power south of the Clysma (Suez) – Aila (Aqaba) line, a role it maintained until the twentieth century. Two references to a mid-tenth-century (or possibly earlier) attack by 'Saracens', causing three hundred monks from Horeb and Ṭūr to seek refuge in Mount Latros in Asia Minor, testify not only to continued insecurity caused by Bedouin aggression but also to considerable numbers of ecclesiastics, numerous enough to withstand emigration.[18]

Although some revenue was left by pilgrims times were often hard, and stories of famine must be connected with difficulties in supplying the distant mountain with grain. The following tradition is attested since the medieval period:

> The monks, [...] terribly plagued with vermin, determined to leave the monastery. Moreover, they had suffered from lack of food. So they ascended the holy mountain with the intention to desert their holy places [...]. On their way, however, the Holy Virgin appear[e]d to them, promising to them to deliver them from their tormentors. She ordered the monks to return, and when they arrived at the monastery, they found one hundred camels laden with provisions waiting for them.[19]

Similar stories survive from desert monasteries in Egypt and Syria and probably derived from a *topos*, a standard formula.[20] The spot where the Virgin Mary appeared to the monks is marked to this day by the chapel of Panagia tou Oikonomou ('Virgin of the Steward', near the Gate of St Stephen), halfway up the Path of Moses.[21] The summit continued to perform a protective role for the desert fathers:

Figure 13. W. Westall (British, draughtsman) and J. Outhwaite (British, engraver), *Mount Sinai*. Engraving on paper. Nineteenth century.

their ascent there would only guarantee them divine protection and surely no means of subsistence.

Itinerant Monks

In his thirty-eighth narration Anastasios told the story of eight hundred Armenian pilgrims, noting that people of this nation frequently travel to Sinai. They witnessed their fellow travellers and their own walking sticks go up in flames for an hour without getting burnt. Anastasios then added that 'the Saracens' mocked this miracle because such phenomena did not appear 'in the synagogues of the Jews or the Arabs'.[22] By the term 'synagogues of the Arabs' he probably referred to mosques, with which he must have been familiar at the time of writing in the mid-seventh century. However, the establishment of Muslim rule and worship seems to have done nothing to curb the pilgrimage zeal of the Armenians. They obviously travelled without much fear of attacks, although the size of their group may indicate an effort to seek safety in numbers.[23]

There are many Armenian inscriptions along the pilgrim routes towards Horeb, especially at Wādī Haggag, along the Aila to Horeb route.[24] More than thirty inscriptions carved by pilgrims have been discovered on Jabal Mūsā, along the stepped 'Path of Moses', around Wādī al-Lajā' to the west of Horeb and on the Justinianic doors of the Monastery *katholikon*. They are names of individuals (clergymen, laymen, a guide and a lady are mentioned) and invocations to *nomina sacra*. Most of these inscriptions, datable on palaeographic evidence, seem to have been carved during the first millennium, between the seventh and the tenth century.[25] Anastasios and the epigraphic evidence testify to a trail of Armenian pilgrims throughout the early Islamic period.[26]

A similar pattern must apply to pilgrims and peripatetic monks of different origin who have not been as well-studied as the Armenians.[27] The several Arabic manuscripts preserved in the Monastery library must have travelled in the baggage of such itinerant monks. Their scriptoria were in Damascus, Mar Sabba, monasteries of the Jordan desert, Clysma (present-day Suez), Cairo and Ṭūr.[28] Among the monks practising monastery-hopping in search for enlightenment, two martyrs were killed by Muslim authorities after professing their Christianity and refusing conversion, Pachōmios, 'a cousin of the caliph' and therefore a Muslim Arab by birth, in the first half of the eighth century, and Qays ibn Rabīʿ ibn Yazīd al-Ghassānī, a Muslim convert originating from an Arab Christian family and living in the mid-ninth century. Both converted (in the case of Qays, converted back) to Christianity, spent time in the Sinai Monastery and eventually met a martyr's end while travelling in Palestine and Syria.[29]

Both monks were remarkably mobile. Qays converted back to Christianity in Baalbek, then visited the patriarch in Jerusalem, became a monk in Mar Sabba in Palestine where he stayed for five years, toured the monasteries around Jerusalem, went to Horeb for another five years (he was made steward, *oikonomos*, there), travelled to al-Ramla in Palestine, returned for seven years (he rose to become superior, *dikaios* or *hēgoumenos*) and was eventually killed in al-Ramla around 860. Pachōmios, having become a Sinai monk, was reported as having been martyred after anathematising 'the religion of the Saracens' before the caliph, supposedly in Damascus. Both Qays and Pachōmios moved freely between the numerous monasteries, churches and pilgrimage sites of Syria, Palestine and Sinai but did not visit Egypt, probably because it was Monophysite territory. They found themselves in danger only when travelling outside the Horeb area, which seems to have been too distant and safely under the monks' control for Muslim threat to Christian converts.

On Jabal Mūsā, two Greek inscriptions have been recorded in cave A:

God of the holy Moses / remember Kosmas and / his children / Timokratēs Sergios and Constantia. / Amen.

+ God of the holy Moses / remember your servant / [---]mios deacon / and *paramonarios* / the writer +[30]

Although no dates have been suggested for these inscriptions on the basis of their palaeography, they must have been carved during the first millennium and most probably after the sixth century. The first one may record a pilgrim's visit whereas the second one commemorates a *paramonarios*, a monastic title known from sources to have been associated with the summit and its basilica and probably still in existence in the late medieval period as two monks are mentioned as 'continually dwelling' on Jabal Mūsā by Felix Fabri in 1483. Both inscriptions are full of spelling mistakes and appeal to 'God of the holy Moses', a typically Sinaitic invocation.

These inscriptions add to the volume of evidence for the continuity of Sinaitic monastic life during the early Islamic period. Christian communities within Muslim lands were isolated from the life of the Church in Byzantium and the 'Latin' West. This isolation was made manifest in the absence of iconoclastic tribulations in Sinai or elsewhere.[31] Although they remained far from theological controversies, eastern monasteries gathered significant numbers of ecclesiastics. The decoration of two marble panels with encaustic scenes in the *katholikon*'s sanctuary, by a painter probably originating from Palestine a few decades after the Muslim conquest, testifies to the continuation of artistic activity.[32]

By the mid-ninth century, Horeb was important enough to attract a certain Fromont (or Frotmond or Frotomundo) and his anonymous brother from Rennes who, instructed by the bishops of King Lothair

II of Lotharingia (835–869, ruled 855–869), travelled to Rome, Jerusalem and Sinai seeking penitence for a murder. They had to remain chained to each other for the duration of their expedition and spent three years on Horeb before returning to Rome and Rennes.[33] The Latin narration of their adventures, written by a monk in Redon (Brittany), contains no reference to difficulties encountered on their journeys apart from the self-inflicted encumbrance of their chains.[34]

Material excavated in Jabal Mūsā that is datable from between the seventh and the eleventh century is sparse. No building activity could be documented, since the erection of the 1934 chapel of Hagia Triada obliterated all signs of buildings postdating the Justinianic basilica. Small finds included fragments of glass vessels (mostly oil lamps, some of the early, undecorated 'mosque lamp' type, eighth to twelfth century) and a little utilitarian pottery (amphorae and table wares).[35] A few green-glazed medium-size vessels, possibly jarlets or jugs, were also found and they are attributable to the Umayyad and early ʿAbbāsid periods (seventh and eighth century). Finally, some unglazed clay oil lamp fragments can be dated between the eighth and the tenth century. The range of pottery shapes testifies to the non-residential character of the site, with the modest number of larger vessels equalling the number of lamps. The former were probably used by the *paramonarioi* of the summit whereas the latter were also carried by occasional visitors.

Conversion of the Laymen

An anonymous text collated at the end of Anastasios's *Narrations* described how the lay population of Horeb was converted to Islam:

> When according to God's fair judgment the nation of Saracens came upon the holy mountain of Sinai, to conquer the place and to make the preexisting Saracens that were previously Christian renounce their faith in Christ, and when [the local Saracens] living nearby and having their tents close to the fortress of Pharan and [the fortress] of the holy bush heard of that, they ascended with their families up to Hagia Koryphē as if it is a fortified place from where to wage war from an elevated spot upon the coming Saracens, which they did; but being too weak to resist for long the

multitude of invaders, they surrendered to save themselves; and to join in their belief.[36]

The author then went on to tell the story of a Bedouin who refused to follow the others and, out of his fervent faith, chose to jump off a cliff rather than be converted. His wife ran after him and implored him to kill her and their children before committing suicide, so that he would spare them the sin of denying their faith. The writer was careful to mention that she addressed her husband in Arabic. Her wish was granted and the husband slaughtered his family before jumping off the southern side of the summit, which is indeed the steepest one.

German historian Peter Grossmann argued that the passage refers to the conversion of the Wādī Fīran population and that the summit was not Jabal Mūsā but a mountain near that oasis.[37] This identification is unjustified since the term *hagia koryphē* is exclusively used for the Horeb summit. Philip Mayerson has suggested that the 'Pharan' fortress was actually a misnomer for the *phylaktērion*,[38] though there is no reason why such a transfer of place name should have happened.

The passage gives interesting insights into an otherwise obscure incident. Firstly, no distinction was made between the locals and their Muslim attackers. They were both called 'Saracens' and both spoke Arabic. It is possible that the aggressors were not actually invaders from outside Sinai but recently Islamicised locals. Secondly, conversion to Islam was forced upon the laymen but not the ecclesiastics. The life of the anchoretic community obviously continued uninterrupted. Thirdly, when the local population had to defend itself against the invaders, the protection offered by Jabal Mūsā was preferred to that of the fortress.

It was the metaphysical protection emanating from Jabal Mūsā rather than its defensive qualities that informed the defenders' choice, although a supply of water and its inaccessible location added to its attraction. The spot from which the faithful Bedouin jumped was probably on the side of the summit furthest away from the point of ascent of the attackers. If his suicide occurred to the southeast, which is very steep, the ascent must have taken place from the northwest, which is the easiest slope to climb, or the northeast, which is to this day the top of the stepped route from Farsh Elias.

The date of the event remained unstated in the anonymous account but it was given by Eutychios:

> As time went by, these slaves had numerous children and prolifer-ated, and, as in the meantime Islam reached its widest expansion during the caliphate of ʿAbd al-Malik ibn Marwān, they attacked and killed one another. Some were killed, others escaped and several have remained Muslims until today and are called Banu Ṣaleh. They are known to this day as 'Children of the Monastery'. From these the Lakhmids also originated. As the slaves converted to Islam and were scattered, the monks destroyed their dwellings, so that nobody would dwell in them anymore. The ruins are pre-served to this day.[39]

The event was placed during ʿAbd al-Malik ibn Marwān's rule (646–705, ruled 686–705). It was also made clear from Eutychios's text that the so-called 'invaders' were local converted Arabs rather than outsiders.

The destruction of their abodes and probably of the *phylaktērion*, too, was securely dated after the conversion in the early years of the eighth century, a dating in accordance with the excavation results which are poor in Islamic pottery in comparison with Jabal Mūsā. The reasons for this demolition must have been the anchoretic com-munity's *hēsychia* (silence, peace) and safety, which would have been compromised by a population unchecked by religious respect. However, such an act of violence on behalf of monks is surpris-ing. Natural forces could have accelerated destruction, for example a rock fall testified by the large boulders still scattered around. The dispersal of the population was probably limited and most remained in the vicinity, eventually becoming the Jabāliyya tribe of 'monas-tery servants'.[40]

The reasons for inflicting such a violent conversion upon a peace-ful and isolated population remain unstated in both texts. The Islam-isation of Palestine and Egypt was slow and it only reached the level of mass conversion between the ninth and the tenth century.[41] It is true that during the rule of ʿAbd al-Malik the Arabisation of the Umayyad caliphate, which until then preserved several Roman elements in administration and economy, accelerated.[42] However, forced conversion was forbidden by Islamic law and exceptions to this rule were rare, such as the forced conversion of 5,000 men of the Christian tribe of Banū Tanukh near Aleppo in the time of the ʿAbbāsid Caliph al-Mahdī (ruled 775–785).[43] It is probable that a small-range event, for example a local dispute between Bedouin tribes, generated this violent outcome. Once more, Jabal Mūsā performed its traditional role as a site of physical prominence and remoteness which offered supernatural protection to those beseeching it.

Collapse of the Basilica

At the time of the conversion of the laymen to Islam in *circa* 700 the terraces supporting the Justinianic basilica complex on Jabal Mūsā were still in place, serving to justify the use of the term 'fortified' by the anonymous author of the narration. More than three centuries later, in the Fāṭimid period, three 'oratories' are mentioned on Horeb in an inscription on a *kursī*, a Qurʾān stand, preserved at the Monastery of Saint Catherine; one of them must have been a mosque at Jabal Mūsā, in all probability built with reused granite blocks from the ruins of the basilica. These are the two *termini* for the basilica's destruction which must have happened sometime between the early eighth and the eleventh century.

The cause of the collapse could provide clues as to a more precise date of the incident. Human agency seems improbable, not only because the site enjoyed the protection of the monks but also because it commanded the respect of the Muslim faithful. There are no contemporary references to violent demolitions of Christian edifices in the Sinai and it seems that during the seventh and the eighth century the iconoclastic rage was stronger within Byzantium than within the caliphate. Even more significant is the negative evidence of the remarkably thorough monastic tradition which mentions no such calamity.

Natural causes seem to be the best explanation for the destruction of the basilica. Although thunderstorms rage violently on the summit and a fire could easily consume the timber roof of the building causing its gradual ruin, a collapse due to earthquake agrees better with the archaeological evidence. The wall supporting the apse of the modern chapel and part of the apse itself were part of the original basilica apse and they stand safely in place, being founded on the granite bedrock. On the contrary, the eastern end of the southern aisle and the northeastern corner of the basilica and narthex have entirely disappeared because they were founded on terraces filled with earth. The dislocation of a few blocks from the retaining walls of the terraces would be enough to bring down the complex. It is also worth noting that no traces of an ash layer, which would support a destructive fire hypothesis, have been found.

Several tremors in the area could have caused the collapse and their dates have been recorded in sources and verified by scientific means. Research so far has focused on Palestine, an area affected by the Dead Sea Transform, the boundary between the African–Sinai and Arabian tectonic plates. The rift extends as far south as Aqaba, a major epicentre of seismic activity close to Horeb.[44] The ruinous earthquake of 18 January 746 (at about 11 a.m.) exceeded grade 9 in the Modified Mercalli intensity scale, resulting in large buildings shifting off their foundations and partially or wholly collapsing. Its epicentre was around Lake Tiberias in present-day Israel. Strong earthquakes (grades 7 to 8, very strong to destructive, causing slight to considerable damage to well-built structures) were recorded on 16 January 738, 8 March 756, in 808 and in December 856 or later.[45]

The earliest reference to an earthquake destruction of the basilical complex appears almost a millennium later, in an account from Balthasar de Monconys following his 1647 travel to Sinai:

There was once on this mountain a beautiful church that was demolished due to a trembling of the earth: they say that God let this happen because the Turks wanted to seize it to make a mosque and wishing to move some stones from the ruins, great flames gushed forth from under the earth.[46]

It is probable that the tradition Monconys recorded alluded to the cause of the catastrophe (earthquake) but also to its date (sometime during the early years of Muslim infiltration into the religious life of Horeb). Therefore, an eighth-century date (perhaps 746) could be tentatively suggested as the time of the disastrous event.

A Virgin Martyr

Soon after the collapse of the Jabal Mūsā basilica, a new figure came to be added to the Sinaitic pantheon alongside Moses and Elijah. Saint Catherine was little-known before the discovery (*inventio*) of her body, miraculously transported from her place of martyrdom in Alexandria to the summit of Jabal Kathrin. However, her prestige expanded all over the Christian world and the Monastery embraced her followers and assumed her name.

Catherine supposedly lived in Alexandria during the rule of the emperor Gaius Valerius Galerius Maximinus (*circa* 270–313, ruled 308–313). She was a young woman of noble birth, indeed of royal descent, great beauty and strong intellect but had vowed to remain chaste rather than follow the prescribed path of marriage. When Maximinus organised sacrifices to pagan gods, Catherine protested publicly. Embarrassed by his inability to counter her learned arguments, uttered in obscure rhetorical Greek, the emperor ordered fifty philosophers to attempt it. They failed, were converted to Christianity by the virgin's words and paid with their lives. Maximinus had the girl tortured on a device of wheels with attached knives but angelic intervention destroyed the contraption encouraging further conversions (and subsequent executions). Catherine finally met a martyr's death by decapitation. Out of her severed neck flowed milk rather than blood. Her body was transferred by angels to the summit of Mount Sinai.[47]

The Saint appeared in various texts from the seventh century onwards and in tenth-century Byzantine wall-painting cycles in Cappadocia and Greece.[48] She gained popularity later in the tenth century, mainly thanks to the story of her life (*vita*) written by Symeon Metaphrastes.[49] The desire for a relic embodying her grace must have proved irresistible and was soon met by the monks of South Sinai.

The exact date of her body's 'discovery' is not known and various moments during the eighth, the ninth and the tenth century have been proposed. The traditional date of *circa* 800 is not supported by evidence. The lack of any reference to the Saint in Eutychios's detailed work (early tenth century) suggests a late tenth-century date for the *inventio*, contemporary to Symeon's work.[50] At about the same time, Egypt fell into the hands of the Fāṭimids and a new capital, Cairo, was founded in 969. The patronage of members of the Fāṭimid elite, the arrival of the Crusaders in the late eleventh century and the popularity of Saint Catherine's relic in the 'Latin' West would define the life of the monastic community on Horeb in the early second millennium.

It is believed that in the late twelfth or the early thirteenth century the Saint's body was transported from the summit of 'Mount Sinai' to the *katholikon* within the walls of the Monastery.[51] A letter by Philippe de Milly (1120–1171), Lord of Nablus (1138/1144–1161) and Transjordan (after 1161) and later Grand Master of the Templars (1169–1171), records a pilgrimage to Sinai in the 1160s and an ascent to the mountain to retrieve a piece of the relic.[52] His visit provides a *terminus post quem* for the 'translation' (miraculous transportation) of her body, which had happened by 1217, when the German magister (master, teacher) Thietmar visited Saint Catherine's sepulchre in the *katholikon*.[53] A date near the time of the 'Latin' conquest of Constantinople by the armies of the Fourth Crusade (1204) is very probable. A chapel was erected on the summit of Jabal Kathrin and others replaced it in following centuries.

Although the adoption of Catherine's name as the Monastery's dedication has been dated to the tenth or the eleventh century, a thirteenth- or fourteenth-century date seems more plausible.[54] A small devotional icon attributed to a thirteenth-century Sinai painter and preserved at the Monastery depicts the Virgin Mary (the Monastery's former patron) holding Jesus with Moses at her feet and Saint Catherine (the new patron) to her right.[55] It eloquently illustrates the transition from one virgin protectress to another. The Greek name of the Monastery, used to this day, can be translated as 'The Holy Monastery of the God-trodden Mount Sinai, Saint Catherine's Monastery', preserving a Jabal Mūsā reference and adding the Saint Catherine dedication as an afterthought.

An interesting point in the story of Saint Catherine's is the transfer of its *inventio* location from 'Mount Sinai' (supposedly Jabal Mūsā) to Jabal Kathrin, where the imprint of her body remains a focus of pilgrimage. In the eleventh-century Latin *Translation and Miracles of Saint Catherine, Virgin and Martyr* her point of rest was clearly stated as Jabal Mūsā:

[…] God transferred her in the hands of angels and had her deposited on the mountain where He once gave to his attendant Moses
the stone tablets inscribed with the Law.[56]

But the tenth-century *vita* (life of a saint) of Symeon Metaphrastes
was not specific and only mentioned 'Mount Sinai' without using the
dedicated Greek words *hagia koryphē*, although this is an *argumen-
tum ex silentio*. The description of the Monastery and its environs
by Abu'l-Makārim in the late twelfth or the early thirteenth century
located the discovery at Jabal Kathrin.[57] Therefore, it is not clear from
the textual record on which summit the body was exposed to pilgrims'
devotions between its tenth-century discovery and its translation.
    However, there is no reason to doubt the monastic tradition which
separates the two summits and assigns the *inventio* to Jabal Kathrin. It
seems that the hagiographical tradition referred to 'Mount Sinai' (the
'Mount of the Law') and this was literally interpreted in 'Latin' versions as the Jabal Mūsā summit.[58] But when Saint Catherine's deposi-
tion point had to be localised in the tenth century by the Sinai brethren,
it was placed away from Jabal Mūsā, which was already charged with
strong Old Testament associations and had been frequented for centuries and therefore could not have hidden such a hallowed relic.
    Soon after its discovery, Catherine's body was dismembered and
most of its pieces were taken to Christian states all over the East and
the West (France, England, Spain, Italy, the Holy Roman Empire, the
Byzantine Empire, Georgia), where shrines to the virgin Saint were
created and gained popularity.[59] The most important shrine was at the
Abbey of the Trinity at Rouen in France, housing three of her fingers
which arrived in the 1020s/1030s with the Syracuse-born Sinai monk
Symeon Pentaglossos, 'the five-tongued' – owing to his fluency in
five languages, and a different Symeon to him who wrote the Saint's
vita a few decades earlier.[60] The fingers had detached themselves
while Symeon was collecting in a glass vial the fragrant oil which
oozed miraculously from the body at its mountaintop shrine.[61] In 1229
Louis IX, king of France (1214–1270, ruled 1226–1270), erected a
church dedicated to the Saint in Paris, marking her peak of fame.[62]
    The spread of Catherine's popularity was both wide and fast. She
was popular with royalty thanks to her lineage, with women and

Figure 14. View from the North-Eastern
Galleries. Wood engraving on paper.

young girls thanks to her strong will and commitment to virginity, and with scholars, students and learned clerics thanks to her education and intellect. She was the patron saint of any profession related to wheels (millers, cart wrights, turners and potters). Finally, she was held worthy of three haloes, a white one for virginity, a green one for learning and a red one for martyrdom.[63] Her numerous admirers flocked to her European shrines but longed to visit the original one. Simone Sigoli, a Florentine lord who visited in 1384, was ecstatic while describing the 'freshness' of her skull:

> And here they have the head and two bones, and truly the relic of the head of St. Catherine is very devout to look upon, for you see all the head from the neck upwards, and it is not covered by any silver ornament: so you can clearly see it with the scalp fresh, as if it were of late, and continually by the grace of God the said head emits manna.[64]

When Johannes Witte de Hese from Utrecht narrated a (probably fictitious) pilgrimage to Sinai in 1489, he focused on the Saint's bones, the oil that oozed from them, but forgot to even mention Jabal Mūsā and the tradition of the Decalogue.[65] Jean Aerts, a Flemish pilgrim (probably a Franciscan priest) who actually travelled to Sinai in late 1481, devoted four pages to his Monastery visit but again failed to mention Jabal Mūsā.[66] Religious fashion had experienced an ephemeral turn and the virgin Saint from Alexandria had eclipsed the 'Mount of the Law' in the eyes of the faithful.

The Age of Pilgrimage
Passage to Heaven
Most of the sources on Horeb from the eleventh to the sixteenth century were narratives of pilgrimage performed by 'Latin' Christians from West and Central Europe. Although the movement of eastern clergymen and pilgrims continued and links with Byzantium remained strong, it was the intensification of western pilgrimage after the creation of Crusader states in Syria and Palestine from 1098 that set these centuries apart. The cultural and religious bond with these Christian principalities (rather than the supposed safety they

offered) encouraged pious travellers to make their way east in search of blessings, exculpation and glory.[67]

Even before the Crusades the interest in Holy Land sites had been revived in Europe through 'replication shrines'. These were either sacred buildings miraculously translated stone by stone to a new location or exact copies built by angels closer to home. The oldest 'replication shrine' was the Holy House of Our Lady of Walsing-ham, founded in 1061 after visions urged the Saxon noblewoman Richeldis de Faverches to rebuild the house of the Annunciation of the Virgin in Nazareth. Since she was unable to make up her mind as to the location, angels undertook the task and produced an exact copy of the house overnight. A similar story marked the end of the Crusader period, when in 1291 (after the fall of Acre) angels trans-ported the actual house of the Virgin Mary (not a copy of it) from Nazareth to Tersatto in present-day Croatia, where shepherds dis-covered it. After a few years the Holy House took off again, this time for Italy, and landed in a wood called Lauretum (thence the name of the shrine today: 'Loreto'). However, it would not stay put and moved a few miles down, to the centre of the town of Recanatti where an impressive basilica celebrates it to this day.[68]

Such miraculous events stoked the desire to possess the (original) Holy Land landmarks. Beyond politics, this desire was the main driving force behind popular support for the Crusades. Soon pil-grims followed the soldiers:

> In the High Middle Ages, pilgrimage to national and international shrines was, pragmatically, as much a pillar of Christendom as the hajj was, theologically, for Islam. […] Protected by ecclesiastical and political authorities, pilgrimage became worldly and fashionable.[69]

Pilgrimage was predominantly an undertaking for wealthy and pow-erful figures who could afford the expense. Less important people either followed the rich and noble as members of their retinue or managed to make their own way into the Holy Land. The experi-ence was life-changing for all. Many contemporary references reveal less-than-edifying aspects of pilgrimage, summarised by the German proverb: 'Go out a pilgrim, come home a whore.'[70] Pilgrims roamed the sacred landscapes as if walking in a parallel world, populated not by contemporaries but by biblical figures and saints.[71] Most fourteenth- and fifteenth-century pilgrims preferred to approach 'Mount Sinai' from Cairo and continue to Jerusalem rather than the other way round, probably because this route was closer to the itinerary of the Exodus.[72] Few took the time for factual descriptions of historical value. Their reluctance to describe, or even mention, actual people is indicative of their excited state of perception and must be taken into account when evaluating the information they provide.

Saint Catherine, venerated in Horeb since the tenth century, was the patroness of pilgrimage. The so-called 'Knights of Saint Catherine' were dedicated to protecting the Holy Land and the pilgrims to it. Their knighthood was probably a symbolic decoration rather than a membership of an organised order and was available to any successful pilgrim who was prepared to make a generous enough donation.[73] In this, the 'knights' resembled modern pilgrims who proudly wear the silver or gold rings of Saint Catherine with her monogram. There seems to have been a special relationship between relics and rings. This is particularly true of Saint Catherine, 'a spouse of Christ' who placed a ring on her finger.[74] Fifteenth-century pilgrims mentioned touching jewellery on Saint Catherine's skull, a practice that was still alive in the seventeenth century. In Christmas 1615 Pietro Della Valle, a wealthy Roman nobleman, purchased and touched no fewer than 'five hundred [rings] of hippopotamus bone for people of no importance, and a good number made of gold and silver for those of distinction'.[75]

The Saint's main shrine on Horeb offered the added attraction of unique Old Testament sites like Jabal Mūsā and the Burning Bush.[76] Therefore, it became a popular destination for the most adventurous pilgrims, although it remained within the hold of the Fāṭimids, Ayyūbids and Mamlūks. The monks were careful to avoid associations with militant Crusader leaders that could upset their Muslim rulers. When Baldwin I (1058?–1118), king of Jerusalem from 1100 to 1118, attempted to visit Sinai in 1115 he was discouraged by the brotherhood.[77] A few years earlier, in 1106, Baldwin's main opponent in the battlefield, the Fāṭimid vizier and regent al-Afḍal, had dedicated a *minbar* (mosque pulpit) to the Monastery (see page

107). Baldwin's visit would have been perceived as a provocation and could upset the sensitive balance of Sinaitic politics.

However, less politically dangerous visitors were welcome. Their routes (set since the sixth century) were long and arduous.[78] They started from (or ended in) Jerusalem. The first followed the Mediterranean coast of the Sinai Peninsula, heading south at Pelusium towards Clysma (present-day Suez) along the western coast before turning east towards Wādī Fīran. The second route continued south from Palestine across the Negev and parallel to the Gulf of Aqaba shore.[79] A third route involved a sea journey to the port of Ṭūr, a relatively short distance away from Jabal Mūsā. These routes were followed with the aid of Bedouin guides, who often charged extortionate rates or turned against the monks and their visitors. Avaricious provincial officials were an additional threat and frequent petitions to the central government in Cairo testify to both these problems.[80]

The Monastery managed to accommodate not only Muslims but also several Christian sects under an Orthodox Christian (Melkite) roof. To this end, chapels dedicated to various rites were consecrated within its walls. In 1816, J.L. Burckhardt was shown the remains of Syrian, Armenian, Coptic and Roman Catholic chapels.[81] The Catholic or 'Latin' one, dedicated to Saint Catherine, was mentioned in several pilgrim accounts and seems to have moved to various locations through the centuries.[82] Its final position was near the western wall and the visitors' cells, where it was seen in 1483 by F. Fabri and visited in 1720 by the Jesuit Father Claude Sicard, *prefetto* of Egypt.[83] In 1697 Antoine Morison, canon of the Church of Saint Peter in Bar-le-Duc, noted that it was infrequently used, perhaps every 15 or 20 years. Richard Pococke, vicar-general of the Protestant Church of Ireland, was one of the last to perform a service in it in 1739.[84]

Similar tolerance (or versatility) was extended to Jabal Mūsā, where a minuscule chapel to the north of the Orthodox one was dedicated to 'Latin' worship (roughly corresponding to the modern *parakella*). It measured five by three *pas* (approximately 3.1 m by 1.86 m) and was dedicated since at least the fourteenth century to the Archangel Michael.[85] A dedication to the Ascension was also mentioned in the seventeenth and the eighteenth century.[86] Thus, the summit accommodated within its limited space the main Christian sects and Muslim devotion. It was in this age of pilgrimage that the first reference to ruins of an ancient structure on Jabal Mūsā was given by the Dominican F. Fabri from Ulm (1483).[87] In 1507 Gregor (or Georg) of Gaming also mentioned an ancient monastery, as did a few others in following centuries.[88]

The number of pilgrimage accounts from Byzantium is relatively small in comparison to those from the 'Latin' West. This was not due to fewer eastern pilgrims but to the mentality of the western ones. They placed their own footprints in those of sacred figures, aspiring to a concrete experience of salvation rather than the spiritual ascent exemplified in Orthodox monasticism by the *Heavenly Ladder*.[89] Pious western travellers counted indulgences obsessively and had a precise idea of the amount of 'indulgence for penance and error' every step bestowed upon them. Indulgences were not granted in an arbitrary fashion; they were regulated by the popes at the request of the Monastery. Pope John XXII (1249–1334, on the throne 1316–1334) granted two *bullae* (papal decrees) in 1328 and 1334 ensuring pilgrims to Sinai a year of indulgence.[90]

A Holy Land visit ensured more than a safe passage to heaven. It also conferred status to the pilgrim on earth. For men of rank who were publicly deemed responsible for improper acts, pilgrimage was an act of redemption.[91] Tokens of its undertaking were necessary for forgiveness; this was one of the reasons why souvenir rings were so popular and also why pieces of Saint Catherine's sepulchre or of the rocks at Jabal Mūsā were frequently chipped off.[92] The achievement was celebrated in written word and 'monumental' souvenirs, either left at the Monastery or erected at public spaces back in the homeland.[93]

Muslim Patronage
The closest that the Sinaitic holy sites and clergy ever came to extinction was in 1008–1009, when the Fāṭimid Caliph al-Ḥākim 'bi ʿAmr Allah' (985–1021, ruled 996–1021) launched an attack on all monasteries and churches under his authority. The culmination of these acts was the demolition of the Church of the Holy Sepulchre in Jerusalem (1009).[94] The fate of the Sinai Monastery was better:

[...] he also sent to the desert a desert Arab, Ibn Gagiat [*sic*, Ibn Ghiyāth] was his name, with a large force, to demolish the Monastery of Sinai and the remaining chapels of this Mountain, that Christians had built up to then. At that time an Egyptian monk named Solomon was in the Monastery, the offspring of noble ancestors and a very wise man, who hoped that the desolation of Melek Dahar [*sic*, the caliph] would not reach in this deepest of deserts and he consoled the Sinai monks who suspected every misfortune. However, when he heard that Gagiat was heading purposely against them and that he destroyed the monasteries of Souveision and many more, then he was overcome by great fear. Nevertheless, he was not desperate or mortified but thought that he could be victorious against the barbarism of Gagiat through gifts. Thence he convened the monks, agreed with them what to do, took with him two or three elders and proceeded at a day's distance to welcome him, bringing humble gifts of food, and others similar. The barbarian, thanks to divine will, received him with a gladdened face and asked him what he wanted. Solomon replied that he had come to prostrate himself in front of him and plead him to have mercy upon his brothers and his Monastery. And he used in his speech all the words that were befitting and could soften his savagery, changing his mind as far as monastic wealth was concerned, and promising him greater benefactions in return for his benevolence, and finally he persuaded Gagiat to stay where he met him, and he would bring him there all the gold and silver vessels of the Monastery, upon receiving which the barbarian changed his mind about destroying the Sinai brethren and departed.[95]

The monastic tradition preserved in this undated Greek text, a *Perigraphē* (*Description*) of the Holy Mount printed in 1710, gives a plausible explanation for the salvation of the Monastery.[96] In the early eleventh-century chronicle of Adémar de Chabannes (988–1034) the rescue is miraculous but no less interesting:

And in the monastery on Mount Sinai, ten thousand Saracen soldiers came to destroy it, but when they were only four miles away, they beheld the whole mountain on fire and flames reaching for

Figure 15. *The Crescent and the Cross.* Wood engraving on paper.

the sky and because of that both buildings and people were spared. When these were reported to the king of Babylon, remorse came upon him and the Saracen people for the evils they caused to the Christians and he declared a law by which the basilica of the glorious Holy Sepulchre was rebuilt.[97]

Adémar's picture of Jabal Mūsā in flames resembles the miraculous rescue narrated by Ammonios and the phenomena described by Anastasios. It was a traditional theme in Sinaitic lore, stressing the shielding action of Jabal Mūsā against aggressors. This time, the summit's protection even inspired the reconstruction of the Holy Sepulchre in Jerusalem, a decision that was actually taken by al-Ḥākim's successor ʿAlī al-Ẓāhir (1005–1039, ruled 1021–1036) in 1027.

Al-Ḥākim's hostility towards Christian institutions was unusual within Fāṭimid policy. Traditional historiography, probably tainted by Sunni hatred for the heterodox Shiʿa ruler, ascribed his behaviour to madness. However, there may have been financial pressures that urged him to confiscate the substantial property of the Christian clergy, a practice not unknown to other caliphs. His aspiration to assume the role of the *Mahdī*, the 'Guided One', the Redeemer of Islam, may also have inspired such extreme acts.[98] It is finally possible that a politically-inspired rapprochement with the Sunni majority of the caliph's realm prompted a distancing from more expressly Shiʿite views towards an eventual Islamisation of the empire and legitimisation of his universal rule.[99]

The role played by the monk Solomon in preventing the destruction of the Monastery extended beyond changing the 'desert Arab' (Bedouin?) Ibn Ghiyāth's mind. Solomon was even mentioned by the Melkite chronicler Yaḥyā ibn Saʿīd al-Anṭākī in the early eleventh century as influencing al-Ḥākim himself into annulling some extreme measures against the Christians towards the end of his rule.[100] Even if the monk's influence upon the ruler was exaggerated, it must be connected with the respect Muslims had for the 'Mount of the Law'. Perhaps the supernatural phenomena described by Adémar were a metaphor for the influence of the Sinaitic clergy, ultimately emanating from Jabal Mūsā.

No contemporary document survives testifying to al-Ḥākim's change of mind. However, an 1169 decree by Shīrkūh, vizier of the Fāṭimid Caliph al-ᶜAḍīd (1149–1171, ruled 1160–1171), referred to 'rules established during al-Ḥākim's time'. Furthermore, a decree, dated 1398, granting privileges to the Monastery from the time of the Mamlūk sultan Barqūq (ruled 1382–1389, 1390–1399) alluded to a now lost decree by al-Ḥākim, probably the 'rules' mentioned by Shīrkūh.[101]

Another incident traditionally associated with al-Ḥākim's aggression was the conversion of the refectory opposite the *katholikon* into a mosque. According to the story, the monks themselves effected the conversion overnight and invited the assailant (Ibn Ghiyāth?) to pray in the 'new' mosque. Since no violence could erupt near a mosque, the Monastery was spared. The story of the mosque's dedication has been dated to different times during the Muslim era, for example in the ninth century or during the rule of Selim I.[102]

Such conversions were not unusual and helped avoid trouble with the Muslim authorities. A chapel had probably been converted into a mosque at Dayr Antush, a few miles east of Horeb, in the ᶜAbbāsid or Fāṭimid period.[103] In 1653, bitter animosity between the archbishop of Sinai Iōasaph (ruled 1617–1660) and the patriarch of Alexandria led to the plundering of the Tzouvania (the Monastery's Cairo priory) by Ottoman militia at the request of the patriarch. Subsequently, a room therein was converted into a mosque (complete with minaret). The Monastery only regained full control of the Tzouvania in 1780.[104]

A piece of wooden mosque furniture preserved in the Monastery, a *kursī* (a Qurʾān stand), bears an inscription providing clues on the date of the conversion and on prayer places at Jabal Mūsā and Wādī Fīran (figure 16):[105]

In the name of God, the Merciful, the Compassionate. He who ordered the making / of this lamp [stand] and blessed *karāsīy* [plural for *kursī*] and the blessed / mosque that is at the higher monastery and the three / oratories that are at the place of the conference of Moses (may peace be with him) / and the mosque that is on the mountain of the monastery of Pharan and the [small] oratory / at the foot of New Pharan and the minaret / on the edge

Figure 16. Monastery of Saint Catherine. *Kursi*. Carved
wood, height 0.46 m. Egypt, early eleventh century.

of the plain is the watchful prince, the chosen one, the light / and
defender of the nation Abū Manṣūr Anūshtakīn, the *amīr*.[106]

Bernhard Moritz identified the donor with an undocumented
official during the period of Caliph al-Āmir (1096–1130, ruled
1101–1130), a view followed by subsequent scholars. He claimed
that the *kursī* should be contemporary with the dated 1106 *minbar*
donated by the Fāṭimid vizier and regent al-Afḍal and supposed that
the Monastery mosque was converted in order to service a 200-men
strong garrison posted to prevent possible Crusader infiltration
into South Sinai.[107] However, it would be preferable to identify
the Abū Manṣūr Anūshtakīn of the *kursī* with the Turkish general
Abū Manṣūr Anūshtakīn ibn ʿAbdallāh al-Dizbirī, an *amīr* (general,
commander) active during the rule of Caliphs al-Ḥākim, al-Zāhir
and al-Mustanṣir (1029–1094, ruled 1036–1094). He was already
a general in 1024, served successfully as governor of Damascus

from 1029 and died there in 1042. The Sinai donation must have taken place before his Syrian appointment in 1029, close to the time the Caliph al-Zāhir decided to allow the reconstruction of the Holy Sepulchre (1027).[108]

The lamp stand mentioned in the inscription should be identified with the cast bronze lamp stand now kept at the Chapel of Saint Stephen in the Monastery. The style and technique of its ornamentation and the calligraphy of its inscriptions, wishing for perfect blessing, complete favour, and happiness to its owner, support a late tenth or early eleventh century date.[109] This evidence reinforces the revised date of the *kursī* and suggests that the lamp stand was also part of Anūshtakīn al-Dizbirī's donation, happening one hundred years earlier than previously thought. It could be suggested that the erection and dedication of the mosques and oratories in Horeb and Wādī Fīran fell within a wider initiative of the Fāṭimid government to reconstruct Christian pilgrimage sites after al-Ḥākim's devastations. This policy could have had the ultimate goal of laying a strong Muslim hold on them rather than obliterating them altogether. Against this background of Muslim devotion, Jabal Mūsā took pride of place because of its Mosaic association and was graced with no fewer than three buildings.

The reference to three 'oratories' on the Mountain of Moses (Horeb) is enigmatic. Moritz identified one of them with the Jabal Mūsā mosque and went on to suggest that the other two were the chapels of Jabal Mūsā and Farsh Elias – a surprising instance of Muslim patronage of Christian cultic buildings.[110] There is little doubt that the first oratory stood where the Jabal Mūsā mosque is today and where some devotional structure must have already been in place since the seventh century. However, no other Muslim cultic building survives from the vicinity or was mentioned in any of the numerous pilgrim and traveller accounts.

A possible explanation is that the *kursī* inscription referred to the restoration of two of the Early Christian prayer niches already discussed (among the fourteen which survive around the mountain). Their remarkable survival must be attributed to several restorations. The monks did not include them among Christian holy sites and did not take care of them, a task obviously performed by the Bedouin.

The reason why they were described as 'oratories' rather than mosques could be their odd orientation towards Jabal Mūsā. 'Open air' mosques are documented from around the Negev and Sinai since the early Islamic period.[111] The Horeb low curved walls may have served as prayer spots for local and visiting Muslims, satellite sites around the summit mosque.[112]

The Jabal Mūsā mosque was referred to by the geographer al-Idrīsī (1100–1165/6), writing *circa* 1154:

> Jabal al-Ṭūr [...] is a high mountain into which you go up by steps, and at its summit is a mosque where there is a well of stagnant water, from which those who come and go may drink.[113]

Al-Idrīsī had not visited Sinai in person but his information, gathered at the court of the Norman king Roger II (1095–1154) in Sicily, was up to date. A Jewish rabbi named Jacob, son of Nathaniel the Cohen, visiting Sinai before 1187, used the term 'synagogue of Ishmaelites' to describe a mosque on Jabal Mūsā.[114] The tradition of Sinai patronage among the Fāṭimid elite continued into the twelfth century as testified by the gifted *minbar* within the Monastery mosque dated by inscription to 1106.[115] The *minbar* was dedicated by al-Afḍal Shāhinshāh (1066–1121), powerful vizier and regent to the throne from 1094 to 1121, during the rule of the Fāṭimid Caliphs al-Mustanṣir, al-Mustaᶜlī (died in 1101, ruled 1094–1101) and al-Āmir. Al-Afḍal was the vizier who fought against the armies of the First Crusade and lost Jerusalem to them in July 1099, a year after recovering it from the Artūqids. He also donated a splendid prayer niche at the mosque of Ibn Ṭūlūn in Cairo. By the time of his Sinai donation he was the most powerful individual in the caliphate. A few months earlier (August 1105) he had been defeated at a battle in al-Ramla by the army of Baldwin, king of Jerusalem. It is likely that his pious donation to the Sinai Monastery mosque was connected with his military campaigns. As already discussed, the reluctance of the monks to accept Baldwin as a pilgrim in 1115 must be related to al-Afḍal's patronage.

The minaret on the northeastern corner of the Monastery mosque also dates from the early twelfth century as demonstrated by dendrochronological analysis of its roof timber. Furthermore, the wooden narthex doors of the *katholikon* have been attributed to the eleventh or the twelfth century. It would not be an overstatement to suggest that this period marked a renaissance of Sinaitic prestige connected more with Muslim patronage than with the presence of Christian Crusaders. Gifts to the Monastery were not only buildings and works of art. Fertile lands were donated by the Fāṭimids. They were under caliphal protection and produced wheat for the needs of the monks and for sale in markets.[116]

While describing the chapel of the Burning Bush to the east of the *katholikon* during his 1217 pilgrimage, Thietmar noted that everybody removed their shoes before entering and added:

> When the Great Sultan, the king of Babylon [Cairo], visited this church, out of respect for the place, he entered with humility and bare feet.[117]

The 'sultan' mentioned has been identified as the Ayyūbid general and ruler al-Malik al-ᶜĀdil I (1145–1218, ruled 1200–1218) who probably visited Horeb on his way to Damascus in 1217 and had issued a decree protecting the Sinai monks in 1176 (much in the Fāṭimid tradition).[118] However, it has been suggested that the 'sultan' was indeed al-ᶜĀdil's brother 'Saladin', Ṣalāḥ al-Dīn Yūsuf ibn Ayyūb (*circa* 1138–1193, ruled 1174–1193), passing through Sinai during the 'Egyptian' phase of his rule (1169–1182), probably around 1174–1176. Saladin was mentioned as appreciating the Monastery and its ornaments and as donating the revenue of a village to the Monastery.[119]

The tradition of Sinaitic veneration among eminent Muslim figures and rulers, begun as early as the seventh century, was revived in the eleventh century and continued into the twelfth or thirteenth. In a 1304 pilgrimage account by five Franciscan monks, the reverence and material support of both '*Saraceni*' and the sultan towards Horeb are mentioned.[120] The reverence even survived until the nineteenth century, when Muḥammad ᶜAlī Pasha (1769?–1849, ruler of Egypt from 1805) was mentioned as visiting the Monastery and praying in its mosque several times, an example followed by his grandson

Figure 17. David Roberts (British, 1796–1864), *Ascent
to the Summit of Mount Sinai*. Lithograph on paper.
Based on drawings executed in February 1839.

ᶜAbbās Pasha in 1853.[121] Moments of tension were also recorded,
like the 1401 plundering of the Monastery and murder of the bishop
(Iōannēs?) by the Mamlūk army and the temporary confiscation of
the Monastery's land holdings in 1431.[122] Nevertheless, violence on

behalf of the official administration was rare and it seems that most incidents of aggression were generated by the Bedouin.

A final piece of evidence for the respect Jabal Mūsā commanded among the followers of Islam was the discovery of a small number of short inscriptions during the site's excavation. They were written with ink or pigment or engraved on pieces of marble and sandstone which were originally part of the *opus sectile* or other revetment decorations of the collapsed Justinianic basilica. Most of them were invocations to God for forbearance, help and mercy, while others referred to pilgrimage or commemorated deceased persons. Although some of them may have been left by Christian pilgrims, others leave no doubt that they were dedicated by Muslims. No dates have so far been suggested for any of them but they obviously post-date the collapse of the basilica.[123] More importantly, they provide concrete evidence from the site itself for the *ziyāra(t)* (visitation) tradition mentioned in sources since the first Islamic century.

Early Medieval Pilgrimage
Even before the first Crusader state (the Kingdom of Jerusalem) was founded in 1099, western travellers to the Holy Land added Mount Sinai to their pilgrim routes. References to and brief descriptions of localities on Horeb in early itineraries testify to knowledge of the place. One of the earliest was the *Commemoratorium on the Churches of Jerusalem*, of *circa* 808, surviving in a single ninth-century manuscript, probably compiled under the auspices of the emperor Charlemagne (Carolus Magnus, 742–814, ruled 768–814).[124] The churches of Horeb were listed:

> On holy Mount Sinai four churches: (1) one where the Lord spoke with Moses on the summit of the mountain; (2) another of St. Elijah; (3) a third of St. [Elisha?]; (4) the fourth the Monastery of St. Mary: the Abbot Elias, 30 monks; there are 7,700 steps for climbing up and down the mountain.[125]

The Jabal Mūsā church was mentioned first and other churches followed in the order they appeared as one descended Horeb. If the third church was indeed dedicated to the prophet Elisha (the reading is conjectural), it could have been near the chapel of Farsh Elias, where a chapel with that name was mentioned in later narrations.[126] The number of steps (7,700) probably referred to their total, counting them on the way up and on the way down.

The work usually referred to by the name of a certain 'Fetellus', who was one of its early editors, must be dated a few decades after the coming of the Crusaders (*circa* 1130). It contains a list of the stations of the Exodus and twelfth among them is Mount Sinai. Its writer drew on sources as diverse as the Bible, Eusebios and later geographers, anecdotal information and first-hand accounts:

> Mount Synai is in Arabia, of very lofty height, and hard of access, the ascent of it being of three thousand and five hundred steps. Of Synai it is said by the most holy hermits and monks who dwell there, that from the time of Moses the place is the constant walking-place of heavenly angels. Mount Synai always smokes and flashes with fiery brightness. Of Synai it is said, and it is true, that every Sabbath heavenly fire flies around it, but does not burn; some it touches, but it does not hurt them, appearing most frequently as if in white fleeces with a slight movement encompassing the mountain, sometimes descending with an intolerable and terrible noise, those most holy inhabitants fleeing thence through the crypts and the cells of the cenobites. On the summit of Synai is a venerable and beautiful church, situated on the spot where God gave to Moses the Law written with His own finger on tablets of stone. Of so venerable dignity is the before-named church, that none dare to enter it, or even to ascend the mountain, unless they have first rendered themselves acceptable by confession, and afflicted themselves by fasting and prayers.[127]

The landmarks of the Sinaitic landscape, the prescribed paths of its visitation, the prohibitions and miraculous events associated with Jabal Mūsā – all had remained unaltered since Anastasios's time. Smoke, flashes, and heavenly fire bring to mind similar phenomena described five centuries earlier, especially the incident of the eight hundred Armenians (see page 84). By 'beautiful church' the writer must have meant the basilica, even though it had been destroyed by his time. Access to the site was still restricted and pilgrims were only admitted after undergoing the cleansing ritual of confession. The persistence of these Jabal Mūsā traditions into the second millennium testifies to the sanctity of the site and the respect it commanded through periods of political and cultural change.

An anonymous work in English verse exemplifies early medieval itineraries which began to be composed in languages other than Latin, thus reaching wider audiences through public recitation. Even though its date of composition is uncertain, the fact that the dedication of the Monastery was to the Virgin Mary rather than Saint Catherine places it before the fourteenth century:

> Now telle we of the Mount of Synai,
> A full denote place sicurly,
> […] In that Mount upon hy,
> Is a Mynstor of our Lady:
> The Mynstor of the Busche men calle hit,
> Wher in the body of Sent Katheryne was put.
> Also behynde the hee Autere,
> Is wher Jesu dud apere,
> In that Chirche to Moisie,
> When he kept Getro Madan schepe trulee.
> In middez of that Hull is a place,
> Where dud his penaunce the Prophet Helias;
> In the hye of that Hull, by Clerkez sawez,
> God yaf to Moises boothe the Lawez:
> Written in Tabelez, wit outen misse,
> Plenor remission ther hit is.
> A Garden ther is witout distaunce,
> Where Onorius dude his penaunce.
> Another Hull also is there,
> To the wiche Angelez dud bere
> The blessed body of Sent Kateryne,
> Sche was a holy Virgyn.[128]

A more detailed narration of a near-contemporary visit was given by Thietmar, visiting Horeb in 1217. His text survived in Latin and Dutch versions, evidence of the popularity such accounts enjoyed.

Thietmar described the Monastery focusing on the *katholikon* and the sepulchre of Saint Catherine, repeated the story of her relic's discovery, examined the life of the monks and detailed his ascent to Jabal Mūsā mentioning the Panagia tou Oikonomou chapel, the two gateways, the Farsh Elias chapel, the summit chapel dedicated to Moses and the caves.[129]

With the addition or omission of a few details, all pilgrimage accounts henceforth would follow the same pattern, only to be fundamentally changed in the nineteenth century, when scholarly questions preoccupied visitors.[130] Ascent to Horeb was effected via the 'Path of Moses', included all landmarks easily accessible around it (but usually not the more distant chapels), culminated at Jabal Mūsā and was often followed by another ascent (on a different day) to Jabal Kathrin. The experience of the pilgrim had changed little since the sixth century and the only new landmarks were the ones associated with the virgin martyr from Alexandria (her mountaintop *inventio* place and her Monastery sepulchre).

The earliest Jewish visitors came to Jabal Mūsā in the Early Christian era. By the Middle Ages, a Jewish pilgrimage tradition had been established, following the Christian tradition and possibly encouraged by the Islamic one. In the second half of the twelfth century, rabbi Jacob provided detailed information which testifies to an actual visit, whereas a contemporary Jewish voyager, Benjamin from the Navarre town of Tudela in the Iberian Peninsula (travelled 1165–1173), gave a vague description which was probably borrowed from other travellers.[131] Illustrations of Mount Sinai in Haggadah and other manuscripts were highly stylised and show no effort to depict Horeb – it was only in the twentieth century that modern European visual material informed Jewish perceptions of the Mount of the Law.[132]

In later years, Jews would appear frequently in the Sinai textual record. Krystoff Harant z Polžic a z Bezdružic, in October 1598, mentioned a group of Jews on pilgrimage miraculously prevented from going through the gateways of the stepped 'Path of Moses' and having to be baptised Christians before continuing to the summit.[133] The story had also been told to F. Fabri in 1483 and was probably a *topos* confirming, nevertheless, a flow of Jewish visitors.[134] John Lloyd Stephens in March 1836 mentioned that the Monastery's superior told him of two

'Asiatic Jews' who had come disguised as Europeans in 1832 but were detected 'under their sheep's clothing' and cast out. Stephens saw on the wall of the Monastery the name of an American Jew.[135]

A little-known piece of information could shed light on this prohibition. Early in the rule of the Ottoman sultan Süleyman I 'the Magnificent' (1494–1566, ruled 1520–1566) a petition was filed on behalf of the powerful Jewish community (*millet*). They requested control of the holy lands of Horeb where Moses had been given the Law. This was avoided by the prompt intervention of the Sinai monks who ensured that two decrees were issued by the sultan in 1522 and 1558 rejecting Jewish claims and preventing their access to Horeb.[136] Four centuries later these claims were forcefully repeated (with success) during the June 1967 'Six-Day War' which started the Israeli occupation of the Peninsula. After Sinai's restitution to Egypt thousands of Jews from Israel (on special 'pilgrim visas') and from around the world continued unhindered to make the ascent to Jabal Mūsā, the birthplace of the Jewish nation.

The material record from Jabal Mūsā for the period in question includes a (proportionately) large quantity of green-glazed, wheel-made lamp fragments with long nozzles, funnel-shaped filling holes and small vertical ring handles. The type is well-documented and dated to the late Fāṭimid or early Ayyūbid periods (late twelfth to thirteenth century).[137] A rare variant is similarly shaped, but cobalt and manganese-splashed rather than green-glazed.[138] The number of lamps was not matched by a similar quantity of table vessels and testifies to the brevity of visits on the site and the absence of building projects which would have left larger utilitarian vessel sherds, as in the sixth century.

Late Medieval Pilgrimage
The volume of pilgrim traffic to Sinai seems to have increased after the Crusaders' loss of Acre in 1291. The fourteenth and the fifteenth centuries represent the highpoint of the pilgrimage phenomenon and a good number of the people attempting the perilous voyage narrated their adventures in writing. They came in groups of at least a dozen. Often one or more of them did not make the journey back and got buried in the Holy Land – a great indulgence indeed.[139] It must be

Figure 18. William Henry Bartlett (British, 1809–1854, painter) and C.
Cousen (British, 1803–1889, engraver), *Refectory of the Convent*. Steel
engraving on paper. Based on drawings executed in October 1845.

stressed that the increased facility of publishing such narrations and
the better rate of their survival is partially responsible for the larger
number of late medieval accounts.

These accounts were also increasingly detailed, although most
repeated similar information on the standard Horeb landmarks.[140]
They included, as one made the ascent from the Monastery, the 'spring
of Moses' or 'of the shoemaker' (a new addition inspired by Exodus
or connected to the Panagia tou Oikonomou story), the Panagia tou
Oikonomou chapel, the two gateways and chapels dedicated to the
prophet Elijah, the prophet Elisha and Saint Mary the Egyptian.

When on the summit pilgrims noticed the rock over cave B and
the cave itself, the chapels on Jabal Mūsā (both the Christian Orthodox one, dedicated to Moses, and the Roman Catholic one of Archangel Michael), by now housing the indispensable relics of saints,

the mosque, cave A and the cisterns. The chapel was adorned with paintings depicting incidents of the Exodus, as first described by the Franciscan Niccolò da Poggibonsi in spring 1349:

> The church is very beautiful and it is small, placed on the summit of the mountain. This church is placed to the east and is separated with a small wall; and on this wall there is a painted panel, how Moses separated the Red Sea with a stick in his hand and how the people of Israel passed, and how the army of the Pharaoh drowned in the Red Sea; [...] In this church the entire story of Moses is painted with images in succession.[141]

The 'small wall' of his account could have been an *iconostasis*, an altar screen, but no icons with similar subjects survive in the Monastery collection, therefore it is possible that the screen was of masonry and painted with frescoes.

Sometime before 1312 Gabriel, the metropolitan of Soupakion (Petra), ascended Jabal Mūsā and found the church in ruins. He decided to dispatch builders to erect a new chapel. In the meantime, the northern and eastern parts of the Monastery walls were damaged in the 30 April – 1 May 1312 earthquakes and the monks urged the builders to mend the walls instead of building a new church. It is unclear whether they also erected the painted chapel.[142]

On the way down fewer attractions were offered and most pilgrims referred to Dayr al-Arbaʿīn and adjacent sites (for example the cave of Saint Onuphrius) before starting their ascent to Jabal Kathrīn, by now safely identified with the finding place of the virgin Saint's body.

Some fourteenth-century accounts resembled earlier medieval itineraries in brevity and lack of detail.[143] Others were entertainingly inaccurate: Rudolf de Frameynsperg, a knight visiting in 1346, reported having seen Moses' tomb in the Monastery, which was founded by the sultan of Cairo.[144] A few were entirely derivative, compiled by authors who had never attempted the journey.[145] Most were unremarkable in the uniformity of their memories.[146]

It is indicative of the margins for misunderstanding that the 1384 account of S. Sigoli identified 'Mount Sinai' with the finding place of Saint Catherine's body, although he distinguished it from the 'Mount of the Law'. The accounts of two of his fellow travellers however, the nobleman Leonardo Frescobaldi and the lord Giorgio Gucci, made the distinction clear, although they were all accompanied by the same guide.[147] Finally, Gucci reported that the reason for only a small part of the Saint's body surviving in the Monastery was its removal and burial by 'Saracens'.[148] Such instances exemplify the limitations of pilgrimage literature as a source of historical information.

However, some accounts provided valuable original details. In September 1335 Jacopo da Verona added to his manuscript the first visual representation of the Horeb holy landscape. It was a summary sketch probably compiled from memory after his ascent. It included the Monastery, its garden, the chapel of Panagia tou Oikonomou, the chapel at Farsh Elias, the Jabal Mūsā chapel and its mosque linked by paths and dominated by the taller summit of Jabal Kathrin.[149] The vraisemblance of the sketch was minimal, each landmark (including the Monastery) being no more than a square building with windows. Its perfunctory nature would typify all depictions of Horeb before the nineteenth century.[150]

Accounts of fifteenth-century pilgrims, despite their number and extent, add little to the above picture of Horeb.[151] The detailed description of F. Fabri in 1483 mentioned nothing of paintings within the Jabal Mūsā chapel, which was by then dedicated to the Saviour (Sōtēr).[152] His testimony is verified by the text of the Cologne Knight Arnold von Harff who visited between 1496 and 1499.[153] It is possible that during the fifteenth century a new chapel had been erected with another dedication and some Greek *proskynētaria* (pilgrim guidebooks) of the sixteenth and the seventeenth century mentioned a dedication to the Transfiguration (of the Saviour), which is often shortened in Greek into 'Sōtēr'. F. Fabri was also shown Jabal Mu´tamr as the place where Moses conversed with God in the company of Aaron and the seventy elders, a new introduction to the Horeb landscape which survives in its Arabic name ('Mount of the Conference').[154]

Pilgrims and their retinues were entertained (and sometimes housed) in the new refectory of the Monastery, a vaulted room to

the south of the *katholikon*. The view that the room was originally
a hostel and a Catholic chapel and only later became a refectory
cannot be accepted since the 1573 paintings on its eastern wall (a
Last Judgement and the Hospitality of Abraham) depict standard
themes in the iconography of Byzantine refectories.[155] Pilgrims left
behind carved and incised graffiti of names, coats of arms and other
heraldic devices. Some can be attributed to known persons, like the
English knight Thomas de Swinburne (1392), Ghillebert de Lannoy
(1401 and 1421/1422) or Anselme Adornes (1470).[156] Although the
room is frequently referred to as 'The Crusader Refectory', the graffiti actually dates from between the fourteenth and the sixteenth
century, after the end of the Crusader era,[157] and testifies to the elevated social standing of western travellers. The cost of Holy Land
pilgrimage was high, but the Sinai diversion was very dangerous and
therefore even more expensive and usually reserved for noblemen,
wealthy merchants and officials.[158]

The archaeological evidence from this period at Jabal Mūsā is
limited. Datable sherds are few and do not agree with the large
numbers of visitors suggested by the sources. The reason for this
must be the nature of items brought to the site by the pilgrims. Clay
lamps must have been replaced by metallic ones, since they practically disappear from the material record. There are very few sherds
of vessels datable to the late thirteenth, the fourteenth and fifteenth
century like a celadon-glazed lip and a few underglaze blue decorated wares.[159]

A description of a meal at the nearby summit of Jabal Kathrin
was given by F. Fabri. He was the only one of his group who carried
food and shared it with the rest: four noble knights, four clerics,
two escorts, their Italian-speaking guide (Father Nikodēmos from
the Monastery, who probably had also shown G. Lengherand around
in 1486) and some Arabs:[160]

> After prayers we sat down, and began to burn with desire for bread
> and water, and each man wished that he had his basket and his
> bottle with him. I know not by what providential means it befell
> that I alone had with me a basket with biscuits, hard-boiled eggs,
> smoked meat, and cheese, which I had brought for myself alone,

whereas the others had left all their provisions with the pilgrims who stayed down below. When they saw that I was so well provided, they congratulated me, and were angry with themselves because of their neglect, and one began to beg me for a scrap of meat, another for a crumb of bread, another for a bit of bread and cheese, and others asked me for a drink of wine. When I saw this I was amused, and gave nothing to any man, but took up my basket, and poured out all that was therein upon the hollow rock close by us, in the place where once St. Catharine's head had lain, and I thus jestingly invited the noblemen and pilgrims [...][161]

Although a deeply pious friar personally devoted to Saint Catherine, Fabri did not hesitate to offer the meal in a receptacle consecrated by tradition – a fitting container. Similar meals must have been served on Jabal Mūsā without the use of any archaeologically traceable objects.

The Ottoman Period

Late fifteenth- and early sixteenth-century accounts by western pilgrims describe the fear experienced by the monks about belligerent Bedouin keen on plunder.[162] The Franciscan monk Francesco Suriano of Venice, who visited in 1494, even mentioned the murder of Bishop Makarios III by armed Arabs.[163] The reason for these unusual disturbances seems to have been the collapse of the Mamlūk administrative machine, especially in a distant and hard to control area like Sinai. The turbulent life of the monks was underlined by the existence of a well-furnished armoury and two small cannons within the Monastery, attested since the later part of the century.[164] In a 1712 Greek engraving, the Monastery is shown under attack by the Bedouin. They are throwing rocks at the monks who, nevertheless, lower through the windlass their daily offering of bread.[165]

Some of the information in pilgrimage accounts of the period was contradictory. Within a few decades, the Monastery was reported as thriving, deserted and thriving once more.[166] It is unlikely that such fluctuations were due to political turmoil, economic instability or actual changes in the number of monks. Probably the travellers compared the modest Horeb community with its populous western equivalents. It is also possible that monks practising *hēsychia* (silence, peace) distanced themselves from such disturbing agents as heterodox visitors,[167] and the fall of Constantinople in 1453 – an event which many Orthodox blamed on the hatred of the 'Latin' West – would also have caused suspicion towards western pilgrims. It should also be considered that a visit during Lent, Easter, Christmas or the festival day of Saint Catherine (November 25), when the anchorites who lived scattered around the Monastery gathered within its walls, would have created a different impression from everyday occasions, when monks concentrated on their duties.

There is another occasion which could have been interpreted by visitors as abandonment of the Monastery. The *kleismos* (closure) was a total isolation of the Sinaitic brotherhood from all outside contacts, a severe search for *hēsychia* in fasting and prayer as if the Monastery were a spiritual Noah's Ark.[168] The *kleismos* was also a way to exert pressure on the Bedouin that depended upon the Monastery for their everyday bread and livelihood. Although no traveller or pilgrim seems to have identified this practice,[169] a brief *kleismos* was experienced by the writer during the first days of Lent in spring 2002. In order to continue excavation work the archaeologist team had to leave the fortress through a hidden door despite the orders of the *dikaios* (superior). The realities of modern life and pressures by the tourist police curtailed the length of this closure, but the Monastery tradition preserves stories of *kleismoi* continuing for years. Every noise was muted and every movement suppressed during these few days and the fortress seemed deserted indeed. However, a total abandonment of the fortress would go against the Sinaitic mentality and would leave hallowed sites uncelebrated, an unacceptable prospect. It is possible that ever since its erection in the sixth century the *katholikon* has had an uninterrupted liturgical life even when the monks' lives were in grave danger. Giorgio Gucci remarked in the account of his 1384 visit:

> And one must believe that out of reverence for St. Catherine and the place where God the Father gave Moses the law, and out of respect for the numberless saints that have been there, God has a love for that place, and has not permitted that that place should be uninhabited, because while these monks are there, by day and by

night the name of God is named, praised, blessed and glorified, and that place is visited, which visited it would not be, if they were not there and if they did not maintain it.[170]

It seems that in the Ottoman period human intervention should be taken into account alongside natural phenomena when the disasters which befell Christian buildings have to be explained. Bedouin efforts to demolish chapels on Horeb appeared in travel records.[171] As in previous centuries, the threat originated from unruly Bedouin rather than organised militia. However, such outbreaks were occasional, while respect towards the summit remained constant. Until the 1770s the Bedouin approached the place dressed in *iḥrām* clothing, a tradition signifying the elevated status enjoyed by the *loca sancta* of Horeb.[172]

The adverse circumstances experienced by the monks and their guests during early Ottoman times were vividly described by the Czech nobleman Krystoff Harant who visited in October 1598.[173] Upon arrival to the Monastery he was subjected in the 'Crusader Refectory' to what he perceived as a revolting gastronomic experience involving hard black bread, raw fava beans in warm water, dried Red Sea fish of a leathery consistency and white cheese tasting of soap. Conversation was offered instead of pudding. (Such menus are familiar to all who have dined at the refectory in modern times.) Harant was an aristo-crat used to the luxuries, indeed extravagances, of the Prague court of the Holy Roman Emperor Rudolf II (1552–1612, ruled 1576–1611) and some excuses have to be made for his spoiled palate. However, his disgust must have been genuine. The 'archpriest', probably the *dikaios*, in an effort to divert his elevated guests, entertained Harant and his two companions by offering them a jug of date wine which they consumed in a porcelain bowl which everyone shared:

The monk who took care of us brought a cup of porcelain. He added some liquor, cutting it with water, and we drank until it was all finished.[174]

The mention of this vessel is remarkable since, despite the frequent use of Chinese porcelain in Mamlūk and Ottoman Egypt, no other reference to an object made of this material exists in Sinaitic bibliography before Friday, 19 January 1923, when Augusta Mary Rachel Dobson saw a 'beautiful large porcelain bowl'.[175] The single instance of a porcelain vessel uncovered within the Monastery walls is a sherd of Chinese blue-and-white porcelain of late Ming date, such as Harant would have seen in the outstanding collection of Rudolf II in Hradčany Castle, Prague.[176] The sherd was uncovered in 1998 in the rubble from the collapsed roof of a cell near the 'Crusader Refectory' and belongs to the so-called '*kraak*' family of wares, widely exported from China in the latter part of the sixteenth century, during the rule of the Wanli emperor (1563–1620, ruled from 1572 to 1620).[177]

The trade routes allowing porcelain to reach Horeb were in place for centuries before the coming of the Ottomans. While standing on the summit of Jabal Kathrin in 1384, L. Frescobaldi noted on the Red Sea:

> We saw in it a great number of sails. They were ships carrying spices from India; and then the caravans take them to Cairo, and on the Nile they go to Alexandria, and by other routes they go to Damascus.[178]

The Castilian nobleman Pero Tafur encountered a caravan fifty years after Frescobaldi and a century and a half before Harant's visit, most probably in Ṭūr. The caravan was on its way back from 'India' (a generic term for South and Southeast Asia and the Far East) with spices, pearls, precious stones, gold, perfumes, linen, parrots, cats and the Venetian ambassador Niccolò da Conti (1395–1469). It could also have carried porcelain vessels.[179] By the early fifteenth century the Red Sea port of Ṭūr was an important trade station, protected from Bedouin attacks by guards dispatched by the Mamlūk government, especially after the 1422–1438 rule of sultan Barsbāy. The Monastery profited from this trade and was reported as receiving a part of the toll paid by anchoring ships.[180]

Excavations at Ṭūr have yielded Chinese sherds, some as early as the Tang dynasty (618–907), several dated to the Ming dynasty (1368–1644).[181] Similar material of a fragmentary nature came to light at Jabal Mūsā. However, the instance of unexpected luxury within the Monastery witnessed by Harant remains unique and all other circumstances described by the disaffected Czech were appalling.[182]

Harant died on the scaffold in Prague on 20 June 1621, a Protestant martyr punished for his belief and politics. He had joined Luther's followers in 1618, twenty years after his Holy Land tour. Had he embraced Protestantism earlier, he would not have attempted the journey. Martin Luther viewed the practice of pilgrimage as an unwanted consequence of the corrupt indulgences system and opposed it vehemently. The steep drop in western pilgrim numbers to Horeb from the seventeenth century onwards must be attributed mainly to religious convictions.[183] Even Catholic believers were reluctant to travel, discouraged by Bedouin banditry and the (justified) suspicion of Ottoman authorities towards the new breed of observant and curious pilgrims who looked a lot like spies. For those attempting the journey, the shortest route was by sea, aboard ships sailing the Red Sea and anchoring at Ṭūr to allow for a short excursion. The itinerary could continue towards the East, adding profit from trade to the blessings of pilgrimage.

The Red Sea trade was affected by the 1488 rounding of the Cape of Good Hope by the Portuguese and the subsequent diversion of sea routes to India and the Far East. A visit to the holy places of Horeb was no longer a brief detour from a lucrative journey but a distant destination, a dangerous endeavour undertaken by fewer and fewer travellers. George Sandys's account of the mountain seems derivative and he probably never added the desert pilgrimage to his travels, which began in 1610.[184] The fictitious London merchant Edward Brown (in a book of his 'adventures' written by John Campbell) did not advance further than Suez in the 1670s and his interest focused on the markets and spectacles of Cairo.[185]

When the British Major Henry Rooke sailed past Ṭūr on 12 April 1782, he claimed to have seen 'Mount Sinai' from his ship, something impossible, and he did not feel compelled to visit the Holy Mountain in person.[186] The mention to the Horeb holy sites and the Monastery in William George Browne's travel narration is only a few lines long.[187] The priorities of these merchant travellers were clearly ordered in the following passage by William Daniel, one of the few British merchants who made the Horeb trip in 1701:

It being a venerable custome among the Greek pilgrims that come there to give five crowns […] I presented them with forty crowns and two pair of spectacles, to pray for King William, the Honourable East India Company, myself, and relations.[188]

While the British focused on trade, the French excelled in diplomacy. The active role assumed by envoys of France within the Ottoman world allowed them to travel as far as Sinai, for example Vincent Stochove, ambassador to the Porte, and Jean Coppin, consul in Damietta between 1643 and 1645.[189] From the account of the Jesuit Charles Jacques Poncet, who stayed at the Monastery for a month in 1701 on his way back from Ethiopia, it can be assumed that Horeb was a meeting place for diplomats taking the Red Sea route to East Africa, India and the Far East.[190] Traders and savants followed in their footsteps.

From the mid-seventeenth century to Napoleon's Egyptian campaign (1798–1801) the accounts of the French provide the most reliable information on Sinaitic life. The monks viewed French monarchs with particular respect, which was only surpassed by their fondness for the (Orthodox) tsars of Russia.[191] Two copper-plate engraving portraits of Louis XIV (1638–1715, ruled 1643–1715) had adventurous lives within the Monastery walls. The first engraving was noted in 1697 at the archbishop's apartment by A. Morison. It was again seen by C. Sicard in 1720, who was also shown the second portrait in the 'Latin chapel'. At approximately the same time it was also mentioned by the diplomat Johannes Ægidius van Egmont. By 1906 the sitter of the one surviving portrait had been identified with Napoleon; it was finally spotted at the library vestibule in the 1930s.[192]

The French geographer André Thevet visited the site in spring 1552 and devoted more lines in his *Cosmography of the Levant* (1554) to the landscape visible from Jabal Kathrin than to the tradition of holy sites around Horeb.[193] His compatriot P. Belon du Mans, a famous naturalist who visited in 1547, noted that he was shown holy sites '*par le menu*' and expressed doubts on the veracity of the story ascribing to Moses the depressions in a stone at the foot of Horeb.[194] He was one of the early doubters who would multiply in later centuries as a new mentality keen on scientific research and verifiable proof became popular in Europe. The distinction between sacred tradition and scientific method was also evident in other accounts.[195] By 1720, even a Jesuit like C. Sicard would use subtle irony when referring to Saint Catherine's relics. During a later visit he also reported the 'camel's footprint' to have been carved by the monks in an effort to appease the Muslims.[196] Finally, when Carsten Niebuhr visited Horeb in 1761, he did not even finish the ascent and turned back without making it to Jabal Mūsā.[197]

The archaeological record from Jabal Mūsā is blank as far as architecture from this period is concerned. J.L. Burckhardt mentioned that the chapel on the summit was severely damaged in 1816 due to the continuous attempts of a Bedouin shaykh to destroy it.[198] It had been rebuilt relatively recently, after another destruction in 1782, of unknown causes.[199] Even earlier (*circa* 1588) an earthquake was responsible for the partial collapse of both the chapel and the mosque.[200] The chapel demolished by this tremor was, according to Jean Palerne who visited in 1581, ten or twelve *pas* long and six *pas* wide (6.2/7.44 m by 3.72 m). J. Coppin in the 1640s gave the dimensions of both chapels as 35 feet long by sixteen or seventeen feet wide, 11.43 m by 5.22/5.55 m.[201]

Small finds were equally sparse. Infrequent visits were attested by few sherds of Kütahya ware and some European porcelain cups. The former was widely available throughout the Ottoman Empire in the seventeenth and the eighteenth century and the latter could have originated in Italian or German kilns. Meissen in Saxony (since the mid-1710s) and Vezzi in Venice (in production 1720–1735) produced cups for the Ottoman market. They came in small sizes, were easy to carry and proved useful for a drink of tea or coffee on site.

Despite the diversion of trade routes, the insecurity of the desert and the decrease in visitor numbers, the Sinaitic clergy managed to extend its influence upon the new rulers of Egypt, preserve its contact with European sovereigns (despite their heterodox views) and produce original scholarly writings. By the early sixteenth century the monks enjoyed a reputation for intellectual ability and cosmopolitanism.[202] A few years before the Ottoman conquest, in 1504, the Mamlūk sultan al-Ashraf Qansuh al-Ghawri (ruled 1501–1516) complained to Pope Julius II (1443–1513, on the throne 1503–1513)

Figure 19. W. Warwick (British, draughtsman and engraver), *Panorama of Lower Egypt, Arabia Petra, Edom and Palestine, shewing the Head of the Red Sea, the Isthmus of Sinai, the Route of the Israelites from Egypt to Canaan...* Steel engraving on paper. Mid-nineteenth century.

about Portuguese expeditions to the Indian Ocean. To perform this delicate task, he chose as his representative a Spanish-born 'superior' from the Monastery.[203]

Sinaitic priories in Constantinople and Cairo were strategically situated near the sultan and his representative in Egypt. The Cairo priory was originally within the walls of the old city. In the early sixteenth century (probably at the time of the Ottoman conquest) it was

moved outside the walls to 'Tzouvania', opposite the 1267–1269
al-Ẓāhir Baybars Mosque in the Husayniyya district.[204] It operated
as the true seat of the archbishop instead of the Horeb Monastery, a
choice dictated by the political necessity of having a high-ranking
clergyman close to the centre of administration and by the practical
need to regulate supplies to the desert community.[205] Furthermore,
every time the archbishop was in residence at the Monastery it was
customary to keep the gates open and to feed the Bedouin, an added
reason to reside in Cairo.[206]

Several decrees survive at the Monastery from the Fāṭimid,
Ayyūbid, Mamlūk and Ottoman periods, the product of petitions on

behalf of the monks to Egyptian authorities. Some more were preserved in the Cairo and Istanbul priories and another one is in the
Ägyptisches Museum in Berlin.[207] They testify to the constant effort
on behalf of the Cairo monks to safeguard their desert brethren and
their property from Bedouin trespassers and avaricious provincial
governors. Gifts of fruit grown at the gardens of Horeb were welcomed by authorities for their symbolic connection with the 'Mount
of the Law'.[208]

When Dom João de Castro (1500–1548), a Portuguese naval
officer, landed on Ṭūr on April 21, 1541, he was told that Saint
Catherine's body had been taken to Tzouvania four months ago in a
'triumphant Chariot, all gilt' to be venerated by the city's Christian
population.[209] Such a well-timed expedition (after the Saint's feast
day on 25 November) would consolidate the Monastery's influence
among Egyptian Christians and its status in the eyes of Ottoman
authorities.

The Horeb Monastery remained popular with Muslim pilgrims.
Although the port of Ṭūr lost its importance for international trade,
it became a main stop along the Red Sea route of the *ḥajj*. This is
attested by Evliya Çelebi's (Ottoman, 1611–1682) mid-seventeenth-
century reference to Ṭūr as the eighth stop from Egypt to Mecca.[210]
Samuel Kiechel mentioned many illustrious 'Turks' (Muslims)
taking a few days to visit the Monastery, pray at the mosque there
and ascend to Jabal Mūsā. One of them had asked the monks' per-
mission to erect a mosque in the garden of Hagioi Apostoloi. When
they rejected his proposal, he petitioned the sultan in Constantinople. Although he was granted his wish, the boat he took back to
Egypt sank and he perished; thus the holy site escaped 'desecration'.
Kiechel also mentioned that the damage caused to the Jabal Mūsā
mosque by the 1588 earthquake had been repaired by both 'Turks'
and monks, because otherwise Muslims would pray in the Christian
chapel and profane it.[211]

The inclusion of the Sinai into the Ottoman Empire brought two
major changes in Sinaitic life. The supreme political authority (the
sultan) was once more – for the first time since the 630s – in Constantinople and the heretofore independent Monastery found itself within
the same religious community, *millet*, and under the Patriarchate

of Constantinople. Therefore, the distancing of the Sinaitic clergy
from the Church of Rome must be connected with the final breach
between Papacy and Orthodoxy after the 1439 Council of Florence
and the fall of Constantinople in 1453. Greeks dominated the ranks
of Sinai monks and the art of the Monastery was hellenised.[212] Jesuit
missions aiming to attract Sinai back into contact with Rome proved
fruitless.[213] However, relationships with ecclesiastical and secular
authorities in European countries persisted. They included doges of
Venice, French, Spanish and Hungarian kings, German emperors,
Austrian archdukes and several popes, responding to pleas for alms
by monks travelling all over Europe and as far as the Americas.[214]

The abbots of the Monastery had borne the title of bishop since the
ninth century and represented the highest authority in the Peninsula.
Their elevation to the title of archbishop and the achievement of
autonomy cannot be dated with certainty but it had happened before
the mid-sixteenth century.[215] The tradition of enlightened clergymen like Grēgorios Sinaitēs (died in 1346) and Philotheos Kokki-
nos (*circa* 1300–1379) continued.[216] Following in their footsteps, the
seventeenth-century Cretan monk Nektarios Pelopidēs (1605–1676),
later to become archbishop of Sinai (1660–1669) and patriarch of
Jerusalem (1661–1669), wrote his *Epitome of Holy and Secular
History* (1659–1660). It was a chronicle focusing on the Monastery
and using original sources, among them some of the aforementioned
decrees. Nektarios's work provides evidence of intellectual activity at the Monastery during the Ottoman period and was the basis
of much later Sinaitic literary production. Its subject matter was
not theological or hagiographical but historical, a choice that was
conscious and political.[217] The *Epitome* was an effort to compile an
encyclopedia of Sinai, to create a compendium of the Monastery's
living memory, to produce a document of Sinaitic identity.

It is from the sixteenth and the seventeenth century that most
Greek manuscripts with pilgrim guides or narrations (*proskynētaria*)
date.[218] They testify to a long tradition which was rarely recorded in
text. Contrary to pilgrims from the West, Orthodox travellers gave
precedence in their narratives to the Mosaic tradition centred around
Jabal Mūsā rather than to the cult of Saint Catherine, although they
venerated her relics, too.

All these accounts focused on Jabal Mūsā and mentioned land-marks familiar from pilgrim accounts already discussed: the steps of the 'Path of Moses' (their count varied considerably: 3,600, 6,000, 6,600, 7,000, 10,000), the chapel dedicated to Moses or to the Trans-figuration, cave B, cave A and the chapel of Archangel Michael. Unusually, two sixteenth-century manuscripts recorded a third chapel dedicated to Moses and Aaron and one *proskynētarion* added a chapel of Saint Marina.[219] However, according to all other texts the chapel of Saint Marina was in the Farsh Elias valley, so the one of Moses and Aaron may have been below Jabal Mūsā, too.

The founder of the main Jabal Mūsā chapel was mentioned in several of the manuscripts as being Germanos, patriarch of Jerusalem, and the erection date was always placed 335 years earlier.[220] However, given that the manuscripts dated between the early sixteenth and the mid-seventeenth century and the original texts are very hard to pinpoint chronologically, the foundation date of the chapel in question is impossible to discover. One sixteenth-century manuscript mentioned the erection of the summit basilica by Justinian, adding it had been destroyed by the time of its writing.[221]

The most original of these accounts was written between 1577 and 1592 by Paisios, a Sinai monk originating from Zakynthos, who was made a bishop (metropolitan) of Rhodes. In charming, collo-quial, decapentasyllabic verse he described the Monastery, Horeb and its landmarks. His Jabal Mūsā description was the most accurate of any *proskynētarion*. The chapel of the (Transfiguration of the) Saviour was to the right of cave B, which in its turn was to the right of the chapel of Archangel Michael. To their west was the mosque and under it a cistern, used by pilgrims for refreshment.[222]

His text was used by another Paisios (died *circa* 1768), former bishop (metropolitan) of Paramythia and Vouthrōton (1750–1754). The latter Paisios never made the Sinai pilgrimage but used available sources (Paisios of Rhodes, Nektarios, the *Perigraphē*) to compose a 'description in rime'.[223] The value of his text and the other *proskynētaria* lies less in their accuracy and more in their gathering of traditions of the Monastery's collective memory.

Place of Devotion

By the early seventh century Jabal Mūsā had already experienced more than three centuries of recorded history. It had been identified as the centrepiece of the Old Testament's most revered sacred landscape on which miracle-working ascetics had added a further layer of sanctity. It had witnessed two building phases, one of them imperially funded and of impressive proportions. It had become the destination of clerics and pilgrims from around Christianity who were serviced by extensive facilities and protected by a dedicated guard. Another glorious church had been built within a strong fortress at its foot. The once peripheral refuge of persecuted martyrs had become a major pilgrimage site and an important monastic centre.

What the twelve centuries that followed had to add was the feat of survival. Through cultural change, religious fanaticism, political turmoil, armed aggression and lengthy isolation, the religious community of Horeb continued to inhabit their fortified refuge and worship in their hallowed locations. They managed to overcome adversities because they shared an identity as custodians of the 'Mount of the Law', as followers in the steps of Moses, Elijah and the desert fathers. This strong Sinaitic identity, already made manifest in the Early Christian period, relied on faith, adaptability, tolerance and tradition.

During the first centuries of the Islamic era the economy of the Sinai Peninsula reverted to nomadism and its urban centres disappeared.[224] The Monastery at the foot of Jabal Mūsā developed into the only constant in the region, an agent of stability among unruly populations.[224] The enumeration of all Bedouin tribes and their affiliations over two pages in the relatively brief *Perigraphē* testifies not to ethnographic curiosity but to the knowledge of (and control over) the Sinai Bedouin by the Monastery.[225] This political power was used in later centuries to ensure the survival of the community but it also burdened it with duties which sometimes attracted the animosity of disaffected parties. Repeated instances of Bedouin aggression were probably due to such political crises and the conversion of the lay population to Islam *circa* 700 must have been such a local phenomenon.

Sinaitic diplomacy excelled in handling heterodox elites. The few threats on the behalf of Muslim authorities (the onslaught of al-Ḥakim's demolition troops in 1009) or violent incidents (the Mamlūk plundering of 1401, the Tzouvania occupation of 1653) had been contained through continuous petitions, building of mosques and welcoming both friends and enemies outside the walls, with open arms full of precious gifts. This is probably the reason why the treasury of the Monastery is relatively poor in liturgical objects made of precious metals.[226]

However, the coexistence with Egypt's Fāṭimid, Ayyūbid, Mamlūk and Ottoman rulers was peaceful most of the time. They wished to control the monks' influence on the Bedouin population and in return granted them protection, enlarged their revenue and bestowed upon their desert seat buildings and works of art. The impressive bronze '*aquamanile*' vessel in the shape of a raptor, traditionally dated to the eleventh or the twelfth century but probably of late ᶜAbbāsid manufacture, could have arrived at the Monastery as such a princely gift.[227] The buildings and furnishings mentioned in the eleventh-century *kursī* inscription and the 1106 *minbar* were also gifts from powerful figures. Beyond political motivations, genuine reverence for the Old Testament landmarks like Jabal Mūsā must have inspired Muslim patrons and visiting rulers sensitive to the tradition of the prophet Moses and to allusions in the Qur'ān.[228]

Such reverence was deeply rooted among the Bedouin and their example was followed by anonymous pilgrims on the *ḥajj* or on *ziyāra(t)*. J.A. van Egmont described within the Jabal Mūsā mosque 'small pieces of cloth, linen handkerchiefs, hair bound up in linen rags, and the like', humble tokens of devotion.[229] Carsten Niebuhr noted that his Muslim guides prayed at the chapels of the Farsh Elias plateau and even kissed the icons, imitating the Christian pilgrims they escorted.[230] A less solemn sign of respect was the Bedouin practice of becoming impregnated on Jabal Mūsā owing to the belief that 'children who are conceived here will be endowed with a holy and prophetic spirit', as witnessed by prior Gregor (or Georg) of Gaming on the night of the 17 October 1507.[231]

The Horeb brethren were able to accommodate Muslim devotion within Christian landmarks, thereby demonstrating both adaptability and tolerance. In this way they ensured the prosperity of their community and its continued existence. The early eleventh century was the moment when Sinai's strongest ties with both 'Latin' West and Muslim East were forged. After escaping al-Ḥākim's threat, the Monastery managed to shield itself against further aggression with mosques strategically placed within its walls, on Jabal Mūsā and probably on two further locations. At the same time Symeon Pentaglossos toured Europe endowing pieces of Saint Catherine's incorruptible, oil-oozing body in return for alms and property.

The success of Symeon's mission (and several later ones) consolidated Saint Catherine's fame and ensured a stream of pilgrims and revenue for five centuries. Once again, dedicated devotional structures, the 'Latin' chapels of Saint Catherine within the Monastery and of Archangel Michael (or the Ascension) at Jabal Mūsā serviced but also contained heterodox piety. For some pilgrims the grace of the virgin Saint obscured even the glory of the Mosaic association. For most, the two traditions merged, as was manifested in the localisation of the Saint's *inventio* not on the summit of Jabal Kathrin, where the Monastery tradition must have always placed it, but on 'Mount Sinai', Jabal Mūsā. During the October 1433 pilgrimage of Philipp, Count of Katzenellenbogen, several noblemen were dubbed 'Knights of Saint Catherine' at the Jabal Mūsā chapel rather than at her sepulchre within the Monastery.[232] Some accounts mentioned manna oozing from her body rather than oil, bringing together the narrative of Exodus with the fourth-century Saint from Alexandria.[233]

The early sixteenth century was another turning point. The Byzantine Empire, the reference for all Orthodox clergy irrespective of distance, had collapsed and the age of discovery had opened new seafaring routes for international trade which diverted visitors. Egypt was merely the province of a large empire and a new way of practising religion reduced the attraction of pilgrimage in Europe. Visitor numbers by the early nineteenth century had dwindled to sixty or eighty per year. The Monastery of Saint Catherine seemed isolated and abandoned to the plundering of the Bedouin, but 'defended itself successfully against all the surrounding tribes by the peculiar arms of its possessors, patience, meekness and money'.[234] This was the time when the priories of the Monastery reached their wider distribution. These satellite institutions influenced centres of power and channelled revenue and information back to the desert, creating a life-giving network. In December 1701, W. Daniel referred to the Greek 'Patriark' (archbishop or *dikaios*) showing him an Italian 'gazet' for European news – although he did not specify how old the newspaper was.[235] It was an era of introspection and resilience strengthened by faith.

The writing of the *Epitomē* by Nektarios in 1659–1660 was the culmination of this period. The book collated historical testimony from the Monastery's library, documents from its archive and, more importantly, its oral memory. This communal memory, harking back to the third-century desert fathers, was the heart of Sinaitic identity. For the monks, their history had begun in the time of Moses, long before their ascetic predecessors arrived at South Sinai. Their tradition connected them with the book of Exodus and the supreme moment of the Old Testament narrative. In this way, the 'Mount of the Law' was the seal of their uniqueness.

By the early nineteenth century Jabal Mūsā had reverted back to its humble Early Christian appearance. The magnificent basilica and even the painted chapel had disappeared. The memory of the basilica's splendour survived in monastic lore and its ruins were incorporated in subsequent structures.[236] In 1999, during the excavation of the southern exterior staircase of the narthex, a hoard of approximately 600 *tesserae* from the mosaic decoration came to light. The minute pieces of glass and stone had been carefully collected and had been buried under the paving of the mosque's entrance way. It was a cache of memory reverentially deposited at a new structure's foundation, a symbol of continuity at a place where even debris assumed a guise of sanctity.

Traditions proved more resilient than buildings and Jabal Mūsā continued to perform the role of an *avaton* offering protection. When the local lay population fled conversion to Islam and when the monks decided to abandon Horeb, Jabal Mūsā was their place of refuge and prayer. When the troops of Ibn Ghiyāth approached, set on destroying the Monastery, Jabal Mūsā erupted. When in the sixteenth century (*circa* 1579) plague struck Egypt, a pair of cells above Farsh Elias offered shelter from contamination.[237] Another miracle, mentioned in the *Epitome* of Nektarios, set Jabal Mūsā within its traditional metaphysical framework:

[...] if someone stands on this summit in the evening, when the sun sets, he can see on the peak, not of the mountain but of its shadow, a light, like the one said to appear on the summit in the Holy Scriptures, when God descended in glory, and fire and darkness, and talked to Moses.[238]

The ancient prohibition against spending the night on the summit was still observed when Georg Christoff von Neitzschitz visited in 1636.[239] However, Antoine Morison slept there on the night of 23 November 1697 because he was too tired to descend. He was joined by fellow travellers and monks from the Monastery and they all celebrated mass the next morning, presumably in the respective Orthodox and Catholic chapels rather than Saint Peter's in Rome, like the *paramonarios* in Anastasios's narration had done.[240]

Jabal Mūsā, a landscape alive with biblical stories, was the cornerstone of Sinaitic identity, the main point of reference through adversity and change. On the one hand, it was immutable, still invested with a concrete set of qualities formulated in the pre-Justinianic period: sacredness, preeminence over other sacred places, protection and limited accessibility. On the other hand, it evolved as centuries progressed with the accumulation of new layers of meaning: it became an imperially-inspired pilgrimage site, an interreligious devotional destination and an all-embracing holy place accommodating pilgrims, buildings, relics and miracles.

Figure 20. Jean de Kergorlay (French), *Au sommet du Sinaï se voient les ruines d'une chapelle*. Photograph. Spring 1906.

Chapter 4

It is good to know the truth and to speak the truth. But it is better
to know the truth and to speak about palm trees.

Freya Stark quoted by G.W. Murray in 'The Land of Sinai',
The Geographical Journal CXIX: 2 (June 1953), 143.

By the end of the twelfth century a complex and unique set of qualities
had come to be assigned to Jabal Mūsā. It was the crown of the sacred
landscape of Horeb, which among other sites included: the Monastery with the relics of Saint Catherine and the Burning Bush, the cave
of the prophet Elijah in Farsh Elias, other landmarks connected with
Moses, and the summit of Jabal Kathrin where the body of the virgin
Saint from Alexandria had miraculously been discovered two centuries earlier. It had become the focal point of an anchoretic community and, later on, of a thriving monastic society. It had been graced
with Justinian's buildings and also with the patronage of rulers and
high-ranking officials of the Fāṭimid state. It had suffered political
tribulations after the advent of Islam and the onslaught of the Crusaders, and had survived as a pilgrimage destination for Christians from
both sides of the schism and Muslims alike. Even Jews had included it
in their itineraries. In short, the majority of Jabal Mūsā's characteristics had crystallised within the first millennium of its recorded history.
However, there remained a last chapter to be written, one that can only
be followed through the scholarly and travel literature devoted to the
site and produced in abundance during the nineteenth century.

   This chapter will focus on works by writers from the British
Isles, France, German-speaking countries and the United States of

America from 1822 to the beginning of World War I in 1914. The former date saw the posthumous publication of J.L. Burckhardt's *Travels in Syria and the Holy Land*, the first book to question the attribution of Jabal Mūsā as the biblical Mount Sinai on the basis of the writer's interpretation of archaeological remains and topographical features.[1] The storm of activity which ensued after its publication is remarkable. Hundreds of books and articles, but also paintings, engravings and photographs, were produced, fiercely arguing for or against contestants for the title of the 'Mount of the Law'. The controversy inspired the first large-scale Ordnance Survey mapping project outside British soil, the 1868–1869 *Ordnance Survey of the Peninsula of Sinai*, published in 1871. The conclusion of this expedition in favour of Jabal Mūsā satisfied most researchers and tourists. However, to this day many scholars seek alternative Mount Sinais in the peninsula, Negev or Arabia.

There are further issues beyond the endless and at times bizarre arguments on whether Jabal Mūsā or some other hill or mountain was the site of the Delivery and Proclamation of the Law. Imperialist aspirations funded the German, French and British missions which mapped the peninsula and were followed by economic penetration into the weakening Ottoman Empire and the eventual annexation of Egypt by the British in 1882. This turn of events seemed inevitable to the handful of European nations which managed to control in one way or the other three quarters of the earth's surface by the late nineteenth century.

Apart from political and economic supremacy, religious fervour of a distinctly Protestant flavour affected the experience of the majority of the pious scholars and visitors to Sinai who recorded their adventures in print. Their attitude was founded on their certainty about the literal truth of the Bible, which often reached the level of Bibliolatry, their rejection of ecclesiastical tradition and their militantly anti-monastic feelings. Only the scriptures could justify the attribution of a biblical site and only rigorous and systematic enquiry of a scientific nature would prove it. Accounts by visiting Roman Catholic priests and travellers did not share the condescending tone of the British, American and German Protestants in their description of the monks and their 'superstitions'.

The self-referential character of this attitude will be made manifest when the history of Horeb in the nineteenth century is examined from two different points of view hereto largely ignored in western scholarship. Firstly, there was the monastic community itself, closely connected with Orthodox Christianity in the Balkans, Russia and the Near East. The 'isolated' and 'ignorant' monks coordinated a network of priories which by the eighteenth century stretched as far as India. Secondly, there was the view of Orthodox, mostly Russian, scholars who first recognised the importance of the Monastery's art treasures. Together with thousands of anonymous pilgrims, they continued to revere Jabal Mūsā and produced a groundbreaking body of literature which remained ignored in Europe and America until the twentieth century.

Between the second and last quarters of the nineteenth century the holy summit of Horeb would be measured, described, sketched and photographed but also questioned and dismissed to an extent that remains unmatched in previous or subsequent years. The amount of information available in print was such that respected scholars could produce volume-long essays on the topography, morphology and climate of the site and large maps without ever having been there.[2] However, in the twentieth century scholarly attention shifted towards a more critical approach to the text of the Bible itself, its sources and formative process,[3] and by the end of World War I the importance of the library, icon collection and mosaics of the Monastery was acknowledged in the western academic world. Until the 1990s, no scholar would contemplate the summit of the mountain or the remains on it. During the twentieth century the pattern of visitation which was established by the late Middle Ages, with prayer, adventure or curiosity as its motivations, was resumed.

Sinai Questioned

In comparison with the pilgrim traffic to Jabal Mūsā up until the sixteenth century, the following two centuries appear quiet. If it was not for the activity of Orthodox clergy connected to the Monastery and for the grandeur of works of art like the painted and gilt wooden screen with its gigantic icons, the work of Maximos, erected in 1612 in the *katholikon*, one could claim that this was a period of decline.[4] From the point of view of European visitor traffic, this was actually true, the change made even more noticeable if compared with the rise of long-distance travel and geographical scholarship in seventeenth-century Europe.

It was an era of encyclopaedic collections of past pilgrims' narrations rather than contemporary pilgrimage. The 1584 compilations by the Frankfurt publisher-printer Sigmund Feyerabend (1528–1590) and the Tübingen professor Martinus Crusius (1526–1607) and the works of Richard Hakluyt (British, 1552/3–1616, published from 1582) and Samuel Purchas (British, 1575–1626, published from 1613) base their information on earlier first-hand accounts rather than actual experience of the places themselves.[5] Even the Italian Franciscan monk Franciscus Quaresmius (1583–1650), a celebrated scholar who had lived in Jerusalem, had visited Sinai himself and published his work in 1639, was more interested in collating older information than adding new.[6] Two of the decisive events which shook Europe during the fifteenth and the sixteenth century and shaped the modern world, the opening of new sea routes towards West and East and the Reformation of the Roman Catholic Church from 1517 onwards, had decisively reduced the attraction of the Holy Land and Mount Sinai for scholars and believers.[7] When their interest was renewed, it was on a level different from that of medieval pilgrimage.

The first wave of scholarly enthusiasm for South Sinai was associated with the so-called 'Sinaitic' inscriptions. In 1636, the alchemist and scholar Athanasius Kircher (German, 1601–1680) identified one of them as Hebrew. It had been transcribed a few years earlier (between 1612 and 1632) by the Franciscan Tommaso Obicini in Wādī al-Lajā'.[8] However, only in 1747, when Robert Clayton (Irish, 1695–1758, the Lord Bishop of Clogher (1745–1758) for the Church of Ireland), inspired by R. Pococke's travel account, urged the London Society of Antiquaries to organise a mission to record these inscriptions and offered a substantial amount to this end, did the scholarly community focus on the Sinaitic 'Hebrew characters'.[9] Missions were dispatched to transcribe as many inscriptions as possible and their authorship, date and decipherment were fervently debated.[10] An early mission, the scope of which included research on the inscriptions, was organised under the protection of the Danish king Frederick V (1723–1766, ruled 1746–1766) and with the general guidance of the scholar Johann Michaelis (1717–1791). The only person to survive it and record his experiences was C. Niebuhr.[11] By the mid-nineteenth century, the Sinai Peninsula was 'a place to be explored, included among the most essential *DESIDERATA* of archaeology' for the Institut National de France, and their enthusiasm was shared by other European scholarly bodies and learned societies.[12] Despite having been correctly identified as Nabatean as early as 1840 by Eduard Friedrich Ferdinand Beer (German, 1805–1841), Sinaitic inscriptions continued to be attributed to the caravan of the Jews fleeing from Egypt or to Early Christian Arabs.[13]

Most passionate among Beer's opponents was the Reverend Charles Forster, Rector of Stisted (British, died 1871), who between 1851 and 1865 published a series of books, pamphlets and articles supporting his theory that the inscriptions were alphabetical and Hebrew in origin. He first expressed an interest in all things Sinaitic in his two-volume, 866-page long diatribe on *The Historical Geography of Arabia*, which he never visited.[14] His essays included concordance tables of characters and even exercises that studious readers could do to gain proficiency in his proposed language system.[15] Whenever the alphabetical characters did not suffice to support his translations, he interpreted some of them as hieroglyphs, while he preferred to consider Egyptian hieroglyphs as pictorial alphabetical characters.[16] The resulting texts were incontrovertibly biblical, for example 'Pilgrimizing the Hebrews / Commit sin at Marah' and 'The People commit adultery congregated in the desert'.[17]

In the third volume of his *The One Primeval Language Traced Experimentally Through Ancient Inscriptions in Alphabetic Characters of Lost Powers from the Four Continents*, he went on to include all 'post-diluvian' dialects in a master linguistic scheme with the aim to trace the 'primeval ante-diluvian' language through them. He concluded by tracing the remains of the lost ten tribes of Israel all over central Asia: 'The fact of their existence, indeed, stands certified by "the sure word of prophecy".'[18] His 1860 contribution *A*

Figure 21. John Frederick Lewis (British, 1805–1876), *A Frank Encampment in the Desert of Mount Sinai. 1842 – The Convent of St. Catherine in the Distance.* Watercolour, gouache and graphite on paper, 64.8x143.3 cm. 1856.

Harmony of Primeval Alphabets incorporated characters from the ruins of Palmyra, Central America and Axum in Ethiopia.[19]

What is surprising is not the eccentricity of his views, which were vehemently rejected by most contemporary authorities, but the fact that his *Sinai Photographed or Contemporary Records of Israel in the Wilderness*, a sumptuous 1862 edition with several photographic

plates, was supported by a long list of influential and high-ranking subscribers.[20] Forster also participated in the 'Mount of the Law controversy', supporting Jabal Sirbāl as the best candidate for the 'Mount of the Law'.[21] This controversy was destined to engage the intellect of nineteenth-century scholars to a larger extent than Sinaitic inscriptions.[22]

The popularity of biblical scholarship in Britain, Germany and the United States of America was a major factor for the second resurgence of Sinaitic studies from the 1820s onwards. It was a time when sermons and theology pamphlets became best-sellers, circulating widely and read by a large part of the literate middle classes. The Methodist and later on the Evangelical movements had impressed upon a willing audience the fundamental principles of Protestant Christianity, namely the predominance of the study of the Bible combined with the rejection of ecclesiastical tradition ('Bible Alone', *Sola Scriptura*) and the ability of any lay student of the scriptures to come to definitive conclusions on matters of biblical exegesis ('Priesthood of All Believers').

Fervent preachers advocated the private and group study of the Bible beyond the confines of the established Church and encouraged bold travellers to stray outside the set paths of pilgrimage, unaltered since the Early Christian period, and to seek fresh evidence. The premise was that only first-hand experience of sacred places and empirical examination of the parameters of the Old Testament narrative would allow for a faithful reconstruction of the scriptural landscapes. New Testament sites (for example the Holy Sepulchre in Jerusalem or the Church of the Nativity in Bethlehem), identified since the Early Christian centuries with plausible accuracy, were under the hold of non-Protestant Christian Church authorities.[23] However, the identification of Old Testament sites was vague and based only on later traditions which were easier to refute if the reading of the Bible allowed it. In the American Stephen Olin's words:

> the Bible […] was always at hand, and it certainly proved the most useful as well as the most interesting book that can be taken by the traveller upon this route.[24]

Olin joined many travellers who roamed Horeb as if no one had ever been there before them. He proclaimed the presence of a chapel below Ra's Ṣafṣāfa as adequate supporting evidence for the identification of this summit with the scriptural Mount Sinai, ignoring the thousands who had visited and worshipped in it before and after him.[25] The potential clarification of the route of the Exodus and the discovery of its remains caught the educated public's imagination. Could there be more godly inspiration hidden in the inaccessible wilderness? Could the Decalogue be verified by archaeological and philological discoveries? The gain from deciphering the ancient riddle would be personal salvation and the justification of the individual before God, according to the principle of 'Faith Alone' (*Sola Fide*).

In doubting the traditional localities of the Old Testament events and seeking new ones, Protestant believers were probably treading down a path already taken by other Christian sects before them. It is possible that in the fifth and the sixth century non-Chalcedonian Christians were trying to establish their alternative *loca sancta*, untainted by heterodox associations and free from the control of the ecumenical church. In this context, it has been suggested that Kosmas Indikopleustēs, a Nestorian sympathiser, opted for Jabal Sirbāl as the 'Mount of the Law' (if indeed his was not an erroneous identification).[26]

What had changed by the nineteenth century were the positivist methods used by the itinerant believers, purporting to validate the metaphysical revelation of Exodus through modern science. The first step in this direction had already been taken in the early eighteenth century, when the *Physica Sacra* by Johann Jakob Scheuchzer (Swiss, 1672–1733), a palaeontologist, palaeobotanist and explorer, was published (1728–1739).[27] In this groundbreaking yet pious work the supernatural incidents of the Bible were explained through physics, medicine and observed phenomena and were illustrated by 750 copper engravings combining religious art with natural history subject matter.[28] On plate CLXVII, 'Mount Sinai' (but not a topographically accurate Jabal Mūsā) was depicted as a volcano. More than a century later, Sir George Biddell Airy (British, 1801–1892), Astronomer Royal from 1835 to 1881, went to some pains to explain in a rigorous and scientific language the theory first illustrated by Scheuchzer.[29] The veracity of the biblical description was beyond doubt but it had to fit within the confines of modern scientific knowledge.

Religious contentions were not the only incentive for arguments on biblical topography. The fact that various secular funding bodies were willing to support the exploration of uncharted areas of the ailing Ottoman Empire, within which the Holy Land was situated, gave an additional motivation for explorers. The years from the 1830s to the 1870s, which mark the highpoint of Sinaitic bibliographical production, also witnessed the rise of West and Central European countries into an unprecedented position of worldwide economic and political prominence. The Treaty of Paris of 1856 ensured better access for Europeans into the Ottoman territory. Improved conditions of travel allowed a greater influx of visitors and several collected intelligence alongside archaeological testimonies.[30] The same means of transport which allowed hundreds of tourists to visit Sinai casually every year were also responsible for a trade network which embraced the globe. The ultimate project of Sinaitic exploration, the *Ordnance Survey of the Peninsula of Sinai*, satisfied the most varied agenda of biblical, scientific, political, economic and military objectives. Gunboats followed in the wake of entrepreneurial businessmen and devoted scholars, and Egypt itself became a dependency of the British Empire in 1882.

In this context, it is not surprising that the earliest scholarly projects in Sinai combined cartographical, meteorological and mineralogical research with biblical scholarship and daring adventure-seeking. Explorers gathered information of a strategic and economical nature as well as specimens and testimonies of the Exodus. The three earliest ventures were U.J. Seetzen's ill-fated mission, J.L. Burckhardt's British-financed tour and Eduard Rüppell's scientific studies.[31] The Scottish entrepreneur John Gardiner Kinnear travelled with his compatriot David Roberts, the celebrated artist, but had his own business agenda, examining the 'prospects' of Muḥammad ʿAlī Pasha's new government.[32] The economic prospects of Sinai were not only examined by Europeans. Muḥammad ʿAlī himself had employed in 1830 and 1853 the Frenchman Louis Maurice Adolphe Linant de Bellefonds (1799–1883), chief engineer of the Suez Canal, to explore Sinai's mineral wealth and routes from Suez to Horeb.[33] Linant wore a different hat when he accompanied Léon Emmanuel Simon Joseph, Marquis de Laborde, in 1828 for a scholarly and art-historical mission to the Monastery (figure 10).[34]

However, most visitors and scholars going to Sinai from the second quarter of the nineteenth century made the journey hoping in earnest to find the biblical Mount Sinai. The questioning of the identification of Jabal Mūsā went hand in hand with an unrelenting denial of all traditions and identifications, an intensely anti-monastic feeling and a militant suspicion against the Orthodox clergy:

> Before we leave Mount Sinai we will add a brief notice on the surroundings. They are replete with silly legends which disturb the gravity of a Protestant traveller, and yet show the deep local impression of the Mosaic events.[35]

Heterodoxy was not enough to justify such scorn. The growing gap between the 'civilised' nations of the West and the 'backward' nations of the East is manifested in the derisory tone of the reports by British, American or German travellers on the monks and their 'naive beliefs'. The Methodist Episcopal John Price Durbin was not alone in considering altogether misguided

> those men in whose eyes tradition of any kind is a sacred thing; who close their own senses and strangle their own reason in obedience to the voice of authority, be it only ancient.[36]

The Greek monks of the Monastery of Saint Catherine were submitted to a scrutiny which bordered on abuse from several of their guests and were often accused of being uneducated, idle, greedy and deceitful, '[...] a dull, stupid class of men'.[37] The Monastery altogether was characterised as '[...] a sort of caravansary [sic] for the entertainment of strangers and pilgrims'.[38] Horatius Bonar was not alone in accusing them of cupidity:

> He [the superior] came, not to give his blessing, as some tourists tell us, but to receive our gold with his own hands. We offered him three sovereigns, -but he held them up in his palm, and told us it was not enough! We told him that we meant to give no more, and bowing in eastern fashion to the group, we left our dragoman to settle with him, which he did by giving a dollar to each of the servants at his own cost. We had to pay dearly for the small amount of cleanliness and comfort which we had experienced. Of hospitality we found nothing.[39]

Two years earlier his compatriot James Hamilton had described a similar incident:

> We were, nevertheless, insensible to the magic of his [the prior's] gray hairs, and with the effrontery of ignorance, presented our single sovereign, which was received, not as we had supposed in silence or with thanks, but with expostulations, which, growing louder, quickened into such violent abuse, that my companion, who slowly relenting already held his purse in his hand, meaning to produce another of those images of our sovereign lady for which the monks showed so great a devotion, replaced it in his pocket.[40]

Another British traveller, Henry Crossley, went further, attributing the identification of Jabal Mūsā with Mount Sinai to greed:

> By a fraud of the Greek monks of St. Catherine, Mount Sinai has been identified with a locality in every respect unsuitable, and irreconcilable with the events which occurred there. [...] Their whole subsequent conduct has been one continued series of similar impositions, so palpable, so extravagant, and in some instances so unblushingly avowed by themselves, that it may be questioned whether, among the genus monk, any species like the monks of St. Catherine ever existed to degrade the Christian religion by their abominable fabrications. [...] It was not till the present century that the world began to awake to the palpable imposture of the monkish Sinai.[41]

The monks were seen not as Christian brethren but as slothful 'Orientals', permeated by the 'immutability [which] is the most striking characteristic of the East'.[42] The ultimate condemnation came from the American Henry Bascom Ridgaway, who identified the Monastery as 'a Botany Bay [penal colony] of the Greek Church, to which refractory monks are sent for punishment'.[43]

An additional accusation referred to the lack of proselytising zeal on behalf of the handful of clerics within the Monastery.[44] E. Robinson mentioned two of the Monastery Bedouin serfs being baptised seven years before his 1838 visit, a piece of information unverified by other sources.[45] The German Friedrich Adolph Strauss mentioned a Bedouin convert attending the '*erhebende griechische Liturgie*', but he could have been an Arab Christian pilgrim instead of a local.[46] The fate awaiting a preacher of any religion outside Islam within a Muslim country was obviously unknown to these opinionated critics, but the monks had explained to the Jesuit missionary M. Jullien that such action would expose them to the wrath of fanatics.[47] Most travellers joined William Henry Davenport Adams in his dismissive aphorism:

> Nor have the monks of Sinai, from their first foundation to the present time, contributed in any way whatsoever to the sum of human knowledge.[48]

In the same vein, the American Samuel Colcord Bartlett wrote:

> Everything in charge of these monks seems to relapse and go to ruin, and nothing to advance. […] We parted company with these cloistered worthies, carrying very little respect for them or their doings.[49]

Such attitudes seem to have been the privilege of mainly Anglo-Saxon writers without knowledge of Greek or any Oriental language. The churchman H. Bonar, despite coming from a centuries-old line of ministers, actually thought that the chanting in the Monastery *katholikon* was in modern Greek.[50] The topographical artist William Henry Bartlett lightheartedly explained the visitors' unremitting condescension as a characteristic peculiar to his nation, part of 'that undaunted sense of privilege and rightness in being British':

> It struck me, indeed, during my stay, that they [the monks] treat travellers with less familiarity now than was their wont when their visits were more rare, and their habits less known; having, perhaps, been annoyed at that odd mixture of ill-timed joking and continual grumbling, which characterises so many of the wandering

islanders, and of which they leave traces whenever the pages of an album offers an escape-vent for their eccentric humours.[51]

The sceptics were not only '*milordi*' (an Italian corruption of 'my lords') but also German, and their works were often translated from English to German and vice versa within months of publication.[52] A. Dauzats in 1830 counted in the Monastery's visitor album one American, twenty-two Frenchmen, three or four thousand Englishmen (a certain exaggeration) and one English woman.[53] Father Marie-Joseph, earlier Ferdinand Baron de Géramb, studied the visitors' book and concluded that most entries belonged to either Englishmen or Germans.[54] Similarities between them were remarkable. The Egyptologist Karl Richard Lepsius echoed his British colleagues:

The whole life of these four priests and twenty-one lay brothers is the reverse of edifying. They gave us the general impression of being, as it were, under a dark rain-cloud, weighed down by the continual pressure of ignorance and indolence, albeit the physical sky under which they vegetate is always cheerful, and the temperature moderate. They are the only inhabitants of the vast desert who can enjoy the refreshing shade of cypresses, palms, and olive trees. The small, but not uncomfortable cells they occupy are built round a neat and well-kept church, in the Basilica style, the inside of which is richly ornamented. They possess besides a library containing about 1500 volumes, an ἰατρεῖον ψυχῆς [soul hospice], in which, had they any taste for it, they might find a remedy for their ennui.[55]

This English translation was made within the same year as the book's original publication in Berlin. Such vibrant publishing activity made the repetition of standard 'experiences' and conclusions between writers separated by distance and language not only possible but also inevitable.

A typical visit, narrated in a typical way, can be found in a book by the printer, publisher and collector of antiquities John Gadsby, who travelled to the Holy Land with his wife and stayed at the Monastery

from 6 to 8 March 1864.[56] Their group celebrated Sunday service in
their rooms within the Monastery walls instead of the *katholikon* and
ascended to the summit on 7 March. He used as his guides works by
the Oxford professor Arthur Penrhyn Stanley, Dean of Westminster
from 1864, S. Olin, William John Beamont and H. Bonar.[57] He discussed their suggestions as to the locality of the scriptural Mount
Sinai and concluded (after much argumentation) that it was Jabal
Mūsā after all. Before departing, he devoted three pages to the customary complaints over surcharging for the hospitality. Give or take
a few details and the presence (or lack) of literary merit, this formula
appears in most accounts of Sinai visits during the third quarter of
the nineteenth century, the period during which the 'Mount of the
Law controversy' raged most fiercely.

The common ground of the narratives examined so far was pri-
marily the Protestant religious conviction of their Anglo-Saxon and
German male writers. Few visitors from other national or religious
groups and even fewer female ones ventured as far as accusing the
monks of fraud or pecuniary greed, even though the Catholic French
abbot Antoine Raboisson connected the Monastery to the murder
of E.H. Palmer and two of his companions in August 1882 by some
Bedouin:[58]

> Furthermore, it is not at all certain that the monks of Saint
> Catherine's would have reached the point of preventing or
> punishing this crime in a similar occasion. Apart from the fact that
> such an enterprise could have been very dangerous for them, they
> were certainly not ignorant of the fact that Palmer had accused
> them of a life of idleness, of shameful ignorance and of a little-
> edifying preference for his brandy and their raki. His person could
> not have been particularly close and precious to them.[59]

Nonetheless, his comment was isolated and apart from him only
the scholar Pierre Victor Lottin de Laval expressed mild disbelief
in the monks' honesty.[60] Travellers from predominantly Roman
Catholic countries were sympathetic or at least respectful, despite
the millennial schism which separated their Church from Orthodox Christianity. These include J.M. Coutelle, the Marquis de

Laborde, Frère Marie-Joseph Géramb, *Monseigneur* Auvergne, Charles, Count de Pardieu, Father Amédée of Damascus, Alexandre Bida and Georges Hachette, Dr H.T.J. Stacquez, Paul Lenoir, travelling with painters Léon Joseph Florentin Bonnat and Jean Léon Gérôme, G. de Lombay, M. Jullien, the Archduke Franz Joseph Otto, Adélaïde Sargenton-Galichon and Count Jean de Kergorlay.[61]

It is possible that the (predominantly French) Roman Catholic writers who supported the traditional identifications felt antagonistic towards the (predominantly British) Protestant writers who doubted them.[62] However, the reasons must have more to do with their devotion to the Church of Rome, which accepted pilgrimage sites, the patristic and ecclesiastical tradition behind their identifications and monasticism. An early instance of the differentiation between Roman Catholic and Protestant writers as far as 'falsified' Sinaitic biblical associations were concerned appears between the subtly doubting (or sometimes plainly descriptive) text of the Jesuit C. Sicard and the scathing anti-monastic footnotes to his text by Robert Clayton.[63] Writers from Roman Catholic countries were more familiar with the Sinaitic way of life and spirituality. The romantic rather than polemical tone of their accounts reveals their attitude, best summarised by Léon Cart: 'The Sinai is a temple; one comes here to contemplate'.[64]

Female travellers were not uncommon in Sinai from the mid-nineteenth century and they were often British, as the amused Father Amédée noted:

> The lady had already been on the Sinai voyage; but she loved the desert; and returned there for her pleasure. [...] The English-woman travelled on a camel. She had adopted a special outfit for the desert.[65]

An early visit by the reformed Dutch courtesan Ida de Saint-Elme (her real name was E. Van Aylde Jongue) in 1828 came to an unfortunate end since she was not admitted to the Monastery (which at the time was still an *avaton* for females).[66] Other lady visitors were luckier and included Miss Platt, Valérie Boissier, Countess de

Gasparin, Jane Loftus, Marchioness of Ely, Agnes Dorothee Bensly *née* von Blomberg, Emily Hornby and A. Sargenton-Galichon.[67] By the time Augusta Mary Rachel Dobson visited Horeb in 1922, the fifteen-person mission she was a part of included eight women and the number of female visitors was enough to justify a different ladies' design for the traditional souvenir rings.[68] Their consideration, even sympathy, for the monks is remarkable when contrasted with the statements of their male equivalents – the Calvinist Gasparin being the sole exception. Their attitude could be due to an actual preference of the monks for these rarely seen creatures, who travelled for weeks on camelback to reach Horeb, just as Egeria had done in 383. Charlotte Rowley noted:

> I never was made so much of in my life as I was by the Greek Superior. I am the second Lady that ever has been there and in consequence he loaded me with all sorts of presents & though he was past 70, he always called me his *Mother*, the only term of endearment or distinction the poor man knew.[69]

Astonishingly, the 'superior' (*dikaios*) offered the ailing Miss Platt butter, eggs and cheese during the severe fasting period of Lent.[70] Nevertheless, not all female visitors were fragile. Adélaïde Sargenton-Galichon climbed Jabal Mūsā and Ra's Ṣafṣāfa (a notoriously difficult task), then rested in Hagioi Tessarakonta and climbed Jabal Kathrin on 22 and 23 February 1902.[71]

The female travellers' positive stance could also be a result of their increased sensitivity, their excitement for a sort of adventure rarely before experienced by members of their sex within their cultural horizon and their reluctance to put on paper their reservations in an aggressive manner deemed inappropriate for the delicate feminine character. As to their opinions on the Sinaitic inscriptions and Mount Sinai controversies, they took a variety of stances which never verged on extremes and usually preferred the traditional identification of the 'Mount of the Law'. Emily Hornby dutifully mentioned contradictory opinions on its location but avoided a conclusion.[72] In Miss Platt's words:

[…] he, who for the mere sake of an hypothesis – which is the case with many opiniative but unscientific travellers – is determined to make some astonishing discovery, or to dispute and ridicule all that has been a subject of belief for centuries, for no other reason than the suspicion of its being of monkish origin, will derive but little pleasure, and less advantage, from the most interesting tour in the world.[73]

Harriet Martineau added:

I am thankful to have seen it; for, whether it be one of the historical holy places or not, its singular wildness renders it quite sacred enough.[74]

Typical of women frequenting Horeb in the nineteenth century but undeniably atypical of Victorian women are the Scottish twin sisters, Agnes Smith Lewis and Margaret Dunlop Gibson. Both fluent in Greek, ancient and modern, and Lewis in Arabic, Hebrew and Syriac, too, the two indomitable scholars visited Sinai several times between 1892 and the outbreak of World War I in search of valuable manuscripts. In their narratives they demonstrate the delicate balance the monastic community struck with its female visitors.[75] Able to communicate with the monks and appreciate both the uniqueness of their life and the importance of the collections they safeguarded, the two ladies nevertheless retained the feelings of superiority and infallibility which typified Victorian travellers. By the time A. Sargenton-Galichon met M. Dunlop Gibson in the Monastery library in 1902, both sisters enjoyed celebrity status.[76] The narratives of their three journeys to Sinai are accurate and reliable but already belong to the era of textual and art-historical scholarship that the twentieth century would prove to be.

The circumstances within which the 'Mount of the Law controversy' was created can therefore be linked to a phase of Western European and American ideology corresponding with the worldwide expansion of capitalist economy and the heyday of colonialism. They have at their root the principles of biblical hermeneutics and empiricism, both spearheaded by Protestant intellectuals, and relate to nineteenth-century narratives of cultural supremacy. The Mount Sinai question was one of the most fiercely debated of its time and brought the distant summit of Jabal Mūsā to the attention of the international scholarly community and a wide educated public. Despite the judicious voices of Catholic and female visitors, the majority of Sinai travellers would not surrender their aspirations to discover a Sinai of their own.

Alternative Sinais

Although the Sinai clergy had been viewed with a certain amount of suspicion from some earlier visitors, the identification of Jabal Mūsā with the biblical Mount Sinai had not been questioned before the 1820s. Even the eccentric Joseph Wolff, whose violent accusations against the monks of the Monastery of Saint Catherine shocked J.R. Wellsted and S. Olin, did not doubt the attribution.[77] As was described with penetrating irony by his travel companion John Carne:

> [...] the rapture of Mr. W.'s feelings on the top of Sinai was inde-scribable; I expected to see him take flight for a better region.[78]

However, the missionary quoted a remarkable statement by a rabbi Soliman from Wilna, whom he met in Jerusalem:

> Would He, therefore, admit or allow that a convent of monks should be built upon that mountain [Sinai]? No. It is, therefore, impossible that that mountain, upon which a convent stands, should be the Mount Sinai where the law was given, amidst thun-ders and lightnings. Mount Sinai is in England. Even Mount Tabor is in Europe.[79]

Even though the rabbi's odd words would find many British travel-lers in the second and third quarter of the nineteenth century agree-ing in principle, the attack against Jabal Mūsā's claim in later times would be more rigorous, based on complex arguments laced with scientific authority.

The first sceptic was J.L. Burckhardt who visited Sinai in spring 1816 and whose account was posthumously published in 1822.

Figure 22. James M. MacDonald (British, 1822–1885), Jebel Serbal from Jebel Tahuneh. Albumen silver print, 16.7 × 20.6 cm. 1869.

Burckhardt was a knowledgeable traveller, fluent in Arabic and well-acquainted with the realities of desert and Bedouin life. The seventh chapter of his *Travels in Syria and the Holy Land*, describing his excursion to the Sinai, remains one of the shrewdest and most accurate accounts of the peninsula, its environment, its inhabitants and their economy, manners and traditions.

It was his inquisitiveness and rational spirit which prompted a discussion of the three summits of Jabal Mūsā, Jabal Kathrin and Jabal Sirbāl. He concluded, on the basis of material remains, that Sirbāl was originally thought to be Mount Sinai by worshippers, whereas, according to Scriptures, the two other mountains had a better claim to being the real holy places.[80] The Swiss traveller peppered his text with intelligent references to the Bible but presented none of the obsessive zeal of his followers and kept a respectful stance towards the monks of the Monastery of Saint Catherine and the Bedouin alike.

Even before the publication of Burckhardt's book, J. Carne was surprised 'at seeing beneath [the summit, where Moses received the Law] so few places where the hosts of Israel could have stood'.[81]

Carne was one of the most interesting visitors to Sinai and his fluency in modern Greek allowed him to write an insightful account of everyday life in the Monastery. Nevertheless, his sharp wit and ironical nature could not avoid some incredulity based on personal experience.

Most doubting writers visited Jabal Mūsā and its rivals and made up their mind based on their own observations and feelings. However, a certain degree of influence from previous visitors whose scholarly authority they held in high esteem is undoubted. It seems that once an alternative was proposed, several advocates would be found. However, few had the courage to admit they had not been to all the localities like W.H. Bartlett:

> Altogether my pilgrimage to the monkish localities of Mount Sinai was shamefully incomplete and heterodox; but happily my deficiencies in this respect have been more than made up by former writers.[82]

Even fewer were prepared to abandon their rigour in favour of a gentler view of tradition, like Reverend Henry Paul Measor, vicar of Kingston-on-Thames:

[...] I am still inclined to believe it to be the true Mount Sinai on which the law was delivered; I am not willing to have the truth of these old traditions doubted, and their scenes transplanted. There is a poetry about old associations which will not bear dislocation, and a prejudice in favour of occupation, which requires strong evidence to make me give a verdict in favour of the new claimant.[83]

In the following pages the main claimants to the title of 'Mount of the Law', or the 'alternative Sinais', will be examined and their pros and cons briefly presented. The aim of this enumeration is not to discover the best candidate anew but to delve into their supporters' frame of mind. In this respect, the *Ordnance Survey* and Dr Beke provide two instructive examples.

On 1 June 1816, J.L. Burckhardt ascended at great danger to himself the extremely steep summits of Jabal Sirbāl, an impressive mountain overlooking the Wādī Fīran oasis. He witnessed there:

[...] steps regularly formed with large loose stones, which must have been brought from below, and so judiciously arranged along the declivity, that they have resisted the devastations of time, and may still serve for ascending.

He then climbed on the eastern peak:

Here is a heap of small loose stones, about two feet high, forming a circle about twelve paces in diameter. Just below the top I found on every granite block that presented a smooth surface, inscriptions, the far greater part of which were illegible.[84]

On the basis of these finds and having noted the absence of similar inscriptions around Horeb and Jabal Kathrin, he concluded that Sirbāl 'was at one period the chief place of pilgrimage in the peninsula'. However, he added:

[...] I am equally convinced, from a perusal of the Scriptures, that the Israelites encamped in the Upper Sinai, and that either Djebel Mousa or Mount St. Catherine is the real Horeb.[85]

The Nabatean peak sanctuary he described on Jabal Sirbāl (and that already discussed on nearby Jabal Mu´tamr) had nothing to do with the biblical identification but his idea introduced the first contender for the title of the 'Mount of the Law'. Later advocates were more fervent in their support of Sirbāl's candidacy. K.R. Lepsius used as arguments the text of Kosmas, the presence of pre-Christian sites, the importance of Wādī Fīran as a religious centre in the Early Christian period and the occurrence of many Sinaitic inscriptions.[86] His views were supported by J. Kitto, another biblical scholar who never travelled to Sinai, C. Forster, E. Lecointre and C.T. Currelly.[87]

Additional advantages making Sirbāl an attractive candidate include the ease with which modern visitors could approach it by sea or land, the inaccessibility of its summit and the commanding aspect of its towering silhouette, a favourite of armchair biblical 'explorers' like Kitto, Forster and Lecointre who never roamed the desert. The frequent encounter of Jabal Sirbāl in engravings and photographs testifies to its popularity as a 'Mount of the Law' contender.

The first author to propose Ra's Ṣafṣāfa as the 'Mount of the Law' was the American Edward Robinson, Professor of Biblical Literature at the Presbyterian Union Theological Seminary. His rejection of Jabal Mūsā was based on his disappointment in the views afforded from it, calling his visit there '[t]he least satisfactory incident in our whole sojourn at Mount Sinai'.[88] After the necessary discussion of biblical texts, he picked the arduously accessible summit at the opposite end of Horeb as his chosen location.

A point of attraction for Ra's Ṣafṣāfa was its position, dominating the plain of al-Rāha, and its volume, which captivated artists like the painter Edward Lear and the photographer Francis Frith.[89] Gathered in the plain, the flock of Moses could see him coming down from the God-trodden summit. Furthermore, Ra's Ṣafṣāfa was the first part of Horeb visible as travellers approached, contrary to Jabal Mūsā which cannot be seen from the traditional route (from Wādī Fīran). Robinson was the most important biblical scholar in nineteenth-century America and his theory remained popular, especially among his compatriots.[90]

The green-hued summit of Jabal Mu´tamr near the Monastery is lower than Jabal Mūsā but cuts a powerful figure against the warm-toned red granite. It was proposed as a possible 'Mount of the Law' by Alexander William Crawford Lindsay, 25th Earl of Crawford and 8th Earl of Balcarres.[91] His idea was reluctantly embraced by J.G. Kinnear.[92] The highest summit in the Sinai Peninsula, Jabal Kathrin, was a good candidate owing to its size. J.L. Burckhardt climbed it and thought it to be an alternative to Jabal Mūsā.[93] His suggestion was supported only by E. Rüppell.[94] The following summits were also identified with the 'Mount of the Law', with one advocate each: Mount Hor;[95] 'Jebel el-'Omjah';[96] Serabit el-Khadim;[97] and 'Jebel Hellal' (*sic*).[98]

The first to insist on the necessity of a trigonometrical survey of the peninsula in order to solve the problems surrounding the location of Mount Sinai was the British Egyptologist Sir John Gardner Wilkinson (1797–1875), who in 1843 published the first guidebook of Egypt.[99] His wish was fulfilled twenty-five years later, when the London-based Palestine Exploration Fund organised the mapping of South Sinai, alongside a systematic gathering of scientific facts, place names, inscriptions, building ground-plans and photographic views. The results of this project would reinforce the identification of Jabal Mūsā with the 'Mount of the Law' and would conclude half a century of passionate arguments.[100]

The *Ordnance Survey* project had military and political agenda to fulfil beyond its biblical inspiration. A first survey of the Red Sea area on behalf of the Bombay government 'relative to the establishment of a steam communication between India and Europe' had been organised by Lieutenant J.R. Wellsted as early as 1833 and again in 1836.[101] The Sinai Peninsula was strategically situated on the sea route from the Mediterranean to India through the Suez Canal which opened to traffic on November 17, 1869, a few months after the conclusion of the Sinai *Survey*.[102] British interests had strongly opposed the construction and control of the Canal by the French and although no direct link appears to survive between the two events, the timing of the scholarly mission to map the Sinai makes it highly probable that it was part of a project to gather information and control this waterway. Later mapping projects, before and during the British annexation of Egypt (1882), had an explicitly imperialist scope.[103] It is typical of the British sense of desert landscape that the whole triangulation of the peninsula used by sub-sequent missions was based on the garden of the Suez Hotel, which had moved to another building, a quarter of a mile away, since the time of the *Ordnance Survey*. This resulted in interesting distortions on paper.[104]

The mission sailed from Southampton on 21 October 1868 and the survey had been concluded with extreme rapidity by May 1869. The results were published in five volumes by 1871. The party included Captain (later Sir) C.W. Wilson (the mission leader), the Reverend Frederick Whitmore Holland, Captain H.S. Palmer, E.H. Palmer (at the time Fellow of Saint John's College Cambridge), C.W. Wyatt, Sergeant-Major James MacDonald (the photographer), three non-commissioned officers of the Royal Engineers and three local guides.[105]

The composition of the group testifies to a typical High Victorian mixture of religion, scholarship and imperialism. The survey, like most early work by the Palestine Exploration Fund, was seen as a British crusade serving God, country and scientific progress.[106] In the words of William Thomson (1819–1890), archbishop of York and the Fund's president:

This country of Palestine belongs to you and to me. It is essentially ours. […] We mean to walk through Palestine in the length and in the breadth of it because that land has been given unto us. […] It is the land to which we may look with as true a patriotism as we do to this dear old England, which we love so much.[107]

The discreet but ardent supporter who underwrote the hazardous and financially risky expedition was Angela Georgina Burdett-Coutts, first Baroness Burdett-Coutts (1814–1906), the richest woman in Britain, a notable philanthropist, patriot and Church of England supporter.[108]

To this day, the volumes of the *Ordnance Survey* remain the most impressive monument to the period's obsession with biblical topography. The answer proposed by C.W. Wilson, H.S. Palmer and their fellow group members was in favour of Jabal Mūsā's candidacy for 'Mount of the Law'. The area had the best natural resources,

Figure 23. Johann Martin Bernatz (German, 1802–1878), *Panorama vom Sinai*. Lithograph on paper. Based on drawings made in March 1837.

its topography was closer to the Bible and routes leading to it conformed best to the book of Exodus. The results also appeared in abridged form, which made the mission's findings available to a wide public.[109]

The outcome of the *Survey* seemed to satisfy most scholars with its stringent method and the scholarly credentials of its members.[110] However, several Protestant scholars remained suspicious of any opinion which agreed with that of the 'corrupted' monks and at best adopted the relaxed attitude of the American Benjamin Bausman:

> Whether this be the identical spot or not, the pure air and toil of climbing mountains, however sacred, creates a desire for food; and here, at a place toward which I had been accustomed to look from my distant home with almost adoring reverence, we soon were seated on the bare rock, each with fowl in hand, stripping off substantial food as best he could, *à la* Bedouin.[111]

Dr Charles Tilstone Beke (British, 1800–1874) provides an interesting comparison with Reverend Charles Forster, in that the eccentricity of his views was counterbalanced by the earnestness with which his contemporaries either accepted or rejected them. His theories proposed an alternative Mount Sinai locality and applied do-it-yourself biblical archaeology and hermeneutics to an unprecedented degree. For these reasons, they deserve an extended

mention as representative products of the psychopathology of their era.[112]

Born in Stepney, Middlesex, Beke practised trade and law before devoting himself to historical, geographical and ethnographical studies. He gained his doctorate from the University of Tübingen, Germany.[113] His travels to Africa and the Holy Land combined geographical curiosity with business acumen and by the end of his life he could afford to indulge in privately-funded explorations which produced lavish yet conjectural volumes of literature.

It was only a matter of time before he devoted himself to the most debated issue of biblical geography, the location of the 'Mount of the Law'. His original contribution, first suggested in 1834, was that biblical Egypt was not in the Nile Delta but in an area to the east, therefore Mount Sinai should be looked for to the east of the Gulf of Aqaba.[114] To prove this, he travelled to Arabia between 8 December 1873 and 19 March 1874, a few months before his death. He refused to be a part of the 'general system of fraud and imposture in which the whole history of the convent [of Saint Catherine] is involved' and agreed with others that '[t]he deliberate fraud and falsehood of the Greek clergy, from the earliest ages of Christianity, are matters of history'. He rejected Jabal Mūsā as 'absolutely destitute of verdure, cultivation, running streams, and even of abundant springs, and with no resources whatsoever' and did not visit Sinai altogether.[115]

Relying on the word of an unnamed person he met in Egypt about a mountain where God spoke to Moses near Aqaba, he circumnavigated the peninsula and landed in the Red Sea port.[116] After a day's ride, he approached 'Jebel-e'-Nūr' (*sic*) and sent his companion John Milne (British, 1850–1913) up the mountain to check for signs of God's presence.[117] Satisfied with his report, he declared this to be the true 'Mount of the Law' and hastened to publish his discovery in *The Times* of 27 February 1874, to the dismay of the authorities of the *Ordnance Survey*, who had concluded in favour of Jabal Mūsā.[118] His widow, editor of the posthumous narrative of his journey, chose the line '*che sara, sara*' to precede her husband's tirades.

Dr Beke was an opinionated and passionate Victorian amateur. Despite the ironical stance of the scholarly community towards his methods, he steadfastly searched for biblical localities 'on the testimony of the Hebrew Scriptures alone, regardless of all traditional interpretations and identifications'.[119] Therefore, his work exemplifies the plight of nineteenth-century Protestant believers on a mission of biblical discovery without the political, economic and military agenda of the *Ordnance Survey* party. On his results, one could quote Professor Ernst Friedrich Karl Rosenmüller's (German, 1768–1835) reaction to his earliest work:

> [...] so many new and hitherto unheard of [views], such as I do not recall having found in any other book of our times.[120]

Orthodox Christianity

In the 1865 account of his 1863 visit, H.T.J. Stacquez acknowledged that most visitors to the Monastery were Russian or Greek, while other nations were rarer.[121] As he based his observation on the visitor album, it may be assumed that the actual numbers of Orthodox pilgrims were larger since they would not sign it, unless they were members of the higher clergy. The fact that many more published narratives of visits survive from Western European countries and the United States simply testifies to the greater publishing activity and demand for original travel accounts in that part of the world. Orthodox pilgrim traffic simply followed the medieval pattern uninterrupted, as it continues to do to this day, with large groups of believers flocking to the Monastery and up Jabal Mūsā.

The experience alone was edifying and exciting and did not necessarily qualify for a written report. Private prayer was deemed more appropriate.

Prints destined for Orthodox audiences were published throughout the eighteenth and the early nineteenth century. They popularised works of named icon painters, like the one by Iakōvos Moschos from the first quarter of the eighteenth century at the Monastery.[122] In it, Old Testament incidents, patristic traditions and modern reality blended into an atemporal view of the place.

However, Russian scholars coming from the only Christian Orthodox state with a scholarly output and a university structure of note before the twentieth century visited Sinai and took an interest in what the Monastery had preserved. Despite being aware of the 'Mount of the Law controversy' raging in Western Europe, their agenda remained different. The Ukrainian monk, later archbishop, Porfiriĭ Uspenskiĭ and even the German Lobegott Friedrich Constantin (von) Tischendorf built their illustrious careers on the desire of the Russian imperial family and academic establishment for testimonies of Orthodoxy's ancient roots. They both removed manuscripts from the Monastery (Uspenskiĭ even took four icons) and presented them to imperial authorities or educational institutions, strengthening Russia's collections of 'relics' and its claims to predominance among Christian nations.

Other Russian scholars were less predatory. Nikodim Kondakov, one of the pioneer historians of Byzantine art, organised in 1881 the first archaeological expedition to Sinai which examined art rather than topography and used a camera to record artefacts.[123] Antonin Kapustin studied the Glagolitic and Cyrillic manuscripts in 1870.[124] Decades later, it would be the work of Vladimir Nikolaevich Beneshevich, who visited Sinai in 1907, 1908 and 1911, which placed the artworks and manuscripts of the Monastery in a central position for the study of Byzantine art.[125] His valuable archive of transcripts and photographs was destroyed between 1928 and 1931 during searches by the Soviet police seeking proof of his alleged spying. Beneshevich was imprisoned (1931–1933) and after a second arrest on suspicion of Nazi sympathies was executed in 1938. His fate is representative of the suspicion faced by Byzantinists under Joseph Stalin's (Georgian, 1878–1953) regime. Their persecution is one of the main reasons why the important contributions of Russian scholars to Sinaitic studies have remained little-known – the language barrier being the other.

Despite the different focus in relation to Western Europe, Russian academia did not operate in a vacuum and the 'Mount of the Law' controversy was discussed by the scholar and statesman Avraam Sergeevich Norov (1795–1869). In his study he covered not only the Sinaitic inscriptions, their resulting scholarly theories, and the 'Mount of the Law', but also the history of the Monastery with an emphasis on its ecclesiastical authorities and their long tradition.[126]

During the eighteenth and the nineteenth century, the Sinaitic clergy was a breeding ground of, and an action field for, a series of important archbishops who distinguished themselves and their Monastery within the hierarchy of the Orthodox Church; the extensive record of nineteenth-century publications in Greek connected with the Monastery serves as proof of its intellectual standing.[127] In 1804 Constantios Vyzantios (1770–1859), an archimandrite of Cretan origin born in Constantinople, was elected archbishop.[128] He had been educated in Constantinople, Italy and Kiev and was exarch of the Sinaitic priories in the Danubian principalities and Cairo, where he negotiated in 1798 the famous Napoleonic decree protecting the Monastery. It is possible that his personality inspired the French general's words in a letter dated 19 December 1799:

> […] the Convent of Mount Sinai is occupied by educated and civilised men, in the middle of barbarians that inhabit the desert they live in.[129]

Typically for an archbishop of Sinai, Constantios lived far from his desert seat, at the Tzouvania priory in Cairo and mostly in Constantinople where he rose to briefly become patriarch while keeping the Sinaitic title (1830–4). His successor, Kyrillos Vyzantios, held the throne of archbishop from 1859 to 1867, when he was unseated by the *synaxis* (council) of the monks for autocratic behaviour. He also spent most of his time in Constantinople.[130] The next archbishop, Kallistratos, was a monk in the Monastery rather than a career cleric, less educated but more devoted to his vocation. He made the fortress on Horeb once again the centre of Sinaitic ecclesiastical life and secured a decree of protection by the Ottoman sultan Abdülaziz (1830–1876, ruled 1861–1876) but his tenure was plagued by financial difficulties.[131] It was during Kallistratos's time that the present belfry next to the *katholikon* was erected by Iakōvos Varoutēs, a mason from Tenos in the Aegean.[132]

Much of the Monastery's wealth originated far from Sinai. The network of priories, *metochia*, extended from France and Italy to the Ottoman Empire, Corfu and even India.[133] They ensured a steady flow of income, with the years between 1845 and 1863 being particularly good, reaching 25,000–30,000 Ottoman pounds a year.[134] Therefore, revenue hardly depended on the generally parsimonious travellers. It took sensitive visitors with language skills like W. Turner and J.L. Burckhardt for the network of priories to get a mention in western bibliography.[135] Things worsened after 1863, when priories in the rich Danubian territories were confiscated, and again in the 1870s, when the Russian priories were dissolved by the government.[136] Kallistratos's successor, Porphyrios I (on the throne from 1885 to 1904), managed to counter the crisis and fill the coffers. He was educated, fluent in several languages and an able diplomat. His successor, Porphyrios II, had studied in Constantinople and Germany and lived in Paris before ascending the Sinai throne in 1904. He remained archbishop until 1926.[137]

The profiles of the archbishops examined above hardly conform to the humble portraits given by western travellers. Although these higher clerics often spent long periods of time outside their desert seat, they left behind them capable representatives. The common accusation of ignorance pressed against the monks seems not to have taken into account that at least one of them in 1887 had formally studied theology in Germany and that he may not have been alone.[138] Even earlier, probably in 1850, the monk Parthenios, who resigned from public life after being rejected by a female member of the French royal family, is reported as being a nephew of the Greek Count Étienne (Stéphane, Stephanos) Zizinia, the consul of Belgium (born in 1823) – clearly not an uneducated person.[139] When Count Zizinia himself visited the Monastery with H.T.J. Stacquez and the Duke of Brabant, later King Leopold II of the Belgians, in 1863 the

Figure 24. Jean de Kergorlay (French), *Ce monastère donne plutôt le sentiment d'être un conte de fée qu'une réalité*. Photograph. Spring 1906.

party was welcomed by the superior with a speech in French. Stacquez noted:

> Far from considering them as ignorant and devoid of all merit, I have to declare that I found among them educated people, pious and extremely praiseworthy.[140]

Many works of art commissioned for and made within the walls of the remote Monastery testify to a lively artistic and spiritual life radiating all over the Orthodox Christian world. Costly decorative items (like the enormous decorated candles) can be dated by inscriptions to the eighteenth and the nineteenth century.[141] The nature of monastic life at Horeb hardly called for many educated clerics. J.L. Burckhardt in 1816 found among the twenty-three monks:

> [...] a cook, a distiller, a baker, a shoemaker, a tailor, a carpenter, a smith, a mason, a gardener, a maker of candles, &c. &c.[142]

The harsh realities of desert life and the onerous duties of ecclesiastic routine were better served by simple, robust and industrious men. The notion entertained by certain western visitors that Monasteries ought to be great centres of learning, the equivalent of European seminaries, certainly did not correspond to the ancient tradition of mystical and private spirituality prevalent in Orthodox asceticism. The Monastery was organised along the lines of a medieval coenobium, faithful to the principles of Early Christian asceticism. Even in the twenty-first century, the small community bears more resemblance to a government with cabinets assigned to each monk than a commune of inspired theologians discussing biblical passages.

Rapacious Scholars

It was the combined effort of biblical scholars and Byzantine art historians that eventually changed the image and fate of Horeb towards the end of the nineteenth century. The first to realise the importance of the Monastery's art treasures was P. Uspenskiĭ, the Ukrainian scholar monk. He trained in the Theological Academy of Saint Petersburg and cultivated an interest in the Early Christian period and was therefore well-equipped to recognise the early date of several icons kept in the Monastery. He managed to remove, under questionable circumstances, four of them to Russia *circa* 1845. He eventually donated them to the Ecclesiastical Academy of Kiev and they are now in the Bohdan and Varvara Khanenko Museum of Art in the same city.[143] He also removed several manuscripts from the library.[144] His clergyman's status and association with Russia, the largest Orthodox state, must have made it easier for the monks to trust him. His background, training and acquisitiveness allowed him to remove some of the earliest and most valuable relics preserved within the Justinianic walls, setting an (unfortunate) example for later scholars.

However, not all contemporary visitors shared Uspenskiĭ's taste. Despite A.W.C. Lindsay's 1838 assessment that '[…] most of them [icons] are modern, but some are very ancient and very interesting for the history of the art; they are almost all in good preservation', the opinion of European visitors and scholars on the works of art in the Monastery was usually negative.[145] The icons were thought to be 'bad pictures; grim-looking saints, and tawdry simpering madonnas, in the flat hard style common in the Greek churches', to use J.G. Kinnear's words, or 'mere daubs' as Thomas Cook's handbook for tourists would put it.[146] The Justinianic doors of the *katholikon* were, according to S. Olin, 'of the rudest workmanship, not at all superior to the cabin which a new settler in the wilds of America hastily constructs with no tools but his axe and auger'.[147] When H. Martineau visited the library, the only thing she managed to examine was a copy of the *Spectator*.[148] S.C. Bartlett noted that of the manuscripts and books in the library 'none of them [are] known to be of any special importance'.[149]

The rejection of these artworks was associated with the low esteem in which westerners held the people worshipping them. In Montague John Rendall's words:

[t]he Greek hand is a true type of the Greek mind: both are hopelessly mediæval and inelastic.[150]

The monks, despite being hurt and offended by the disapproval of their visitors, obviously realised the importance of their icon collection since they had them numbered and catalogued.[151] Similar care was extended to the manuscripts, and the first dedicated library building was erected in 1734.[152] At approximately the same time the monks became aware of the acquisitiveness of library visitors. C. Sicard, in 1720, noted the difficulty he had in persuading the monks to open the library because they were suspicious of theft.[153] The first to realise the importance of the Monastery library was the young Frenchman François-Auguste de Thou, who travelled in 1628 but left no detailed account of his voyage; several scholars were dispatched after him, specifically ordered by the minister Jean-Baptiste Colbert (1619–1683) to remove manuscripts for the royal library of Louis XIV, but they were unsuccessful.[154] Alexander W.C. Lindsay's ironic tone disguises his *ennui* for the attention of a monk's careful handling of the outstanding *Codex* 204, a Gospel book of imperial provenance illuminated in Constantinople around 1000:

In the archbishop's apartment, now used as the Treasury, we were shown a most beautiful manuscript of the Gospels in Greek, on vellum, in uncial, or capital, letters of gold; I thought the good father would never have done turning over the preliminary leaves of illuminations, and arranging the silk screens interposed between them. Would that it were in the British Museum![155]

Miss Platt, writing in 1842, mentioned that an English traveller a little while before her 1839 visit offered '300 pounds' (either Ottoman *lira* or pounds sterling) for this manuscript but the archbishop forbade its sale. She hastened to add:

Thus English travellers too frequently, by impudently offering such high prices for things of this kind, give to Orientals an impression that they must be of immense value, and consequently at once defeat their object of obtaining possession of them.[156]

Apart from the aversion of travellers towards the Orthodox clergy, aesthetic preferences influenced their perspective. Protestant visual standards called for simplicity and in H. Bonar's words 'a high, large, bare, rocky hall would have satisfied our idea of a chapel for Sinai'.[157] The British Oliver Brockbank, visiting Horeb in 1914, noted that the 'fine old building' of the *katholikon* was 'spoilt with eikons and hundreds of tawdry lamps'.[158]

The publication in 1846 and 1862 of C. Tischendorf's exciting 'find', the celebrated *Codex Sinaiticus*, was to be the turning point in the appreciation of the Monastery's holdings by western scholars. Interestingly, the change did not start from one of the superbly illuminated codices but from the most important relic for the study of the Bible, the austere fourth-century Greek manuscript preserving the earliest and most complete version of the Holy Scriptures known to date.

The story of the removal of the *Codex* remains a contested issue. The German scholar arrived at Sinai in 1844 searching for early manuscripts of the Bible. He spotted some leaves of the *Codex* (he claimed they were waiting to stoke the ovens) and stealthily removed forty-three of them to Leipzig, where he had them published without mentioning their provenance. He returned in 1853 for the remainder of the manuscript but left empty-handed, probably because of the monks' suspicion. His third visit, in 1859, was supported by Aleksandr (Alexander) II Nikolaevich, Emperor (tsar) of the Russian Empire (1818–1881, ruled 1855–1881), and yielded results. On the last day of his stay he came across the rest of the manuscript, which the monks had bound into quires. He asked to remove it to the Cairo priory (Tzouvania) for a closer study and when in Cairo borrowed it with the intention of showing it to his imperial patron. Instead, he presented the book as a gift to the tsar and never returned to Sinai again.[159]

Given the care extended by the monks upon their holdings, it is unlikely that they had put the parchment leaves in a basket to be burned in the ovens. In March 1845, a year after Tischendorf removed the first portion of the *Codex Sinaiticus*, the monks refused to show F.A. Strauss the *Codex* 204, a reaction unrecorded by other travellers that was probably connected with the previous year's incident.[160] Since medieval times it was forbidden to remove books from the Monastery or the church and curses were scribbled at the margins of manuscripts.[161] Thanks to his actions, a step had been taken for the scholarly community of the West toward realising that the main lure of Horeb was not biblical landmarks, which caused interminable controversy, but the Monastery library, which propelled Uspenskiĭ and Tischendorf to professorships, international status, even nobility (in 1869 the tsar awarded the latter the style of 'von' Tischendorf).

In the wake of Tischendorf's sumptuous publications, the eminent Egyptologist Heinrich Ferdinand Karl Brugsch published the few leaves of the *Codex Sinaiticus* remaining in Sinai and Georg Moritz Ebers assessed with considerable erudition the importance of the mosaics and the architecture of the Monastery.[162] When Prince Johann Georg, Duke of Sachsen, visited Sinai in October 1910, he devoted most of his account to works of art rather than biblical theories, a sign of a change in orientation among scholars as well as visitors.[163] A few years later, the 1914 German expedition attempted to produce a systematic catalogue of all the works of art at the Monastery, with a pioneering focus on Islamic material.

Their research was sadly dispersed and mostly lost due to the out-break of World War I.[164] Since the publication of the Sōtērious' seminal work on the icons in the Monastery, art historians have been making the desert pilgrimage with high hopes of making new discoveries.[165] Horeb is no longer an uncharted territory hiding traces of the Exodus, but a Noah's Ark preserving unique works of art to be published in scholarly studies and exhibited to interna-tional audiences.[166]

Sinai Represented

Thanks to the writings of scholars and aspiring amateurs the Sinai journey found enthusiastic followers who could gain unprecedented access to its natural features and man-made wonders through the works of pictorial artists. Their work, the product of arduous effort under adverse circumstances, was instrumental in making the Horeb localities recognisable throughout the Christian world.[167]

Rudimentary depictions of the Horeb landscape had been included in pilgrimage accounts printed since the fourteenth century. They were little more than sketches, obviously executed from memory after the return of the writer and with the aid of an artist who had not attempted the journey. Such sketches combined the stations of the pilgrimage in an abstract mountain setting, a visual enumeration of landmarks rather than the picture of a landscape.

However, by the nineteenth century several more accomplished views were published and some had claims both to artistic merit and a degree of realistic detail. Depictions of 'Mount Sinai' in popular editions of the Bible assumed a character of accuracy which satis-fied a public accustomed to the conventions of modern mapping and topographical views. They were different from earlier illustrations in which the biblical incident was situated in a nonspecific setting. The Sinai landmarks were now presented without Moses or the Israelites, as containers of past biblical incidents caught in present time through the eyes of contemporary travellers.

The accuracy of even these representations was often flawed since they were not executed on the spot. It is from the late 1830s that precise depictions of the Horeb sites became available to the Euro-pean and American public through the work of itinerant artists. One

Figure 25. Edward Thomas Daniell (British, 1804–1842),
Summit of Mount Sinai or Jebel Musa. Watercolour,
gouache and graphite on paper, 33.2x49.4 cm. 1840.

of the earliest painters to record the Horeb landmarks *en plein air*
was the Oxford-educated British Reverend Edward Thomas Daniell.
Well-travelled and talented, he produced a valuable watercolour of
Jabal Mūsā where one half of an arch from the sixth-century basilica
is seen standing to the south of the small chapel (figure 25). Despite
its merits, his work was not reproduced in engravings and therefore never became widely known. Francis Arundale's drawings and
W.H. Bartlett's watercolours were engraved and included in books,
however the text took precedence over the images (figure 18).[168]

Popularity would be the achievement of the Scottish David
Roberts, who travelled to the Holy Land, Egypt and Sinai in 1838–
1839 and made drawings and watercolours which combined visual
accuracy and inspiring atmosphere. His works were engraved in
1840 by Louis Haghe (British, 1806–1885), published by Sir Fraser
Graham Moon, 'Her Majesty's Printseller', and met with success
with a public eager for exotic landscapes with religious associations
(figures 1, 9, 17 and 26).[169]

Comparisons between his works and places which have survived essentially unchanged testify both to the precision of his
details and the romanticism of his gaze, which made subjects truly
majestic, indeed sublime. His view of the Monastery with Horeb
in the background remains to this day the most iconic image of the
sacred landscape of Mount Sinai (figure 1). His lithograph of Jabal
Mūsā juxtaposed the Muslim mosque and the Christian chapel
in a carefully balanced composition (figure 26). The picture was
charged with symbolic meaning as the artist placed the Christian
and Muslim places of worship opposite each other on the solid
rocks of the 'Mount of the Law' and stressed their ruinous state as
a sign of humility. It was also accurate in its depiction of masonry
and geophysical features. However, it seems that the magnificence
of the landscape, the panoramic expanse of void around the modest
remains, was Roberts's focus. He painted 'the terrible wilderness',
a biblical narrative set in stone.

The American painter Miner Kilbourne Kellogg visited Sinai
in 1844 and sketched Jabal Mūsā from Jabal al-Dayr on 6 March.
Horeb was just one of the stations in his 24-year-long journey in
Europe and the Near East, a journey inspired both by American
patriotism and Swedenborgian religious fervour. In his travels he
produced a large body of work, mostly sketches in pencil, watercolour and oil, later to be reinterpreted in large compositions in oil
on canvas. His own image was often included in the composition,
as an added note, a piece of evidence of his presence at the place
depicted. In the watercolour of the Farsh Elias chapel the figures of
Kellogg and his attendant are missing, only to be added in the finished oil on canvas version. His ambitious agenda aimed to expand
the horizons of the American public using his experience and the
visual material he collected on his travels.[170] Even though his plans
remained unfulfilled, he embodied the missionary artist ideal better
than any of his contemporaries.

One of the first works Kellogg completed after his return to the
United States in 1865 was the now lost canvas *Mount Sinai and the
Valley of Es-Seba'îyeh*, a visual statement not only of his experiences
in the Holy Land but also of his convictions as to the identification
of biblical landmarks with actual places: although accepting Jabal

Figure 26. David Roberts (British, 1796–1864), *Summit of Mount Sinai shewing the Christian and Mahometan Chapels*. Lithograph on paper. Based on drawings executed in February 1839.

David Roberts, R.A.

Figure 27. Francis Frith (British, 1822–1898), *The Convent of Sinai.*
Albumen silver print, 15.9 × 22.4 cm. Negative about 1858; print 1862.

Mūsā as the 'Mount of the Law', Kellogg added his own idea in the
debate, dismissing al-Rāha as the 'Plain of the Encampment' of the
wandering Jews and proposing a valley to the east of Horeb. The
painting materialised not only his memories from the place but also
his convictions, expressing in line and colour an argument of biblical scholarship. He even used it in public lectures delivered between
1867 and 1870 as illustrative material, proof of the soundness of his
contribution to scriptural geography.[171]

Kellogg's example demonstrates that, in the heated controversy
of biblical identifications, the subject, angle, size and orientation of
the subject matter of a seemingly innocuous painting assumed the
active role of an argument. The contemporary critical acclaim for
his rather dry work was due less to its artistic merits and more to
its importance as evidence of the actual whereabouts of a contested
biblical incident.[172]

Admiration similar to that bestowed upon Kellogg's paintings in
America was expressed across the Atlantic for the works of John
Frederick Lewis, exhibited in Britain at approximately the same

Figure 28. James M. MacDonald (British, 1822 – 1885),
Convent of St. Katherine, with Jebel Músá in the Background.
Albumen silver print, 16 × 20.8 cm. 1869.

time. His work *A Frank Encampment in the Desert of Mount Sinai,
1842 – The Convent of Saint Catherine in the distance*, executed in
1856, presented an Orientalist vision of a languid English visitor
(Frederick William Stewart) relaxing in Arab dress under a tent
(figure 21).[173] Even though the Horeb landscape was secondary in
visual terms, the location (*'Desert of Mount Sinai'*, *'The Convent of
Saint Catherine'*) occupied most of the title. It seems that the biblical
setting heightened the importance of the scene and gave it an added
gravitas in the eyes of Victorian viewers.

Less well-known today than Roberts's prints or Kellogg's paintings but popular in their time nevertheless were the engravings
accompanying G.H. von Schubert's work on the Holy Land, executed after paintings by Johann Martin Bernatz.[174] The panorama of
the view from Jabal Mūsā in the 1839 and 1856 editions remains a
valuable source for the archaeology of the site, although the artist
used the roof of the chapel as a standpoint, thus excluding it from the
frame (figure 23). The possibility of artistic freedom should not be

excluded given the romantic style of Bernatz's work, not dissimilar to the style of Roberts. But the ruins and standing buildings can be identified in their right places. In Bernatz's engravings the shift was made from the sublime (Roberts) and the didactic (Kellogg) to the accurate, a move which would soon be completed with the use of the new medium of photography.

The first noteworthy photographer to work at South Sinai was Francis Frith, a prolific artist who travelled to the Holy Land in 1856–1857 and created large format views extremely popular with researchers and armchair tourists alike. Frith had to overcome unforeseen impediments (for example, the collodion he used on his plates boiled when the temperature in his dark tent reached 54 degrees Celsius) but the volume and quality of the work he managed to produce is admirable.[175] When it came to the text accompanying his beautiful albumen prints, Reginald Stuart Poole, an archaeologist, offered the necessary scholarly authority to the publication.[176] For the first time Horeb was recorded in detail and the only interference by the artist was the placing of his camera. The Sinaitic desert did not disappoint its public. There was no squalor or ugly buildings to hide or picturesque poverty to forget (as was the case of the Jerusalem or Cairo city views), only the clean, awe-inspiring rock formations, as sublime as in Roberts's engravings (figures 5, 27 and 30).

James MacDonald, the photographer of the *Ordnance Survey*, also recorded the localities of Horeb in 1868–1869.[177] His views worked together with the texts of scholars and the line drawings and maps of draughtsmen and were 'drier' but no less accomplished than Frith's (figures 12, 22 and 28).[178] Despite the spread of photographic reproductions in the 1850s and the pioneering work of Frith and MacDonald, books richly illustrated with engravings remained popular.[179] The British Reverend Samuel Manning's *The Land of the Pharaohs. Egypt and Sinai: Illustrated by Pen and Pencil*, first published in 1875, featured many picturesque images and was translated into French and German.[180]

Roberts, Kellogg, Bernatz, Frith and MacDonald used their firsthand experience of Horeb and the possibilities offered by their media (watercolour, oil painting, lithography and photography) to produce works of art which were at once sources of information, arguments for scholarship, materials for metaphysical contemplation, tourist enticements and statements on the essence of the Sinaitic landscape. Their views of Horeb succeeded in embedding specific vistas into popular imagination, even if they were distinctly individual. They made the rocks of Horeb iconic, instantly recognisable thanks to their attributes: barren expanses of desert, vertical cliff faces, panoramas across mountain tops, strategically placed lonely trees, humble traces of human piety. This visual vocabulary was created between the 1830s and 1870s but is alive and used to this day.

Intrepid Tourists

Despite the negative proclamations of scholars and savants, Jabal Mūsā remained a perennial favourite among adventurous travellers. Since the 1830s popular magazines abridged detailed accounts, like the one by J.L. Burckhardt, in order to familiarise their audience with a destination which combined religious interest with the allure of the exotic.[181] The London publishing firm of John Murray produced the first handbooks for the intrepid tourist from 1843 onwards.[182] The travel agents Henry Gaze & Sons had already organised three Holy Land tours by 1868.[183]

However, it was Thomas Cook who made the Holy Land and Sinai popular with the affluent middle classes of Britain and other countries.[184] His reconnaissance tour in the Near East took place in 1868 and the first tourists followed the next year.[185] Sinai was in Cook's tour schedule from the start and the word 'Sinai' appeared on the cover of his *Programmes of Personally-Conducted and Independent Palestine Tours [...] for the Season of 1874–5* in larger lettering than any other place name, even Italy.[186] The railway connecting Cairo and Suez (since 1855) had made the journey easier, safer and faster.[187]

The 'Cookii', as the Bedouin nicknamed them, opted for camping outside the Monastery walls and enjoyed familiar delicacies like Yorkshire bacon and potted salmon, usually included in the agent's fee.[188] French visitors unsurprisingly enjoyed a better diet: 'Two soups, four first courses, three roasts, salads, various puddings, and on top of all that unlimited mustard. It was a first class wedding meal with *bombe glacée à la manne*!'[189] Their fare was fundamentally different from the severe eating habits of the monks who abstained from most foods every Monday, Wednesday, Friday, through several fasting periods and in Lent, as visitors continue to discover to this day:

> They never eat flesh, and in lent, nothing that is the produce of flesh, as cheese or the like; and they are permitted to eat oil and shell-fish only on Saturdays, Sundays, and feast days, in lent; [...] and any one may conclude how coarsely they fare, when I hardly saw any other dishes there than rice ill dressed with oil, vinegar, and onions, and sometimes with onions and dried fish, the same sort of fish dressed in a soup, dried horse beans sodden in water, sallad, and cheese.[190]

The Monastery kitchens must have also catered to the needs of visitors (as in the case of Miss Platt), something seldom noted or appreciated.[191]

When on Jabal Mūsā, options were limited. George Fisk described a meal of 'very coarse brown bread, goat's milk cheese, black olives dressed in oil, delicious coffee, fresh water from the spring, and a little flask of date spirit to qualify it'. David Austin Randall got arak, dried dates and figs, brown bread and coffee. Paul Lenoir had breakfast, coffee and liqueurs in what was the best Jabal Mūsā picnic ever. He even complained that it was unlikely that the crows fed the Monastery's stale bread to the prophet Elijah (1 Kings 17) and suggested that the birds were fattening the godly man to eat him themselves – without bread. H.T.J. Stacquez refused to believe the same bread was not granite until he actually held it in hand. His menu included hard-boiled eggs, oranges, date preserve and coffee. Isabella Bird, despite abstaining from food herself, found traces of a rather elegant meal, including an empty champagne bottle which 'profaned this summit'. She 'threw it with indignation over the southern precipice more than 1,000 feet in depth'. M.J. Rendall had brown bread, almonds, raisins and water.[192]

It was probably these European, especially British, travellers who brought with them transfer-printed stoneware vessels, the sherds of which appear on Jabal Mūsā and testify to meals served in style on Staffordshire tableware. Similar wares produced in England were even decorated with prints bearing Sinai-inspired names, like 'Horeb'.[193] When in the Monastery, the souvenirs which could be purchased to commemorate a visit included 'sausages of Sinai dates, with almonds, araki, villanous Crete wine, and little silver rings, blessed at St. Catharine's shrine; [...] also were to be bought little boxes of manna, and mandrepores, and star-fish from Tor'.[194]

The lists of royals and nobles added to the end of Cook's guide-books testify to the elevated status of the travellers, and the Monastery's visitors' book came to read like a royal register. The Prince of Wales, future king Edward VII (1841–1910), visited the Holy Land in February–June 1862 under the guidance of A.P. Stanley. Royal visitors also included Louis-Philippe-Albert of Orléans, Count of Paris and his brother Robert-Philippe, Duke of Chartres who travelled to the Monastery in great style in 1860.[195] Another classic guide-book was published by the German house of Karl Baedeker and was promptly translated into English. It included coloured maps, detailed descriptions and called the journey to Sinai 'the most interesting of Oriental expeditions'.[196] French equivalents include the *Descriptive, historical and archaeological itinerary of the East* by Émile Isambert, published in 1881 in the *Guides Joanne* series, and Barnabé Meistermann's 1909 guidebook.[197] Periklēs Grēgoriadēs' *The Holy Monastery of Sinai according to its topographical, historical and administrative aspects*, published in Jerusalem in 1875, was a richly detailed book only accessible to a small Greek-speaking audience.[198]

The fathers of the Monastery adapted to the stream of visitors admirably well.[199] When William Charles Maughan was robbed of his gold by Bedouin and had to cash a cheque at the Monastery, he noted:

[...] considering that the monks knew nothing of us, and that, although the magic autograph of Messrs. Coutts & Co. at the foot of a bill is held in profound respect on all the exchanges of Europe, still their operations hardly extend to the wilderness of Sinai; when one took these circumstances into view, the monks might well have declined the transaction.[200]

Figure 29. *Les montagnes de Sinaï. Sinaigebirge.*
Postcard. Sent on 23 December 1906.

Of course, the monks had centuries of experience in pilgrimage and even though resentful Europeans complained about the service, one has to be reminded that the bulk of visitors consisted of Russian pilgrims.[201]

By the last years before World War I the British rulers of Egypt would casually carry themselves in 'Jæger waistcoats, mackintoshes, and thick dressing gowns' round the desert.[202] They even offered afternoon tea to monks, who 'did not understand that sort of meal at all'.[203] However, by 1899, when E. Hornby offered them tea, biscuits, raisins, coffee with a nip of whisky and cigarettes, monks seem to be fairly well-acquainted with the etiquette.[204] Piety was combined with curiosity and frugality with comfort by these precursors of modern tourists. They advertised their adventures on postcards printed with views of by now familiar landmarks of South Sinai.

The end of the Great War in 1918 also marked the conclusion of an era of adventurous travel. Cars covered the distance from Cairo to Horeb in a fraction of the time it took on camelback. When

Agamemnōn Zachos examined the visitors' book, he found it occupied by names of British tourists (633 out of 1,935), Indian and British soldiers (341) and only a modest number of Russians (220), Americans (190), French (153) and Greeks (59). The small number of Russians must be due to the 1917 revolution which damaged pilgrim traffic.[205]

People attempting the less than arduous, indeed quite safe, journey were pilgrims (the Greeks and Russians mainly fall in this category), art historians, palaeographers, tourists or simply curious intellectuals in search of alternative lifestyles. Their stance towards the Sinai clergy was positive overall. Even Claude Scudamore Jarvis, governor of Sinai from 1923 to 1936 and as paternalistic as an imperialist could be, was quick to admit that 'one cannot dismiss the monks of Mount Sinai without a testimony to their wondrous hospitality and kindness'.[206] The splendid works of interwar British travel literature by Henry Vollam Morton and Louis Golding contemplated the austerity of monastic life with thoughtful sympathy.[207] However, none of the above groups focused on Jabal Mūsā in particular. It was just another feature of the Horeb landscape, a picturesque destination among several others, which had the added attractions of being less known and more exotic.[208] In recent times, environmentalists and the Monastery have striven to limit the flood of tourists who ascend to the mountain.[209] Many go there for the view and the biblical echoes but are mostly unaware of the long history of visitation and worship. The mass adoration of art objects and ease of travel have obscured the religious significance of the place, 'for the Holy Mountain is a spiritual, not a physical experience'.[210]

Object of Enquiry

The nineteenth century was the last stage in the 'biography' of Jabal Mūsā, a major turning point of an interreligious pilgrimage destination into an archaeological site and then into a tourist attraction. The backwater that Sinai had become in the eyes of the western world during the seventeenth and the eighteenth century owing to the Reformation of the Catholic Church and the popularity of global sea travel was brought back into the focus of the scholarly and artistic communities and the general public.

The first stimulus was the search for 'Sinaitic' inscriptions on desert rocks. Although they had been associated with the Old Testament narrative of Exodus since the Early Christian period, their biblical connection was only put under scrutiny in the late eighteenth and the early nineteenth century by people collecting and trying to decipher them. The bizarre theories advocated by some created a pattern which would be repeated again in later decades. By the 1840s the Jews were finally dissociated from the inscriptions but a new controversy had already started, questioning this time the identification of Jabal Mūsā with the biblical 'Mount of the Law'. Scholars and explorers, tourists and artists criss-crossed the peninsula on foot and camelback in search of the best candidate for the sacred location.

The reasons why there should be an alternative Mount Sinai at all relate to the state of biblical studies in nineteenth-century Western Europe. Protestant theologians in Germany, Britain and the United States advocated critique over tradition, independent worship over the established Church, private study of the Bible over accepted exegeses and scientific rigour over 'blind' belief. Protestant churches were also keen to get their own strongholds at the Holy Land, untainted by heterodox associations. The paradoxical claim that the metaphysical phenomena related in the book of Exodus could be clarified using quasi-scientific methods based on sensory experience was typical of the way theologians tried to balance faith and the principles of post-Enlightenment positivism. Therefore, it is not surprising that most of the doubters of Jabal Mūsā were Protestant and came from Germany, Britain and America.

Apart from religious convictions, political, economic and military motives supported organised scholarly projects and individual explorers. The Suez Canal between the Mediterranean and the Red Sea was the first large-scale enterprise to facilitate international military campaigns and trade. Its strategic role attracted soldiers, spies and businessmen in the Sinai desert, usually under the guise of biblical exploration. Egypt was one of the first lands of the Ottoman Empire to be included within a colonialist empire and the maps drafted by 'Mount of the Law' enthusiasts even before the 1880s aided its administration. By the early twentieth century, scholars would mainly be motivated by a search for oil.[211]

The volume of publications describing the Sinaitic desert and especially the localities of Horeb was such that Professor Carl Ritter (German, 1779–1859) was able to write by 1848 hundreds of pages on Sinaitic landmarks without ever having visited the place.[212] His digested account was so popular that almost twenty years later it was translated and published in England, at the height of the 'Mount of the Law' controversy and only three years before the ultimate work of exodial topography, the *Ordnance Survey of the Peninsula of Sinai*.[213]

The background of the *Ordnance Survey* was indicative of the complex motivations behind the 'Mount of the Law' controversy. The mixture of scholars, soldiers, clerics and adventurers that comprised the *Survey* team embodied the aspirations and convictions of Victorian imperialist policy. On the other hand, Charles Beke represented the passionate amateur who followed his own groundbreaking views despite scholarly rejection. This species was ideally embodied by the German businessman Heinrich Schliemann (1822–1890) who in the 1870s identified and excavated Homeric Troy and Mycenae. His British counterpart was less fortunate and his contributions have since been forgotten.

The reports of this extensive geographical and textual research, published in English and German and often translated from one language into the other, were not as innocuous and detached as their learned character suggested. Feelings of religious, cultural and racial superiority translated into abuse against the monks of the Monastery, deemed to be avaricious, ignorant, deceitful and unable to spread the word of militant Christianity. Offensive comments extended beyond the grave:

> When a monk dies he is buried for one year, after which his withered mask, as empty as the life it lived, is disinterred, and added to the ghastly stack which has been slowly piling up for a thousand years.[214]

The anti-monastic feelings of Protestant writers sanctioned in their eyes the acts of C. Tischendorf, the scholar who removed the *Codex Sinaiticus*:

I, for one, am glad that the great White Father of the north [the tsar] borrowed, and forgot to return, the chief treasure which it [the library] contained.[215]

The 'end-justifies-means' mentality of the scholarly establishment supported Tischendorf in his defiance to the Monastery's calls to return the *Codex* because, in the words of Philip Schaff, Professor of Biblical Learning at the Union Theological Seminary, New York, and an eminent biblical scholar of the time:

[…] these ignorant monks could never have made use of it, and Biblical scholars could not travel to Mount Sinai to examine it. […] They lead a simple, temperate life, idle, monotonous, and stupid life.[216]

It mattered little if the manuscript was Tischendorf's in the first place and if he could 'present' it to Alexander II, tsar of Russia. What mattered was that he 'rescued' the relic from its 'medieval prison' for the world of western academia.

It was a short step from the general contempt for the Sinai monastic community to the rejection of all the traditions they had preserved and Jabal Mūsā's identification with the 'Mount of the Law' was the most questioned one. Sinai had to be discovered by Protestant scholars using their Bibles and should not be tainted with Oriental superstition. It would be untouched since the time of Moses, to be worshipped and preferably owned as well by the illuminated West. To this end, every traveller had to review the bibliography, visit all the candidate sites and record his memories in a journal which would end with a customary diatribe suggesting his preferred 'Mount of the Law'.

The connection between anti-monastic feelings, western cultural superiority and Protestant biblical criticism is best demonstrated in the accounts of Roman Catholic visitors. Their heterodox views and traditional animosity towards the Orthodox clergy should have aligned them with Protestants. However, this was rarely the case. They focused on the long tradition of pilgrimage and generally accepted the Jabal Mūsā candidacy. The same was true for female visitors of all Christian dogmas, although the reasons for their attitude were more complex: they conformed to ideals of ladylike behaviour, responded to alternative stimuli and allowed their sensitivities to go beyond polemical issues of biblical topography which obsessed their male companions.

Despite doubts of its biblical past, Jabal Mūsā remained a popular destination for audacious tourists who were attracted to its long history and natural beauty. The image of Horeb became familiar throughout Christendom thanks to the multitude of paintings, engravings and photographs depicting it. Artists made open-air sketches and took long-exposure photographs trying to captivate the sublime views of the Old Testament site. Their gaze was not neutral, indeed some of them engaged in the controversy and contributed to the wider public's understanding of the debate through the viewpoints they chose for their works.

The search for the 'Mount of the Law' continues to this day. biblical scouts are reconnoitring sites and possible locations are being proposed, Jabal Mūsā being one among them, although not a popular one. Attention has shifted since the late 1860s and early 1870s: art historians and philologists are investigating the Monastery library, icon store and mosaics instead of climbing mountain tops. This change of focus is due to the pioneering work of a few art historians and biblical scholars. Several of them originated from Russia, a Christian Orthodox country with a long tradition in Byzantine studies, and their works brought to the attention of the scholarly community both the vibrant intellectual history of Sinaitic clergy and the importance of the relics they preserved within their monastic enclave.

Admiration for artefacts went as far as arranging their removal to the metropolis of Eastern Christianity, Saint Petersburg, an act seen as re-appropriation rather than larceny by the Russian imperialist establishment. The most famous example of 're-appropriated' treasure is the *Codex Sinaiticus* manuscript, eventually presented by C. Tischendorf to the tsar in return for a title. The *Codex* affair was a turning point for the fates of both the Monastery and Jabal Mūsā. It marked the nadir of ill-treatment of the monks by their guests, since verbal abuse gave way to their deprivation of their greatest treasure. It was not the first time that items had been removed from the library or the chapels, since Uspenskiĭ had already taken some icons. Even before him, in 1815, William John Bankes had removed manuscripts, which were, surprisingly, returned to the Monastery.[217]

However, the *Codex* was beyond comparison with anything previously discovered and coincided well with the nineteenth-century obsession with the Bible. It stimulated the scholarly community's interest in the manuscripts of the Monastery. Finally, it shifted the specialists' and public's attention from scriptural identifications to medieval artefacts housed in the 'living museum' at Horeb's foot, not any more a Botany Bay of ignorant monks but a treasure house ripe for the picking of the illuminated few.

At the same time that Tischendorf was publishing his discourse on the first instalment of the *Codex* he took to Leipzig, the following passage from the novel *Tancred* was being written. Benjamin Disraeli's (British, 1804–1881) lines epitomised the Victorian fascination with Sinai. However, his vision was individual for his time. Ignoring those questions of exodial topography which preoccupied contemporary Sinaitic bibliography, unaware of the preoccupations with biblical textual history that would come to monopolise it soon, his text perceived Jabal Mūsā as the focus of an ancient tradition. The imagination of the writer, and later British prime minister, was set alight with religious fervour and surrendered to the sublime beauty and romantic associations of a landscape he never visited. In this, he touched the essence of the Jabal Mūsā romance:[218]

Between the Egyptian and Arabian deserts, formed by two gulfs of the Erythræan sea, is a peninsula of granite mountains. It seems as if an ocean of lava, when its waves were literally running mountains high, had been suddenly commanded to stand still. [...] On one of these elevations, more than five thousand feet above the ocean, is a convent; again, nearly three thousand feet above this convent, is a towering peak, and this is Mount Sinai.

On the top of Mount Sinai are two ruins, a Christian church and a Mahometan mosque. In this, the sublimest scene of Arabian glory, Israel and Ishmael alike raised their altars to the great God of Abraham. Why are they in ruins? Is it that human structures are not to be endured amid the awful temples of nature and revelation; and that the column and the cupola crumble into nothingness in sight of the hallowed Horeb and on the soil of the eternal Sinai?

Ascending the mountain, about halfway between the convent and the utmost height of the towering peak, is a small plain surrounded by rocks. In its centre are a cypress tree and a fountain. This is the traditional scene of the greatest event of time.

Figure 30. Francis Frith (British, 1822–1898), *The Summit of Gebel Moosà*. Albumen silver print, 16 × 23 cm. 1858.

Epilogue

'But now and again you get the impression, for instance, that a scholar is trying to build up a new theory, not because he really believes in it, but merely because he wants to upset the theory of the man in front of him.'

'Darn good thing!' the Colonel endorsed. 'Makes books worth writing.'

'And another thing. When you actually get on the spot, you sometimes realize for the first time the fellow's never been there. And never hinted that he's been there, either.'

'Who?'

'I mean the scholar, the one who's put out such a clever theory about such-and-such a place.'

'A clever theory's better than a foolish theory', said the Colonel sternly.

Louis Golding, *In the Steps of Moses the Lawgiver*, London 1938, viii-ix.

The theories, clever or not, developed during the nineteenth-century 'Mount of the Law' controversy were at the epicentre of the last chapter in this 'biography' of Jabal Mūsā. Golding's Colonel Smith would undoubtedly be upset since Mount Sinai's original location remains to be discovered. However, he would also be satisfied, as the 'Mount Sinai' is now more visited than ever before. The ways of perceiving and using the site remain unchanged: monks observe, Bedouin accommodate, believers pray, doubters question, scholars study and tourists sightsee.

It could be argued that Jabal Mūsā inspired the efforts of the State of Israel to annex the Sinai Peninsula and thus assumed a further, political role. One of the popular incentives for the operations was indeed the 're-possession' of the 'Mount of the Law' but the strategic and economic realities which dictated armed action had little to do with biblical landmarks. The approach of Israeli archaeologists active during the years of the occupation resulted in high-quality contributions. However, even the recent excavation, investigating in unprecedented depth Jabal Mūsā's material record, affected little the importance or meaning of the site. It translated a narrative of religious devotion and centuries-old tradition into categories of culture and tourism management, simply expressing in twenty-first-century parlance that the site is unique, significant and worth protecting.[1]

Jabal Mūsā's 'biography' was created from the bringing together of an actual and a textual place, from the identification of the 'Mount of the Law' with a granite summit. This summit acquired the characteristics of sacredness, preeminence, protection and (selective) inaccessibility. Its role as a pilgrimage destination was promoted by an imperial building programme which monumentalised the summit and its surroundings and ensured their defence. In the following centuries the summit expanded its audience across three religions and became the solid core around which a distinct Sinaitic identity was forged. Finally, in the nineteenth century it experienced an outburst of scholarly attention before reverting to its ancient qualities and function.

What makes Jabal Mūsā interesting for the scholar, fascinating for the visitor, and hallowed for the believer is the layering of worship; the stratigraphy of devotion. The place continues to inspire awe, to be seen as a refuge and to attract pilgrims. The immutability of its rituals is the measure of its importance. Arguably, some prohibitions are not respected any more and the night-time *avaton* is breached almost daily. Modernity denies or ignores tradition. For some, Jabal Mūsā is just a mountaintop. For most, it remains a holy place.

Notes

Introduction

1. Tilley 1994: 25, 34; Casey 1998: 230.

Geography

1. On Sinaitic place names, see Wilson & Palmer 1869: part I, 26–7, 51, 273–308; Bénédite 1891: 1; Hobbs 1995: 198–9; Greenwood 1997: xi-xii, 4
2. Palmer 1871: 118; Eckenstein 1921: 119–20; Aharoni 1961: 164–5. 'Horeb' could have been a name for the Mount of the Law in later biblical traditions, see Herrmann 1975: 71–2; Vaux 1978a: 426–7.
3. Eusebius 1966: 172; author's translation. On the '(desert of) Sin', see Eusebius 1966: 172, 152; Kerkeslager 1998: 197–9; Briend 2003: 2080–1.
4. Eusebius 1966: 173; Wilkinson 1977: 1–2; Briend 2003: 2082–3.
5. Description based on Wilson & Palmer 1869: part I, 230–1; Barron 1907: 53, plate X; Awad 1951: 157–9; Avnimelech 1965: 140, 176–80; Avnimelech 1969: 152–4; Garfunkel 1979a: 41–51, 46–8, 61–7; Arad & Bartov 1981; Kamil 1991: 7–8; Hobbs 1995: 14; Greenwood 1997: 11–25, 26–50, 104–13; Briend 2003: 1973–5. For overviews of scientific research in Sinai, see Rothenberg 1979a: 7–8; Hobbs 1995: 243–4.
6. On the Jabal Mūsā area, see Wilson & Palmer 1869: part I, 110–7; Barron 1907: 213; Awad 1951: 158–9; Daumas 1951: 365–70; Hobbs 1995: 6; Greenwood 1997: 39–46; Dahari 2000: 3, 25; *Master Plan* 2010: 27–30, 33–43.
7. Wilson & Palmer 1869: part I, 112, 220; Barron 1907: 67; Meistermann 1909: 148; Daumas 1951: 378; Perevolotsky 1981: 335–6.
8. Marthalēs 1710: no pagination. On Marthalēs, see Eckenstein 1921: 181; Popescu-Belis & Mouton 2006: 199.

9. Stochove *et al.* 1975: 122. Stochove's text was plagiarised by his fellow traveller Gilles Fermanel (died in 1661); see Stochove *et al.* 1975: 123. On V. Stochove, see Saint-Génois 1846: volume II, 123; Labib 1961: 94.

10. Nektarios 1980: 50; *Proskynētaria* 2003: 139.

11. Wilson & Palmer 1869: part I, 208, plate VIII, figure 1: I and II; Palmer 1871: 110–11. Many variations appear as to these identifications; see Lagrange 1897: 120.

12. Wilson & Palmer 1869: part I, 114–15, 207–9; Daumas 1951: 371–3; Greenwood 1997: 45–6.

13. Wilson & Palmer 1869: part I, 114–5; Palmer 1871: 105–6; Barron 1907: 71; Daumas 1951: 372; Dahari 2000: 47.

14. Ševčenko 1966: 257, 263, figures 11A, 11B.

15. *Egeria* 2008: 83; Koufopoulos & Myriantheos-Koufopoulou 2010: 110.

16. Wilson & Palmer 1869: part I, 115; Palmer 1871: 132–4; Barron 1907: 14, 71–2; Eckenstein 1921: 185–6; Zachos 1937: 61–2; Daumas 1951: 221–2, 222 note, 372; Hamilton 1993: 15–8; Greenwood 1997: 46.

17. Wilson & Palmer 1869: part I, 11–2, 113, 147, 240–5; Barron 1907: 69–70; Daumas 1951: 365–6; Goring-Morris 1987: volume I, 29–44; Zafrir *et al.* 1991: 124; Tsafrir 1993c: 316–8; Moustafa & Klopatek 1995; Hobbs 1995: 12–3; Greenwood 1997: 45; Briend 2003: 1975–6. For the latest work on the area's climate, see *Master Plan* 2010: 30–2.

18. Perevolotsky 1981: 335–6; Hobbs 1995: 7–8.

19. Hull 1886: 25–6; Hobbs 1995: 11; Moustafa & Klopatek 1995: 387; Meshel 2000: 146.

20. Hart 1891: 20–1.

21. Field 1952: 72; Hobbs 1995: 8–11; Greenwood 1997: 51–64.

22. *Synaxis* 1998: 123–4, 134–5.

23. Eckenstein 1921: 90–1; Bar-Yosef 1982: 9; Goldberg & Bar-Yosef 1982: 401–4; Nevo 1991: 4–5; Dahari 1993: 350; Greenwood 1997: 24

24. Finkelstein 1993: 334, 336–7, 340; Dahari 1993: 349–50; Koufopoulos & Myriantheos 2014: 1127.

25. Dahari 1993: 350. For cultivation in the Negev, see Evenari *et al.* 1982: 95–125; Nevo 1991.

26. Dahari 2000: 38–40.

27. Wilson & Palmer 1869: part III, volume I, 32.

28. Hart 1891: 18; Post 1933: 800–1; Shabetai 1940: 45; Hobbs 1995: 19.

29. Barron 1907: 70; Field 1952: 73–4; Danin 1979: 77–83; Moustafa & Klopatek 1995: 387–94; Hobbs 1995: 16–21. Latest research in *Master Plan* 2010: 44–6.

30. Tchernov 1979: 93–9; Hobbs 1995: 21–31.

Chapter 1

1. Goldberg & Bar-Yosef 1982: 400; Rabinowitz 1985: 216–25.
2. Palmer 1871: 78; Tsafrir 1993c: 318; Bowersock 1996: 10.
3. Wilson & Palmer 1869: part I, 194–7; Petrie 1906: 243–4, figures 176–8; Eckenstein 1921: 90; Albright 1948; Field 1952: 75–6, 81–91; Rothenberg 1971: 21; Ronen 1971; Oren 1979: 181–91; Rothenberg 1979b: 109–27; Goring-Morris 1987; Hershkovitz 1988: 47; Finkelstein & Perevolotsky 1990: 69; Briend 2003: 1982.
4. Bar-Yosef 1982: 11–2.
5. Meshel 2000: 121–42; Finkelstein & Perevolotsky 1990: 69.
6. Eckenstein 1921: 17–29, 52–63; Skrobucha 1966: 4–5; Rothenberg 1971: 15; Rothenberg 1979c: 137–66; Beit-Arieh 1982: 13–8. On Egyptian presence in Sinai: Weill 1904; Breasted 1906: volume I, 6, 75–6, 275, 314–23; Breasted 1906: volume II, 352; Breasted 1906: volume IV, 204; Petrie 1906.
7. Aharoni 1961: 166; Rothenberg 1971: 17–8; Briend 2003: 1980–6, 2042–53.
8. Thompson 1975: 3, 24–9; Hershkovitz 1988: 47; Finkelstein & Perevolotsky 1990: 74–9; Briend 2003: 1977–80.
9. Eckenstein 1921: 83; Kamil 1991: 8; Bowersock 1996: 5.
10. On references in Diodorus and Strabo, see Eckenstein 1921: 83–5; Negev 1986: 113–5.
11. Eckenstein 1921: 91; Sartre 1982: 37–40; Nevo 1991: 111–12 note 7; Mayerson 1994: 232–3; Bowersock 1996: 76–89, 94–5, 102–3.
12. Cosmas 1970: 85 (V.53). Translated in Cosmas 1897: 159–60. French translation in Cosmas 1970: 84. Another edition of the Greek text in Cosmas 1909: 154. See also Eckenstein 1921: 88–9; Wolska 1962: 3; Champdor 1963: 18–19; Ševčenko 1966: 255–6 note 2; Cosmas 1968: 15–19; Wilkinson 1977: 6; Maraval 1985: 75, 307; Dahari 2000: 22–3. It has been argued that Kosmas identified the Mount of the Law with Jabal Sirbāl rather than Jabal Mūsā, but the case of an error is much more likely; see Lagrange 1897: 128–9; Ševčenko 1966: 255–6 note 2; Vaux 1978a: 429; Tsafrir 1993c: 327.
13. Petrus 1965: 102 (Y14). Translation from Egeria 1971: 208; Cosmas 1970: 85–6 note 53². On Petrus Diaconus, see Manley & Abdel-Hakim 2006: 247.

14. Negev 1967: 254–5; Meshel 2000: 144, 149 note 1; Taylor 2001: 154; Briend 2003: 1987–8.
15. Negev 1977b; Negev 1981; Negev 1986: 6–7; Meshel 2000: 144.
16. Negev 1986: 9.
17. Negev 1982: 23–4; Negev 1986: 109, 111, 115; Negev 1991: 209.
18. Rothenberg 1971: 18; Hourani 1995: 22, map II opposite page 36.
19. Meshel 2000: 149 note 1. On the term 'Saracen', *Sharqiyīn*, see Moritz 1920: 2387–90; Eckenstein 1921: 95; Égérie 1982: 137 note 3; Shahîd 1984a: 123–41; Mayerson 1986: 36; Exeria 1991: 47 note 13; Shahîd 1995: 968; Figueras 2000: 71, 73–7; Dahari 2000: 8–9.
20. Gutwein 1981: 5–40, 314–21; Sartre 1982: 74; Shahîd 1984b: 399–400, 548; Mayerson 1986: 40–5; Mayerson 1988: 65–6; Mayerson 1989: 72–3; Mayerson 1994: 233.
21. Nilus 1860: 611–14 (third narration). For a Latin translation, see Nilus 1860: 611–14; for general discussions, see Degenhart 1915: 8–9, 33–7; Eckenstein 1921: 106–9; Devreesse 1940: 220, 220 note 4; Labib 1961: 8–10; Mayerson 1963: 160–2; Skrobucha 1966: 30–2; Ševčenko 1966: 256, 256 note 5; Christides 1973: 40–6; Mayerson 1975: 51–8; Huber 1979: 203–6; Mayerson 1980: 133–4; Shahîd 1989: 134–9; *Synaxis* 1998: 156, 175–6.
22. Lagrange 1905: 257–9; Murray 1935: 197–8; Henninger 1955: 97–148; Albright 1968: 207–9; Christides 1973: 46–50; Mayerson 1975: 56–7, 60; John 1992: 129; King 2009: 81–93.
23. Mayerson 1975: 64–5; Isaac 1984: 194, 196; Tsafrir 1993c: 320.
24. Mayerson 1975: 52–3; Shahîd 1995: 984–6.
25. Perevolotsky 1981: 353–5.
26. Negev 1977b: 78; Gutwein 1981: 23–6, 246–8; Tsafrir 1993c: 318–20.
27. Perevolotsky 1981: 353; Finkelstein & Perevolotsky 1990: 79–80; Mayerson 1994 (1987): 232–42.
28. Eckenstein 1921: 107–8; Mayerson 1975: 67–8; Mayerson 1986: 40–5; Mayerson 1989: 73–4.
29. For Christianisation, see Ammonius 1912: 4–5; Shahîd 1984b: 298–302, 308; Shahîd 1989: 524–6; Mayerson 1989: 74; John 1992: 129. For Wādī Fīran and Ṭūr, see Shahîd 1984b: 298–305, 555–6; Grossmann 1989: 1901–4, 1906–8; Shahîd 1995: 986–9; Grossmann *et al.* 1996.
30. Hershkovitz 1988: 53, 56–8.
31. Shahîd 1984b: 302, 306, 319–24.
32. Nevo 1991: 125–35.
33. Shahîd 1984b: 301–2, 328; for the differentiation between *al-Badw* and *al-ᶜArab*, see Shahîd 1995: 968–9, 972–4.

34. Hershkovitz 1988: 53, 58; Tsafrir 1993c: 322–3.

35. Shahîd 1989: 136.

36. Burckhardt 1822: 554–64; Newbold 1847: 71–2; Ritter 1866: 384–6; Wilson & Palmer 1869: part I, 57; Palmer 1871: 74–100; Murray 1935: 265–6; Oppenheim 1943: 135–9, 165–6; Daumas 1951: 17; Field 1952: 78–9, 106–17; Aharoni 1961: 145; Skrobucha 1966: 62–3; Bonné *et al.* 1971: 397, 407; Marx 1977: 37–8; Ben-David 1977–8: i–iv; Nandris 1981: 608–9; Arad & Michael 1984; Nandris 1984; Nandris 1990; Bailey 1991: 5–6; Tetsuo 1992: ix–xi; Hobbs 1995: 139–51; Basile 1998; Goren 1999: 8–9, 43, 60; Popescu-Belis 2001: 140–1.

37. Field 1952: 78; Shahîd 1984b: 306, 306 note 82, 385 note 133; Shahîd 1995: 977–80; Popescu-Belis 2001: 107–46.

38. Lavie 1990: 268.

39. Wilson & Palmer 1869: part III, volume I, 26; Perevolotsky 1981: 337–56; Hobbs 2001: 207–11.

40. Burckhardt 1822: 564.

41. Field 1952: 93; Marx 1977: 36.

42. Paphnutius 1781: 123 (IV). Author's translation. Latin translation in Paphnutius 1781: 123. On Onuphrius, see Eckenstein 1921: 95–6; Skrobucha 1966: 20; Hobbs 1995: 129–30; Dahari 2000: 22, 66; *Egeria* 2008: 87.

43. Brown 1996: 81–101; Brown 1998: 51–9.

44. Théodoret 1977: 356–57 (VI.8). Translated in Theodoret 1985: 65–6; for a French translation, see Théodoret 1977: 356–7.

45. Eckenstein 1921: 94–5; Tsafrir 1993c.

46. Klopfenstein 1979: 17–31.

47. Vaux 1978a: 432–9; Maiberger 1984: 73–82; Tsafrir 1993c: 316; Kerkeslager 1998: 180–8.

48. Aharoni 1961: 126; Tsafrir 1993c: 315; Kerkeslager 1998: 153–79, 188–92.

49. Greene 1883: 139–52; Herrmann 1975: 73; Vaux 1978a: 434–7; Vaux 1978b: 560–2, 560–1 notes 26, 27; Coleman & Elsner 1995: 40–5; Peters 1996: 40, 464–5 notes 3, 5; Wilken 1996: 120–4; Friedman 1996: 136–46; Kerkeslager 1998: 104–46, 148–50.

50. Negev 1977b: 79–80

51. Herrmann 1975: 72–3, 77; Vaux 1978a: 426–39; Blum 1998; Kerkeslager 1998: 152 note 218, 210–13; Anati 1993: 19–89; Briend 2003: 2062.

52. Kerkeslager 1998: 203 note 366.

53. Golding 1938: 341.

54. Amantos 1953: 7; Champdor 1963: 19–20; Huber 1979: 201–2.

55. Labib 1961: 4–10; Shahîd 1984b: 302–5; Finkelstein 1985: 39; Hershkovitz 1988: 47; Tsafrir 1993c: 322; Shahîd 1995: 968–72, 983–4.

56. On Wādī Fīran, see Rothenberg 1971: 20–1; Dahari 2000: 17–20, 113–37; Grossmann 2002: 30 note 51. On Ṭūr, see *De Vitis Patrum* 1849: 1008; Eckenstein 1921: 96; Dahari 2000: 138–46.

57. Dahari 2000: 41.

58. Finkelstein 1985: 42–60; Tsafrir 1993c: 324–5; Finkelstein 1993: 336–8; Dahari 2000: 48, table 3.

59. Dahari 2000: 49–54.

60. Symeon 1864a: 101–2 (IA΄). Author's translation. For a Latin translation, see Symeon 1864a: 101–2.

61. Symeon 1864a: 104–8; Eckenstein 1921: 97–8; Zachos 1937: 76–7; Skrobucha 1966: 19; Tsafrir 1993c: 320–1; *Synaxis* 1998: 138–9, 147–8; Dahari 2000: 21.

62. Sozomenus 1960: 288–89 (VI.32). Translated in Sozomen 1891: 370, with an addition by the author. On Silvanos and his time at Horeb, see Le Nain de Tillemont 1705: 450–3; Wilson & Palmer 1869: part I, 198; Eckenstein 1921: 96–7; Chitty 1995: 71–3, 168; *Synaxis* 1998: 187–8.

63. Eckenstein 1921: 104–5; Labib 1961: 2–3; Mayerson 1964: 178; Skrobucha 1966: 26; Huber 1979: 206; Sartre 1982: 140–4; Shahîd 1984b: 152–8, 555–6; Tsafrir 1993c: 322; Dahari 2000: 19.

64. Grossmann 1988: 556–8, Abb. 3; Grossmann 1989: 1904–6, Abb. 27.

65. English translation in Mayerson 1978: 36; Latin translation in Eutychius 1863: 1071–2; German translation in Eutychios 1985: 89.

66. Turner 1820: 441. On W. Turner, see Manley & Abdel-Hakim 2006: 250. Arundale 1837: 33; Robinson 1867: 98–9; Wilkinson 1843: 411; Wilkinson 1847: 219.

67. Shahîd 1984b: 305–8, 313, 313 note 107, 315, 480–1.

68. Pococke 1814: 287, 289; Burckhardt 1822: 544; Eckenstein 1921: 99; Aharoni 1961: 159; Labib 1961: 8; Champdor 1963: 15; Skrobucha 1966: 19–20; *Perigraphē* 1978: 111; Kamil 1991: 18–9; Dahari 2000: 21, 59.

69. Negev 1977b: 62–7; Walser 1979: 224; Oren 1982: 211.

70. Marcianus 1933: [491] 132. On the letter, see Eckenstein 1921: 110; Amantos 1953: 10; Skrobucha 1966: 35; Chitty 1995: 169; Dahari 2000: 22.

71. Tsafrir 1993c: 315, 333; Shahîd 1995: 983–4.

72. Greek text and Latin translation in Joannis 1860b: 2855–8, 2957–60, 2979–88, 3001–2; French translation in Jean 1946; on John Moschos, see Skrobucha 1966: 29; Baldwin 1991; Dahari 2000: 23.

73. Maraval 1985: 72; Dahari 1993: 350; Tsafrir 1993c: 332; Dahari 2000: 151

74. Grēgoriadēs 1875: 38–40; Shahîd 1984b: 298; Hershkovitz 1988: 49; Tsafrir 1993c: 322.

75. *Synaxarium* 1902: 391$_{1-13}$ (Mensis Ianuarius 14). Author's translation.

76. English translation in Mayerson 1978: 36–7; Latin translation in Eutychius 1863: 1071–2; German translation in Eutychios 1985: 88–9; for a discussion, see Shahîd 1995: 976–7.

77. For Saint George of Arselas, see Eckenstein 1921: 113; for the area, see Wilson & Palmer 1869: part I, 136–7; for monastic remains, see Finkelstein 1985: 60–73; Ovadiah 1985; Dahari 2000: 102–3; for the cannabis, see Burckhardt 1822: 536; Hobbs 1995: 181; Hobbs 1996: 17–18; Marx 1999: 353–4; Hobbs 2001: 208; for Bedouin folklore on buried treasures, see Wilson & Palmer 1869: part I, 68.

78. Michaēl 1999: 45.

79. Lavie 1990: 55.

80. Pococke 1814: 288; Palmer 1871: 118–19; Rogers 1883: 231; Meistermann 1909: 151; Murray 1935: 152–4; Champdor 1963: 50; Michaēl 1999: 27, 36.

81. Dumas 1839a: 62. Translated quote from Dumas 1839a: 62; Dumas 1839b: 220.

82. Burckhardt 1822: 595; Skrobucha 1966: 57; *Perigraphē* 1978: 117–18; Kamil 1991: 36–7; Tetsuo 1992: x.

83. Henniker 1823: 229. On F. Henniker, see Manley & Abdel-Hakim 2006: 243.

84. Wilson & Palmer 1869: part I, 63–4; Palmer 1871: 57.

85. Rendall 1911: 122–3.

86. Burckhardt 1822: 567–8; Wilson & Palmer 1869: part I, 64; Palmer 1871: 65–6, 75–7, 85; Skrobucha 1966: 60; Hobbs 1995: 164–5.

87. *Perigraphē* 1978: 118.

88. Burckhardt 1822: 519. On J.L. Burckhardt, see Manley & Abdel-Hakim 2006: 241.

89. Turner 1820: 447–8.

90. Murray 1935: 153.

91. Panayotidi & Kalopissi-Verti 2007: no pagination; Kalopissi-Verti & Panayotidi 2010: 93.

92. Panagiōtidē *et al.* 2002: 69–73, 75–7; Kalopissi-Verti 2006: 279–80; Kalopissi-Verti & Panayotidi 2010: 87–9; Koufopoulos & Myriantheos-Koufopoulou 2010: 108–10. See also *Egeria* 2008: 80.

93. Wilson & Palmer 1869: part I, 208; Panagiōtidē *et al.* 2002: 73 note 20.

94. Dahari 2000: 163.

95. Finkelstein 1985: 42–60; Finkelstein 1993: 337.

96. Burckhardt 1822: 612; Negev 1977a, 219–20, figure 1; Cohen 1979; Evenari *et al.* 1982: 346; Negev 1982: 25; Negev 1986: 116–18; Dahari 2000: 7; Taylor 2001: 168–70; Briend 2003: 2008–9. There is another mount named Jabal Muʿtamr near Horeb, to the east of the Monastery; a third Jabal Muʿtamr is in West-Central Sinai.

97. Negev 1986: 117–18; Dahari 2000: 7.

98. For a *corpus*, see Stone 1992a: 31–5, 37, 38, 42, 45; Stone 1992b: 138, 159, 183.

99. Rothenberg 1971: 19.

100. The 'Nabatean theory' has been suggested by Aharoni 1961: 170; Negev 1986: 116.

101. Scholars have misunderstood the succession of buildings on Jabal Mūsā: Lagrange 1897: 118–20; Anastase 1902b: 10–1 note 5; Meistermann 1909: 149–51, figure 33; Éthérie 1948: 34, 104 note 1; Daumas 1951: 378; Égérie 1982: 132 note 1; Maraval 1985: 309, 309 notes 471, 472.

102. Theodosius 1965: 123 (27). English translation in Wilkinson 1977: 70. On the date and sources of the work, see Wilkinson 1977: 184–91. For the value of various measurements given in these early works, see Wilkinson 1977: 16–20. See also Stone 1982a: 28–9.

103. Koikylidēs 1897: 10, 20–1; Avi-Yonah 1954: 43, plates 5, 10; Donner & Cüppers 1977: XI–XVI, 25, 27, 73, 160; Fontaine 1955: 56–9; Cosmas 1968: 148–50; Wilkinson 1977: 7; Piccirillo 1993: 26–33, 91; Bowersock 1996: 172, 184.

104. Bosio 1983: 76–7. Author's translation. On Agrippa's map, see Kubitschek 1919: 2100–11. On the *Tabula Peutingeriana*, see Ritter 1866: 22–7; Kubitschek 1919: 2126–44; Eckenstein 1921: 94–5; Fontaine 1955: 54–5; Bosio 1983: 47, 50, 76–7, 165–74; Dahari 2000: 9–10; Briend 2003: 2085.

105. Bowersock 1996: 168.

106. Silvia 1887: 35–44; Silvia 1897: 11–15; Eckenstein 1921: 114–20; Éthérie 1948: 14–16, 96–119; Amantos 1953: 9; Fontaine 1955: 55–6; Egeria 1960: 1–8; Labib 1961: 17–22; Champdor 1963: 14–18; Egeria 1965: 37–45; Devos 1967: 188–94; Forsyth 1968: 3–4; Egeria 1971: 7–8, 29, 300–3; Huber 1979: 206–8; Égérie 1982: 120–49, 120 note 1; Shahîd 1984b: 295–7; Finkelstein 1985: 41; Exeria 1991: 41–53; Tsafrir 1993c: 327; Chitty 1995: 71, 168; Wilken 1996: 127–30; Egéria 1998: 78–99; Dahari 2000: 20, 29; Briend 2003: 2080; Manley & Abdel-Hakim 2006: 242.

107. Gregorius 1891: 279–80; see also Eckenstein 1921: 131; Labib 1961: 22–3; Skrobucha 1966: 35–6.

108. Petrus 1965: 100–3 (previously published in Silvia 1887: 142–3); see also Eckenstein 1921: 115; Devos 1967: 192–3. On Petrus, see Amann 1933; Grossmann 2002: 43–4, 44 note 89; Briend 2003: 2083.

109. Égérie 1982: 120–49 (2.3, 3.1–2, 3.3). English translation in Egeria 1971: 91, 93–4.

110. Égérie 1982: 120–49 (3.5, 3.7, 3.8). English translation in Egeria 1971: 94–5.

111. Mian 1970: 222–3, map on page 210. Questioned in Égérie 1982: 126–7 note 4.

112. Forsyth *et al.* 1973: 6; Mayerson 1978: 34, 37; Tsafrir 1993b: 14; Tsafrir 1993c: 328.

113. Egeria 1971: 214; Égérie 1982: 133 notes 4 and 5; Devreesse 1940: 208–11.

114. Skrobucha 1966: 27–8; Egeria 1971: 18; Bowman 2001: 8–10.

115. Greek text and French translation in Théodoret 1977: 222–5, 354–7; for an English translation, see Theodoret 1985: 29, 67, 35 note 10, 68 note 5; German and Italian translations in Theodoret 1926: 42–3, 78; Teodoreto 1986: 59–60, 100; on the date of the *History of the Monks of Syria*, see Théodoret 1977: 30–1. See also Eckenstein 1921: 98–9; Théodoret 1977: 245 note 2; *Perigraphē* 1978: 141–2; Dahari 2000: 21, 28–9.

116. Theodoret 1985: 35 note 1; Chitty 1995: 168; *Synaxis* 1998: 158–9; Grossmann 2002: 20 note 19.

117. Théodoret 1977: 222–5 (II.13). English translation in Theodoret 1985: 29. On the method of collecting water, see Théodoret 1977: 223 note 1.

118. Amantos 1953: 10. On the ecclesiastical office of *apokris(i)arios*, see Magdalino 1991b.

119. Ephraem 1972a: 61–2, 71–3, for the Syriac original; Ephraem 1972b: 66–7, 75–7, for a German translation; Dahari 2000: 28–9, for a partial English translation. On Ephraem, see Baldwin & Ševčenko 1991; Chitty 1995: 168. Nektarios 1980: 208.

120. Theodoret 1985: 68 note 1; see also Théodoret 1977: 365 note 1, where Pierre Canivet proposed a 375–380 date for his death, a view espoused by Dahari 2000: 28; Chitty 1995: 168.

121. Théodoret 1977: 354–7 (VI.12). English translation in Theodoret 1985: 67. Also mentioned in the *Synaxarium of the Church of Constantinople* (*Synaxarium* 1902: 426$_{7-12}$, Mensis Ianuarius 26).

122. Le Nain de Tillemont 1706: 574; Eckenstein 1921: 100–4; Skrobucha 1966: 20–6; Finkelstein 1985: 41; Maraval 1985: 71 note 38; Chitty

1995: 170–1; Dahari 2000: 22; Grossmann 2002: 35; Manley &
Abdel-Hakim 2006: 239.

123. Epiphanius 1864: 265–8 (for Sinai), Greek with Latin translation;
English translation in Wilkinson 1977: 119, 198–9 (for commentary).
On Epiphanios, see Kazhdan 1991.

124. Mayerson 1976: 377–9; Mayerson 1978: 35–6; Mayerson 1980;
Shahîd 1984b: 308–19, 327–8; Mayerson 1994: 238–9.

125. Amantos 1953: 7–9, 8 note 5.

126. English translation of the seventh- or eighth-century Syriac text in
Ammonius 1912: 2. See Mayerson 1980: 137–40; Shahîd 1984b: 312.

127. Procopius 1971: 354–56 (V.viii). English translation in Procopius
1971: 355–7; other English translations in Procopius 1886: 146–7;
Wilkinson 1977: 76. On Prokopios, see Manley & Abdel-Hakim
2006: 248.

128. Mayerson 1978: 35–6.

129. Platon 1958: no pagination, 80e–81a. English translation in Plato
1993: 32 and ix.

130. On *formulae*, see Cameron 1985: 96–7.

131. John 1992: 130.

132. Antoninus 1965a: 148–9 (37–8). English translation in Antoninus
1897: 29–30. For a discussion of this passage, see Mayerson
1964: 187. A similar text can be found in Antoninus 1965b: 171;
alternatively *De Locis Transmarinis Sacris Beati Antonini Martyris*
in Antoninus 1879b: 131–2. On the second text, see Wilkinson 1977:
6–7. For other editions, see Antoninus 1879a: 112–13; Antoninus
1889: 26–7; Antoninus 1965a: 148–9. See also Wilson & Palmer
1869: part I, 200–1; Eckenstein 1921: 125; Devreesse 1940: 214–15.;
Fontaine 1955: 51–3; Shahîd 1984b: 319–24; Finkelstein 1985: 41;
Dahari 2000: 23, 30; Grossmann 2002: 37 note 69; Briend 2003:
2079.

133. Egeria 1971: 215.

134. Another seventh-century Anastasios is perhaps identified with
Anastasios of Sinai; see Anastase 1902b: 8; Anastase 1903: 56–8;
Caranikolas 1955; Chitty 1995: 171–2, 175–6; Dahari 2000: 23–4.

135. On Anastasios, see Anastase 1902b: 3–6; Eckenstein 1921: 111–3;
Synaxis 1998: 128.

136. For the duties of *paramonarios,* see Magdalino 1991a.

137. Anastase 1902a: 61. Author's translation.

138. Anastase 1902a: 82–3. Author's translation. The narration
survived in sixteenth- and seventeenth-century Greek manuscript
proskynētaria (pilgrim guidebooks); see *Proskynētaria* 2003: 74,
84–5, 91, 117, 147–8.

139. Anastase 1902a: 81. Author's translation.
140. Stone 1982a: 35–6.
141. Anastase 1902a: 81–2. Author's translation. For a discussion, see Eckenstein 1921: 126; Mayerson 1994: 239; Chitty 1995: 175.
142. For Elbert Farman's experience of similar phenomena in 1908, see Manley & Abdel-Hakim 2006: 183–5. On E. Farman, see Manley & Abdel-Hakim 2006: 242.
143. Anastase 1902a: 60–1; Hobbs 1995: 19–20.
144. Finkelstein 1981; Finkelstein 1985: 56; Finkelstein 1993: 338–9; Coleman & Elsner 1995: 211; Dahari 2000: 47.
145. Finkelstein 1985: 66, 66 note 27.
146. Nilus 1860: 631; Mayerson 1975: 62–3.
147. Shahîd 1995: 973–4.
148. Severus 1845: 194. English translation in Eckenstein 1921: 96.
149. Exodus 19:12–13 and 20–24, 24:1–2, 34:3; Peters 1996: 37–8.
150. Finkelstein 1985: 60; Finkelstein 1993: 334, 340; *Synaxis* 1998: 132.
151. Joannis 1860a: 812–14. Author's translation. For the Greek text and a Latin translation, see Joannis 1860a: 812–14; for another English translation, see John 1959: 120–1. On Stephen, see Nektarios 1980: 211–12; Eckenstein 1921: 112; *Synaxis* 1998: 189–90.
152. Ševčenko 1966: 257, 263; Dahari 2000: 45.
153. Finkelstein 1993: 336–9; Dahari 2000: 38–49.
154. Hobbs 1995: 234.
155. Champdor 1963: 51; Dansette 2001: 69. The connection was first encountered in the *Perigraphē*; see *Perigraphē* 1978: 139–40).

Chapter 2
1. Maraval 1985: 70 1.
2. Maraval 1985: 78–9.
3. Procopius 1971: 354–6 (V.viii). English translation in Prokopius 1971: 355–7. For a discussion, see Eckenstein 1921: 121–2; Labib 1961: 10–11; Skrobucha 1966: 32; Paisios 1978: 78–9.
4. Mayerson 1978: 33–6; Mayerson 1982: 52.
5. Cameron 1985: 96.
6. Forsyth 1968: 4–6; Forsyth 1980: 52–4.
7. Grēgoriadēs 1875: 53–5; Forsyth 1968: 14–15 note 17; Dahari 2000: 29–34, 61.
8. Evagrius 1865: 2803; Dahari 2000: 55; Grossmann 2002: 35–6.
9. Mayerson 1978; Isaac 1984: 196–7; Cameron 1985: 96–8; Mayerson 1986: 35–6, 38–9.
10. English translation in Mayerson 1978: 36–7, continued in Skrobucha 1966: 34; Latin translation in Eutychius 1863: 1071–2; German

translation in Eutychios 1985: 88–90. On Eutychios, see Breydy
1983: 1–11; Eddé *et al.* 1997: 158–9. On the text, see Eckenstein
1921: 122–4; Labib 1961: 11; Mayerson 1964: 181–2, 182 note 83;
Skrobucha 1966: 32–4; Dahari 2000: 30.

11. Grēgoriadēs 1875: 40–53.

12. Dahari 2000: 30.

13. Dahari 2000: 37, 44–5.

14. Anastase 1902a: 61–2. Author's translation.

15. *Synaxarium* 1902: 229$_{31-6}$ (Mensis November16). Author's
translation. On the text, see Amantos 1953: 11 note 1; Paisios 1978:
79.

16. Mouton & Popescu-Belis 2006: 1–6, 53.

17. Author's translation, after the French translation in Mouton &
Popescu-Belis 2006: 49, 52.

18. Mouton & Popescu-Belis 2006: 19–20.

19. Martoni 1895: 572, 605–10; Harff 1946: 140; Jacopo 1950: 73.

20. Mouton & Popescu-Belis 2006: 15–18.

21. Mouton & Popescu-Belis 2006: 21–4.

22. Translated by the author after the French translation in al-Makrizi
1908: 204. Greek translation in Grēgoriadēs 1875: 82–3. See also
Jacopo 1950: 198 note 243.

23. Mouton & Popescu-Belis 2006: 34.

24. Mouton & Popescu-Belis 2006: 12–13.

25. The most recent description in *Master Plan* 2010: 48–54.

26. Liphschitz & Waisel 1976: 42.

27. Ševčenko 1966: 262, figure 1. Author's translation. Amantos 1953:
12; Paisios 1978: 80; Dahari 2000: 58.

28. Rabino 1938: 39–40, 42, 107.

29. Meistermann 1909: 133. On V. Posniakov, see Khitrowo 1889:
287–8; Eckenstein 1921: 176.

30. Forsyth 1968: 7–8; Forsyth 1980: 55–6; Kamil 1991: 51; Dahari
2000: 59.

31. Manginis 2015b: 214.

32. Liphschitz & Weisel 1976: 42–3.

33. Forsyth 1968: 6–7, 6–7 note 5; Forsyth 1980: 56.

34. Forsyth 1968: 5–6; Forsyth 1980: 52; Dahari 2000: 60.

35. Rabino 1935: 32, 33, 83, 84; Sōtēriou & Sōtēriou 1958: 5; Weitzmann
1980: 87.

36. Forsyth 1980: 52, 63–4; Dahari 2000: 60.

37. Forsyth 1968: 7–18.

38. Abel 1907: 109–11, plates III–IV.

39. Amantos 1953: 15; Forsyth 1968: 8–9, 8–9 note 7; Liphschitz & Waisel 1976: 41–2; Forsyth 1980: 57; Koufopoulos *et al.* 2004: 563, 567.
40. Ševčenko 1966: 262. Author's translation. Rabino 1935: 27, 79–80. See also Pococke 1814 (1743): 290; Amantos 1953: 13; Paisios 1978: 81. There is also a fourth, recently discovered inscription, see Koufopoulos *et al.* 2004: 567.
41. Sōtēriou & Sōtēriou 1958: 6–7; Weitzmann 1980: 82.
42. Gutwein 1981: 23.
43. Ševčenko 1966: 256–7; Forsyth 1968: 9; Forsyth 1980: 57.
44. Abel 1907: 109, plate II2; Rabino 1935: 45, 45 notes 1–2, plates IX–X; Skrobucha 1966: 89–90. On the sixth-century date of the doors, see Forsyth 1968: 10; Liphschitz & Weisel 1976: 42; Forsyth 1980: 58; Weitzmann 1980: 81–2.
45. Forsyth 1968: 10; Forsyth 1980: 59.
46. Eckenstein 1921: 130; Rabino 1935: 31, 82; Daumas 1951: 390 note ***; Sōtēriou & Sōtēriou 1958: 3–4; Skrobucha 1966: 86–7.
47. Beamont 1861: 61; Grēgoriadēs 1875: 17 note 1; Rabino 1935: 27, 80; *Perigraphē* 1978: 127–8.
48. First studied by Léon E.S.J. de Laborde (1830: 67–8, plate 20) and restored in 1847 and 2005–2008; see Sōtēriou & Sōtēriou 1958: 4–6; Weitzmann 1982b: 5–18; Nardi & Zizola 2014.
49. Ševčenko 1966: 263, figures 7A, 7B, 7C. Author's translation. See also Amantos 1953: 12; Ševčenko 1966: 258–61.
50. Abel 1907: 105–9, plate I.
51. Meyendorff 1968; Weitzmann 1980: 84.
52. Forsyth 1968: 13, 14 note 17; Weitzmann 1980: 85.
53. Rabino 1935: 30, 82; Forsyth 1968: 12; *Perigraphē* 1978: 128; Weitzmann 1980: 83; Forsyth 1980: 60.
54. Weitzmann 1966: 6–10.
55. Forsyth 1968: 8; Forsyth 1980: 57.
56. Forsyth 1980: 62.
57. Petrie 1906: 237.
58. Popescu-Belis 2000: 385–6.
59. Mourelatos 2005.
60. Gutwein 1981: 321–38.
61. Dahari 2000: 56.
62. Mayerson 1963: 170–1; Mayerson 1964: 186; Mayerson 1994: 241.
63. Kawatoko 1995: 51–9; Dahari 2000: 57.
64. Kawatoko 1998: 75–91, plates 31–52; Dahari 2000: 14–15.
65. The 1868–1869 *Ordnance Survey of the Peninsula of Sinai* recorded the buildings present at the time on Jabal Mūsā in ground-plan;

in February 1897, Father Marie-Joseph Lagrange of the Dominican convent of Saint Étienne in Jerusalem published a ground-plan of the ruins on the summit and some drawings of architectural fragments; a few years later another missionary, Father Barnabé Meistermann, published a similar plan; see Maughan 1873: 112–13. Lagrange 1897: 117–21; on Lagrange's mission, see Labib 1961: 140 Meistermann 1909: 150–1, figures 32–3.

66. Jacopo 1950: 198 note 243; Daumas 1951: 378; Amantos 1953: 17. The only reference to the Jabal Mūsā ruins in the literature produced by the Michigan, Princeton and Alexandria expedition under Kurt Weizmann (1904–1993) appears in a footnote, see Forsyth 1968: 14 note 17. Peter Grossmann briefly dealt with what was visible in the 1980s, see Grossmann 1989: 1906–7. A longer discussion and a reconstruction were published in 2000 by Uzi Dahari, see Dahari 2000: 29–34.

67. Panagiōtidē *et al.* 2002; Kalopissi-Verti 2006; Panayotidi & Kalopissi-Verti 2007; Koufopoulos & Myriantheos-Koufopoulou 2010; Kalopissi-Verti & Panayotidi 2010; *Master Plan* 2010: 55–6; Koufopoulos & Myriantheos 2014: 110–13, figures 1–5. See also *Egeria* 2008: 79–80.

68. Koufopoulos & Myriantheos-Koufopoulou 2010: 110.

69. Panayotidi & Kalopissi-Verti 2007: no pagination; Kalopissi-Verti & Panayotidi 2010: 90.

70. Koufopoulos & Myriantheos-Koufopoulou 2010: 115.

71. For a comparative section of the two basilicas, see Koufopoulos & Myriantheos-Koufopoulou 2010: 114, figure 5.

72. Koufopoulos & Myriantheos 2014: 110–13.

73. Ševčenko 1966: 263, figures 12A and 12B. Author's translation.

74. Panayotidi & Kalopissi-Verti 2007: no pagination; Kalopissi-Verti & Panayotidi 2010: 93–6; based on research by Charikleia Diamanti and Maria Skordara. Also see Gorin-Rosen 2000: 238–42; Calderon 2000: 186; Ballet 2001: 45–6

75. Dahari 2000: 29–34.

76. Dahari 2000: 30.

77. Dahari 2000: 32–4; Dansette 2001: 70; Koufopoulos & Myriantheos-Koufopoulou 2010: 117.

78. Panayotidi & Kalopissi-Verti 2007: no pagination; Kalopissi-Verti & Panayotidi 2010: 82.

79. Dahari 2000: 60.

80. Kraemer 1958: 251–60; Mayerson 1963: 165–6, 169; Mayerson 1964: 188; Mayerson 1994: 239. On the value of *solidi*, see John 1992: 110–11, 231–2.

81. Anastase 1884: 398; Grēgoriadēs 1875: 72–6; Labib 1961: 33, 71; Weitzmann 1980: 91, 153–4; Meimarēs 1985: 11, 15, 66; Tarnanidēs 1988: 22–7; Mayerson 1994: 238–9; Chitty 1995: 168, 170; Dansette 2001: 78; Wolff 2003: 210; Aleksidze *et al.* 2005: 361–2; Ratliff 2008: 15–16.
82. Maraval 1985: 310.
83. Dahari 2000: 30.
84. For the Greek text and a Latin translation, see Joannis 1860a; for an English translation, see John 1959. Also see Anastase 1902b: 6; Amantos 1953: 20–1; John 1959: 13–17; Skrobucha 1966: 37–42; Huber 1979: 210–11; Kazhdan & Nelson 1991; Chitty 1995: 172–5; *Synaxis* 1998: 161–2; Duffy 1999: 2, 2 notes 4–5; Dahari 2000: 23.
85. Labib 1961: 12; Dahari 2000: 69; *Egeria* 2008: 87–8.
86. Eddé *et al.* 1997: 102.
87. Gregorius 1899: 261; Eckenstein 1921: 130–1; Amantos 1953: 22; Labib 1961: 23; Maraval 1985: 308 note 467; Chitty 1995: 170, 173; Dahari 2000: 23.
88. Mayerson 1983: 55–6; John 1992: 37.
89. Skrobucha 1966: 43–4; Huber 1979: 202–3.
90. Finkelstein 1985: 42–60, figures B–S, 1–16; Dahari 2000: 38–49, 150–8.
91. Mansi 1771: 194; Meistermann 1909: 120; Eckenstein 1921: 137; Amantos 1953: 25, 28, 82; Skrobucha 1966: 35; Kamil 1991: 27; Dahari 2000: 54.
92. Dahari 2000: 94, table 4.
93. Mayerson 1986: 44; Popescu-Belis 2001: 111; Grossmann 2002: 36–9, 54–6.
94. Mayerson 1964: 191; Grossmann 2002: 39.
95. English translation in Dahari 2000: 29.

Chapter 3

1. Walser 1979: 224–5; Cytryn-Silverman 2001: 5–6.
2. Henniker 1823: 234. The story was also told to A. Morison in 1697; see Morison 1704: 95. Also see Manginis 2015b: 215.
3. Burckhardt 1822: 546–8; Pigafetta 1837: 37; Eckenstein 1921: 134–5; Golubovich 1923: 90–105; Rabino 1938: 39–40; Amantos 1953: 26–7; Skrobucha 1966: 57–9; *Perigraphē* 1978: 118; Hobbs 1995: 159–61; Mouton & Popescu-Belis 2006: 33; *Egeria* 2008: 243–4.
4. Ratliff 2008: 14–15; Manginis 2015b: 215.
5. Skrobucha 1966: 53–4; Hobbs 1995: 165–8.
6. El Cheikh 2004: 3.

7. Mukaddasi 1897: 65; Le Strange 1890: 73. On al-Muqaddasī, see Le Strange 1890: 5–6; Eckenstein 1921: 143–4; Manley & Abdel-Hakim 2006: 246.

8. Anastase 1902a: 61. Author's translation. Anastase 1902a: 61; Anastase 1902b: 10 note 4, 45–6 note 3.

9. Kraemer 1958: 205–6, papyrus 72; Negev 1977b: 78; Mayerson 1982: 47 note 10; Negev 1986: 129; Mayerson 1994: 242; Hoyland 2006: 401, 401 note 33.

10. Kraemer 1958: 207–8, papyrus 73; Negev 1977b: 78; Mayerson 1982: 47 note 10; Negev 1986: 129; Mayerson 1994: 242.

11. Kraemer 1958: 257; Mayerson 1989: 73; Manginis 2015b: 216.

12. On Yāqūt, see Le Strange 1890: 8–9. Translated by the author after the French tradition in al-Makrizi 1908: 202–3.

13. Matthews 1949: xii, 16, 143 note 47.

14. Matthews 1949: xiii, 76.

15. Ḥijjāwī 1996: 227–8.

16. Mayerson 1964: 156–69, 177–99; Kamil 1991: 10.

17. Kawatoko 1995: 53–9; Kawatoko 1996: 67–77; Grossmann 2002: 41–2.

18. Baronius 1869: 91; *Vita Pauli* 1892: 33; Eckenstein 1921: 138.

19. Quote from Meinardus 1970: 253–4 note 2. See also Meistermann 1909: 142–3; Champdor 1963: 49; Kamil 1991: 71–2; Dansette 2001: 68–9.

20. Meinardus 1970: 253–5; Dansette 2001: 69. The story appears several times, often with variations, see Thietmarus 1857: 46–7; Anglure 1878: 49; Poggibonsi 1881: 146–9; Martoni 1895: 608; Thietmar 1936: 60–6; Poggibonsi 1945: 129–30; Frescobaldi *et al.* 1948: 60–1, 114–16, 200–1; Jacopo 1950: 74–5; Coppin 1971: 269; Nektarios 1980: 201–4; Mouton & Popescu-Belis 2006: 36–7. For a variant, see Tafur 1874: 92–3; Tafur 1926: 82; Tafur 1934: 70–1.

21. *Egeria* 2008: 83, 89–90.

22. Anastase 1902a: 81–2.

23. Stone 1982a: 35.

24. Stone 1982a: 36–52; Stone 1982b: 28–31; Mayerson 1982: 44–57; Mayerson 1994: 239.

25. Stone 1982a: 5–6, 16, 22–3, 65–86; Stone 1982b: 28.

26. Ševčenko 1966: 258; Stone 1982b: 30–1; Talbot 2008: 39.

27. On Georgians, see Stone 1982b: 31.

28. Meimarēs 1985: 11, 66–7.

29. Swanson 2001: 109–15, 116–17, 116–17 note 42, 126; Ratliff 2008: 16.

30. Ševčenko 1966: 264, figures 13, 14. Author's translation.

31. El Cheikh 2004: 119.

32. Weitzmann 1980: 86–7; Weitzmann 1982c: 63–80, 93.
33. Anonymous 1680: 220.
34. Eckenstein 1921: 136–7; Labib 1961: 23–4; Skrobucha 1966: 68; Hobbs 1995: 224–5.
35. Panayotidi & Kalopissi-Verti 2007: no pagination; Kalopissi-Verti & Panayotidi 2010: 98–100; based on research by Charikleia Diamanti and Maria Skordara.
36. Anastase 1902a: 87. Author's translation; see also Eckenstein 1921: 135–6; Murray 1935: 266; *Perigraphē* 1978: 113; Chitty 1995: 176; Hobbs 1995: 158–9.
37. Grossmann 2002: 40–1, 41 note 80.
38. Mayerson 1964: 197.
39. Translation by Christos Bitzis-Politis from the German translation in Eutychios 1985: 90.
40. Popescu-Belis 2000: 379, 382–4, 385–6.
41. Décobert 1992: 279–80; Levy-Rubin 2000: 261–5.
42. Eddé *et al.* 1997: 36, 150; El Cheikh 2004: 55.
43. Eddé *et al.* 1997: 69; Levy-Rubin 2000: 268; Swanson 2001: 124, 124 note 75.
44. Degg 1990: 301, figure 5; Nur & Ron 1996: 75–6, figure 2.
45. Amiran 1950–1: 226–7; Amiran 1952: 49–51; Ambraseys 1962: 78; Russell 1985: 39, 46–9. For the 746 earthquake, see www.ngdc.noaa.gov.
46. Monconys 1973: 101. Author's translation. On Monconys, see Eckenstein 1921: 178; Labib 1961: 95–7.
47. The synopsis of Saint Catherine's life and martyrdom here is based on the Greek text of Symeon 1864b: 275–302.
48. Walsh 2007: 24–7; 34–8.
49. Symeon 1864b: 276–302. On the *vita*, see Eckenstein 1921: 138–9; Walsh 2007: 28–9.
50. Kamil 1991: 23; Wolff 2003: 209; Lewis 2006: 115; Walsh 2007: 40–1; *Egeria* 2008: 81–3.
51. Kamil 1991: 24; Walsh 2007: 40, 44.
52. Walsh 2007: 44, 44 note 29. On P. de Milly, see Barber 2003: 60–78.
53. Thietmarus 1857: 42–3; Thietmar 1936: 44–54.
54. Kamil 1991: 24; Dahari 2000: 2; Dansette 2001: 73–4; Walsh 2007: 42.
55. Nelson & Collins 2007: 266–7; *Egeria* 2008: 270–1.
56. *Translatio* 1903: 427. Author's translation. Also see Michelant & Raynaud 1882: 63.
57. Mouton & Popescu-Belis 2006: 38.
58. Mouton & Popescu-Belis 2006: 38.

59. Kamil 1991: 28–9; Wolff 2003: 218–19.

60. Mabillon 1707: 341–3. For a Latin narration of Symeon Pentaglossos' travels and of the Saint's miracles, see *Translatio* 1903: 423–38. See also Eckenstein 1921: 139; Amantos 1953: 30, 34; Skrobucha 1966: 68–73; Kamil 1991: 23; Lewis 2006: 115.

61. Mabillon 1707: 342; Hugo 1881: 252–3; Eckenstein 1921: 140–1; Labib 1961: 29.

62. Kamil 1991: 24.

63. Eckenstein 1921: 161–2; Skrobucha 1966: 65; Wolff 2000: 35.

64. Sigoli 1843: 97. English translation in Frescobaldi *et al.* 1948: 196–7.

65. Hese 1870: 181. On J.W. de Hese, see Saint-Génois 1846: volume I, 36–7; Eckenstein 1921: 167 note 2, 168.

66. Aerts 1873: 563–6. On Jean Aerts, see Saint-Génois 1846: volume II, 205; Eckenstein 1921: 168.

67. Tōmadakēs 1990: 16; Amantos 1953: 42–3; Sōtēriou & Sōtēriou 1958: 9; Kraack 2001: 87–9.

68. Turner & Turner 1978: 175–80, 233.

69. Turner & Turner 1978: 187–8, 197.

70. Skrobucha 1966: 78; Hobbs 1995: 226.

71. Deluz 2001: 187.

72. Dansette 2001: 67, 68.

73. Giustiniano 1672: 121–3; Meistermann 1909: 122; Eckenstein 1921: 139, 160–1; Zachos 1937: 32–3; Rabino 1938: 65 note 2; Labib 1961: 84–5, plate VIII; Skrobucha 1966: 91–2; Turner & Turner 1978: 175–6; Kamil 1991: 28; Dansette 2001: 74–5; Kraack 2001: 93.

74. Labib 1961: 26.

75. Morison 1704: 111; Fabri 1897: 600–1; Harff 1946: 142; Blunt 1953: 68; Holt 1998: 21. On P. Della Valle, see Holt 1998: 15.

76. Eddé *et al.* 1997: 100–2.

77. Albertus 1611: 376; Wilken 1813: 402–3; Albericus 1894: 708; Grēgoriadēs 1875: 80; Meistermann 1909: 120; Eckenstein 1921: 147; Daumas 1951: 384; Amantos 1953: 34–5, 43; Labib 1961: 34; Skrobucha 1966: 96; Kamil 1991: 28; Hobbs 1995: 226; Walsh 2007: 44.

78. Eckenstein 1921: 170–1; Hobbs 1995: 227–31.

79. Gutwein 1981: 247–8; Grossmann 2002: 31–3.

80. Stern 1964a: 39, 50, 55, 61–2, 67, 72–3, 78–9, 83, 171–4; Deluz 2001: 184–96.

81. Burckhardt 1822: 542–3.

82. Rabino 1938: 35–6; Kraack 2001: 92–3, 96–7.

83. Taifel 1598: 27; Fabri 1897: 612–14; Teufel 1972: 169; Sicard 1982: 131. On C. Sicard, see Eckenstein 1921: 180; Manley & Abdel-Hakim 2006: 248.

84. Morison 1704: 109; Pococke 1814: 293.

85. Anglure 1878: 51; Meistermann 1909: 150–1; Rabino 1938: 36–7; Labib 1961: 45; Palerne 1991: 151; Dahari 2000: 31.

86. Bremond 1680: 144–5; Pitts *et al.* 1949: 81.

87. Fabri 1843: 459; Fabri 1897: 559–60; Prescott 1957: 86–7. On Fabri, see Röhricht & Meisner 1880: 280; Davies 1911: v–vi; Eckenstein 1921: 168; Manley & Abdel-Hakim 2006: 242.

88. Georgius 1721: 498; Van Egmont & Heyman 1759: 169; Prefetto 1810: 242–3; Prefetto 1812: 283; Turner 1820: 436–7; Burckhardt 1822: 566; Wellsted 1838: 105–6; Schubert 1839: plates 6–8; Seetzen 1855: 83–4 (also quoted in Ritter 1866: 210); Schubert *et al.* 1856: plates 10–11; Ritter 1866: 210; Hull 1885: 53; Lombay 1892: 76; Jullien 1893: 127.

89. Dansette 2001: 83; Talbot 2008: 39.

90. Fabri 1897: 608–10; Eckenstein 1921: 153; Jacopo 1950: 8; Labib 1961: 56.

91. Saint-Génois 1846: volume I, 14–15.

92. Fabri 1897: 625.

93. Fabri 1897: 613–14; Kraack 2001: 88–9, 93–106.

94. Manginis 2015b: 214.

95. *Perigraphē* 1978: 123–4. Author's translation.

96. *Perigraphē* 1978: 123–4. On this tradition, see Van Egmont & Heyman 1759: 163; Grēgoriadēs 1875: 78–80; Amantos 1953: 31; Sōtēriou & Sōtēriou 1958: 8; Nektarios 1980: 193–4; Eddé *et al.* 1997: 71–2.

97. Adémar 1897: 169–70 (III: 47). Author's translation, from the Latin original and the French translation in Adémar 1947: 186–7 (chapter XLVII). On the text, see Eckenstein 1921: 144.

98. Manginis 2015b: 214.

99. Pruitt 2013.

100. Pruitt 2013.

101. Manginis 2015b: 214.

102. Manginis 2015b: 214–15.

103. Dahari 2000: 100–1.

104. Amantos 1953: 55–6; Skrobucha 1966: 95.

105. Manginis 2015b.

106. Moritz 1918: 52–3. Translation by Melanie Gibson and the author. German translation in Moritz 1918: 53; French translation in Rabino

1935: 36, 87–8, 215, inscription 54, plate XI and Rabino 1938: 41–2, 107.
107. Moritz 1918: 57–60; Skrobucha 1966: 62.
108. Manginis 2015b: 215.
109. Nelson & Collins 2007, 222–5, entry by Linda Komaroff.
110. Moritz 1918: 56–8.
111. Finkelstein & Perevolotsky 1990: 69; Avni 1994: 84–91, 95.
112. Manginis 2015b: 216–17.
113. Le Strange 1890: 73. French translation in Édrisi 1836: 332. On al-Idrīsī, see Eckenstein 1921: 146; Le Strange 1890: 7.
114. Negev 1977b: 80.
115. Moraitou 2007: 186–7, figure 15; Manginis 2015b: 213.
116. Mouton & Popescu-Belis 2006: 27–8.
117. Thietmarus 1857: 42 and Thietmar 1936: 40. Author's translation.
118. Thietmarus 1857: 42 note 504; Eckenstein 1921: 151; Thietmar 1936: 41 note 64; Mouton & Popescu-Belis 2006: 42.
119. Mouton & Popescu-Belis 2006: 27–8, 42–5, 52; Heidemann *et al.* 1997: 81–107.
120. Fratres Minores 1919: 72. For similar mentions, see Frescobaldi *et al.* 1948: 60.
121. Pardieu 1851: 189; Eckenstein 1921: 185–6; Mouton & Popescu-Belis 2006: 43 note 132.
122. Grēgoriadēs 1875: 81–2; Luke 1927: v, 58; *Perigraphē* 1978: 124–5.
123. Panayotidi & Kalopissi-Verti 2007: no pagination; Kalopissi-Verti & Panayotidi 2010: 102–4; material studied by Ioannis Meimaris.
124. Wilkinson 1977: 12.
125. English translation in Wilkinson 1977: 138. On the text, see Eckenstein 1921: 137.
126. Dahari 2000: 38.
127. English translation in Fetellus 1897: 15–16.
128. Anonymous 1625: 1243. Lina Eckenstein (1921: 163–4) dated it around 1425.
129. Thietmarus 1857: 41–8 (Latin); Thietmar 1936 (Dutch): 69. On Thietmar, see Eckenstein 1921: 150–2.
130. Mouskes 1836: CCVII–CCXXVII, 422–3; Michelant & Raynaud 1882: 63–4, 82–3, 98, 119, 185–6, 196–7; Albertus 1906: 183, 185; Anonymous 1906: 403; *De Via* 1906: 406; *Itinerarium* 1906: 409; Labib 1961: 31–3; Deluz 2001: 186.
131. Benjamin 1840: 159; Benjamin 1983: 135. On Benjamin, see Eckenstein 1921: 146.
132. Vilnay 1963: XXXVI, XL, 217–19.

133. Harant 1608: 89–90; Harant 1855: 74; French translation in Harant 1972: 117–18.

134. Fabri 1897: 553–4. On the prohibition, see Eckenstein 1921: 172. The story appeared centuries later in Dumas 1839a: 93; Dumas 1839b: 250.

135. Stephens 1837: 284; Stephens 1970: 194–5; on Stephens, see Davis 1996: 32–5; Manley & Abdel-Hakim 2006: 249.

136. Amantos 1953: 47.

137. Kubiak 1970: 13–15, figures 10a–b, 11a–b, plates 2/12, 3/13 ('*type I*'); Rosenthal & Sivan 1978: 153 (lamp 633).

138. Kubiak 1970: 14; Philon 1980: 61, figure 133.

139. Dansette 2001: 65.

140. Skrobucha 1966: 80–2; Hobbs 1995: 234–5; Dansette 2001: 68–71.

141. Poggibonsi 1945: 131. Author's translation. On N. da Poggibonsi, see Poggibonsi 1881: 123–63; Poggibonsi 1927: 1, 15; Poggibonsi 1945: 122–34; Frescobaldi *et al.* 1948: 10; Wolff 2000: 36–45; Wolff 2003: 97, 197, 210, 221–4. The paintings were also seen by N. de Martoni in September 1394; see Martoni 1895: 609.

142. Paisios 1978: 70–5, 109–10; Nektarios 1980: 197–8.

143. Michelant & Raynaud 1882: 104; Fratres Minores 1919: 72; *Peregrinationes* 1927: 355. Similarly brief are accounts of or references to other pilgrimages: Röhricht & Meisner 1880: 59, 468–9; Robert 1884: 13; Labib 1961: 41, 42.

144. Frameynsperg 1725: 358–9; Röhricht & Meisner 1880: 468; Eckenstein 1921: 158; Dansette 2001: 66.

145. Eckenstein 1921: 157, 158; Letts 1949: 47; Labib 1961: 36–40; Milton 1996: 169–95; Manley & Abdel-Hakim 2006: 245.

146. For fourteenth-century pilgrims, see List of Pilgrims and Travellers and Baldensel 1725: 343–5; Suchen 1848: 13; Anglure 1878: 46–53; Röhricht & Meisner 1880: 465–7; Brygg 1884: 382; Sudheim 1884: 346–8; Reboldis 1890: 153, 166–9; Reboldis 1919: 329, 335–42; Eckenstein 1921: 157; Sudheim 1937: 134–6; Frescobaldi *et al.* 1948: 10–11; Labib 1961: 43–7; Champdor 1963: 25; Dansette 2001: 66.

147. Frescobaldi *et al.* 1948: 58, 196. See also Jacopo 1950: 77; Poggibonsi 1945: 133. Fifteenth-century pilgrims were equally undecided; see Fabri 1897: 550, 570, 584–7; Harff 1946: xxv. On Frescobaldi, Gucci and Sigoli, see Frescobaldi *et al.* 1948: 20–4; Eckenstein 1921: 158; Dansette 2001: 66; Wolff 2003: 208.

148. Frescobaldi *et al.* 1948: 111.

149. Jacques 1895: 155–302, sketch on page 235; Eckenstein 1921: 158–60; Jacopo 1950: 72–9; Vilnay 1963: XIV. On Jacopo, see Eckenstein 1921: 157; Frescobaldi *et al.* 1948: 10.

150. Blunt 1953: 64.
151. For fifteenth-century pilgrims, see List of Pilgrims and Travellers and Breidenbach *et al.* 1625: 1381; Georgius 1721: 495–507; Saint-Génois 1846: volume I, 33–4, 34–6, 155–92; Lengherand 1861: viii–ix, 158–66, 238–9 notes 153–8; Morin 1862: 1–9; Röhricht & Meisner 1880: 104, 114, 313, 487–8, 499, 522–3; Eckenstein 1921: 167–8; Labib 1961: 51–3, 54–60, 61–5; Mitchell 1965: 143–8; Capodilista 1966: 33, 227–32; Brasca 1966: 135–9; Wolff 2003: 56. The account of Bernhard von Breydenbach's 1483 Holy Land pilgrimage was the first to be printed with woodcuts, see Breidenbach *et al.* 1625: 1380; Röhricht & Meisner 1880: 129, 142–3; Davies 1911: i–xx, xxix; Eckenstein 1921: 167–8; Fontaine 1955: 60; Vilnay 1963: XIV.
152. Fabri 1897: 558. Also see Bianchi 1500: no pagination; Bianchi 1800: 128; Eckenstein 1921: 170; Vilnay 1963: XV.
153. Eckenstein 1921: 168.
154. Fabri 1897: 597–9.
155. Rabino 1938: 54, 110; Weitzmann 1980: 88; Kraack 2001: 97.
156. Lannoy 1840: 46, 67; Saint-Génois 1846: volume I, 30–2, 127–53; Lannoy 1878: xviii–xix, 68–9, 94–5; Adornes 1893: 168–9; Eckenstein 1921: 167 Labib 1961: 47.
157. Rabino 1935: 55, 57–60; Rabino 1938: 66–79; Labib 1961: 82–3, plate VII; Kamil 1991: 30, 52.
158. Champdor 1963: 22–5.
159. Yumiba 1984: 67/191, 196–8, 129–30; Féhérvári 2000: 251, number 313; Watson 2004: 404, 417–25, 420–3.
160. Fabri 1897: 549; Lengherand 1861: 161–3.
161. Fabri 1843: 462. English translation in Fabri 1897: 564. For the pilgrim group, see Fabri 1897: 563, 565.
162. Rabino 1938: 40; Hobbs 1995: 155–7.
163. Wolff 2003: 212. On F. Suriano, see Manley & Abdel-Hakim 2006: 249.
164. Kiechel 1866: 349; Kiechel 1972: 60; Turner 1820: 443, 445–8; Burckhardt 1822: 556; Amantos 1953: 48.
165. Athanasius 1727.
166. Grēgoriadēs 1875: 141–2; Rabino 1938: 2–3, table on page 3; Skrobucha 1966: 60, 93; Kamil 1991: 30, 31; Hobbs 1995: 90; Dansette 2001: 76–7; Mouton & Popescu-Belis 2006: 30–1, 36–7.
167. Dansette 2001: 80–2.
168. Grēgoriadēs 1875: 85; Amantos 1953: 33, 53–4.
169. For a possible three-year *kleismos*, see Taifel 1598: 33–4; Röhricht & Meisner 1880: 546; Teufel 1972: 176. J. Palerne witnessed a single

monk guarding the Monastery; see Palerne 1991: 146–54; on J. Palerne, see Labib 1961: 78–9.

170. Frescobaldi *et al.* 1948: 116. English translation by Theophilus Bellorini and Eugene Hoade.

171. Harant 1608: 89; Harant 1855: 74; Harant 1972: 117.

172. Burckhardt 1822: 566–7; Eckenstein 1921: 127.

173. Harant 1608: 83–111; French translation in Harant 1972: 109–43; Czech simplified version in Harant 1855: 69–90 and Czech abridged version in Harant 1988: 130–8. On K. Harant, see Harant 1972: 1–13; Wolff 2000: 45–58; Wolff 2003: 214–15.

174. Harant 1608: 85–6. Author's translation, from the French translation in Harant 1972: 113. Ten years earlier, on 10 June 1588, Samuel Kiechel was also offered some wine by the 'vicarius' in a cup; see Kiechel 1866: 359; Kiechel 1972: 77.

175. Dobson 1925: 55–6. On A.M.R. Dobson, see Manley & Abdel-Hakim 2006: 241–2.

176. Evans 1997: 178, 191–2. On Chinese pottery in Rudolf II's collections, see Venturi 1885: 9; Zimmermann 1905: XXVI–XXVII, XXXIII, LII–LIII, LXII, LXV; Morávek 1937: 27; Scheicher 1997: 104–11.

177. Rinaldi 1989: 71, decoration V and 88, figure 68 (dated to 1575–1615); Carré *et al.* 1994: 340–1; Shulsky 1998–9: 90–1, figure 7.

178. Frescobaldi *et al.* 1948: 64. English translation by Theophilus Bellorini and Eugene Hoade; it has not been possible to find the Italian original. The Ṭūr port was also described by F. Fabri (1897: 574).

179. Fiorentino 1550: 368v; Bracciolini 1723: 139; Tafur 1874: 92–8; Tafur 1934: 70–5; English translation in Tafur 1926: 8–9, 83–6. On P. Tafur, see Mas Latrie 1884: 283; Eckenstein 1921: 166; Vives 1938: 132–3; Kamil 1991: 30; Manley & Abdel-Hakim 2006: 249. On the date of his Horeb visit, see Vives 1938: 157; Dansette 2001: 66.

180. Fabri 1897: 575; Hobbs 1995: 84; Dansette 2001: 68, 71.

181. Kawatoko 1995: 54, plate 35; Kawatoko 1996: 37–8, plate 32; Kawatoko 1998: 47, plates 22–23.

182. For other sixteenth-century pilgrims, see List of Pilgrims and Travellers and Crusius 1584: 229–36, 527–8; Breidenbach *et al.* 1625: 1377, 1379; broadside print in Furtenbach 1653; Pigafetta 1837: 31–41; Röhricht & Meisner 1880: 444, 528, 530, 532–3, 533–6, 536–8, 538–9, 541–2; Labib 1961: 65–70, 73–8, 7–82; Lichtenstein 1972: 18–20; Fernberger 1999: 29–33.

183. Hobbs 1995: 221.

184. Sandys 1625: 905–6. On G. Sandys, see Fedden 1958: 8–10.

185. Brown 1739. On Edward Brown's 'voyages', see Fedden 1958: 11, 11 note 1.
186. Rooke 1783: 71.
187. Browne 1799: 179.
188. Pitts *et al.* 1949: 82. Another British traveller was Thomas Shaw; see Shaw 1738: 350–3. On T. Shaw, see Manley & Abdel-Hakim 2006: 248.
189. Coppin 1971: 265–75, xii–xiii.
190. Eckenstein 1921: 180; Pitts *et al.* 1949: 163–4; Labib 1961: 101.
191. Eckenstein 1921: 176–8.
192. Morison 1704: 113, on Morison, see Labib 1961: 98–100; Van Egmont & Heyman 1759: 178; Kergorlay 1911: 65; Rabino 1935: 69; Labib 1961: 102; Sicard 1982: 131.
193. Thevet 1984: 147–8. On A. Thevet, see Labib 1961: 72–3.
194. Belon du Mans 1970: 127, 128b. On P. Belon du Mans, see Eckenstein 1921: 175; Labib 1961: 71–2; Manley & Abdel-Hakim 2006: 240.
195. Palerne 1991: 152; Coppin 1971: 268; Labib 1961: 96.
196. Prefetto 1810: 242; Prefetto 1812: 283; Labib 1961: 102–3; Sicard 1982: 131.
197. Niebuhr 1776: 198–9; Niebuhr 1973: 50–1; Niebuhr 1994: 195. On C. Niebuhr, see Manley & Abdel-Hakim 2006: 246–7.
198. Burckhardt 1822: 566.
199. Sōtēriou & Sōtēriou 1958: 1.
200. Taifel 1598: 29; Teufel 1972: 171; Kiechel 1866: 354; Kiechel 1972: 69–70.
201. Coppin 1971: 270; Palerne 1991: 151.
202. Skrobucha 1966: 97–8.
203. Barros 1552: 92r–93r; Barros 1932: 291–4; Jullien 1893: 106.
204. Grēgoriadēs 1875: 88–9; Amantos 1953: 46. On the mosque and the district, see Behrens-Abouseif 2007: 121–6.
205. Stern 1964a: 6, 41, 51, 74, 80, 100; Labib 1961: 74; *Perigraphē* 1978: 122–3; Dansette 2001: 83–4.
206. Grēgoriadēs 1875: 144; Skrobucha 1966: 86; *Perigraphē* 1978: 122.
207. Stern 1960: 439–55; Stern 1964a; Stern 1964b: 10–32; Stern 1966: 233–76; Humbsch 1976: 186–90, 195–8, 238–47, 349–52, 413–14, 433–43, 456–65, 478–90; Heidemann *et al.* 1997: 81–107; Mouton & Popescu-Belis 2006: 26–8, 42–5, 52.
208. Fabri 1897: 583, 626.
209. Castro 1625: 1141. It seems that no Portuguese travellers attempted the Sinai pilgrimage. For a brief mention, see Barbessa 1550: 310r, 313v.

210. Tshelebi 1980: 33.
211. Kiechel 1866: 349–60; Kiechel 1972: 60–79.
212. Jullien 1893: 106; Skrobucha 1966: 78–9; Tōmadakēs 1990: 16.
     On the Hellenisation of art, see Weitzmann 1980: 96, 154. On the
     destruction of Latin manuscripts, see Weitzmann 1980: 154.
213. Libois 1993: 63.
214. Grēgoriadēs 1875: 97–116; Eckenstein 1921: 148–50, 166; Amantos
     1953: 38–42, 48–50, 59; Labib 1961: 75; Tōmadakēs 1990: 16.
215. Rabino 1938: 4; Amantos 1953: 49; Tōmadakēs 1990: 14; Dansette
     2001: 77.
216. Grēgoriadēs 1875: 76–8; Amantos 1953: 44–6; Skrobucha 1966:
     43–7.
217. Nektarios 1980. On Nektarios, see Stern 1960: 439–43; Stern 1964a:
     5–6; Popescu-Belis 2001: 117–18; Popescu-Belis & Mouton 2006:
     190, 192–5.
218. *Proskynētaria* 2003.
219. *Proskynētaria* 2003: 72, 80, 89, 97, 98, 112, 113, 123, 124, 139, 143,
     146; Skrobucha 1966: 80.
220. *Proskynētaria* 2003: 77, 98, 109–10, 124.
221. *Proskynētaria* 2003: 139.
222. Paisios 1978: 59–60; *Proskynētaria* 2003: 60–67, 151–221.
223. Paisios 1978: 30–41, 109–10.
224. Mouton 2001b: 198–9, 206; Hobbs 1995: 158.
225. *Perigraphē* 1978: 114–15.
226. Weitzmann 1980: 158.
227. Weitzmann 1980: 159; Ettinghausen & Grabar 1987: 198, figure 187.
228. Richards 2001: 150.
229. Van Egmont & Heyman 1759: 168.
230. Niebuhr 1776: 198–9; Niebuhr 1973: 51; Niebuhr 1994: 195.
231. Georgius 1721: 498. Translated in Skrobucha 1966: 80. See
     Eckenstein 1921: 127–8; Hobbs 1995: 169.
232. Röhricht & Meisner 1880: 472; Katzenellenbogen 1882: 355; Kraack
     2001: 90, 90 note 11.
233. Frescobaldi *et al.* 1948: 58 (for Frescobaldi), 197 (for Sigoli).
234. Burckhardt 1822: 485, 552, 547, 586.
235. Pitts *et al.* 1949: 80.
236. Koufopoulos & Myriantheos-Koufopoulou 2010: 108.
237. Labib 1961: 77.
238. Nektarios 1980: 168. Author's translation.
239. Neitzschitz 1666: 211–2; Neitzschitz 1674: 170–1. On von
     Neitzschitz, see Eckenstein 1921: 178.
240. Morison 1704: 97.

Chapter 4

1. Burckhardt 1822: 488–596.
2. Ritter 1848; Knobel 1857: 187–95; Kiepert 1859; Altmüller 1861.
3. Aharoni 1961: 170; Nicholson 1973; Vaux 1978a: 393–452; Meshel 1982; Niehaus 1995; Briend 2003: 2053–8.
4. Rabino 1935: 28, 82; Amantos 1953: 46–69; Sōtēriou & Sōtēriou 1958: 4; Skrobucha 1966: 87.
5. Feyerabend 1584; Crusius 1584: 229–36, 261–3, 527–8. On Purchas, see Breidenbach *et al.* 1625: 1377, 1379–81; Castro 1625: 1141; Sandys 1625: 905–6; on Sinai in Purchas, see Beckingham 1997: 226–7. Also see Fiorentino 1550; Barros 1552; Barros 1932.
6. Quaresmius 1639: 438, 954–9, 985, 992–6, 1001–5.
7. Saint-Génois 1846: volume I, 37–8; Turner & Turner 1978: xviii, 201.
8. Kircher 1636: 204–19. See Blunt 1953: 67–8; Monconys 1973: 28–9, 108–9; Bottini 1995: 98, 101.
9. Pococke 1814: 284, 289. On R. Pococke, see Eckenstein 1921: 181; Manley & Abdel-Hakim 2006: 248. His account was often quoted; see Conder 1830: 136–202; Thompson *et al.* 1977: 435–50. On R. Clayton, see Manley & Abdel-Hakim 2006: 241. Also see Prefetto 1810: 217–18; Prefetto 1812: 253–5; Grēgoriadēs 1875: 137 note.
10. Eckenstein 1921: 89.
11. Niebuhr 1994: i–v.
12. Author's translation after Lottin de Laval 1855–9a: 1–31. On Lottin de Laval, see Labib 1961: 130–1.
13. Major studies: *CIS* 1907: 152–72; Cantineau 1930: 22–5; Cantineau 1932: 47–8; Stone 1992b: 85–97, 99. Recent reviews: Taylor 2001: 148–51; Briend 2003: 1991–9.
14. Forster 1844.
15. Forster 1851: plate VII, opposite page 163; Forster 1852: plate XV.
16. Forster 1851: plate IV, opposite page 95; Forster 1852: 11–15, plate I opposite page 46.
17. Forster 1862: 233, 241.
18. Forster 1854: 238–343, quote from page 237.
19. Forster 1860.
20. Forster 1856; Forster 1862: v–vii.
21. Forster 1865: 171–222.
22. Manginis 2015a.
23. Manginis 2015a: 67.
24. Olin 1843: 383. On S. Olin, see Manley & Abdel-Hakim 2006: 247.
25. Olin 1843: 401.
26. Maraval 1985: 75, 307; Hobbs 1995: 68.

27. Scheuchzer 1732: 26–7, 84–7, 87–95, 100–08, 114–6, 119–20, plates CXVII, CXLIX–CLI, CLII–CLV, CLIX–CLX, CLXIV, CLXVII.
28. Kempe 2006: 114–19.
29. Airy 1876: 55–6, 78–9.
30. Koller 1842; Vaczek & Buckland 1981: no pagination; Moscrop 2000: 45–8.
31. Seetzen 1855: 69–105, especially 81–6. On Seetzen's mission, see Stephens 1970: xxxi; *Seetzen* 1995: 17–21; Schienerl 2000: 64–7. Burckhardt 1822: 488–587. Rüppell 1829: 251–64; Rüppell 1838: 114–25.
32. Kinnear 1841: 77–93. On D. Roberts' trip, see Roberts 1994: 44–61; Manley & Abdel-Hakim 2006: 248. On J.G. Kinnear, see Manley & Abdel-Hakim 2006: 244.
33. Mazuel 1937: 17–22; Labib 1961: 114–16.
34. Mazuel 1937: 99–103. On Laborde, see Vilnay 1963: XXI–XXII; Manley & Abdel-Hakim 2006: 244.
35. Schaff 1878: 193. On Philip Schaff, see Manley & Abdel-Hakim 2006: 248.
36. Durbin 1845: 147.
37. Randall 1867: 289. For his Horeb trip, see Randall 1867: 285–345; Randall 1886: 34–420.
38. Olin 1843: 413.
39. Bonar 1857: 243. On H. Bonar, see Manley & Abdel-Hakim 2006: 240–1. Similar accusations were phrased by Burckhardt 1822: 579–81; Henniker 1823: 226–7; Olin 1843: 408, 412; Dawson Borrer, see Borrer 1845: 346; Durbin 1845: 150; Hamilton 1993: 21–2, 33–4; Bartlett 1862: 92; Bartlett 1879: 265; Schaff 1878: 186–7; Brockbank 1914: 32–3; Beadnell 1927: 172–3. See Hobbs 1995: 136–8, 233, 256–7.
40. Hamilton 1993: 34. On J. Hamilton, see Manley & Abdel-Hakim 2006: 243.
41. Crossley 1860: 5, 16, 17.
42. Warburton 1845: v.
43. Ridgaway 1876: 66.
44. Robinson 1867: 143–4; Platt 1842: 154–8; Fisk 1843: 150–1 note 1; Olin 1843: 412; Gasparin 1848: 57–64, 82; Ritter 1848; Ritter 1866: 242; Bonar 1857: 220; Beamont 1861: 72–5; Beamont 1871: 121; Schaff 1878: 192; Field 1883: 104–87; Jullien 1893: 105; Sutton 1913: 94.
45. Robinson 1867: 137.
46. Strauss 1848: 158–9; Strauss 1849: 125–6.
47. Jullien 1893: 105.

48. Adams 1879: 105.

49. Bartlett 1879: 275, 284. On S.C. Bartlett, see Manley & Abdel-Hakim 2006: 239.

50. Bonar 1857: 219. The same mistake was made by Arthur Warwick Sutton; see Sutton 1913: 101.

51. Bartlett 1862: 76; on W.H. Bartlett, see Manley & Abdel-Hakim 2006: 239–40. Short quote in Hazleton 1980: 3.

52. Wellsted 1838 and Wellsted 1842; Lepsius 1846a, Lepsius 1846b and Lepsius 1852; Olin 1843 and Olin 1848; Ritter 1848 and Ritter 1866; Strauss 1848 and Strauss 1849; for translations from French into English, see Laborde 1830 and Laborde 1836; Géramb 1839 and Geramb 1840.

53. Dumas 1839a: 104; Dumas 1839b: 260.

54. Géramb 1839: 225–6; Geramb 1840: 331. On M.-J. Géramb, see Labib 1961: 119–22.

55. Lepsius 1846a: 7. Translated in Lepsius 1846b: 10. On R. Lepsius, see Manley & Abdel-Hakim 2006: 245.

56. Gadsby 1864: 27–40. On J. Gadsby, see Manley & Abdel-Hakim 2006: 243.

57. Stanley 1887: 3–62. On A.P. Stanley, see Moscrop 2000: 46; Manley & Abdel-Hakim 2006: 248–9. Olin 1843: 375–422. Beamont 1861: 56–85. On W.J. Beamont, see Manley & Abdel-Hakim 2006: 240. Bonar 1857: 217–43.

58. Raboisson 1886: 308–10, plates 62–75; Raboisson 1887: 5–67. On A. Raboisson, see Labib 1961: 137–8.

59. Raboisson 1887: 53. Author's translation. On Palmer's murder, see Kitchener 1885: 199–200; Hazleton 1980: 4–8; Kamil 1991: 13–14; Moscrop 2000: 138–42.

60. Lottin de Laval 1855–9a: 163–74.

61. Coutelle 1832: 201–15; Laborde 1830: 66–8, translated into English in Laborde 1836: 228–45; Géramb 1839: 211–53, translated into English in Geramb 1840: 321–49; Auvergne 1854: 210–19; Pardieu 1851: 184–98 (on Pardieu, see Labib 1961: 129–30); (Amédée) de Damas 1864: 207–22, 243–65 (on Amédée, see Labib 1961: 131); Bida & Hachette 1864: 10–14; Stacquez 1865: 350–69 (on H.T.J. Stacquez, see Labib 1961: 133–6); Lenoir 1872: 232–55 (on Lenoir, see Labib 1961: 136–7; Manley & Abdel-Hakim 2006: 244–5); Lombay 1892: 73–80; Jullien 1893: 102–54; Francis Joseph 1895: 48–56; Sargenton-Galichon 1904: 70–106; Kergorlay 1911: 37–90.

62. Moscrop 2000: 41–2.

63. Prefetto 1810: 243, 248, 250, 250–1; Prefetto 1812: 284, 289, 291, 291–3.

64. Cart 1915: 148. Author's translation. For an account of his visit, see Cart 1915: 114–72.

65. (Amédée) de Damas 1864: 267–8. Author's translation.

66. Labib 1961: 112–3.

67. Platt 1842: 144–91; Gasparin 1848: 67–90; Loftus 1870: 176–187; Bensly 1896; Hornby 1907: 39–58 (on E. Hornby, see Manley & Abdel-Hakim 2006: 243). To this list should be added: Miss Bennet, see Dumas 1839a: 99; Dumas 1839b: 257; Charlotte Rowley, see Rowley-Conwy *et al.* 1998: 110; the Marquise de Roche-Dragon, see Labib 1961: 126; Miss Brocklehurst and Miss Booth, see Schaff 1878: 187; and Mary Eliza Rogers, see Rogers 1883: 230–8.

68. Dobson 1925: 1–4, 34–141.

69. Rowley-Conwy *et al.* 1998: 110.

70. Platt 1842: 150–1.

71. Sargenton-Galichon 1904: 85–94.

72. Hornby 1907: 46.

73. Platt 1842: 169.

74. Martineau 1848: 315. On H. Martineau, see Manley & Abdel-Hakim 2006: 246.

75. Lewis & Gibson 1999, a reprint of Gibson 1893 and Lewis 1898. On M. Dunlop Gibson, see Manley & Abdel-Hakim 2006: 243. On A. Smith Lewis, see Manley & Abdel-Hakim 2006: 245.

76. Sargenton-Galichon 1904: 83; Cart 1915: 159–61.

77. Wolff was a German Jew who converted to Christianity and lived in Britain; see Wolff 1824: 174–80; Wolff 1827a: 7–8; Wolff 1827b: 39–41. On J. Wolff, see Manley & Abdel-Hakim 2006: 250. See Wellsted 1838: 53–5, 80–106 (83–4, 84 note * for Wolff); German translation in Wellsted 1842: 69–85; Olin 1843: 375–422 (410–11 for Wolff); German translation in Olin 1848.

78. Quote from Carne 1830a: 223; see also Carne 1830b: 340–2. On J. Carne, see Manley & Abdel-Hakim 2006:241.

79. Wolff 1860: 198–9.

80. Burckhardt 1822: 609.

81. Carne 1885: 106. For J. Carne's Horeb stay, see Carne 1830a: 208–28; Carne 1885: 104–8.

82. Bartlett 1862: 91–2.

83. Measor 1844: 142.

84. Burckhardt 1822: 607.

85. Burckhardt 1822: 609.

86. Lepsius 1846a: 13–52; Lepsius 1846b: 21–92; Lepsius 1852: 338–71. On Lepsius' theory, see Kutscheit 1846: 19–28; Poole 1854: 12.

87. Kitto 1850: 137; Kitto 1860: 173–5. Forster 1862: 87–113; Forster 1865: 171–222. Lecointre 1882: 73–4, 77–9, 81–4. Lecointre never visited either Horeb or Sirbāl; see Raboisson 1887: 9–36. Petrie 1906: 247–54.

88. Robinson 1867: 106. On E. Robinson, see Davis 1996: 34–7, 113–15; Moscrop 2000: 19; Manley & Abdel-Hakim 2006: 248.

89. On E. Lear's Sinai experience, see Khatib 2001: 197–211. Frith *et al.* 1860b: plates *The Convent of Sinai, and Plain of er-Ráhà* and *Approach to the Convent of Sinai.*

90. Russegger 1847: 44–9; Martineau 1848: 317–18; Anderson 1852: 83–4; Frith *et al.* 1860a; Frith *et al.* 1860b; Beamont 1861: 55, 78–9, 81–3 (later to change his opinion; see Beamont 1871: 121–6); Bartlett 1862: 74; Loftus 1870: 186; Maughan 1873: 115–16; Manning 1875: 216–21; Adams 1879: 74–5, 108–9; Hall 1907: 246; Sutton 1913: 91. For American supporters, see Olin 1843: 393–9; Durbin 1845: 142–8; Bausman 1861: 133; Randall 1867: 319; Ridgaway 1876: 75–7; Schaff 1878: 174, 178–9; Field 1883: 113–17.

91. Lindsay 1858: 194–7. On A.W.C. Lindsay, see Manley & Abdel-Hakim 2006: 245.

92. Kinnear 1841: 90–1.

93. Burckhardt 1822: 609.

94. Lepsius 1846a: 6; Lepsius 1846b: 12; Beke 1878: 15–16.

95. Greene 1883: 156–7; Greene 1884: 230–7. John Baker Greene himself never visited Sinai.

96. Crossley 1860: 20–36.

97. Eckenstein 1921: 74–82.

98. Jarvis 1931: 171–2.

99. Wilkinson 1843: 412–13; Wilkinson 1847: 220. He had not visited Sinai and borrowed his information from E. Robinson, see Wilkinson 1843: 402; Wilkinson 1847: 215.

100. Manginis 2015a: 69.

101. Wellsted 1838: 1 and German translation in Wellsted 1842.

102. Moscrop 2000: 58–60. See also Hobbs 1995: 244.

103. Wilson & Palmer 1869: part I, 5–15, 139–49; Moscrop 2000: 81. For a list of various expeditions in the Sinai, see Murray 1953: 151–3.

104. Murray 1953: 152.

105. Wilson & Palmer 1869, in five volumes. Also see Holland 1871: 514–15; Howe 1997: 40–1; Moscrop 2000: 81.

106. Vaczek & Buckland 1981: no pagination; Moscrop 2000: 2–3, 102–4.

107. Moscrop 2000: 70–1.

108. Howe 1997: 40.

109. Palmer 1878: 164–82; Palmer 1892: 173–91.

110. Scholars that supported Jabal Mūsā before the *Ordnance Survey* publication include: Burckhardt 1822: 609 (alongside Jabal Kathrin); Wellsted 1838: 54–5, 100–3; Wellsted 1842: 86–92; Fisk 1843: 155; Borrer 1845: 330; Gasparin 1848: 76; Kellogg 1848: 44; Ritter 1848 and Ritter 1866: 216–25; Pardieu 1851: 194; Graul 1854: 213–15; Lottin de Laval 1855–9a: 208–10, 225–8; Stanley 1887; Bonar 1857: 234, 237–8; Hamilton 1993: 30; Bräm 1859: 238–99; Tyrwhitt 1864: 346; Gadsby 1864: 33–7; (Amédée) de Damas 1864: 221; Brocklebank 1865: 177–8; Kræmer 1866: 356–8; Beamont 1871: 121–6. After the 1871 publication of the *Ordnance Survey*, more followed: Holland 1870: 21–6; Holland 1871: 519–25; Clarke 1884: 101; Dawson 1885: 43–4; Hull 1885: 186–7; Lombay 1892: 75; Jullien 1893: 121, 132–7; Bensly 1896: 145–6; Sargenton-Galichon 1904: 68–9; Rendall 1911: 167; Closen 1935: 23–4.

111. Bausman 1861: 128–50.

112. Manginis 2015a: 70–1.

113. For his work *Origines Biblicæ*; see Beke 1834.

114. Beke 1834: 154–96; Beke 1835; Beke 1862: 9–12; Beke 1871; Beke 1873.

115. Quotes from Beke 1878: 31, 32 and 34 respectively.

116. Beke 1878: 226–7.

117. Beke 1878: 406–12.

118. Beke 1878: 560–3, 567–9, 575–80.

119. Beke 1862: 9.

120. Quoted in Beke 1873: 3. Author's translation.

121. Stacquez 1865: 356. See also Burckhardt 1822: 485, 552; Gadsby 1864: 29; Randall 1867: 290; Robinson 1867: 131; Buxton *et al.* 1895: 131–2; Bensly 1896: 124; Hobbs 1995: 221–2.

122. *Egeria* 2008: 273–4.

123. Weitzmann 1982b: 8–9.

124. Tarnanidēs 1988: 32–3.

125. Beneshevich 1925. On his work, see Weitzmann 1982b: 5 note 1, 9; Tarnanidēs 1988: 32–3.

126. Norov 1878: 61–135.

127. Bibliography in Konidares 1971: 537–50.

128. Amantos 1953: 68–9; Labib 1961: 149; Isaias 2000: 26–7.

129. Grēgoriadēs 1875: 130–1 note 1; Renaudin 1900: 319–21. Author's translation. Amantos 1953: 70–2 (Greek translation). See also Turner 1820: 443–4; Coutelle 1832: 205 note 1; Grēgoriadēs 1875: 126–35; Meistermann 1909: 124, 141; Eckenstein 1921: 183–4; Rabino 1935: 70, 85 inscription 39; Amantos 1953: 68; Labib 1961: 105–6;

Skrobucha 1966: 82, 99–100; Kamil 1991: 32–3; *Description* 1994: 682; *Egeria* 2008: 218–19.

130. Amantos 1953: 73–5.
131. Grēgoriadēs 1875: 133–5; Meistermann 1909: 124 note 1; Amantos 1953: 75–6; Labib 1961: 149; Skrobucha 1966: 86.
132. Rabino 1935: 34, 86, inscriptions 42–4; Skrobucha 1966: 90.
133. Wādī Fīran, Ṭūr and other sites in the Sinai; Alexandria; Palestine (in Jerusalem and Jaffa); Syria (in Damascus, Laodicea and Antioch); Lebanon (see *Egeria* 2008: 91–2); Cyprus; Crete; Constantinople (see *Egeria* 2008: 91–2); Danubian Principalities; Bulgaria; and several other places. The Bombay and Calcutta priories were created in 1772 and 1777; see Amantos 1953: 67. For lists of priories, see Pitra 1885: 562–3, 589–90; Jullien 1893: 106; Amantos 1953: 99–100; Skrobucha 1966: 91; Hobbs 1995: 83. See also Grēgoriadēs 1875: 88–97; Meistermann 1909: 121; Eckenstein 1921: 188; Amantos 1953: 35–8; Labib 1961: 56; Kamil 1991: 29; Manaphēs 1990: 380; Dansette 2001: 79–80; Mouton & Popescu-Belis 2006: 26–7. On Cypriot priories, see Giovanni 1919: 342.
134. Grēgoriadēs 1875: 147–8.
135. Turner 1820: 443–4; Buckhardt 1822: 549, 556–7.
136. Grēgoriadēs 1875: 123–4, 147–8; Rabino 1938: 4; Kamil 1991: 35.
137. Amantos 1953: 76–7.
138. Raboisson 1886: 309; Lombay 1892: 77.
139. Lottin de Laval 1855–9a: 173–4.
140. Stacquez 1865: 355, note 1. Author's translation. Stacquez 1865: 350–69.
141. Koufopoulos *et al.* 2000: 267–75.
142. Burckhardt 1822: 550.
143. Galavares 1990a: 92; Dahari 2000: 62; Cormack & Vassilaki 2008: 360, 460.
144. Aleksidze *et al.* 2005: 357–8.
145. Lindsay 1858: 159–204. For positive evaluations of icon painting, see Turner 1820: 431; Dumas 1839a: 89; Dumas 1839b: 245; Pardieu 1851: 188.
146. Kinnear 1841: 80; Cook 1897: 312. See also Coutelle 1832: 202; Géramb 1839: 215, 221–15; Geramb 1840: 324, 328–31; Fisk 1843: 150; Wilkinson 1843: 410; Wilkinson 1847: 219; Anderson 1852: 82; Hamilton 1993: 24; Maughan 1873: 105; Ridgaway 1876: 67, 88; Adams 1879: 98; Jullien 1893: 112–5; Bensly 1896: 111; Sargenton-Galichon 1904: 76; Kergorlay 1911: 73.
147. Olin 1843: 407.
148. Martineau 1848: 312; her Horeb visit on pages 310–34.

149. Bartlett 1879: 262–84.

150. Rendall 1911: 128.

151. Robinson 1867: 99 ; Jullien 1893: 114.

152. Amantos 1953: 62–3; Weitzmann 1980: 155.

153. Labib 1961: 103–4; Sicard 1982: 132.

154. Labib 1961: 108–9.

155. Lindsay 1858: 189. The *Codex* 204 was often shown to visitors and the monks were especially proud of it; see Stephens 1837: 197; Stephens 1970: 288; Dumas 1839a: 89–90; Dumas 1839b: 246; Russegger 1847: 39–40; Bida & Hachette 1864: 12; Stacquez 1865: 355 – a viewing commented on by Labib 1961: 135–6; Ritter 1866: 237–8; Randall 1867: 296; Robinson 1867: 98–9; Loftus 1870: 183; Schaff 1878: 189; Raboisson 1887: 43–4. On *Codex* 204, see Weitzmann & Galavaris 1990: 42–7, figures 92–108, plates III–VIII; Galavares 1990b: 314, figures 3–6 on page 329; Justin Sinaites 2007.

156. Platt 1842: 173–4.

157. Bonar 1857: 219.

158. Brockbank 1914: 27. On O. Brockbank, see Manley & Abdel-Hakim 2006: 241.

159. Tischendorf 1846; Tischendorf 1862; Tischendorf 1863: 3–24. Smaller parts of the manuscript remain in the Monastery, see Sophronios 1998: 27–49; more pages are in the National Library of Russia, Saint Petersburg; see *Egeria* 2008: 221–2. Also see Bentley 1985; Kamil 1991: 63–9; Hobbs 1995: 245–6, 259–60; Skeat 2000: 313–15; *Egeria* 2008: 221–2.

160. Strauss 1848: 159; Strauss 1849: 126.

161. Meimarēs 1985: 17.

162. Brugsch 1866: 34–54; Brugsch 1875a; Brugsch 1875b; Ebers 1872: 250–379; Ebers & Guthe 1884: 358–410.

163. Sachsen 1912: 6–30, plates IV–X.

164. Schmidt & Moritz 1926: 26–34; Stern 1960: 445; Stern 1964a: 7–10.

165. Sōtēriou & Sōtēriou 1956, Sōtēriou & Sōtēriou 1958. For early work on the Monastery library, see Skrobucha 1966: 104. For research on the icons, see Skrobucha 1966: 106–8.

166. Rice 1960: 4–8.

167. On artists, see Manginis 2015a: 72–5, figures 1–3.

168. Bartlett 1862; Arundale 1837. On Bartlett, see Vilnay 1963: XXIV.

169. Roberts 1842–9.

170. Kellogg 1848; on M.K. Kellogg, see Davis 1996: 101–26.

171. Kellogg 1848: 45–6; Davis 1996: 115–26.

172. Davis 1996: 118.

173. Llewellyn & Newton 2001: 37–9, figure 1; Weeks 2001: 187, figure 23.
174. Schubert & Bernatz 1839: plates 6, 7 and 8; Schubert *et al.* 1856: plates 10 and 11. For another album, see Schubert *et al.* 1868: plate 5 for Jabal Mūsā. For J.M. Bernatz, see Vilnay 1963: XXIII.
175. Vaczek & Buckland 1981: no pagination; Williams 1998: 172.
176. Frith *et al.* 1860a; Frith *et al.* 1860b. On F. Frith, see Williams 1998: 168–78.
177. Howe 1997: 40–4.
178. Vaczek & Buckland 1981: no pagination.
179. Vilnay 1963: XXVI–XXVII.
180. Manning 1875: 214–21. On S. Manning, see Manley & Abdel-Hakim 2006: 245–6.
181. Kitto 1835a: 433–4; Kitto 1835b: 449–52. On Sinai tourism, see Manginis 2015a: 75–7.
182. Wilkinson 1843: 396–417; Wilkinson 1847: 212–20; Moscrop 2000: 46. For tourists and travellers to Sinai before the 'Thomas Cook Age', see Manley & Abdel-Hakim 2006: 18, 59–60, 64–5, 74–5, 76, 93–4, 104, 105–6, 110–11, 112, 122, 139, 146, 151–2, 175, 178–9, 197–8, 222, 234, 241, 244, 249.
183. Brendon 1992: 120.
184. Labib 1961: 137, 144–5.
185. Brendon 1992: 124–6.
186. Cook 1874. For an extended section on Sinai, see Cook 1897: 310–18.
187. Labib 1961: 143.
188. Hornby 1907: 52; Brendon 1992: 132.
189. Lenoir 1872: 245–6. Author's translation. See also Dumas 1839a: 86; Dumas 1839b: 224.
190. Pococke 1814: 291.
191. Pococke 1814: 292.
192. Dumas 1839a: 99; Dumas 1839b: 257; Döbel 1842: 22–4; Fisk 1843: 159 ; Borrer 1845: 328; (Amédée) de Damas 1864: 256; Stacquez 1865: 358, 366 ; Randall 1867: 313, 319 ; Lenoir 1872: 250–1 ; Bensly 1896: 151; Rendall 1911: 142; Manley & Abdel-Hakim 2006: 223, 240.
193. Manginis 2015a: 76, figure 4.
194. Hamilton 1993: 22.
195. Bensly 1896: 159; Cook 1899; Zachos 1937: 33–4; Labib 1961: 132–3.
196. Baedeker 1878: 459–513; Baedeker 1895: 230–80.
197. Isambert 1881: 718–36; Meistermann 1909.
198. Grēgoriadēs 1875.

199. Hamilton 1993: 21.

200. Maughan 1873: 128; for his Horeb visit, see Maughan 1873: 73–102.

201. Zachos 1937: 12. On Russian travellers to Sinai from the sixteenth century onwards, see Manley & Abdel-Hakim 2006: 65, 160, 164, 191, 212, 243, 244, 247, 250. See also Labib 1961: 142.

202. Sutton 1913: 90–112, plates 40–59.

203. Buxton *et al.* 1895: 126–38.

204. Hornby 1907: 44.

205. Dobson 1925: 83; Zachos 1937: 82.

206. Jarvis 1931: 230. Jarvis also recorded his Sinai experience in Jarvis 1938 and Jarvis 1939. On C.S. Jarvis, see Rabino 1938: 56 note 1; Manley & Abdel-Hakim 2006: 244.

207. Morton 1938; Golding 1938: 270–345. On H.V. Morton, see Manley & Abdel-Hakim 2006: 246; on L. Golding, see Manley & Abdel-Hakim 2006: 243.

208. Sherman 1997: 30–1.

209. Hobbs 1995: 261–88; Hobbs 1996: 1–21; Alexander 2001: 60–6.

210. Golding 1938: 341.

211. Beadnell 1927: 3; Murray 1953: 151 note 3; Kamil 1991: 13. 'Mountain oil' was mentioned by R. Pococke and J.L. Burckhardt, see Pococke 1814: 284; Burckhardt 1822: 468–9.

212. Ritter 1848.

213. Ritter 1866: 1–253.

214. Buxton 1898: 148.

215. Buxton 1898: 148–9.

216. Schaff 1878: 191–2.

217. Turner 1820: 443–4 note *. On W.J. Bankes, see Usick 1998: 52, 55; Manley & Abdel-Hakim 2006: 239.

218. Disraeli 1847: 240–1.

Epilogue

1. For steps taken and suggestions made on the future of the Horeb landscape, see *Master Plan* 2010.

List of Pilgrims and Travellers

This list of names and dates of travellers to Horeb and Jabal Mūsā is not meant to be comprehensive and only those who visited between the fourth and the early twentieth century and were discussed or mentioned in the book are included. Sinai monks or itinerant monks like Julian Saba and Symeon the Elder, John Moschos, Qays and Pachōmios or Bononius, whose visits were longer and of a different character, are not included. Although most travellers must have made their way to Jabal Mūsā, the dates of their ascent are not always stated. Only two clearly did not ascend (Miss Platt and Carsten Niebuhr).

Nationalities: (Am) American, (A) Arab, (Au) Austrian, (B) British, (Be) Belgian, (C) Canadian, (Cz) Czech, (D) Dutch, (Da) Danish, (E) Egyptian, (F) French, (Fl) Flemish, (Fr) Frank, (G) German (includes Prussians, Bavarians etc.), (H) Greek, (I) Italian, (J) Jewish, (K) Kurdish, (R) Roman / Byzantine, (Ru) Russian, (Sp) Spanish, (Sv) Swedish, (Sw) Swiss, (U) Ukrainian.

An asterisk (*) denotes a probably fictitious account or an uncertain visit. Accounts widely acknowledged as fabricated (for example by 'Johan de Mandeville') are not included.

Months in italic Latin numerals.

NAME	DATES	AT HOREB	ON JABAL MŪSĀ
ᶜAbbās Pasha (E)	1812–1854	1853	
Abū ʾl-Mughīra (A)	7th century	*III* 684 (669, 699)	
Adams, William Henry D. (B)	1828–1891	before 1879	
Adornes, Anselme (Fl)	15th century	*VIII* 1470	
Aerts, Jean (Fl)	15th century	1481	
Affagart, Greffin (F)	1490/5–1557	1534	
Amédée of Damascus (F)	19th century	1859	
Anglure, Ogier d' (F)	14th century	6–10 *XI* 1395	
Anonymous (?)	13th century		
Anonymous (?)	13th century		
Anonymous (?)	13th century	*circa* 1231	
Anonymous (?)	13th century	before 1265	
Anonymous (?)	13th century	before 1265	
Anonymous (F)	14th century		
Anonymous (?)	14th century		
Anonymous (?)	15th century	16–19 *X* 1486	17 *X* 1486
Anonymous (?)	16th century	mid-16th century	
Arundale, Francis (B)	1807–1853	*IX* 1833	
Auvergne, *Monseigneur* (F)	1793–1836	21–22 *V* 1835	21 *V* 1835
Van Aylde Jongue, Ida: see Saint-Elme			
Baldensel, Wilhelm von (G)	14th century	1336	
Bankes, William John (B)	1786–1855	1815	
Barron, T. (B)	19th century	before 1868–1869	
Bartlett, Samuel Colcord (Am)	1817–1898	19–23 *II* 1874	20 *II* 1874

NAME	DATES	AT HOREB	ON JABAL MŪSĀ
Bartlett, William Henry (B)	1809–1854	12–20 *X* 1845	
Baudouin, Lord of Launay (F)	17th century	10–13 *X* 1631	
Baumgarten, Martin (G)	15–16th century	17–20 *X* 1507	17 *X* 1507
Bausman, Benjamin (Am)	1824–1909	16–20 *III* 1861	17 *III* 1861
Beadnell, Hugh J.L. (B)	1874–1944	1921, 1923–1924	
Beamont, William John (B)	1828–1868	1853, 5–7 *XII* 1860	6 *XII* 1860
Beck, Georg (G)	16th century	13–16 *XI* 1565	
Belon du Mans, Pierre (F)	1518–1564	1547	
Beneshevich, Vladimir N. (Ru)	1884–1938	1907, 1908, 1911	
Bennet, Miss (B)	19th century	before 1830	
Bensly, Agnes Dorothee (G)	19th century	5 *II* (or later) – 20 *III* 1893	*III* 1893
Bern, Jacob von (G)	14th century	10 *IX* 1346	
Bernatz, Johann Martin (G)	1802–1878	28 *II* – 7 *III* 1837?	2 *III* 1837?
Bianchi, Noe (I) *	15th century	15th century	
Bida, Alexandre (F)	1823–1895	28 *II* – 4 *III* 1861	2 *III* 1861
Bird (Bishop), I. (B)	1831–1904	1878 or later	
Bonar, Horatius (B)	1808–1889	26–29 *I* 1856	28 *I* 1856
Bonnat, Léon Joseph Florentin (F)	1833–1922	*c.* 1868	
Booth, Miss (B)	19th century	late 1870s	
Borrer, Dawson (B)	19th century	23–27 *III* 1843	24 *III* 1843
Brabant, Duke of (Be)	1835–1909	7–9 *II* 1863	8 *II* 1863
Brasca, Santo (I)	1444–1522	1480	
Bräuning, Johann Jacob (G)	16th century	19 *VIII* 1579	

NAME	DATES	AT HOREB	ON JABAL MŪSĀ
Brémond, Gabriel de (F)	17th century	between 1643 and 1645	
Breydenbach, Bernhard von (G)	died in 1497	22–27 *IX* 1483	
Brockbank, Oliver (B)	19–20th century	1914	
Brocklehurst, Miss (B)	19th century	late 1870s	
Broquière, Bertrandon de la (F)	15th century	1432	
Browne, William George (B)	1768–1813	after 22 *III* 1793	
Brugsch, Heinrich F.K. (G)	1827–1894	1–4 *V* 1865 and later	
Burckhardt, Johann Ludwig (Sw)	1784–1817	1–4, 18–30 *V* 1816	20 *V* 1816
Buxton, Edward North (B)	1840–1924	15–17 *II* 1894	17 *II* 1894
Capodilista, Gabriele (I)	15th century	18–22 *VIII* 1458	
Carlier de Pinon, Jean le (F)	16th century	1579	
Carne, John (B)	1789–1844	6–10 *XI* 1821	9 *XI* 1821
Cart, Léon (F)	1869–1916	before 1915	
Catherwood, Frederick (B) *	1799–1854		
Chartres, Robert-Philippe Duke of (F)	1840–1910	1860	
Conyngham, Francis (B)	19th century	1868	
Cook, Thomas (B)	1808–1892	1868 and possibly later	
Coppin, Jean (F)	17th century	mid-1640s	
Coutelle, J.-M. (F)	1748–1835	24–28 *X* 1800	26? *X* 1800
Crossley, Henry (B)	19th century	before 1860	
Currelly, Charles Trick (C)	1876–1957	spring 1906	

Name	Dates	At Horeb	On Jabal Mūsā
Daniel, William (B)	17–18th century	*XII* 1701	
Daniell, Edward Thomas (B)	1804–1842	1841	
Dauzats, Adrien (F)	1804–1868	1830	
D(e)ardel, Jean de (F)	14th century	1377	
Della Valle, Pietro (I)	1586–1652	24–26 *XII* 1615	
Didier, Charles (Sw)	1805–1864	1845	
Döbel, Ernst Christof (G)	19th century	27 *X* – 6 *XI* 1833	28 or 29 *X* 1833
Dobson, Augusta Mary Rachel (B)	1872–1923	*XII* 1922 – *I* 1923	
Dorndorff, Rupertus Lentulus (G)	16th century	1583?	
Durbin, John Price (Am)	1800–1876	4–7 *II* 1843	5 *II* 1843
Ebers, Georg Moritz (G)	1837–1898		
Ecklin von Aarau, Daniel (G)	16th century	1553	
Egeria (R)	4th century	*XI* 383 – *I* 384	17 *XII* 383
Van Egmont, Johannes Ægidius (D)	1697–1747	*c.* 1720	
'Ernoul' (F) *	13th century		
Fabri, Felix (Sw)	*c.*1441–1502	22–27 *IX* 1483	
Farman, Elbert (Am)	1831–1911	1908	
Fauvel, Robert (F)	17th century	10–13 *X* 1631	
Fermanel, Gilles (F)	died 1661	10–13 *X* 1631	
Fernberger von Egenberg, A.G.C. (G)	1557–1594	18–25 *X* 1580	
Field, Henry Martyn (Am)	1822–1907	spring 1882	
Fisk, George (B)	19th century	21–25 *V* 1842	23 *V* 1842
Fraas, Oscar (G)	1824–1897		
Frameynsperg, Rudolf de (G)	14th century	1346	

NAME	DATES	AT HOREB	ON JABAL MŪSĀ
Franciscan monks (five) (?)	14th century	1304	
Franz Joseph Otto, Archduke (Au)	1865–1906	6–7 *III* 1894	
Frescobaldi, Leonardo (I)	14th century	28 or 29 *X* – 2 *XI* 1384	
Frith, Francis (B)	1822–1898	between 1856 and 1857	
Fromont and his brother (Fr)	9th century	mid-9th century	
Fumet, Lord of (F)	16th century	1547	
Fürer von Haimendorf, Christoph (G)	16th century	13–16 *XI* 1565	
Furtenbach, David (G)	16th century	17–29 *XI* 1561	
Gabriel of Soupakion (H)	13–14th century	before 1312	
Gadsby, John (B)	*c.*1809–1893	6–8 *III* 1864	7 *III* 1864
Gasparin, Valérie Boissier de (F)	1813–1894	24–28 *III* 1848	25 *III* 1848
Géramb, M.-J. (earlier F.) (F)	1772–1848	25 *II* – 5 *III* 1833	1 *III* 1833
Gérôme, Jean Léon (F)	1824–1904	*c.* 1868	
Ghistelle, Josse van (Fl)	15th century	between 1481 and 1484	
Gibson, Margaret Dunlop (B)	1843–1920	1892 and later	
Gogara, Basil [*sic*] (Ru)	17th century	*c.* 1634	
Golding, Louis (B)	1895–1958	before 1938	
Gotch, Paul (B)	1915–2008	before 1945	
Graul, Carl (G)	1814–1864	*III* 1853	5 *III* 1853
Gregor (or Georg) of Gaming (G)	15–16th century	17–20 *X* 1507	17 *X* 1507
Gucci, Giorgio (I)	14th century	28 or 29 *X* – 2 *XI* 1384	

Name	Dates	At Horeb	On Jabal Mūsā
Hachette, Georges (F)	1838–1892	28 *II* – 4 *III* 1861	2 *III* 1861
Hamilton, James (B)	19th century	1854	
Harant, Krystoff (Cz)	1564–1621	*X* 1598	18 *X* 1598
Harff, Arnold von (G)	15th century	between 1496 and 1499	
Hart, Henry Chichester (B)	19th century	*XI* 1883	20 *XI* 1883
Hellfrich, Johann (G)	16th century	*II* 1566	
Henniker, Sir Frederick (B)	1793–1825	21?-24 *IV* 1820	22? *IV* 1820
Hese, Johannes Witte de (D)*	15th century	1489	
Holland, Frederick Whitmore (B)	19th century	1868–1869	
Hornby, Emily (B)	1834–1906	2–6 *III* 1899	3 *III* 1899
Hull, Edward (I)	1829–1917	19–22? *XI* 1883	20 *XI* 1883
Hume, W.F. (B)	19–20th century	before 1906	
Hyde, John (B)	died in 1825	1819	
Jacob, rabbi (J)	12th century	before 1187	
Jacopo da Verona (I)	14th century	arrived 10 *IX* 1335	
Jarvis, Claude Scudamore (B)	1879–1952	1920s-1930s	
Jaschaw, Georg (G)	16th century	17–29 *XI* 1561	
Jullien, M. (F)	19th century	*XI* 1889	18 *XI* 1889
Kapustin, Antonin (Ru)	1817–1894	1870	
Katzenellenbogen, Philip von (G)	15th century	*X* 1433	
Kellogg, Miner Kilbourne (Am)	1814–1889	*II-III* 1844	
Kergorlay, Jean de (F)	19–20th century	spring 1906	
Kiechel, Samuel (G)	1563–1619	8–11 *VI* 1588	

NAME	DATES	AT HOREB	ON JABAL MŪSĀ
Kinnear, John Gardiner (B)	19th century	18–22 *II* 1839	
Koller, Baron (B)	19th century	*III* 1840	
Kondakov, Nikodim (Ru)	1844–1925	1881	
Kondokoff, N.P. [*sic*] (Ru)	16th century	between 1582 and 1594	
Korobeinikoff, Triphon [*sic*] (Ru)	16th century	between 1582 and 1594	
Kosmas (R?)	6–10th century		
Kosmas 'Indikopleustēs' (R)	6th century	first half of 6th century	
Kræmer, Robert Fredrik von (Sv)	1791–1880	17–20 *IV* 1862	
Laborde, Léon E.S.J. Marquis de (F)	1807–1869	1828	
Lagrange, Marie-Joseph, formerly Albert Marie-Henri Lagrange (F)	1855–1938	1893, *II* 1897	26 *II* 1897
Lannoy, Ghillebert de (F)	1386–1462	1401, 1421/1422	
Lear, Edward (B)	1812–1888	25–28 *I* 1849	
Leman, Ulrich (G)	15th century	*VI-VII* 1473	
Lengherand, Georges (F?)	died in 1500	16–19 *X* 1486	17 *X* 1486
Lenoir, Paul (F)	1826–1881	*c.* 1868	
Lepsius, Karl Richard (G)	1810–1884	23–27 *III* 1845	24 *III* 1845
Lewis, Agnes Smith (B)	1843–1926	1892 and later	
Lewis, John Frederick (B)	1805–1876	1842?	
Lichtenstein, Hans Ludwig von (G)	16th century	1–7 *IX* 1587	3 *IX* 1587

Name	Dates	At Horeb	On Jabal Mūsā
Linant de Bellefonds, L.M.A. (F)	1799–1883	1828	
Lindsay, Alexander W.C. (B)	1812–1880	16 *III* – 17 *IV* 1837	21 *III* 1837
Loftus, Jane (B)	19th century	6–10 *III* 1868	7 *III* 1868
Lombay, G. de (F)	19th century	*III* 1887	
Loti, Pierre (F)	1850–1923	1894	
Lottin de Laval, Pierre Victor (F)	1810–1903	*III* 1850	8 *III* 1850
Löwenstein, Count Albrecht zu (G)	16th century	17–29 *XI* 1561	
MacDonald, James (B)	1822–1885	1868–1869	
Manning, Samuel (B)	1822–1881	before 1875	
Martineau, Harriet (B)	1802–1876	*III* 1846	
Martoni, Niccolò de (I)	14th century	*IX* 1394	
Maughan, William Charles (B)	died in 1914	29 *II* – 4 *III* 1872	2 *III* 1872
Measor, Henry Paul (B)	died 1865	26?–29 *III* 1842	28 *III* 1842
Meggen, Jodocus van (Sw)	16th century	1542	
Meingre de Boucicault, Jean le (F)	14th century	1389	
Meistermann, Barnabé (F)	19–20th century	before 1909	
Meuillon, Guillaume de (F)	14th century	between 1390 and 1391	
Milly, Philippe de (F)	1120–1171	1160s	
Mirebel, Claude (F?)	15th century	mid-15th century	
Monconys, Balthasar de (F)	1608–1665	26 *IV* – 2 *V* 1647	29 *IV* 1647
Monopole, Antoine de (F)	14th century	1377	
Morison, Antoine (F)	17th century	20 *XI* – 2 *XII* 1697	23 – 24 *XI* 1697

Name	Dates	At Horeb	On Jabal Mūsā
Morton, Henry Vollam (B)	1892–1979		
Mouskes, Philippe (F)	*c.*1220–1282	second half of 13th century	
Muḥammad ᶜAlī Pasha (E)	*c.*1769–1849		
Münster, Hans Ludwig von (G)	16th century	1–7 *IX* 1587	3 *IX* 1587
Neitzschitz, Georg Christoff von (G)	17th century	*VII* 1636	7 *VII* 1636
Neuhaus, Otto von: see Baldensel			
Newbold, Captain (B)	19th century	*VI* 1847?	
Niebuhr, Carsten (Da)	1733–1815	*IX* 1761	Did not ascend.
Obicini, Tommaso (I)	1585–1632	between 1612 and 1621	
Oerttel von Augsburg, Emanuel (G)	16th century	1561	
Olin, Stephen (Am)	1797–1851	13–18 *III* 1840	14 *III* 1840
Orléans, Louis-Philippe-Albert of (F)	1838–1894	1860	
Ouspensky, B. [*sic*] (Ru ? U ?)	19th century	*c.* 1845	
Palerne, Jean (F)	16th century	21–24 *VIII* 1581	
Palmer, Edward Henry (B)	1840–1882	1867–1868 and later	
Palmer, Henry Spencer (B)	1838–1893	1868–1869 and later?	
Pardieu, Charles Count de (F)	19th century	8–11 *X* 1849	
Philippe d'Alsace (F)	1143–1191	1117	
Philippe d'Artois (F)	14th century	1389	
Piacenza, pilgrim of (R)	6th century	550s	

Name	Dates	At Horeb	On Jabal Mūsā
Piellat, Count de (F)	19th century	1897?	
Pigafetta, Filippo (I)	16th century	after 14 *II* 1577	
Platt, Miss (B)	19th century	28 *III* – 2 *IV* 1839	Did not ascend.
Pococke, Richard (B)	1704–1765	Easter 1739	
Poggibonsi, Niccolò da (I)	14th century	spring 1349	
Poncet, Charles Jacques (F)	17–18th century	1701	
Poole, Reginald Stuart (B) *	1832–1895		
Posniakov, Vasiliĭ (Ru)	16th century	between 1558 and 1561	
Quaresmius, Franciscus (I)	1583–1650	before 1639	
Raboisson, Antoine (F)	19th century	*III* 1882	13 *III* 1882
Randall, David Austin (Am)	1813–1884	3–6 *III* 1861	4 *III* 1861
Rauter, Ludwig von (G)	died in 1615	*I* – *II* / 1569	
Raynald de Châtillon (F)	1125–1187	12th century	
Reboldis, Antonius de (I)	14th century	26 *I* – 4 *II* 1331	29 *I* 1331
Rendall, Montague John (B)	1862–1950	10?-13 *III* 1911 or before	12 *III* 1911 or before
Ridgaway, Henry Bascom (Am)	1830–1895	16–21 *III* 1874	17 *III* 1874
Rieter, Sebald (G)	15th century	1479	
Roberts, David (B)	1796–1864	18–22 *II* 1839	
Robinson, Edward (Am)	1794–1863	23–29 *III* 1838	26 *III* 1838
Roche-Dragon, Marquise de (F)	19th century	1845	
Rogers, Mary Eliza (B) *	19th century	before 1883?	
Rotenham (G)	16th century	1–7 *IX* 1587	3 *IX* 1587
Rowley, Charlotte (B)	born in 1811	Christmas 1835	

NAME	DATES	AT HOREB	ON JABAL MŪSĀ
Rumpff, Sigmund (G)	16th century	17–29 *XI* 1561	
Rüppell, Eduard (G)	1794–1884	*V* 1822, *IV* 1826, *V* 1831	7 *V* 1831
Russegger, Joseph Ritter von (Au)	1802–1863	22 *X* – 1 *XI* 1838	28 *X* 1838
Rusticiana (R)	6th century	between 592 and 594	
Sachsen, Johann Georg Duke of (G)	1869–1938	*X* 1910	
Saint-Elme, Ida de (D)	19th century	1828	
Ṣalāḥ al-Dīn Yūsuf ibn Ayyūb (K)	*c.*1138–1193	1174–1176	
Sandys, George (B) *	1577–1644	after 1610	
Sanseverino, Roberto da (I)	1417–1487	18–22 *VIII* 1458	
Sargenton-Galichon, Adélaïde (F)	19–20th century	20–24 *II* 1902	22 *II* 1902
Schaff, Philip (Am)	1819–1893	late 1870s	
Schubert, Gotthilf H. von (G)	1780–1860	28 *II* – 7 *III* 1837	2 *III* 1837
Schulenburg, Alexander von (G)	16th century	13–16 *XI* 1565	
Schuueicker, Solomon (G)	16th century	1581	
Seetzen, Ulrich Jasper (G)	1767–1811	*IV* 1807	13 or 16 *IV* 1807
Séjourné, R.P. (F)	19th century	1893	
Shaw, Thomas (B)	1694–1751		
Sicard, Claude (F)	18th century	1720, 12 *IX* – 1 *X* 1722	16 *IX* 1722
Sigoli, Simone (I)	14th century	28 or 29 *X* – 2 *XI* 1384	
Sparnau, Peter (G)	14th century	1385	
Stacquez, H.T.J. (Be?)	19th century	7–9 *II* 1863	8 *II* 1863

NAME	DATES	AT HOREB	ON JABAL MŪSĀ
Stanley, Arthur Penrhyn (B)	1815–1881	between 1852 and 1853	
Stephens, John Lloyd (Am)	1805–1852	*III* 1836	
Stewart, Frederick William (B)	1805–1872	1842?	
Stewart, Robert Walter (B)	19th century	1854	
Stochove, Vincent (Be)	1605–1679	10–13 *X* 1631	
Strauss, Friedrich Adolph (G)	1817–1888	28 *II* – 5 *III* 1845	1 *III* 1845
Sudheim, Ludolf von (G)	14th century	between 1336 and 1341	
Suriano, Francesco (I)	1450–*c.*1529	1494	
Sutton, Arthur Warwick (B)	1854–1925	16–19 *III* 1912	
Swinburne, Thomas de (B)	14th century	*XI* 1392	
Tafur, Pero (Sp)	1406/10–*c.*1484	1435 or 1437	
Tennstädt, Ulrich von (G)	14th century	1385	
Teufel von Krottendorf, Hans C. (G)	1567–1642	18–23 *X* 1588	
Thenaud, Jean (F)	15–16th century	*VII* 1512	
Thevet, André (F)	1516–1592	spring 1552	
Thietmar (G)	12–13th century	1217	
Thou, François Auguste de (F)	1607–1642	1628	
Tischendorf, L.F. Constantin (G)	1815–1874	1844, 1853, 1859	
Tobin, Catherine (B)	19th century	1853	

NAME	DATES	AT HOREB	ON JABAL MŪSĀ
Tucher, Johannes (G)	15th century	1479	
Turner, William (B)	1792–1867	*VIII* 1815	5 *VIII* 1815
Tyrwhitt, Richard St John (B)	1827–1895	*II* 1862	
Ubayya (A)	7th century	*XII* 683	
Ulrich II of Mecklenburg-Stargard (G)	15th century	autumn 1470	
Uspenskiĭ, Porfiriĭ (U)	1804–1885	1845	
Valimbert, Jacques de (F)	16th century	1584	
Vichensky, Hippolyte [*sic*] (Ru)	17–18th century	*c.* 1708	
Wallenfels (G)	16th century	1–7 *IX* 1587	3 *IX* 1587
Wellsted, James Raymond (B)	1805–1842	after 11 *I* 1833, after 23 *IX* 1836	
Wilson, Sir Charles William (B)	1836–1905	1868–1869 and later?	
Wolff, Joseph (G)	1795–1862	6–10 *XI* 1821, 1836	
Wurmser, Jacob (G)	16th century	17–29 *XI* 1561	
Wyatt, Claude W. (B)	19th century	1868–1869	
Zachos, Agamemnōn (H)	20th century	25 *VIII* – 14 *IX* 1925	31 *VIII* 1925
Zizinia, Étienne (H)	born in 1823	7–9 *II* 1863	8 *II* 1863
Zülnhart, Wolf von (G)	15th century	30 *X* – early *XI* 1495	

Image Credits

Frontispiece and figures 3 and 6: From Clarke 1884: 114, 111 and plate opposite page 106 (respectively); author's collection.

Figures 1, 4, 9, 11, 13, 17, 18, 19, 23, 26 and 29: Author's collection.

Figures 2 and 10: From Laborde 1830, no plate numbering; General Research Division, The New York Public Library.

Figures 5 and 30: The Miriam and Ira D. Wallach Division of Art, Prints and Photographs: Photography Collection, The New York Public Library.

Figure 7: Photograph by the author, October 1998.

Figures 8, 14 and 15: From Rogers 1883: 233, 232 and 235 (respectively); author's collection.

Figures 12, 22 and 28: The J. Paul Getty Trust 84.XO.1248.3.1.29, 84.XP.728.47 and 84.XO.1248.3.1.28 (respectively).

Figure 16: Photograph by the author, May 2003.

Figures 20 and 24: From Kergorlay 1911: plate 16 opposite page 56 and plate 11 opposite page 40 (respectively); author's collection.

Figures 21 and 25: Yale Center for British Art, Paul Mellon Collection, New Haven, Connecticut, U.S.A.

Figure 27: General Research Division, The New York Public Library.

Endpapers: Based on Baedeker 1895: map insert and *Master Plan* 2010: 56, figure 4.26.

Bibliography

AA	*Archäologischer Anzeiger.*
AB	*Analecta Bollandiana.*
AnIsl	*Annales Islamologiques.*
AOL	*Archives de l'Orient Latin.*
BAR	British Archaeological Reports.
BASOR	*Bulletin of the American Schools of Oriental Research.*
BiblArch	*Biblical Archaeologist.*
BSOAS	*Bulletin of the School of Oriental and African Studies.*
Byzantion	*Byzantion. Revue Internationale des Études Byzantines.*
BZ	*Byzantinische Zeitschrift.*
CCSL	Corpus Christianorum Series Latina.
CSCO	Corpus Scriptorum Christianorum Orientalium.
DOP	*Dumbarton Oaks Papers.*
DTC*	*Dictionnaire de Théologie Catholique.*
IEJ	*Israel Exploration Journal.*
JSL	*Journal of Sacred Literature.*
LA	*Studii Biblici Franciscani Liber Annuus.*
Madras Journal	*Madras Journal of Literature and Science.*
MGH	Monumenta Germaniae Historica.
ODB	*The Oxford Dictionary of Byzantium.*
PEQ	*Palestine Exploration (Fund) Quarterly (Statement).*
PG*	J. P. Migne, editor, *Patrologiæ Cursus Completus, Series Græca.*

PL*	J. P. Migne, editor, *Patrologiæ Cursus Completus, Series Prima.*
QEDEM	Monographs of the Institute of Archaeology, The Hebrew University of Jerusalem.
QSA	*Quaderni di Studi Arabi.*
RB	*Revue Biblique (Internationale).*
RC	*Revue Catholique.*
RE*	*Paulys Real-Encyclopädie der classischen Altertumswissenschaft*, neue Bearbeitung, begonnen von Georg Wissowa.
SA	Σιναϊτικά Ανάλεκτα (*Analecta Sinaitica*).
Tel Aviv	*Tel Aviv. Journal of the Tel Aviv University Institute of Archaeology.*
ZDPV	*Zeitschrift des Deutschen Palaestina-Vereins.*

* References to *DTC*, Mansi 1771, *PG*, *PL* and *RE* are to columns and not pages.

All biblical quotations are from *The Holy Bible*, New International Version, Cross Reference Edition with Concordance, London 1998. All Qurʾānic quotations are from *The Koran*, translated with notes by N.J. Dawood, London 1999.

Abel, F.M. (1907) 'Mélanges III. Notes d'archéologie chrétienne sur le Sinaï', *RB* NS 4, number 1, 105–12.

Adams, William Henry Davenport (1879) *Mount Sinai, Petra, and the Desert Described and Illustrated. By the author of 'The Catacombs of Rome'*, London.

Adémar de Chabannes (1897) *Chronique publié d'après les manuscrits par Jules Chavanon*, Paris.

Adémar de Chabannes (1947) 'Chronique (Partie originale)' in *L'an mille. Œuvres de Liutprand, Raoul Glaber, Adémar de Chabannes, Adalberon, Helgaud réunies, traduites et présentées par Edmond Pognon*, Paris, 145–209.

Adornes, Anselme (1893) E. Feys, 'Voyage d'Anselme Adornes au mont Sinaï et à Jérusalem en 1470, d' après un manuscrit de Romboudt de Doppere', *Annales de la Société d'Émulation pour l'étude de l'Histoire & des Antiquités de la Flandre*, 5e série tome IV, XLIe volume de la collection, 135–222.

Aerts (1873) Emmanuel Neeffs, 'Un voyage au XVᵉ siècle. Vénétie, Terre-Sainte, Égypte, Arabie, Grandes-Indes', *RC* N.S. 9 / XXXV, 268–91, 321–36, 425–51, 553–81.

Aharoni, Yohanan (1961) 'Kadesh-Barnea and Mount Sinai' in Beno Rothenberg, in collaboration with Yohanan Aharoni and Avia Hashimshoni, *God's Wilderness. Discoveries in Sinai*, translated by Joseph Witriol, London.

Airy, Sir G.B. (1876) *Notes on the Early Hebrew Scriptures*, London.

Albericus Aquensis (1894) 'Historia Hierosolymitanae Expeditionis', *PL* CLXVI, Parisiis, 389–716.

Albertus Aquensis (1611) 'Historia Hierosolimitanæ Expeditionis Edita ab Alberto Canonico ac Custode Aquensis Ecclesiæ super passagio Godefridi de Bullione, & aliorum Principum', *Gesta Dei per Francos, sine Orientalium Expeditionum, et Regni Francorum Hierosolimitani. Orientalis Historiæ Tomus Primus*, Hanoviæ.

Albertus (1906) '1240. – Fr. Albertus Stadensis: – 1. Iter trans mare versus Iherusalem – 2. Itinerarium Terrae Sanctae' in Golubovich 1906, 181–5.

Albright, W.F. (1948) 'Exploring in Sinai with the University of California African Expedition', *BASOR* 109 (February), 5–20.

Albright, William Foxwell (1968) *Yahweh and the Gods of Canaan. A Historical Analysis of Two Contrasting Faiths*, London.

Aleksidze, Zaza *et al.* (Mzekala Shanidze, Lily Khevsuriani, Michael Kavtaria) (2005) *Catalogue of Georgian Manuscripts Discovered in 1975 at St. Catherine's Monastery on Mount Sinai*, English translation by M. Shanidze, Athens.

Alexander, Doug (2001) 'Desert dilemma', *Geographical* May 2001, 60–6.

Altmüller, H.W. (1861) *Sinai & Golgatha oder Plastische Darstellung des Heiligen Landes und seiner Umgebungen*, Cassel.

Amann, É. (1933) 'Pierre Diacre', *DTC* 12, Paris, 1929–30.

Amantos, K. (1953) Σύντομος Ἱστορία τῆς Ἱερᾶς Μονῆς τοῦ Σινᾶ, Thessaloniki.

Ambraseys, N.N. (1962) 'A Note on the Chronology of Willis's List of Earthquakes in Palestine and Syria', *Bulletin of the Seismological Society of America* 52, number 1 (January), 77–80.

(Amédée) de Damas, Le R.P. (1864) *En Orient. Voyage au Sinaï*, Paris.

Amiran, D.H. Kallner (1950–1) 'A Revised Earthquake-Catalogue of Palestine', *IEJ* 1, 223–46.

Amiran, D.H.K. (1952) 'A Revised Earthquake-Catalogue of Palestine', *IEJ* 2, 48–65.

Ammoniia (1890) *Повесть о убиенных св. отцах в Синае и Раифе*, издалъ И. Помяловскій, Saint Petersburg.

Ammonio (1826) *Martirio de' Santi Padri del Monte Sinai e dell' Eremo di Raitu composto da Ammonio Monaco volgarizzamento fatto nel buon secolo della nostra lingua non mai stampato*, Milano.

Ammonius (1912) *The Forty Martyrs of the Sinai Desert and the Story of Eulogios from a Palestinian Syriac and Arabic Palimpsest*, transcribed by Agnes Smith Lewis, Horae Semiticae number IX, Cambridge.

Anastase (1902a) 'Le texte grec des récits du moine Anastase sur les saints pères du Sinaï' (F. Nau), *Oriens Christianus* 2, 58–89.

Anastase (1902b) *Les récits inédits du moine Anastase; contribution à l'histoire du Sinaï au commencement de VIIe siècle. (Traduction française.) Avec un résumé des récits édifiants d'Anastase le Sinaïte* (F. Nau) Paris (extrait de la *Revue de l'Institut Catholique de Paris*, numbers 1 et 2).

Anastase (1903) 'Le texte grec des récits utiles à l'âme d'Anastase (le Sinaïte)' (F. Nau), *Oriens Christianus* 3, 57–90.

Anastase d'Arménie (1884) 'Les LXX couvents Arméniens de Jérusalem. Introduction critique et traduction de P. Léonce Alishan', *AOL* II, Documents III. Voyages, 395–9.

Anati, Emmanuel (1993) *Har Karkom in the Light of New Discoveries*, Studi Camuni volume XI, English edition, Capo di Ponte.

Anderson, Reverend John (1852) *Wanderings in the Land of Israel and through the Wilderness of Sinai, in 1850 and 1851. With an Account of the Inscriptions in Wady Mokatteb, or the Written Valley*, Glasgow and London.

Anglure (1878) *Le Saint Voyage de Jherusalem du Seigneur d'Anglure*, publié par François Bonnardot & Auguste Longnon, Paris.

Anonymous (1625) 'Here beginneth the way that is marked, and made wit Mount Joiez from the Lond of Engelond unto Sent Jamez in Gallis, and from thennez to Rome, and from thennez to Jerusalem: and so againe into Engelond, and the namez of all the Citeez be their waie, and the maner of her governanuce, and namez of her silver that they use be alle these waie' in Samuel Purchas, *His Pilgrimes. The Second Part. In Five Bookes.* The Eighth Booke: *Peregrinations, and Travels by Land into Palestina, Natolia, Syria, Arabia, Persia, and Other Parts of Asia*, chapter V, 1230–45.

Anonymous (1680) 'De Gestis Sanctorum Rotonensium, Conwoionis, et aliorum, Libri Tres. Auctore Monacho Rotonensi anonymo, Conwoionis discipulo. Ex ms. codice Rotonensi annorum 700. Liber Tertius de virtutibus sanctorum Episcoporum Marcellini urbis

Romæ Episcopi, & Hypotemii Andegavensis Episcopi: necnon & de liberatione sancti loci à barbaris, precibus sancti Conwoionis Abbatis' in Lucas d'Achery and Johannes Mabillon, *Acta Sanctorum Ordinis S.Benedicti in Sæculorum Classes Distributa. Sæculum IV quod est ab Anno Christi DCCC ad DCCCC*, pars secunda, Lutetiæ Parisiorum, 214–22.

Anonymous (1906) 'Sec. XIII. – Anonymi Minoritae (?): – A) De Saracenis et de ritu ipsorum etc. – B) Brevis descriptio Orbis' in Golubovich 1906, 399–404.

Antoninus (1879a) 'Antonini Martyris Perambulatio Locorum Sanctorum [circa 570]' in Tobler & Molinier 1879.

Antoninus (1879b) 'De Locis Transmarinis Sacris Beati Antonini Martyris' in Tobler & Molinier 1879.

Antoninus (1889) *Antonini Placentini Itinerarium*, im unentstellten Text mit deutscher Übersetzung, herausgegeben von J. Gildemeister, Berlin.

Antoninus (1897) *Of the Holy Places visited by Antoninus Martyr*, translated by Aubrey Stewart and annotated by Col. Sir C.W. Wilson, London 1887, in *The Library of the Palestine Pilgrims' Text Society*, volume II, London.

Antoninus Placentinus (1965a) 'Itinerarium', cura et studio P. Geyer, *CCSL* CLXXV (*Itineraria et alia Geographica*): V, Turnholti, 127–53.

Antoninus Placentinus (1965b) 'Itinerarium (recensio altera)', cura et studio P. Geyer, *CCSL* CLXXV (*Itineraria et alia Geographica*): V, Turnholti, 155–74.

Arad, Schlomo and Sami Michael (1984) *Bedouins. The Sinai Nomads*, Jerusalem.

Arad, V. and Y. Bartov (1981) *Geological Research in Sinai. Bibliography*, Jerusalem.

Arundale, F. (1837) *Illustrations of Jerusalem and Mount Sinai; Including the most Interesting Sites between Grand Cairo and Beirout [...] with a Descriptive Account of his Tour and Residence in those Remarkable Countries*, London.

Athanasius Sacri Montis Sinai in Arabia Archiepiscopus (1727) *Illustrisse DDVV Humillimi in Christo Athanasius et Devotissimi Religiosi S. Montis Sinai in Arabia per Hieromonachum nostrum Dionisium humillime presentatus.*

Auvergne, Monseigneur (1854) *Ses voyages à Rome, à Naples, au mont Liban, au Sinaï; sa mort; la translation de son corps de Diarbékir au mont Liban; d'après ses lettres, ses relations et les documents adressés par les consuls de Syrie*, Lille.

Avi-Yonah, Michael (1954) *The Madaba Mosaic Map*, Jerusalem.

Avni, Gideon (1994) 'Early Mosques in the Negev Highlands: New Archaeological Evidence on Islamic Penetration of Southern Palestine', *BASOR* 294 (May), 83–100.

Avnimelech, M.A. (1965) *Bibliography of Levant Geology including Cyprus, Hatay, Israel, Jordania, Lebanon, Sinai and Syria*, Jerusalem.

Avnimelech, M.A. (1969) *Bibliography of Levant Geology including Cyprus, Hatay, Israel, Jordania, Lebanon, Sinai and Syria*, Jerusalem.

Awad, Hassân (1951) *La montagne du Sinaï Central: étude morphologique*, Le Caire.

Baedeker, K., editor (1878) *Egypt. Handbook for Travellers.* Part First: *Lower Egypt, with the Fayûm and the Peninsula of Sinai*, Leipsic and London.

Baedeker, Karl, editor (1895) *Egypt. Handbook for Travellers.* Part First: *Lower Egypt and the Peninsula of Sinai*, Leipsic and London, third edition.

Bailey, Clinton (1991) *Bedouin Poetry from Sinai and the Negev; Mirror of a Culture*, Oxford.

Baldensel, Guilielmus de (1725) 'Nobilissimi Guilielmi de Baldensel, Equitis Aurati Hierosolymitani, Hodoeporicon ad Terram Sanctam. Anno 1336 […] editum […] Matthiæ Eberspergeri' in Canisius 1725, 331–57.

Baldwin, Barry (1991) 'Moschos, John', *ODB*, New York and Oxford, 1415.

Baldwin, Barry and Nancy Patterson Ševčenko (1991) 'Ephrem the Syrian', *ODB*, New York and Oxford, 708.

Ballet, Pascale (2001) 'Un atelier de potiers aux "Sources de Moïse" (ʿUyūn Mūsā)', in Mouton 2001a, 37–50.

Barber, Malcolm (2003) 'The career of Philip of Nablus in the kingdom of Jerusalem' in Peter Edbury and Jonathan Phillips, editors, *The Experience of Crusading 2. Defining the Crusader Kingdom*, Cambridge.

Barbessa, Odoardo (1550) 'Libro di Odoardo Barbessa Portoghese' in *Delle Nauigationi et Viaggi nel qual si contiene La Descrittione dell'Africa, Et del Paese del Prete Ianni, con uarii uiaggi, dal mar Rosso à Calicut, & insin all'isole Molucche, doue nascono le Setierie, Et la Nauigatione attorno il mondo*, primo volume, Venetia, 310–348v.

Baronius, Cæsar S.R.E. Card. (1869) *Annales Ecclesiastici denuo excusi et ad nostra usque tempora perducti ab Augustino Theiner*, tomus sextusdecimus 934–1045, Romæ.

Barron, T. (1907) *The Topography and Geology of the Peninsula of Sinai (Western Portion)*, Cairo.

Barros, João de (1552) *Asia de Joam de Barros, dos feitos que os Portugueses fizeram no descobrimento e conquista dos mares e terras do Oriente, Da primeira decada*, Lisboa.

Barros, João de (1932) *Ásia de Joam de Barros, dos feitos que os Portugueses fizeram no descobrimento e conquista dos mares e terras do Oriente, primeira decada, quarta edição revista e prefaciada por António Baião conforme a edição princeps, Livro octavo*, Coimbra.

Bartlett, S.C. (1879) *From Egypt to Palestine through Sinai the Wilderness and the South Country; Observations of a Journey made with Special Reference to the History of the Israelites*, New York.

Bartlett, W.H. (1862) *Forty Days in the Desert, on The Track of the Israelites; or, A Journey from Cairo, by Wady Feiran, to Mount Sinai and Petra*, London, fifth edition.

Bar-Yosef, Ofer (1982) 'Pre-Pottery Neolithic Sites in Southern Sinai', *BiblArch* 45 number 1 (winter), 9–12.

Basile, Christopher (1998) 'The dimension of sound' in David Parsons (producer), *The Music of Islam. Volume Two: Music of the South Sinai Bedouins*, CD, Tucson.

Bausman, Benjamin (1861) *Sinai and Zion; or, A Pilgrimage through the Wilderness to the Land of Promise*, Philadelphia.

Beadnell, H.J. Llewellyn (1927) *The Wilderness of Sinai. A Record of Two Years' Recent Exploration*, London.

Beamont, Reverend W.J. (1861) *Cairo to Sinai and Sinai to Cairo; Being an Account of a Journey in the Desert of Arabia, November and December, 1860*, Cambridge and London.

Beamont, William (1871) *To Sinai and Syene and Back in 1860 and 1861*, London.

Beckingham, C.F. (1997) 'North and north-east Africa and the Near and Middle East' in L.E. Pennington, editor, *The Purchas Handbook. Studies of the life, times and writings of Samuel Purchas 1577–1626 with bibliographies of his books and of works about him*, London.

Behrens-Abouseif, Doris (2007) *Cairo of the Mamluks. A History of the Architecture and its Culture*, London.

Beit-Arieh, Itzak (1982) 'New Discoveries at Serâbît el-Khâdîm', *BiblArch* 45 number 1 (winter), 13–18.

Beke, Charles Tilstone (1834) *Origines Biblicæ; or Researches in Primeval History*, London.

Beke, Charles T. (1835) *On the Localities of Horeb, Mount Sinai, and Midian, in Connexion with the Hypothesis of the Distinction Between Mitzraim and Egypt*, reprinted from the *British Magazine*, London.

Beke, Charles T. (1862) *A Few Words with Bishop Colenso on the Subject of the Exodus of the Israelites and the Position of Mount Sinai*, London.

Beke, Charles T. (1871) *The Idol in Horeb: Evidence that the Golden Image at Mount Sinai was a Cone, and not a Calf*, London.

Beke, Charles T. (1873) *Mount Sinai A Volcano*, London, second edition.

Beke, Charles (1878) *The Late Dr. Charles Beke's Discoveries of Sinai in Arabia and of Midian. With Portrait, Geological, Botanical, and Conchological Reports, Plans, Map, and Thirteen Wood Engravings. Edited by his Widow*, London.

Belon du Mans, Pierre (1970) *Voyage en Egypte de Pierre Belon du Mans 1547*, présentation et notes de Serge Sauneron, Le Caire.

Ben-David, Joseph (1977–8) *The Bedouin Tribes in Southern Sinai*, Jerusalem (in Hebrew with English summary).

Bénédite, Georges (1891) *La péninsule Sinaïtique*, Paris.

Beneshevich, V.N. (1925) *Monumenta Sinaitica archaeologica et palaeographica*, volume I, Leningrad.

Benjamin of Tudela (1840) *The Itinerary of Rabbi Benjamin of Tudela*, translated and edited by A. Asher, volume I, London and Berlin.

Benjamin of Tudela (1983) *The Itinerary of Benjamin of Tudela. Travels in the Middle Ages*, introductions by Michael A. Singer, 1983, Marcus Nathan Adler, 1907, A. Asher, 1840, translation by Masaʻot shel Rabi Binyamin, Malibu.

Bensly, Agnes Dorothee (1896) *Our Journey to Sinai. A Visit to the Convent of St. Catarina. With a Chapter on the Sinai Palimpsest. Illustrated from Photographs Taken by the Author*, London.

Bentley, James (1985) *Secrets of Mount Sinai: The Story of the Codex Sinaiticus*, London.

Bianchi, Noe (1500) *Viazo da venesia al sancto iherusalez, et al monte sinai sepulcro de sancta chaterina piu copiosamente et verissimame(n)te descrito, che nesuno deli altri cum dessegni de paesi citade porti y chiesie y sancti luoghi y molte altr(e) sanctimo(n)ie ch' qui se trouva(n)o designate et descrite chome sono ne li logi lor ppri. yc.*, Venice.

Bianchi, Noe (1800) *Viaggio da Venezia al Santo Sepolcro, ed al Monte Sinai col disegne delle Città, Castelli, Ville, Chiese, Monasteri, Isole, Porti, Fiumi, che sin la si ritrovano; ed una breve regola di quanto si deve osservare nel detto Viaggio; e quello che si paga da luogo a luogo, sì di Dazi, come d'altre cose. Composto dal R. Padre F. Noe' dell' Ordine di S. Francesco*, Treviso.

Bida and Hachette, Georges (1864) 'Excursion au Mont Sinaï, par deux voyageurs Français. 1862. – Texte inédit. – Dessins inédits par M.H.

Pottin d'après M. Bida', *Le Tour du Monde. Nouveau Journal des Voyages* IX/209 (prémier sémestre), 1–16.

Blum, Howard (1998) *The Gold of the Exodus. The Discovery of the Most Sacred Place on Earth*, London.

Blunt, Wilfrid (1953) *Pietro's Pilgrimage. A Journey to India and back at the beginning of the Seventeenth Century*, London.

Bonar, Horatius (1857) *The Desert of Sinai: Notes of a Spring-Journey from Cairo to Beersheba*, London.

Bonné, Batsheva *et al.* (Marilyn Godber, Sarah Ashbel, Arthur E. Mourant and Donald Tills) (1971) 'South-Sinai Beduin. A Preliminary Report on Their Inherited Blood Factors', *American Journal of Physical Anthropology* 34.3 (May), 397–408.

Borrer, Dawson (1845) *A Journey from Naples to Jerusalem, by Way of Athens, Egypt, and the Peninsula of Sinai, Including a Trip to the Valley of Fayoum; Together with a Translation of M. Linant de Bellefond's 'Mémoire sur le lac Mœris'*, London.

Bosio, Luciano (1983) *La Tabula Peutingeriana. Una descrizione pittorica del mondo antico*, Rimini.

Bottini, Giovanni-Claudio (1995) 'Tommaso Obicini (1585–1632) Custos of the Holy Land and Orientalist' in Anthony O'Mahony, Göran Gunner and Kevork Hintlian, *The Christian Heritage in the Holy Land*, Cavendish, 97–101.

Bowersock, Glen Warren (1996) *Roman Arabia*, Cambridge Massachusetts.

Bowman, Glenn (2001) 'A Textual Landscape: The Mapping of a Holy Land in the Fourth-Century *Itinerarium* of the Bordeaux Pilgrim' in Paul and Janet Starkey, editors, *Unfolding the Orient*, Reading, 7–39.

Bracciolini, Poggius (1723) *Poggii Bracciolini Florentini Historiæ de Varietate Fortunæ Libri Quatuor, ex Ms. Codice Bibliothecæ Ottobonianæ nunc primum editi, & Notis illustrati Adominico Georgio*, Lutetiæ Parisiorum.

Bräm, A. (1859) *Israels Wanderung von Gosen bis zum Sinai*, Elberfeld.

Brasca, Santo (1966) 'Viaggio in Terrasanta di Santo Brasca 1480', a cura di Anna Laura Momigliano Lepschy, in Marenco 1966, 17–158.

Breasted, James Henry (1906) *Ancient Records of Egypt. Historical Documents from the Earliest Times to the Persian Conquest, Collected Edited and Translated with Commentary*, volume I: *The First to the Seventeenth Dynasties*, volume II: *The Eighteenth Dynasty*, volume IV: *The Twentieth to the Twenty-Sixth Dynasties*, Chicago.

Breidenbach *et al.* (Baumgarten, Bellonius and Christopher Furer of Haimendorf) (1625) 'Mount Sinai, Oreb, and the adioyning parts of Arabia, described out of the foure Journals of Breidenbach,

Baumgarten, Bellonius, and Christopher Furer of Haimendorf' in Samuel Purchas, *His Pilgrimes. The Second Part. In Five Bookes.* The Eighth Booke: *Peregrinations, and Travels by Land into Palestina, Natolia, Syria, Arabia, Persia, and Other Parts of Asia*, chapter XIII, 1376–82.

Bremond, Gabriel (1680) *Descrittioni esatte dell' Egitto Superiore, et Inferiore, Monte Sinai, Libano, Terra Santa, e altro Provincie di Siria, come anche del Peregrinaggio de Mahomettani dal Cairo, e Damasco, alla Meka, e Sepolcro di Mahometto nella Città di Medina. Con varie, e curiose osservationi di costumi, Leggi, riti, e habiti di più nationi, e belissime notitie di successi così antichi, come moderni. Tradotta dal Francese dal Sig. Angelo Riccardo Ceri Rom.*, Roma.

Brendon, Piers (1992) *Thomas Cook. 150 Years of Popular Tourism*, London.

Breydy, Michel (1983) *Études sur Saʿīd ibn Baṭrīq et ses sources*, CSCO Volumen 450 Subsidia Tomus 69, Lovanii.

Briend, Jacques, editor (2003) *Terre Sainte. Cinquante ans d'archéologie.* Volume 2. *De la Judée au Sinaï*, Paris.

Brockbank, Oliver (1914) *Diary of a Journey through the Sinai Peninsula and Arabia in 1914*, n.p.

Brocklebank, John (1865) *Continental and Oriental Travels: Being Excursions in France, Italy, Egypt, Sinai, Palestine, and Syria. With Biblical Elucidations and Historical Notes*, London.

Brown, Edward (1739) *The Travels and Adventures of Edward Brown, Esq; Formerly a Merchant in London*, London.

Brown, Peter (1996) *The Making of Late Antiquity*, Cambridge Massachusetts.

Brown, Peter (1998) *Late Antiquity*, Cambridge Massachusetts and London, second edition.

Browne, W.G. (1799) *Travels in Africa, Egypt, and Syria, from the year 1792 to 1798*, London.

Brugsch, Heinrich (1866) *Wanderung nach den Türkis-Minen und der Sinai-Halbinsel*, Leipzig.

Brugsch-Bey, Henri (1875a) *L'Exode et les Monuments Égyptiens. Discours prononcé à l'occasion du Congrès International d'Orientalistes à Londres*, Leipzig.

Brugsch Bey, Heinrich (1875b) *Neue Bruchstücke des Codex Sinaiticus aufgefunden in der Bibliothek des Sinai-Klosters*, Leipzig.

Brygg, Thomas (1884) *'Itinerarium in Terram Sanctam Domini Thomæ de Swynburne, castellani Ghisnensis et postea Burdigalensis majoris.* Introduction critique de comte Riant', *AOL* II, Documents III. Voyages, 378–88.

Burckhardt, John Lewis (1822) *Travels in Syria and the Holy Land*, edited by William Martin Leake, London.

Buxton, Edward North *et al.* (Hannah Maud Buxton, Clare Emily Buxton and Theresa Buxton) (1895) *On Either Side of the Red Sea. With Illustrations of the Granite Ranges of the Eastern Desert of Egypt, and of Sinai*, London.

Buxton, Edward North (1898) *Short Stalks. Second Series. Comprising Trips to Somaliland, Sinai, the Eastern Desert of Egypt, Crete, the Carpathian Mountains, and Daghestan*, London.

Calderon, Rivka (2000) 'Byzantine Pottery from South Sinai' in Dahari 2000, 183–231.

Cameron, Averil (1985) *Procopius and the Sixth Century*, London.

Canisius, Henricus (1725) *Thesaurus Monumentorum Ecclesiasticorum et Historicorum, sive Henrici Canisii Lectiones Antiquæ, ad Sæculorum Ordinem Digestæ Variisque Opusculis Auctæ, quibus Præfationes Historicas, Animadversiones Criticas, et Notas in Singulos Auctores Adjecit Jacobus Basnage*, tomus IV, Antverpiæ.

Cantineau, J. (1930) *Le Nabatéen I. Notions générales, Écriture, Grammaire*, Paris.

Cantineau, J. (1932) *Le Nabatéen II. Choix de textes, Lexique*, Paris.

Capodilista, Gabriele (1966) 'Itinerario di Gabriele Capodilista 1458', a cura di Anna Laura Momigliano Lepschy, in Marenco 1966, 159–241.

Caranikolas, Panteleimon (1955) *A Note on Anastasius of Sinai*, Athens (extract from *Theology* XXVI).

Carne, John (1830a) *Letters from the East: Written during a Recent Tour through Turkey, Egypt, Arabia, the Holy Land, Syria, and Greece*, volume I, London, third edition.

Carne, John (1830b) *Recollections of Travels in the East; a Continuation of the Letters from the East*, London.

Carne, John (1885) *Letters 1813–1837*, Edinburgh (number 23 of a privately printed edition of 100 copies).

Carré, Dominique *et al.* (Jean-Paul Desroches, Franck Goddio) (1994) *Le San Diego; Un trésor sous la mer*, Paris.

Cart, Léon (1915) *Au Sinaï et dans l'Arabie Pétrée*, extrait du tome XXIII du *Bulletin de la Société Neuchâteloise de Géographie*, Neuchâtel.

Casey, Edward S. (1998) *The Fate of Place. A Philosophical History*, Berkeley/ Los Angeles/ London.

Castro, Don John of (1625) 'A Rutter of Don John of Castro, of the Voyage which the Portugals made from India to Zoez. [...]' in Samuel Purchas, *His Pilgrimes. The Second Part. In Five Bookes. The Seventh Booke: Navigations, Voyages, and Discoveries of the*

Sea-Coasts and Inland Regions of Africa, which is generally called Æthiopia: By Englishmen and Others, chapter VI, 1123–48.

Champdor, Albert (1963) *Le Mont Sinaï et le Monastère Sainte-Catherine*, Paris.

Chitty, Derwas J. (1995) *The Desert a City. An Introduction to the Study of Egyptian and Palestinian Monasticism under the Christian Empire*, Crestwood N.Y.

Christides, Vassilios (1973) 'Once Again the "Narrations" of Nilus Sinaiticus', *Byzantion* XLIII Hommage à Marius Canard, 39–50.

CIS (1907) *Corpus Inscriptionum Semiticarum, Pars Secunda; Inscriptiones Aramaicas continens, Tomus II, Fasciculus Primus*, Parisiis.

Clarke, Reverend C. Pickering (1884) 'Sinai' in Colonel Sir Charles W. Wilson, editor, *Picturesque Palestine; Sinai and Egypt*, London, volume IV, 1–120.

Closen S.J., G.E. (1935) *Ad Montes Sinai et Nebo. Iter Pontificii Instituti Biblici in Paeninsulam Sinaiticam Factum a Die 3 ad 13 Octobris A. 1934*, Romae.

Cohen, Nira (1979) 'A Note on Two Inscriptions from Jebel Moneijah', *IEJ* 29, 219–20.

Coleman, Simon and John Elsner (1995) *Pilgrimage. Past and Present in the World Religions*, London.

Conder, Josiah (1830) *The Modern Traveller. A Description, Geographical, Historical, and Topographical, of the Various Countries of the Globe*, Volume the Fourth, *Arabia*, London.

Cook, Thomas (1874) *Programmes of Personally-Conducted and Independent Palestine Tours, with Extensions to Egypt and the Nile, Sinai, Petra, Moab, the Hauran, Turkey, Greece, and Italy, for the Season of 1874–5*, London.

Cook, Thomas (1897) *Cook's Tourist's Handbook for Egypt, the Nile and the Desert*, London.

Cook, Thomas (1899) *Cook's Tours in Palestine, Egypt, Moab, Sinai, Petra, etc. Programme of Arrangements*, London.

Coppin, Jean (1971) *Voyages en Egypte de Jean Coppin 1638–1639 1643–1646*, présentation et notes de Serge Sauneron, Le Caire.

Cormack, Robin and Maria Vassilaki (2008) *Byzantium, 330–1453*, London.

Cosmas (1897) *The Christian Topography of Cosmas, an Egyptian Monk*, translated from the Greek, and Edited, with Notes and Introduction by J.W. McCrindle, London.

Cosmas (1909) *The Christian Topography of Cosmas Indicopleustes*, edited with geographical notes by E.O. Winstedt, Cambridge.

Cosmas Indicopleustès (1968) *Topographie Chrétienne*, tome I, introduction, texte critique, illustration, traduction et notes par Wanda Wolska-Conus, Paris.

Cosmas Indicopleustès (1970) *Topographie Chrétienne*, tome II, introduction, texte critique, illustration, traduction et notes par Wanda Wolska-Conus, Paris.

Coutelle, J.M.J. (1832) 'Extrait des observations sur la topographie de la presqu'ile de Sinai; Les moeurs, les usages, l'industrie, le commerce et la population des habitants' in S. Cahen, *La Bible, traduction nouvelle, avec l'Hébreu en regard, Pentateuque* tome second. *L'Exode*, Paris, 190–215.

Crossley, H. (1860) 'Sinai, Kadesh, and Mount Hor; or, a Critical Enquiry into the Route of the Exodus', *The Journal of Sacred Literature and Biblical Record* XXI (April), 1–60.

Crusius, Martinus (1584) *Turcogrœciœ libri octo*, Basileæ.

Cytryn-Silverman, Katia (2001) 'The Settlement in Northern Sinai during the Islamic Period' in Mouton 2001a, 3–36.

Dahari, Uzi (1993) 'Remote Monasteries in Southern Sinai and Their Economic Base' in Tsafrir 1993a, 341–50.

Dahari, Uzi (2000) *Monastic Settlements in South Sinai in the Byzantine Period. The Archaeological Remains*, with contributions by R. Calderon, W.D. Cooke, Y. Gorin-Rosen and O. Shamir, Jerusalem.

Danin, Avinoam (1979) 'The Flora. Wild and Cultivated Plants' in Rothenberg *et al.* 1979, 77–83.

Dansette, Béatrice (2001) 'Le Sinaï, lieu de solitude, centre de relations et d'échanges spirituels ? Essai d'interprétation des récits des pèlerins occidentaux au Sinaï aux derniers siècles du Moyen Âge' in Mouton 2001a, 63–85.

Daumas, J. (1951) *La péninsule de Sinaï*, Le Caire.

Davies, Hugh W.M. (1911) *Bernhard von Breydenbach and his Journey to the Holy Land 1483–4. A Bibliography*, London.

Davis, John (1996) *The Landscape of Belief. Encountering the Holy Land in Nineteenth-Century American Art and Culture*, Princeton.

Dawson, Sir J. William (1885) *Egypt and Syria. Their Physical Features in Relation to Bible History*, London.

Décobert, Christian (1992) 'Sur l'arabisation et l'islamisation de l'Égypte médiévale' in Christian Décobert, editor, *Itinéraires d'Égypte. Mélanges offerts au père Maurice Martin s.j.*, Le Caire.

Degenhart, Friedrich (1915) *Der Hl. Nilus Sinaita (Sein Leben und Seine Lehre von Mönchtum)*, Münster in Westf.

Degg, Martin R. (1990) 'A Database of Historical Earthquake Activity in the Middle East', *Transactions of the Institute of British Geographers* New Series 15 number 3, 294–307.

Deluz, Christiane (2001) 'Bédouins et pèlerins d'Occident au Sinaï, une difficile rencontre' in Mouton 2001a, 183–96.

Description (1994) *Description de l'Égypte, ou Recueil des Observations et des Recherches qui ont été faites en Égypte pendant l'Éxpédition de l'Armée Française, publié par les Ordres de Sa Majesté l'Empereur Napoléon le Grand*, I-*Planches*, *Etat Moderne*, volume II, Köln.

De Via (1906) 'Sec. XIII. – De Via eundi de Iope in Ierusalem, et de Santo Sepulcro, et aliis locis' in Golubovich 1906, 405–8.

De Vitis Patrum (1849) 'De Vitis Patrum Liber Quintus sive Verba Seniorum', interprete Pelagio S.R.E. Diacono, *PL* LXXIII, Parisiis, 851–992.

Devos, Paul (1967) 'La date du voyage d'Égerie', *AB* 85, 165–94.

Devreesse, Robert (1940) 'Le Christianisme dans la péninsule sinaïtique, des origines à l'arrivée des Musulmans', *RB* NS 49 number 2, 205–23.

Disraeli, B. (1847) *Tancred: or, the New Crusade*, volume II, London.

Döbel, E. Ch. (1842) *Wanderungen im Morgenlande. Herausgegeben von Ludwig Storch*, zweiter Band, Gotha.

Dobson, A. Mary R. (1925) *Mount Sinai. A Modern Pilgrimage. With a Preface by Rendel Harris*, London.

Donner, Herbert and Heinz Cüppers (1977) *Die Mosaikkarte von Madeba*, Teil I: Tafelband, Wiesbaden.

Duffy, John (1999) 'Embellishing the Steps: Elements of Presentation and Style in *The Heavenly Ladder* of John Climacus', *DOP* 53, 1–17.

Dumas, Alexandre (1839a) *Quinze jours au Sinaï*, tome second, Bruxelles.

Dumas, Alexandre (1839b) *Travelling Sketches in Egypt and Sinai; Including a Visit to Mount Horeb, and Other Localities of the Exodus, Translated, Corrected and Abridged from the French by a Biblical Student*, London.

Durbin, John P. (1845) *Observations in the East. Chiefly in Egypt, Palestine, Syria, and Asia Minor*, volume I, New York.

Ebers, Georg (1872) *Durch Gosen zum Sinai. Aus dem Wanderbuche und der Bibliothek*, Leipzig.

Ebers, Georg and Hermann Guthe (1884) *Palästina in Bild und Wort. Nebst der Sinaihalbinsel und dem Lande Gosen. Nach dem Englischen Herausgegeben*, zweiter Band, Stuttgart und Leipzig.

Eckenstein, Lina (1921) *A History of Sinai*, London.

Eddé, Anne-Marie *et al.* (Françoise Micheau and Christophe Picard) (1997) *Communautés chrétiennes en pays d'Islam du début du VIIe siècle au milieu du XIe siècle*, Paris.

Édrisi (1836) *Géographie d'Édrisi. Traduite de l'Arabe en Français d'après deux manuscrits de la Bibliothèque du Roi et accompagnée de Notes par P. Amédée Jaubert*, tome premier, Paris.

Egeria (1960) *Itinerarium Egeriae (Peregrinatio Aetheriae)*, Herausgegeben von Otto Prinz, Heidelberg.

Egeria (1965) 'Itinerarium Egeriae', cura et studio Aet. Francheschini et R. Weber, *CCSL* CLXXV (*Itineraria et alia Geographica*): II, Turnholti, 27–90.

Egeria (1971) *Egeria's Travels*, newly translated with supporting documents and notes by John Wilkinson, London.

Egéria (1998) *Viagem do Ocidente à Terra Santa, no Séc. IV*, edição de Alexandra B. Mariano e Aires A. Nascimento, Lisboa.

Egeria (2008) *Egeria. Monuments of Faith in the Medieval Mediterranean*, an edition of the Hellenic Ministry of Culture and the Participants of the EGERIA Programme, Athens.

Égérie (1982) *Journal de Voyage (Itinéraire)*, introduction, texte critique, traduction, notes, index et cartes par Pierre Maraval et Valérius de Bierzo, *Lettre sur la B^{se} Égérie*, introduction, texte et traduction par Manuel C. Díaz y Díaz, Paris.

Van Egmont and John Heyman (1759) *Travels Through Part of Europe, Asia Minor, The Islands of the Archipelago, Syria, Palestine, Egypt, Mount Sinai, &c.* […] *Translated from the Low Dutch*, volume II, London.

El Cheikh, Nadia Maria (2004) *Byzantium Viewed by the Arabs*, Cambridge Massachusetts and London.

Ephraem des Syrers (1972a) *Hymnen auf Abraham Kidunaya und Julianos Saba*, Herausgegeben von Edmund Beck, *CSCO* Volumen 322, Scriptores Syri Tomus 140, Louvain.

Ephraem des Syrers (1972b) *Hymnen auf Abraham Kidunaya und Julianos Saba*, Übersetzt von Edmund Beck, *CSCO* Volumen 323, Scriptores Syri Tomus 141, Louvain.

Epiphanius Monachus Hagiopolitis (1864) 'Ad Modum Descriptionis Situs Orbis, Enarratio Syriæ, Urbis Sanctæ, et Sacrorum Ibi Locorum', *PG* CXX, Parisiis, 259–72.

Éthérie (1948) *Journal de Voyage*, texte latin, introduction et traduction de Hélène Pétré, Paris.

Ettinghausen, R. and O. Grabar (1987) *The Art and Architecture of Islam 650–1250*, London.

Eusebius (1966) *Das Onomastikon der Biblischen Ortsnamen*, herausgegeben von Erich Klostermann, Hildesheim.

Eutychios (1985) *Das Annalenwerk des Eutychios von Alexandrien. Ausgewählte Geschichten und Legenden kompiliert von Saᶜid ibn Baṭrīq um 935 A.D.*, Übersetzt von Michael Breydy, *CSCO* Volumen 472, Scriptores Arabici Tomus 45, Lovanii.

Eutychius (1863) 'Contextio Gemmarum sive Eutychii Patriarchæ Alexandrini Annales', Joanne Seldeno chorago; interprete Edwardo Pocockio, *PG* CXI, Parisiis, 889–1232.

Evagrius Scholasticus (1865) 'Historiæ Ecclesiasticæ libri sex', *PG* LXXXVIb, Parisiis, 2406–882.

Evans, Helen C. (2004) *Saint Catherine's Monastery, Sinai, Egypt. A Photographic Essay*, with photographs by Bruce White, New Haven and London.

Evans, R.J.W. (1997) *Rudolf II and his World. A Study in Intellectual History 1576–1612*, London, second edition.

Evenari *et al.* (Leslie Shanan and Naphtali Tadmor with chapters by Yehoshua Itzaki and Amiram Shkolnik) (1982) *The Negev. The Challenge of a Desert*, Cambridge Massachusetts and London, second edition.

Exeria (1991) *Viaxe a Terra Santa*, traducción, introducción e notas de X. Eduardo López Pereira, Madrid.

Fabri, Felix (1843) *Fratris Felicis Fabri Evagatorium in Terræ Sanctæ, Arabiæ et Egypti Peregrinationem*, edidit Cunradus Dietericus Hassler, Volumen Secundum, στη Bibliothek des Literarischen Vereins in Stuttgart III.

Fabri (1897) *The Wanderings of Felix Fabri, Volume II. (Part II.)*, translated by Aubrey Stewart, in *The Library of the Palestine Pilgrims' Text Society*, volume X, London.

Fedden, Robin (1958) *English Travellers in the Near East*, London.

Féhérvári, Géza (2000) *Ceramics of the Islamic World in the Tareq Rajab Museum*, London.

Fernberger, Georg Christoph (1999) *Reisetagebuch (1588–1593) Sinai, Babylon, Indien, Heiliges Land, Osteuropa. Lateinisch-Deutsch. Kritische Edition und Übersetzung von Ronald Burger und Robert Wallisch*, Beiträge zur Neueren Geschichte Österreichs Band 12, Frankfurt am Main.

Fetellus (1897) 'Description of Jerusalem and the Holy Land. By Fetellus' in *The Library of the Palestine Pilgrims' Text Society*, volume V, London.

Feyerabend, Sigmund (1584) *Reyssbuch dess Heyligen Lands, das ist, ein grundtliche Beschreibung aller und jeder Meer und Bilgerfahrten zum Heyligen Lande* [...] , Franckfort am Mayn.

Field, Henry M. (1883) *On the Desert: with a Brief Review of Recent Events in Egypt*, New York.

Field, Henry (1952) *Contributions to the Anthropology of the Faiyum, Sinai, Sudan, Kenya*, Berkeley and Los Angeles.

Figueras, Pau (2000) *From Gaza to Pelusium. Materials for the Historical Geography of North Sinai and Southwestern Palestine (332 BCE–640 CE)*, Beer-Sheva. Studies by the Department of Bible and Ancient Near East volume XIV, Beer-Sheva.

Finkelstein, Israel (1981) 'Byzantine Prayer Niches in Southern Sinai', *IEJ* 31, 81–91.

Finkelstein, Israel (1985) 'Byzantine Monastic Remains in the Southern Sinai', *DOP* 39, 39–75.

Finkelstein, Israel (1993) 'Byzantine Remains at Jebel Sufsafeh (Mt. Horeb) in Southern Sinai' in Tsafrir 1993a, 334–40.

Finkelstein, Israel and Avi Perevolotsky (1990) 'Processes of Sedentarization and Nomadization in the History of Sinai and the Negev', *BASOR* 279 (August), 67–88.

Fiorentino, Poggio (1550) 'Viaggio di Nicolò di Conti Venetiano Scritto per Messer Poggio Fiorentino' in Giovanni Battista Ramusio, editor, *Delle Nauigationi et Viaggi nel qual si contiene La Descrittione dell'Africa, Et del Paese del Prete Ianni, con uarii uiaggi, dal mar Rosso à Calicut, & insin all'isole Molucche, doue nascono le Setierie, Et la Nauigatione attorno il mondo*, primo volume, Venetia, 365–368v.

Fisk, Reverend George (1843) *A Pastor's Memorial of Egypt, the Red Sea, the Wildernesses of Sin and Paran, Mount Sinai, Jerusalem, and Other Principal Localities of the Holy Land, visited in 1842; with Brief Notes of a Route through France, Rome, Naples, Constantinople, and up the Danube*, London.

Fontaine, A.L. (1955) *Monographie cartographique de l'isthme de Suez, de la péninsule du Sinaï, du Nord de la chaîne arabique suivie d'un catalogue raisonné sur les cartes de ces régions*, Mémoires de la Société d' Études Historiques et Géographiques de l'Isthme de Suez, tome II, Le Caire.

Forster, Reverend Charles (1844) *The Historical Geography of Arabia; or, the Patriarchal Evidences of Revealed Religion: A Memoir, with Illustrative Maps; and an Appendix, Containing Translations, with an Alphabet and Glossary, of the Hamyaritic Inscriptions Recently Discovered in Hadramaut*, vols I and II, London.

Forster, Reverend Charles (1851) *The One Primeval Language Traced Experimentally Through Ancient Inscriptions in Alphabetic Characters of Lost Powers from the Four Continents; Including The Voice of Israel from the Rocks of Sinai; and The Vestiges of Patriarchal Tradition from the Monuments of Egypt, Etruria, and Southern Arabia*, Part I: *The Voice of Israel from the Rocks of Sinai: or, The Sinaitic Inscriptions Contemporary Records of the Miracles and Wanderings of the Exode*, London.

Forster, Reverend Charles (1852) *The One Primeval Language Traced Experimentally Through Ancient Inscriptions in Alphabetic Characters of Lost Powers from the Four Continents; Including The Voice of Israel from the Rocks of Sinai; and The Vestiges of Patriarchal Tradition from the Monuments of Egypt, Etruria, and Southern Arabia*, Part II: *The Monuments of Egypt, and Their Vestiges of Patriarchal Tradition*, London.

Forster, Reverend Charles (1854) *The One Primeval Language Traced Experimentally Through Ancient Inscriptions in Alphabetic Characters of Lost Powers from the Four Continents; Including The Voice of Israel from the Rocks of Sinai; and The Vestiges of Patriarchal Tradition from the Monuments of Egypt, Etruria, and Southern Arabia*, Part III: *The Monuments of Assyria, Babylonia, and Persia: with a New Key for the Recovery of the Lost Ten Tribes*, London.

Forster, Reverend Charles (1856) *The Israelitish Authorship of the Sinaïtic Inscriptions Vindicated Against the Incorrect 'Observations' in the 'Sinai and Palestine' of the Rev. Arthur Penrhyn Stanley, M.A. Canon of Canterbury. A Letter to the Right Honourable The Lord Lyndhurst*, London.

Forster, Reverend C. (1860) *A Harmony of Primeval Alphabets*, London.

Forster, Reverend Charles (1862) *Sinai Photographed or Contemporary Records of Israel in the Wilderness*, London.

Forster, Reverend Charles (1865) *'Israel in the Wilderness'; or, Gleanings from the Scenes of the Wanderings. With an Essay on the True Date of Korah's Rebellion*, London.

Forsyth, George H. (1968) 'The Monastery of St. Catherine at Mount Sinai: The Church and Fortress of Justinian', *DOP* 22, 1–19, figures 1–50.

Forsyth, George H. (1980) 'The Monastery of St. Catherine at Mount Sinai: The Church and Fortress of Justinian' in Galey 1980, 49–64.

Forsyth, George H. *et al.* (Kurt Weitzmann with Ihor Ševčenko and Fred Anderegg) (1973) *The Monastery of Saint Catherine at Mount Sinai. The Church and Fortress of Justinian*, plates, Ann Arbor.

Frameynsperg, Rudolphus de (1725) 'Itinerarium Nobilis Viri Rudolphi de Frameynsperg, &c. in Palæstinam, ad Montem Sinai, et in Ægyptum. Anno Domini M.CCCXLVI. A Canisio publici juris factum' in Canisius 1725, 358–60.

Francis Joseph Otto Archduke of Austria (1895) *Drei Wochen auf der Halbinsel Sinai*, 2. Auflage, Wien.

Fratres Minores (1919) 'De Fratribus Minoribus visitandibus captivos in Babylonia' in Golubovich 1919, 68–72.

Frescobaldi *et al.* (1948) *Visit to the Holy Places of Egypt, Sinai, Palestine and Syria in 1384 by Frescobaldi, Gucci & Sigoli*, translated from the Italian by Fr. Theophilus Bellorini O.F.M. and Fr. Eugene Hoade O.F.M. with a preface and notes by Fr. Bellarmino Bagatti O.F.M., Jerusalem.

Friedman, Mark (1996) 'Jewish Pilgrimage after the Destruction of the Second Temple' in Rosovsky 1996, 136–46.

Frith, Francis *et al.* (1860a) *Egypt, Sinai, and Jerusalem: A Series of Twenty Photographic Views by Francis Frith, with Descriptions by Mrs. Poole and Reginald Stuart Poole*, London.

Frith, Francis *et al.* (1860b) *Cairo, Sinai, Jerusalem, and The Pyramids of Egypt: A Series of Sixty Photographic Views by Francis Frith, with Descriptions by Mrs. Poole and Reginald Stuart Poole*, London.

Furtenbach, David (1653) *Furtenbachische Reiss-Beschreibung von Venedig biss zu dem Berg Sinai*, Stuttgart.

Gadsby, John (1864) *Mount Sinai and the Holy Land in 1864*, London.

Galavarēs, Giōrgos (1990a) «Πρώιμες εἰκόνες στὸ Σινὰ ἀπὸ τὸν 6ο ὡς τὸν 11ο αἰώνα» in Manaphēs 1990, 91–101.

Galavarēs, Giōrgos (1990b) «Εἰκονογραφημένα χειρόγραφα» in Manaphēs 1990, 311–45.

Galey, John (1980) *Sinai and the Monastery of St. Catherine*, London.

Garfunkel, Zvi (1979a) 'Geography. Contrasting Landscapes' in Rothenberg *et al.* 1979, 41–51.

Garfunkel, Zvi (1979b) 'Geology. Dramatic Upheavals' in Rothenberg *et al.* 1979, 61–7.

Gasparin, Valérie de (1848) *Journal d'un Voyage au Levant par l'Auteur du Mariage au point de vue Chrétien*, tome III, *Le Désert et la Syrie*, Paris.

Georgius (1721) Georgij Prioris Gemnicensis Ord. Cart, 'Ephemeris Sive Diarium Peregrinationis Transmarinæ, Videlicet Ægypti, Montis Sinai, Terræ Sanctæ ac ultimo Syriæ Anno Domini 1507. Et sequenti' in A.R.P. Bernardo Pezio, *Thesaurus Anecdotorum Novissimus: seu Veterum Monumentorum, præcipuè Ecclesiasticorum, ex Germanicis potissimùm Bibliothecis adornata Collectio recentissima*, tomus II, Pars III, Augustæ Vindelicorum & Græcii, 455–640.

Géramb, Marie-Joseph de (1839) *Pélerinage à Jérusalem et au Mont-Sinaï en 1831, 1832 et 1833*, tome troisième, Paris, fifth edition.

Geramb, Marie-Joseph de (1840) *A Pilgrimage to Palestine, Egypt, and Syria*, volume II, London.

Gerstel, Sharon E.J. and Robert S. Nelson (2010) *Approaching the Holy Mountain. Art and Liturgy at St Catherine's Monastery in the Sinai*, Turnhout.

Gibson, Margaret Dunlop (1893) *How the Codex was Found. A Narrative of Two Visits to Sinai, from Mrs Lewis's Journals, 1892–1893*, Cambridge.

Giovanni (1919) '1328–34. – Monte Sinai. – Papa Giovanni XXII e i Monaci Basiliani greci del Sinai' in Golubovich 1919, 342.

Giustiniano, Bernardo (1672) *Historie Cronologiche della Vera Origine di tutti gl'Ordini Equestri, e Religioni Cavalleresche, consagrate alla Sacra Maestà Cattolica di D. Carlo II. Monarca delle Spagne, &c.*, Venetia.

Goldberg, Paul and Ofer Bar-Yosef (1982) 'Environmental and Archaeological Evidence for Climatic Change in the Southern Levant' in John L. Bintliff and Willem Van Zeist, editors, *Palaeoclimates, Palaeoenvironments and Human Communities in the Eastern Mediterranean Region in Later Prehistory*, part ii, *BAR* International Series 133 (ii), Oxford, 399–418.

Golding, Louis (1938) *In the Steps of Moses the Lawgiver*, London.

Golubovich, Girolamo (1906) *Biblioteca Bio-Bibliografica della Terra Santa e dell' Oriente Francescano*, tomo I (1215–1300), Firenze.

Golubovich, Girolamo (1919) *Biblioteca Bio-Bibliografica della Terra Santa e dell' Oriente Francescano*, tomo III (dal 1300 al 1332), Firenze.

Golubovich, Girolamo (1923) *Biblioteca Bio-Bibliografica della Terra Santa e dell' Oriente Francescano*, tomo IV (dal 1333 al 1345), Firenze.

Golubovich, Girolamo (1927) *Biblioteca Bio-Bibliografica della Terra Santa e dell' Oriente Francescano*, tomo V (dal 1346 al 1400), Firenze.

Goren, Orna (1999) *Traditionelle Handwerksformen der Beduinen in Israel und im Sinai*, Jerusalem.

Goring-Morris, A. Nigel (1987) *At the Edge. Terminal Pleistocene Hunter-Gatherers in the Negev and Sinai*, *BAR* International Series 361 (i+ii), Oxford.

Gorin-Rosen, Yael (2000) 'Glass from Monasteries and Chapels in South Sinai' in Dahari 2000, 233–45.

Graul, Carl (1854) *Reise nach Ostindien über Palästina und Egypten von Juli 1849 bis April 1853. Zweiter Theil: Reise durch Egypten und nach dem Sinai*, Leipzig.

Greene, J. Baker (1883) *The Hebrew Migration from Egypt. A Historical Account of the Exodus, based on a Critical Examination of the Hebrew Records and Traditions*, London, second edition.

Greene, J. Baker (1884) 'The Route of the Exodus', *PEQ*, 230–7.

Greenwood, Ned H. (1997) *The Sinai: A Physical Geography*, Austin.

Grēgoriadēs, Periklēs (1875) Ἡ Ἱερὰ Μονὴ τοῦ Σινᾶ. Κατὰ τὴν τοπογραφικήν, ἱστορικὴν καὶ διοικητικὴν αὐτῆς ἔποψιν, Jerusalem.

Gregorius I (1891) *Registrum Epistolarum*, tomus I, libri I–VII, ediderunt Paulus Ewald et Ludovicus M. Hartmann, *MGH, Epistolarum* tomus I, Berolini.

Gregorius I (1899) *Registrum Epistolarum*, tomus II, libri VIII–XIV cum indicibus et praefatione, edidit Ludovicus M. Hartmann, *MGH, Epistolarum* tomus II, Berolini.

Grossmann, Peter (1988) 'Neue baugeschichtliche Untersuchungen im Katharinenkloster im Sinai', *AA*, Heft 3, 543–58.

Grossmann, Peter (1989) 'Neue frühchristliche Funde aus Ägypten' in *Actes du XIᵉ Congrès International d'Archéologie Chrétienne*, Collection de l'École Française de Rome, *Studi di Antichità Christiana* XLI, Rome, 1843–908.

Grossmann, Peter (1990) «Ἀρχιτεκτονική» in Manaphēs 1990, 29–57.

Grossmann, Peter (2002) Ἡ ἀρχαία πόλις Φαρὰν, ἀρχαιολογικὸς ὁδηγός, Athens.

Grossmann, Peter *et al.* (Michael Jones and Andreas Beichert) (1996) 'Report on the Season in Firan-Sinaï (February–March 1992)', *BZ* 89, Heft 1, 11–36.

Gutwein, Kenneth C. (1981) *Third Palestine. A Regional Study in Byzantine Urbanization*, Washington, D.C.

Hall, H.R., editor (1907) *Handbook for Egypt and the Sudan*, London, 11th edition.

Hamilton, James (1993) *Sinai, the Hedjaz, and Soudan: Wanderings around the Birth-Place of the Prophet, and Across the Æthiopian Desert, from Sawakin to Chartum*, Reading (reprint of the 1857 edition).

Harant z Polžic a z Bezdružic, Krystoff (1608) *Putowánj, aneb cesta z kralowstwj Cžeského do města Benátek: Odtud po Móri do Země Swaté, země Jüdské, a dále do Egypta [...] Potom na Horu Oreb, Synai a swaté Panny Kateřiny, w pusté Arabij* [...] *na dwa Djly rozdělená*, Pražském.

Harant z Polžic a z Bezdružic a na Pecce, Kristof (1855) *Kristofa Haranta z Polžic a z Bezdružic a na Pecce atd. Cesta z královstvi Českého do Benátek, Odtud do země Svaté, země Judské a dále do Egypta a potom na Horu Oreb, Sinai a sv, Kateřiny v pusté Arabii*, díl. II, v Praze.

Harant de Polžic et Bezdružic, Christophe (1972) *Voyage en Egypte 1598, introduction, traduction et notes de Claire et Antoine Brejnik*, Le Caire.

Harant z Polžic a z Bezdružic, Kryštof (1988) *Cesta Kryštofa Haranta z Polžic a z Bezdružic a na Pecce z království Českého do Benátek, odtud do země Svaté, země Judské a dále do Egypta, a potom na horu Oreb, Sinai a sv. Kateřiny v pusté Arábii. Podle vydáni z roku 1854 (v komisi u Fr. Řivnáče) přepsal. František Kožík*, Praha.

Harff, Arnold von (1946) *The Pilgrimage of Arnold von Harff, Knight, from Cologne, through Italy, Syria, Egypt, Arabia, Ethiopia, Nubia, Palestine, Turkey, France and Spain, which he accomplished in the years 1496 to 1499*, translated from the German and edited with notes and an introduction by Malcolm Letts, London.

Hart, Henry Chichester (1891) *Some Account of the Fauna and Flora of Sinai, Petra, and Wâdy 'Araba*, London.

Hazleton, Lesley (1980) *Where Mountains Roar. In Search of the Sinai Desert*, London.

Heidemann, Stefan *et al.* (Christian Müller, Yūsuf Rāġib) (1997) 'Un décret d'al-Malik al-ᶜĀdil en 571/1176 relatif aux moines du Mont Sinaï', *AnIsl* 31, 81–107.

Henniker, Sir Frederick (1823) *Notes during a Visit to Egypt, Nubia, the Oasis, Mount Sinai, and Jerusalem*, London.

Henninger, Joseph (1955) 'Ist der sogenannte Nilus-Bericht eine brauchbare religionsgeschichtliche Quelle?', *Anthropos* 50, 81–148.

Herrmann, Siegfried (1975) *A History of Israel in Old Testament Times*, translated by John Bowden, Philadelphia.

Hershkovitz, Israel (1988) 'The Tell Mahrad Population in Southern Sinai in the Byzantine Era', *IEJ* 38, 47–58.

Hese, Joannis de (1870) 'Itinerarius' in Gustav Oppert, *Der Presbyter Johannes in Sage und Geschichte. Ein Beitrag zur Voelker- und Kirchenhistorie und zur Heldendichtung des Mittelalters*, Berlin, 180–93.

Ḥijjāwī al-Qaddūmī, Ghāda, editor (1996) *Book of Gifts and Rarities (Kitāb al-Hadāyā wa al-Tuḥaf). Selections Compiled in the Fifteenth Century from an Eleventh-Century Manuscript on Gifts and*

Treasures, translated from the Arabic, with introduction, annotations, glossary, appendices, and indices by Ghāda Ḥijjāwī al-Qaddūmī, Cambridge Massachusetts.

Hobbs, Joseph J. (1995) *Mount Sinai*, Austin.

Hobbs, Joseph J. (1996) 'Speaking with People in Egypt's St. Katherine National Park', *The Geographical Review* 86, number 1 (January), 1–21.

Hobbs, Joseph J. (2001) 'The Sinai Bedouin at the Dawn of the Twenty-First Century' in Mouton 2001a, 207–15.

Holland, Reverend F.W. (1870) *Sinai and Jerusalem; or, Scenes from Bible Lands: Illustrated by Twelve Colored Photographic Views, Including a Panorama of Jerusalem, with Descriptive Letterpress*, London.

Holland, Reverend F.W. (1871) 'Explorations in the Peninsula of Sinai' in Capt. Wilson and Capt. Warren, *The Recovery of Jerusalem. A Narrative of Exploration and Discovery in the City and the Holy Land*, London, 513–47.

Holt, Peter M. (1998) 'Pietro Della Valle in Ottoman Egypt 1615–1616' in Starkey & Starkey 1998, 15–23.

Hornby, Emily (1907) *Sinai and Petra. The Journals of Emily Hornby, in 1899 and 1901*, London and Liverpool.

Horne, The Rev. Thomas Hartwell (1837) *The Biblical Keepsake: or, Landscape Illustrations of the Most Remarkable Places Mentioned in the Holy Scriptures, Arranged in the Order of the Several Books and Chapters, Made from Original Sketches Taken on the Spot, and Engraved by W. and E. Finden, with Descriptions of the Plates*, third series, London.

Hourani, George F. (1995) *Arab Seafaring in the Indian Ocean in Ancient and Early Medieval Times*, revised and expanded by John Carswell, Princeton.

Howe, Kathleen Stewart (1997) *Revealing the Holy Land: The Photographic Exploration of Palestine*, Santa Barbara.

Hoyland, Robert (2006) 'New documentary texts and the early Islamic state', *BSOAS* 69, issue 3, 395–416.

Huber, Paul (1979) 'Monks, Pilgrims and Saracens. Sinai in Early Christian Times' in Rothenberg *et al.* 1979, 201–11.

Hugo Flaviniacensis Abbas (1881) 'Chronicon', *PL* CLIV, Parisiis, 9–404.

Hull, Edward (1885) *Mount Seir, Sinai and Western Palestine. Being a Narrative of a Scientific Expedition*, London.

Hull, Edward (1886) *Memoir of the Geology and Geography of Arabia Petræa, Palestine, and adjoining districts. With special reference to the mode of formation of the Jordan–Arabah depression and the Dead Sea*, London.

Humbsch, Robert (1976) *Beiträge zur Geschichte des osmanischen Ägyptens. Nach arabischen Sultans- und Statthalterurkunden des Sinai-Klosters*, Islamkundliche Untersuchungen Band 39, Freiburg.

Isaac, Benjamin (1984) 'Bandits in Judaea and Arabia', *Harvard Studies in Classical Philology* 88, 171–203.

Isaias Simonopetritis, Archimandrite of the Ecumenical Throne (2000) 'A Synoptic View of the Orthodox Ascetical Tradition of Mount Sinai' in *Religious Heritage and Mass Culture in the Third Millennium. Symposium Proceedings*, London, 19–27.

Isambert, Émile (1881) *Itinéraire descriptif, historique et archéologique de l'Orient. Deuxième partie: Malte, Égypte, Nubie, Abyssinie, Sinaï*, Paris.

Itinerarium (1906) 'Sec. XIII. – Itinerarium Sanctorum Locorum' in Golubovich 1906, 408–10.

Jacopo de Verona (1950) *Liber Peregrinationis di Jacopo da Verona*, a cura di Ugo Monneret de Villard, Roma.

Jacques de Vérone (1895) 'Le pèlerinage du moine augustin Jacques de Vérone (1335), publié par R. Röhricht', *Revue de l'Orient Latin* III, 155–302.

Jarvis, Major C.S. (1931) *Yesterday and To-day in Sinai*, Edinburgh and London.

Jarvis, C.S. (1938) *Desert and Delta*, London.

Jarvis, C.S. (1939) *Back Garden of Allah*, London.

Jean Moschus (1946) *Le Pré Spirituel*, introduction et traduction de M.-J. Rouët de Journel, *Sources Chrétiennes* 12, Paris.

Joannis Climaci, S.P.N. (1860a) 'Scala Paradisi', *PG* LXXXVIII, Parisiis, 631–1164.

Joannis Eucrate, Beati (1860b) 'Liber qui inscribitur Pratum', *PG* LXXXVII, pars tertia, Parisiis, 2851–3112.

John Climacus (1959) *The Ladder of Divine Ascent*, translated by Lazarus Moore, with an introduction by M. Heppell, London.

John Moschos (1992) *The Spiritual Meadow (Pratum Spirituale)*, Introduction, Translation and Notes by John Wortley, Kalamazoo.

Jullien, R.P.M. (1893) *Sinaï et Syrie. Souvenirs bibliques et chrétiens*, Lille.

Justin Sinaites, Father (2007) 'The Sinai Codex Theodosianus: Manuscript as Icon' in Nelson & Collins 2007, 56–77.

Kalopissi-Verti, Sophia (2006) 'Excavating on the Holy Summit (Gebel Musa) at Mt Sinai: a proposal of heritage management' in Elizabeth Jeffreys, editor, *Proceedings of the 21st International Congress of*

Byzantine Studies, London 21–26 August 2006, volume II, *Abstracts of Panel Papers*, London, 279–80.

Kalopissi-Verti, Sophia and Maria Panayotidi (2010) 'Excavations on the Holy Summit (Jebel Mūsā) at Mount Sinai: Preliminary Remarks on the Justinianic Basilica' in Gerstel & Nelson 2010, 73–106.

Kamil, Jill (1991) *The Monastery of Saint Catherine in Sinai. History and Guide*, Maps and Photographs by Michael Stock, Cairo.

Katzenellenbogen (1882) Reinhold Röhricht and Heinrich Meisner, 'Die Pilgerreise des Letzten Grafen von Katzenellenbogen (1433–1434)', *Zeitschrift für Deutsches Alterthum und Deutsche Litteratur* 26, 348–71.

Kawatoko, Mutsuo (1995) *Al-Ṭūr. A Port City Site on the Sinai Peninsula. The 11th Expedition in 1994 (A Summary Report)*, Tokyo.

Kawatoko, Mutsuo (1996) *Al-Ṭūr. A Port City Site on the Sinai Peninsula, The 12th Expedition in 1994 (A Summary Report)*, Tokyo.

Kawatoko, Mutsuo (1998) *Al-Ṭūr. A Port City Site on the Sinai Peninsula. The 13th Expedition in 1996 (A Summary Report)*, Tokyo.

Kazhdan, Alexander (1991) 'Epiphanios Hagiopolites', *ODB*, New York and Oxford, 714.

Kazhdan, Alexander and Robert S. Nelson (1991) 'John Klimax', *ODB*, New York and Oxford, 1060–1.

Kellogg, Miner K. (1848) 'The Position of Mount Sinai Examined', *The Literary World* 55 (volume III, number 3) 19 February, 44–6.

Kempe, Michael (2006) 'Sermons in Stone. Johann Jacob Scheuchzer's Concept of the Book of Nature and the Physics of the Bible' in Klaas van Berkel and Arjo Vanderjagt, editors, *The Book of Nature in Early Modern and Modern History*, Groningen Studies in Cultural Change volume 17, Leuven, 111–120.

Kergorlay, Cte Jean de (1911) *Sites délaissés d'Orient (du Sinaï à Jérusalem)*, Paris.

Kerkeslager, Allen (1998) 'Jewish Pilgrimage and Jewish Identity in Hellenistic and Early Roman Egypt' in David Frankfurter, editor, *Pilgrimage and Holy Space in Late Antique Egypt*, Leiden, 99–225.

Khatib, Hisham (2001) 'Edward Lear's Travels to the Holy Land: visits to Mount Sinai, Petra and Jerusalem' in Searight & Wagstaff 2001, 197–211.

Khitrowo, Mme B. de (1889) *Itinéraires russes en Orient traduits pour la Société de l'Orient Latin*, I, 1, Genève.

Kiechel, Samuel (1866) *Die Reisen des Samuel Kiechel. Aus drei Handschriften Herausgegeben von Dr K.D. Haszler*, Bibliothek des Litterarishen Vereins in Stuttgart LXXXVI, Stuttgart.

Kiechel, Samuel (1972) 'Voyage de Samuel Kiechel 25 avril–16 septembre 1588', traduit de l'allemand par Ursula Castel, présentation et notes de Serge Sauneron, in *Voyages* 1972, 27–143.

Kiepert, H. (1859) *Karte der Sinai-Halbinsel nach den Itinerarien von Burckhardt, Rüppell, Laborde, Callier, Koller, Russegger, Robinson, Abeken und R. Lepsius construirt und gezeichnet von H. Kiepert*, Berlin.

King, Geoffrey (2009) 'Camels and Arabian *balîya* and other forms of sacrifice: a review of archaeological and literary evidence', *Arabian Archaeology and Epigraphy* 20, 81–93.

Kinnear, John G. (1841) *Cairo, Petra, and Damascus, in 1839. With Remarks on the Government of Mehemet Ali, and on the Present Prospects of Syria*, London.

Kircher, Athanasius (1636) *Prodromus Coptus sive Ægyptiacus* [...] *in quo Cùm linguæ Coptæ, siue Aegyptiacæ, quondam Pharaonicæ, origo, ætas, vicissitudo, inclinatio; tùm hieroglyphicæ literaturæ instauratio, vti per varia variarum eruditionum, interpretationumque difficillimarum specimina, ita noua quoque & insolita methodo exhibentur*, Romæ.

Kitchener, H.H. (1885) 'Major Kitchener's Report' in Hull 1885, 199–222.

Kitto, John (1835a) 'Mount Sinai', *The Penny Magazine of the Society for the Diffusion of Useful Knowledge* 231 (November 7), 433–5.

Kitto, John (1835b) 'Convent of Mount Sinai', *The Penny Magazine of the Society for the Diffusion of Useful Knowledge* 233 (November 21), 449–52.

Kitto, John (1850) *The Bible History of the Holy Land*, London, second edition.

Kitto, John (1860) *The Illustrated Commentary on the Old and New Testaments, Chiefly Explanatory of the Manners and Customs Mentioned in the Sacred Scriptures; and also of the History, Geography, Natural History, and Antiquities; Being a Republication of the Notes of the Pictorial Bible, of a Size which will Range with The Authorised Editions of the Sacred Text; with Many Hundred Woodcuts, from the Best and Most Authentic Sources*, volume I, London.

Klopfenstein, Martin A. (1979) 'Exodus, Desert, Mount of God. Biblical Traditions of Sinai' in Rothenberg *et al.* 1979, 17–32.

Knobel, August (1857) *Die Bücher Exodus und Leviticus*, Leipzig.

Koikylides, Kleops M. (1897) Ὁ ἐν Μαδηβᾷ Μωσαϊκὸς καὶ Γεωγραφικὸς Περὶ Συρίας, Παλαιστίνης καὶ Αἰγύπτου Χάρτης, Jerusalem.

Koller, Baron (1842) 'Extract from Baron Koller's Itinerary of his Tour to Petra, describing an Inland Route from Mount Sinai to Akabah', *Journal of the Royal Geographical Society of London* 12, 75–9.

Konidarēs, Gerasimos (1971) «Γενικὴ βιβλιογραφία περὶ Σινᾶ» in Gerasimos Konidarēs, editor, *Πανηγυρικὸς τόμος ἐπὶ τῇ 1400ῇ ἀμφιετηρίδι τῆς Ἱερᾶς Μονῆς τοῦ Σινᾶ*, Athens.

Koufopoulos, Petros *et al.* (Marina Myriantheōs-Koufopoulou and Daniēl Sinaitēs) (2000) «Παρατηρήσεις στην παραγωγή και χρήση του κεριού στη Μονή Σινά» in *Η Μέλισσα και και Προϊόντα της, Στ΄ Τριήμερο Εργασίας, Νικητή, 12–15 Σεπτεμβρίου 1996*, Athens.

Koufopoulos, Petros, Marina Myriantheos-Koufopoulou, Costas Zambas, Amerimni Galanou and Ioanna Dogani (2004) 'The 6th century timber roof of St Catherine Sinai: identification, research and proposals for its protection' in Clara Bertolini, Tanja Marzi, Elisabeth Seip and Panos Touliatos, editors, *Interaction between Science, Technology and Architecture in Timber Construction*, Paris.

Koufopoulos, Petros and Marina Myriantheos-Koufopoulou (2010) 'The Architecture of the Justinianic Basilica on the Holy Summit' in Gerstel & Nelson 2010, 107–17.

Koufopoulos, Petros and Marina Myriantheos (2014) 'Water Management at the Monastery of Mount Sinai during the 6th Century AD' in I.K. Kalavrouziotis and A.N. Angelakis, editors, *IWA Regional Symposium on Water, Wastewater and Environment: Traditions and Culture*, Patras, 109–18.

Kraack, Detlev (2001) 'Chivalrous Adventures, Religious Ardour and Curiosity at the Outer Periphery of the Medieval World. Inscriptions and Graffiti of Later Medieval Travellers' in Mouton 2001a, 87–106.

Kraemer Jr., Casper J. (1958) *Excavations at Nessana*, volume 3, *Non-literary Papyri*, Princeton.

Kræmer, Robert von (1866) *En Vinter i Orienten. Reseanteckningar från Egypten, Nubien, Sinai och Palestina*, Stockholm.

Kubiak, Wladyslaw B. (1970) 'Medieval Ceramic Oil Lamps from Fusṭāṭ', *Ars Orientalis* 8, 2–18.

Kubitschek, K. (1919) 'Karten', *RE*, Stuttgart, 2022–149.

Kutscheit, Joh. Val. (1846) *Hr. Professor Dr. Lepsius und der Sinai. Prüfung und Beseitigung der von dem gennanten Herrn Professor auf seiner Reise nach der Halbinsel des Sinai für die biblische Geographie gewonnen Resultate*, Berlin.

Labib, Mahfouz (1961) *Pèlerins et voyageurs au Mont Sinaï*, Le Caire.

Laborde, Léon de (1830) *Voyage de l'Arabie Pétrée par Léon de Laborde et Linant*, Paris.

Laborde, Léon de (1836) *Journey through Arabia Petræa, to Mount Sinai, and the Excavated City of Petra, the Edom of the Prophecies*, London.

Lagrange, M.-J. (1897) 'Chronique II. – Le Sinaï', *RB* 6, 107–30.

Lagrange, Marie-Joseph (1905) *Études sur les religions sémitiques*, deuxième édition, revue et augmentée, Paris.

Lannoy, Guillebert de (1840) *Voyages et Ambassades de Messire Guillebert de Lannoy, Chevalier de la Toison d'or, Seigneur de Santes, Willerval, Tronchiennes, Beaumont et Wahégnies. 1399–1450*, Mons.

Lannoy, Guillebert de (1878) *Oeuvres de Ghillebert de Lannoy. Voyageur, Diplomate et Moraliste. Recueillies et publiées par Ch. Potvin. Avec des notes géographiques et une carte par J.-C. Houzeau*, Louvain.

Lavie, Smadar (1990) *The Poetics of Military Occupation*, Berkeley Los Angeles and Oxford.

Lecointre, E. (1882) *La Campagne de Moïse pour la Sortie d'Égypte*, Paris.

Le Nain de Tillemont, Louis Sébastien (1705) 'Silvain, Abbé du Mont Sinaï et de Gerares' in Louis Sébastien Le Nain de Tillemont, *Mémoires pour servir à l'histoire ecclesiastique des six premiers siècles*, tome dixième, Paris, 448–58.

Le Nain de Tillemont, Louis Sébastien (1706) 'Les Saints Anacoretes Paul, Isaïe, Sabbas, et les autres tuez par les barbares dans les solitudes de Sinaï et de Raïthe' in Louis Sébastien Le Nain de Tillemont, *Mémoires pour servir à l'histoire ecclesiastique des six premiers siècles*, tome settieme, Paris, 573–80.

Lengherand, Georges (1861) *Voyage de Georges Lengherand, mayeur de Mons en Haynaut, à Venise, Rome, Jérusalem, Mont Sinaï & le Kayre, 1485–1486, avec Introduction, Notes, Glossaire, &c. par le Marquis de Godefroy Ménilglaise*, Mons.

Lenoir, Paul (1872) *Le Fayoum le Sinaï et Pétra. Expédition dans la Moyenne Égypte et l'Arabie Pétrée sous la direction de J.L. Gérome*, Paris.

Lepsius, R. (1846a) *Reise des Professors Dr. R. Lepsius von Theben nach der Halbinsel des Sinaï vom 4. März bis zum 14. April 1845*, Berlin.

Lepsius, R. (1846b) *A Tour from Thebes to the Peninsula of Sinai, between March 4 and April 14, 1845, translated from the German, by Charles Herbert Cottrell*, London.

Lepsius, Richard (1852) *Discoveries in Egypt, Ethiopia, and the Peninsula of Sinai, in the Years 1842–1845, during the Mission sent out by His Majesty Fredrick William IV. of Prussia. Edited, with Notes, by Kenneth R.H. Mackenzie*, London.

Le Strange, Guy (1890) *Palestine under the Moslems. A Description of Syria and the Holy Land from A.D. 650 to 1500*, translated from the works of the mediæval Arab geographers, London.

Letts, Malcolm (1949) *Sir John Mandeville. The Man and his Book*, London.

Levy-Rubin, Milka (2000) 'New Evidence Relating to the Process of Islamization in Palestine in the Early Muslim Period – The Case of Samaria', *Journal of the Economic and Social History of the Orient* 43, number 3, 257–76.

Lewis, Agnes Smith (1898) *In the Shadow of Sinai: a Story of Travel and Research from 1895 to 1897*, Cambridge.

Lewis, Agnes Smith and Margaret Dunlop Gibson (1999) *In the Shadow of Sinai: Stories of Travel and Biblical Research*, Brighton.

Lewis, Katherine J. (2006) 'Catherine of Alexandria' in Margaret Schaus, editor, *Women and Gender in Medieval Europe: An Encyclopedia*, London, 115–16.

Libois S.J., Charles (1993) *Monumenta Proximi-Orientis II. Égypte (1547–1563)*, in *Monumenta Historica Societatis Iesu a Patribus Eiusdem Societatis Edita* volumen 145, *Monumenta Missionum Societatis Iesu* volumen LVIII, *Missiones Orientales*, Roma.

Lichtenstein, Hans Ludwig von (1972) 'Voyage de Hans Ludwig von Lichtenstein 7 juillet–19 octobre 1587', traduit de l'allemand par Ursula Castel, présentation et notes de Serge Sauneron, in *Voyages* 1972, 1–25.

Lindsay, Lord (1858) *Letters on Egypt, Edom, and the Holy Land*, London, fifth edition.

Liphschitz, Nili and Yoav Weisel (1976) 'Dendroarchaeological Investigations in Israel (St. Catherine's Monastery in Southern Sinai)', *IEJ* 26, 39–44.

Llewellyn, Briony and Charles Newton (2001) 'John Frederick Lewis: "In Knowledge of the Orientals Quite One of Themselves"' in Paul and Janet Starkey, editors, *Interpreting the Orient. Travellers in Egypt and the Near East*, Reading, 35–50.

Loftus, Jane, Marchioness of Ely (1870) *Mafeesh, or, Nothing New; The Journal of a Tour in Greece, Turkey, Egypt, the Sinai-Desert, Petra, Palestine, Syria, and Russia*, volume I, London.

Lombay, G. de (1892) *Au Sinaï. Palestine et Syrie*, Paris.

Lottin de Laval (1855–9a) *Voyage dans la Péninsule Arabique du Sinaï et l'Égypte Moyenne. Histoire, Géographie, Épigraphie*, Paris.

Lottin de Laval (1855–9b) *Voyage dans la Péninsule Arabique du Sinaï et l'Égypte Moyenne. Histoire, Géographie, Épigraphie*, livraisons 9 à 16, planches (lithographies in-folio), Paris.

Luke, Harry Charles (1927) *A Spanish Franciscan's Narrative of a Journey to the Holy Land, translated from the 16th-Century Latin MS. [...] and Edited with Notes*, London.

Mabillon, Johanne (1707) *Annales Ordinis S.Benedicti Occidentalium Monachorum Patriarchæ. In quibus non modo res monasticæ, sed etiam ecclesiasticæ historiæ non minima pars continetur, tomus quatrus, complectens res gestas ab anno Christi DCCCCLXXXI. ad annum MLXVI. inclusive, cum Appendice, & Indicibus necessaris*, Luteciæ-Parisiorum.

Magdalino, Paul (1991a) 'Prosmonarios', *ODB*, New York and Oxford, 1739.

Magdalino, Paul (1991b) 'Apokrisiarios', *ODB*, New York and Oxford, 136.

Maiberger, Paul (1984) *Topographische und historische Untersuchungen zum Sinaiproblem. Worauf beruht die Identifizierung des Ǧabal Mūsā mit dem Sinai?*, Orbis Biblicus et Orientalis 54, Göttingen.

al-Makrizi (1908) 'Les couvents des Chrétiens. Traduction de l'Arabe d'Al-Makrizi', *Revue de l'Orient Chrétien* deuxième série III (XIII), 192–204.

Manaphēs, Kōnstantinos A., editor (1990) Σινά. Οἱ θησαυροὶ τῆς Ἱ. Μονῆς Ἁγίας Αἰκατερίνης, Athens.

Manginis, George (2000) 'Hagia Koryphe, Sinai, after the coming of Islam: The pottery evidence', *Assemblage* 6, http://www.assemblage. group.shef.ac.uk /issue6/manginis.htm.

Manginis, George (2015a) 'Pillar of Fire or Dust? Jabal Mūsā in the Nineteenth Century' in *Proceedings of the Multidisciplinary Conference on the Sinai Desert, Cairo 29–30 November 2014*, Cairo, 66–83.

Manginis, George (2015b) 'On a Fāṭimid Kursī in the Monastery of Saint Catherine at Mount Sinai' in *Aegis: Essays in Mediterranean Archaeology Presented to Matti Egon by Scholars of the Greek Archaeological Committee UK*, Oxford, 211–20.

Manley, Deborah and Sahar Abdel-Hakim (2006) *Traveling through Sinai from the Fourth to the Twenty-first Century*, with illustrations by W.H. Bartlett, Cairo and New York.

Manning, Rev. Samuel (1875) *The Land of the Pharaohs. Egypt and Sinai: Illustrated by Pen and Pencil*, London.

Mansi, Joannes Dominicus (1771) *Sacrorum Conciliorum Nova et Amplissima Collectio*, tomus decimus sextus, *ab anno DCCCLXIX usque ad ann. DCCCLXXI inclusive*, Venetiis.

Maraval, Pierre (1985) *Lieux saints et pèlerinages d'Orient. Histoire et géographie des origines à la conquête arabe*, Paris.

Marcianus Imperator (1933) 'Epistula ad Macarium Episcopum et Monachos in Monte Sina' in *Acta Conciliorum Oecumenicorum*, tomus alter, volumen primum, pars prima, *Concilium Universale Chalcedonense*, volumen primum, pars prima, Berolini et Lipsiae, [490] 131–[491] 132.

Marenco, Franco, editor (1966) *I Cento Viaggi*, volume 4, Milano.

Marthalēs ho Glykys, Nikēphoros (1710) *Βιβλίον περιέχον τὴν ἀκολουθίαν τῆς ἁγίας Αἰκατερίνης, τό τε προσκυνητάριον τοῦ ἁγίου Ὄρους Σινὰ μετὰ τῶν πέριξ καὶ πάντων τῶν ἐν αὐτῷ καὶ περὶ αὐτό, τήν τε τάξιν τῆς ἀκολουθίας τοῦ μοναστηρίου, καὶ τοὺς ἐν αὐτῷ μέχρι τοῦδε ἀρχιεπισκοπήσαντας, καὶ ἐγκώμιόν τι εἰς τὸ Σινὰ Ὄρος*, Trieste.

Martineau, Harriet (1848) *Eastern Life, Present and Past*, Philadelphia.

Martoni, Nicolas de (1895) 'Relation du pèlerinage à Jérusalem de Nicolas de Martoni, notaire italien (1394–1395), publié par Léon Legrand', *Revue de d'Orient Latin* III, 566–669.

Marx, Emanuel (1977) 'Communal and Individual Pilgrimage: The Region of Saint's Tombs in South Sinai' in R.P. Werbner, *Regional Cults*, London, 29–51.

Marx, Emmanuel (1999) 'Oases in South Sinai', *Human Ecology* 27, number 2 (June), 341–57.

Mas Latrie, Comte de (1884) 'Histoire des Archevêques Latins de l'Île de Chypre', *AOL* II, 207–328.

Master Plan (2010) The Holy Monastery of Saint Catherine, Mount Sinai, *Master Plan for Wadi el Deir*, edited by Petros M. Koufopoulos and Marina Myriantheos-Koufopoulou, Cairo.

Matthews, Charles D. (1949) *Palestine – Mohammedan Holy Land*, Yale Oriental Series, Researches, volume XXIV, New Haven.

Maughan, William Charles (1873) *The Alps of Arabia. Travels in Egypt, Sinai, Arabia and the Holy Land*, London.

Mayerson, Philip (1963) 'The Desert of Southern Palestine According to Byzantine Sources', *Proceedings of the American Philosophical Society* 107, 160–72.

Mayerson, Philip (1964) 'The First Muslim Attacks on Southern Palestine (A.D. 633–634)', *Transactions and Proceedings of the American Philological Association* XCV, 155–99.

Mayerson, Philip (1975) 'Observations on the "Nilus" *Narrationes*: Evidence for an Unknown Christian Sect?', *Journal of the American Research Center in Egypt* 12, 51–74.

Mayerson, Philip (1976) 'An Inscription on the Monastery of St. Catherine and the Martyr Tradition in Sinai', *DOP* 30, 375–9.

Mayerson, Philip (1978) 'Procopius or Eutychius on the Construction of the Monastery at Mount Sinai: Which Is the More Reliable Source?', *BASOR* 230 (April), 33–8.

Mayerson, Philip (1980) 'The Ammonius Narrative: Bedouin and Blemmye Attacks in Sinai' in Gary Rendsburg, Ruth Adler, Milton Arfa and Nathan H. Winter, editors, *The Bible World. Essays in Honor of Cyrus H. Gordon*, New York, 133–48.

Mayerson, Philip (1982) 'The Pilgrim Routes to Mount Sinai and the Armenians', *IEJ* 32, 44–57.

Mayerson, Philip (1983) 'Codex Sinaiticus: An Historical Observation', *BiblArch* 46 number 1 (winter), 54–6.

Mayerson, Philip (1986) 'The Saracens and the *Limes*', *BASOR* 262 (May), 35–47.

Mayerson, Philip (1988) 'Justinian's Novel 103 and the Reorganisation of Palestine', *BASOR* 269 (February), 65–71.

Mayerson, Philip (1989) 'Saracens and Romans: Micro–Macro Relationships', *BASOR* 274 (May), 71–9.

Mayerson, Philip (1994) 'Urbanisation in Palaestina Tertia: Pilgrims and Paradoxes' in Philip Mayerson, *Monks, Martyrs, Soldiers and Saracens. Papers on the Near East in Late Antiquity (1962–1993)*, Jerusalem, 232–58 (originally published in 1987).

Mazuel, Jean (1937) *L'œuvre géographique de Linant de Bellefonds. Étude de géographie historique*, Le Caire.

Measor, Reverend H.P. (1844) *A Tour in Egypt, Arabia Petræa, and the Holy Land, in the Years 1841–2*, London.

Meimarēs, Iōannēs (1985) Κατάλογος τῶν νέων Ἀραβικῶν χειρογράφων τῆς Ἱερᾶς Μονῆς Ἁγίας Αἰκατερίνης τοῦ Ὄρους Σινᾶ, Athens.

Meinardus, Otto (1962) *Atlas of Christian Sites in Egypt*, Le Caire.

Meinardus, Otto F.A. (1970) *Christian Egypt. Faith and Life*, Cairo.

Meistermann, P. Barnabé (1909) *Guide du Nil au Jourdain par le Sinaï et Pétra sur les traces d'Israël*, Paris.

Meshel, Zeev (1982) 'An Explanation of the Journeys of the Israelites in the Wilderness', *BiblArch* 45 number 1 (winter), 19–20.

Meshel, Ze'ev (2000) *Sinai. Excavations and Studies*, *BAR* International Series 876, Oxford.

Meyendorff, John (1968) 'Justinian, the Empire and the Church', *DOP* 22, 43–60.

Mian, Franca (1970) '"Caput Vallis" al Sinai in Eteria', *LA* XX, 209–23.

Michaēl Monachos (1999) Βεδουῖνοι, οι αγνοημένοι άρχοντες της ερήμου, Athens.

Michelant, Henri and Gaston Raynaud, editors (1882) *Itinéraires à Jérusalem et descriptions de la Terre Sainte rédigés en français aux Xie, XIIe & XIIIe siècles*, Genève.

Milton, Giles (1996) *The Riddle and the Knight. In Search of Sir John Mandeville, the World's Greatest Traveller*, New York.

Mitchell, R.J. (1965) *The Spring Voyage. The Jerusalem Pilgrimage in 1458*, London.

Monconys, Balthasar de (1973) *Voyage en Egypte de Balthasar de Monconys 1646–1647*, présentation et notes d'Henry Amer, Le Caire.

Moraitou, Mina (2007) 'The reconstruction of a wooden screen in the Fatimid style', *Μουσείο Μπενάκη* 7, 181–96.

Morávek, Jan (1937) *Nově Objevený Inventář Rudolfinských Sbírek na Hradě Pražském*, Praha.

Morin, E. (1862) *Notice sur un Manuscrit de la Bibliothèque Publique de Rennes inscrit dans le Catalogue imprimé des Manuscrits de cette bibliothèque sous le n° 157, avec ce titre: Voyage à la Terre-Sainte, au Mont Sinaï et au Couvent de Sainte-Catherine*, Rennes.

Morison, A. (1704) *Relation historique, d'un voyage nouvellement fait au mont de Sinaï et à Jérusalem.* […], Toul.

Moritz, Prof. Dr. B. (1918) *Beiträge zur Geschichte des Sinái-Klosters im Mittelalter nach Arabischen Quellen*, Berlin.

Moritz, B. (1920) 'Saraka', *RE*, Stuttgart, 2387–90.

Morton, H.V. (1938) *Through Lands of the Bible*, London.

Moscrop, John James (2000) *Measuring Jerusalem. The Palestine Exploration Fund and British Interests in the Holy Land*, London and New York.

Mourelatos, Dionysios (2005) 'Early Byzantine workshops in a settlement near St Catherine's monastery (Mount Sinai, Egypt)' in *Proceedings of the 21st International Congress of Byzantine Studies, Abstracts of Communications* III, London, 338–9.

Mouskes, Philippe (1836) *Chronique rimée de Philippe Mouskes*, publiée par Le Baron de Reiffenberg, tome I, Bruxelles.

Moustafa, Abdel Raouf A. and Jeffrey M. Klopatek (1995) 'Vegetation and landforms of the Saint Catherine area, southern Sinai, Egypt', *Journal of Arid Environments* 30, 385–95.

Mouton, Jean-Michel, editor (2001a) *Le Sinaï de la conquête arabe à nos jours*, *Cahier des Annales Islamologiques* 21, Le Caire.

Mouton, Jean-Michel (2001b) 'Saladin et les Bédouins du Sinaï' in Mouton 2001a, 197–206.

Mouton, Jean-Michel and Andrei Popescu-Belis (2006) 'Une description du monastère Sainte-Catherine du Sinaï au XIIe siècle: Le manuscrit d'Abū l-Makārim', *Arabica* LIII, 1, 1–53.

Mukaddasi (1897) *Description of Syria, Including Palestine*, translated from the Arabic and annotated by Guy Le Strange, in *The Library of the Palestine Pilgrims' Text Society*, volume III, London.

Murray, G.W. (1935) *Sons of Ishmael. A Study of the Egyptian Bedouin*, London.

Murray, G.W. (1953) 'The Land of Sinai', *The Geographical Journal* CXIX:2 (June), 140–54.

Nandris, J.G. (1981) 'The Role of "Vlah" and its Rulers on Athos and Sinai', *Revue des Études Sud-Est Européenes* XIX number 3 (juillet-septembre), 605–10.

Nandris, J.G. (1984) 'Sinai and Vlah: An Ethnoarchaeological Link with South-East Europe', *Dritter Internationaler Thrakologischer Kongress zu Ehren W. Tomascheks, 2.–6. Juni 1980, Wien*, Band I, Sofia, 297–303.

Nandris, John G. (1990) 'The Jebaliye of Mount Sinai, and the Land of Vlah', *QSA* 8, 45–90.

Nardi, R. and C. Zizola (2014) 'The Conservation of the 6th century Mosaic of the Transfiguration in the Monastery of Saint Catherine in the Sinai' in *Proceedings of the Multidisciplinary Conference on the Sinai Desert*, Cairo 29–30 November 2014, Cairo.

Negev, A. (1967) 'New Dated Nabatean Graffiti from the Sinai', *IEJ* 17, 250–5.

Negev, Avraham (1977a) 'A Nabatean Sanctuary at Jebel Moneijah, Southern Sinai', *IEJ* 27, 219–31.

Negev, Avraham (1977b) *The Inscriptions of Wadi Haggag, Sinai*, *QEDEM* 6, Jerusalem.

Negev, Avraham (1981) 'Nabatean, Greek and Thamudic Inscriptions from the Wadi Haggag – Jebel Musa Road', *IEJ* 31, 66–71.

Negev, Avraham (1982) 'Nabatean Inscriptions in Southern Sinai', *BiblArch* 45 number 1 (winter), 21–5.

Negev, Avraham (1986) *Nabatean Archaeology Today*, New York and London.

Negev, Avraham (1991) *Personal Names in the Nabatean Realm*, *QEDEM* 32, Jerusalem.

Neitzschitz, George Christoff von (1666) *Sieben-jährige und gefährliche Welt Beschauung durch die vornehmsten drey Theil der Welt Europa, Asia und Africa*, Budißin.

Neitzschitz, George Christoff von (1674) *Sieben-jährige und gefährliche Neu-verbesserte Europæ, Asiæ, und Africanische Welt-Beschauung*, Nürnberg.

Nektarios ho Krēs (1980) Ἐπιτομὴ τῆς Ἱεροκοσμικῆς Ἱστορίας, ἐπιμελείᾳ Παν. Φ. Χριστοπούλου, Athens.

Nelson, Robert S. and Kristen M. Collins, editors (2007) *Holy Image, Hallowed Ground; Icons from Sinai*, Los Angeles (third printing).

Nevo, Yehuda D. (1991) Nevo, *Pagans and Herders; a re-examination of the Negev runoff cultivation systems in the Byzantine and Early Arab periods*, Jerusalem.

Newbold, Captain (1847) 'Visit to Mount Sinai, to which is prefixed a brief Geological Sketch of the Peninsula of Sinai', *Madras Journal* XIVii (number 33) July–December, 47–73.

Nicholson, E.W. (1973) *Exodus and Sinai in History and Tradition*, Oxford.

Niebuhr, Carsten (1776) *Voyage en Arabie & en d'autres Pays circonvoisins*, tome premier, traduit de l'Allemand, Amsterdam and Utrecht.

Niebuhr, Carsten (1973) *Entdeckungen im Orient. Reise nach Arabien und anderen Ländern 1761–1767*, herausgegeben und bearbeitet von Robert und Evamaria Grün, Tübingen und Basel.

Niebuhr, Carsten (1994) *Travels through Arabia, and other Countries in the East, performed by M. Niebuhr, now a Captain of Engineers in the Service of the King of Denmark*, translated into English by Robert Heron; with notes by the translator; and illustrated with engravings and maps, volume I, Reading.

Niehaus, Jeffrey J. (1995) *God at Sinai. Covenant and Theophany in the Bible and Ancient Near East*, Carlisle.

Nilus monachus (1860) 'Narrationes quibus cædes monachorum Montis Sinæ et captivitas Theoduli ejus filii describuntur', *PG* LXXIX, Parisiis, 583–694.

Norov, A.S. (1878) *Іерусалимъ и Синай. Зариски втораго путешествія на востокъ*, Saint Petersburg.

Nur, Amos and Hagai Ron (1996) 'And the Walls Came Tumbling Down: Earthquake History in the Holyland' in S. Stiros and R.E. Jones, *Archaeoseismology*, Fitch Laboratory Occasional Paper 7, Athens, 75–85.

Olin, Reverend Stephen (1843) *Travels in Egypt, Arabia Petræa, and the Holy Land*, volume I, New York.

Olin, Stephen (1848) 'Mittheilungen über Stephen Olin's Reise in das Morgenland', *Zeitschrift der Deutschen morgenländischen Gesellschaft*, zweiter band, 315–35.

Oppenheim, Max Freiherr von (1943) *Die Beduinen*, unter Mitbearbeitung von Erich Bräunlich und Werner Caskel, Band II, *Die Beduinenstämme in Palästina, Transjordanien, Sinai, Hedjaz*, Leipzig.

Oren, Eliezer D. (1979) 'Land Bridge Between Asia and Africa. Archaeology of Northern Sinai up to the Classical Period' in Rothenberg *et al.* 1979, 181–91.

Oren, Eliezer D. (1982) 'Excavations at Qasrawet in North-Western Sinai. Preliminary Report', *IEJ* 32, 203–11.

Ovadiah, Asher (1985) 'Greek Inscriptions in Deir Rumḥan, Sinai', *DOP* 39, 77–9.

Paisios (1978) Σπυρίδωνος Δημ. Κοντογιάννη, *Τοῦ ἐπισκόπου Παραμυθίας Παϊσίου Περιγραφὴ τοῦ Ἁγίου καὶ Θεοβαδίστου Ὄρους Σινᾶ*, Athens.

Palerne, Jean (1991) *D'Alexandrie à Istanbul. Pérégrinations dans l'Empire Ottoman 1581–1583*, introduction et annotations d'Yvelise Bernard, Paris.

Palmer, E.H. (1871) *The Desert of the Exodus: Journeys on foot in the Wilderness of the Forty Years' Wanderings*, parts I and II (in two volumes), Cambridge, London and New York.

Palmer, H.S. (1878) *Ancient History from the Monuments. Sinai from the Fourth Egyptian Dynasty to the Present Day*, London.

Palmer, H.S. (1892) *Ancient History from the Monuments. Sinai from the Fourth Egyptian Dynasty to the Present Day. A New Edition – Revised Throughout by Rev. Professor Sayce*, London.

Panayotidi, Maria and Sophia Kalopissi-Verti (2007) 'Excavation of the Justinian Basilica on the Holy Summit (Jabal Musa) at Mount Sinai', unpublished paper presented at the *Ideologia e Cultura Artistica Tra Adriatico e Mediterraneo Orientale (IV–X secolo): Il Ruolo dell'Autorità Ecclesiastica alla Luce di Nuovi Scavi e Ricerche* International Conference, Bologna and Ravenna 26–29 November.

Panagiōtidē, M. *et al.* (S. Kalopisē-Vertē, N. Physsas, G. Manginēs and G. Phoukanelē) (2002) «Ανασκαφή στην Αγία Κορυφή του Όρους Σινά (Gebel Musa). Προκαταρτικά πορίσματα», *SA* 1, 69–90.

Paphnutius (1781) 'Vita et Acta Sancti Patris Nostri Onuphrii' in *Bibliotheca Veterum Patrum Antiquorumque Scriptorum Ecclesiasticorum*, cura et studio Andreæ Galandii, tomus XIV, Venetiis, Appendix, 122–7.

Pardieu, Cte de (1851) *Excursion en Orient. L'Égypte, le Mont Sinaï, l'Arabie, la Palestine, la Syrie, le Liban*, Paris.

Peregrinationes (1927) 'Peregrinationes tocius Terre Sancte' in Golubovich 1927, 350–5.

Perevolotsky, Avi (1981) 'Orchard Agriculture in the High Mountain Region of Southern Sinai', *Human Ecology* 9, number 3 (September), 331–57.

Perigraphē (1978) Περιγραφὴ τοῦ θεοβαδίστου ὄρους Σινᾶ, ἐπιμελείᾳ
Παναγιώτου Φ. Χριστοπούλου, Athens.

Peters, F.E. (1996) 'The Holy Places' in Rosovsky 1996, 37–59.

Petrie, W.M. Flinders (1906) *Researches in Sinai,* London.

Petrus (1965) 'Petri Diaconi Liber de Locis Sanctis' in 'Appendix
ad Itinerarium Egeriae', cura et studio R. Weber, *CCSL* CLXXV
(*Itineraria et alia Geographica*): II, Turnholti, 93–103.

Philon, Helen (1980) *Benakı Museum Athens; Early Islamic Ceramics,
Ninth to Twelfth Centuries,* London.

Piccirillo, Michele (1993) *The Mosaics of Jordan,* edited by Patricia M.
Bikai and Thomas A. Dailey, American Center for Oriental Research
Publications number 1, Amman.

Pigafetta, Filippo (1837) 'Viaggio di Filippo Pigafetta dal Cairo al Monte
Sinai nell' anno MDLXXVII' in Giovanni da Schio da Costazza,
Viaggi vicentini inediti compendiati, 17–42.

Pitra, Joannes Baptista Cardinalis (1885) *Analecta Novissima. Spicilegii
Solesmensis. Altera Continuatio. Tom. I. De Epistolis et Registris
Romanorum Pontificum* (Paris).

Pitts, Joseph *et al.* (William Daniel and Charles Jacques Poncet) (1949)
*The Red Sea and Adjacent Countries at the Close of the Seventeenth
Century as Described by Joseph Pitts, William Daniel and Charles
Jacques Poncet,* edited by Sir William Foster, London.

Plato (1993) *Phaedo,* translated and edited by David Gallop, Oxford.

Platon (1958) *Platonis Opera,* recognovit breviqve adnotatione critica
instrvxit Ioannes Burnet, tomus I, Oxonii.

Platt, Miss (1842) *Journal of a Tour through Egypt, the Peninsula of
Sinai, and the Holy Land, in 1838, 1839,* volume II, London.

Pococke, Richard (1814) 'Travels in Egypt' in John Pinkerton, editor,
*A General Collection of the Best and Most Interesting Voyages and
Travels in All Parts of the World; Many of Which are Now First
Translated into English. Digested on a New Plan,* volume 15, London,
163–402.

Poggibonsi, Fra Niccolò da (1881) *Libro d'Oltramare,* pubblicato da
Alberto Bacchi Della Lega, volume secondo, Bologna.

Poggibonsi (1927) '1346–50. – Terra Santa. – Fr. Nicolò di Poggibonsi e
il suo Libro d'Oltramare' in Golubovich 1927, 1–24.

Poggibonsi, Fra Niccolò da (1945) *Libro d'Oltramare (1346–1350),* testo
di A. Bacchi Della Lega riveduto e riannotato dal P.B. Bagatti O.F.M.
a ricordo del sesto centenario, Gerusaleme.

P(oole), R(eginald) S(tuart) (1854) *Egypt, Ethiopia, and the Peninsula of
Sinai,* reprinted from the *JSL* July, London.

Popescu-Belis, Andrei (2000) 'Le Dār al-ᶜabīd du mont Sinaï: une hypothèse', *AnIsl* 34, 375–86.

Popescu-Belis, Andrei (2001) 'Légende des origines, origines d'une légende: les Ğabāliyya du mont Sinaï' in Mouton 2001a, 107–46.

Popescu-Belis, Andrei and Jean-Michel Mouton (2006) 'Un aperçu des descriptions grecques et arabes du Sinaï et du monastère Sainte-Catherine au XVIIIᵉ siècle', *Collectanea Christiana Orientalia* 3, 189–241.

Post, George E. (1933) *Flora of Syria, Palestine and Sinai. A Handbook of the Flowering Plants and Ferns, Native and Naturalized from the Taurus to Ras Muhammad and from the Mediterranean Sea to the Syrian Desert*, second edition, extensively revised and enlarged by John Edward Dinsmore, volume II, Beirut.

Prefetto (1810) *A Journal from Grand Cairo to Mount Sinai, and back again. Translated from a Manuscript written by the Prefetto of Egypt, by the Right Rev. Robert Clayton, Lord Bishop of Glogher*, in Henry Maundrell, *A Journey from Aleppo to Jerusalem, at Easter, A.D. 1697 [...] To which is added, A Faithful Account of the Religion and Manners of the Mahometans. By Joseph Pitts*, London, 215–70.

Prefetto (1812) *A Journal from Grand Cairo to Mount Sinai, and back again, in Company with some Missionaries De Propaganda Fide at Grand Cairo. Translated from a Manuscript, written by the Prefetto of Egypt, by the Right Rev. Robert Clyton, Lord Bishop of Glogher*, in Henry Maundrell, *A Journey from Aleppo to Jerusalem, at Easter, A.D. 1696*, Edinburgh, 251–313.

Prescott, H.F.M. (1957) *Once to Sinai. The further pilgrimage of Friar Felix Fabri*, London.

Procopius (1886) *Of the Buildings of Justinian*, translated by Aubrey Stewart and annotated by C.W. Wilson and Hayter Lewis, London.

Procopius (1971) *Buildings*, with an English translation by H.B. Dewing with the collaboration of Glanville Downey, Cambridge Massachusetts.

Proskynētaria (2003) Σωτηρίου Ν. Καδᾶ, *Προσκυνητάρια τοῦ ἁγίου καὶ θεοβαδίστου Ὄρους Σινᾶ ἀπὸ δέκα ἑλληνικὰ χειρόγραφα 16ου–17ου αἰ.*, Athens.

Pruitt, Jennifer (2013) 'Method in Madness: Recontextualising the Destruction of Churches in the Fatimid Era', *Muqarnas* 30, 119–39.

Quaresmius, Fr. Franciscus (1639) *Historica Theologica et Moralis Terræ Sanctæ Elucidatio: In qua pleraque ad veterem & præsentem eiusdem Terræ statum spectantia accuratè explicantur, varij errores refelluntur, veritas fideliter exacteque discutitur ac comprobatur. Opus non tantùm ad Terram Sanctam proficiscentibus, sed etiam*

Sacræ Scripturæ studiosis & divini verbi præconibus vtilissimum, Tomus II, Antverpiæ.

Rabino, H.L. (1935) 'Le Monastère de Sainte-Catherine (Mont-Sinaï). Souvenirs épigraphiques des anciens pélerins', *Bulletin de la Société Royale de Géographie d'Égypte* XIX 1er fascicule, 21–126, planches I–XX.

Rabino, H.L. (1938) *Le Monastère de Sainte-Catherine du Mont Sinaï*, Le Caire.

Rabinowitz, Dan (1985) 'Themes in the Economy of the Bedouin of South Sinai in the Nineteenth and Twentieth Centuries', *International Journal of Middle East Studies* 17, number 2 (May), 211–28.

Raboisson, L'Abbé (1886) *En Orient. Récits et Notes d'un Voyage en Palestine et en Syrie par l'Égypte et le Sinaï. Première partie comprenant l'Égypte et le Sinaï*, Paris.

Raboisson, L'Abbé (1887) *En Orient. Récits et Notes d'un Voyage en Palestine et en Syrie par l'Égypte et le Sinaï. Seconde partie comprenant la Palestine et la Syrie*, Paris.

Randall, Reverend D.A. (1867) *The Handwriting of God in Egypt, Sinai, and the Holy Land: The Records of a Journey from the Great Valley of the West to the Sacred Places of the East*, Philadelphia.

Randall, Reverend D.A. (1886) *Ham-Mishkan, The Wonderful Tent. An Account of the Structure, Signification, and Spiritual Lessons of the Mosaic Tabernacle Erected in the Wilderness of Sinai*, Cincinnati.

Ratliff, Brandie (2008) 'The Monastery of Saint Catherine at Mount Sinai and the Christian Communities of the Caliphate', *Sinaiticus* 14–17.

Reboldis, Antonius de (1890) 'Antonius de Cremona, Itinerarium ad Sepulcrum Domini (1327, 1330). Mitgetheilt von Reinhold Röhricht', *ZDPV* XIII, 153–74.

Reboldis, Antonius de (1919) '1327–30. – Terra Santa-Egitto. – Fr. Antonii de Reboldis de Cremona Ord. Min.: Itinerarium ad Sepulcrum Domini (1327), et ad Montem Sinai (1330)' in Golubovich 1919, 326–42.

Renaudin, Paul (1900) 'Le Monastère de Sainte-Catherine au Sinaï', *Revue de l'Orient Chrétien* 5, 319–21.

Rendall, M.J. (1911) *Sinai in Spring or The Best Desert in the World*, London.

Rice, Howard C. (1960) *Mount Sinai and the Monastery of St. Catherine. An Exhibition based on the Expedition sponsored by the University of Michigan, Princeton University, and the University of Alexandria*, Princeton.

Richards, D.S. (2001) 'St Catherine's Monastery and the Bedouin: archival documents of the fifteenth and sixteenth centuries' in Mouton 2001a, 149–81.

Ridgaway, Henry B. (1876) *The Lord's Land: A Narrative of Travels in Sinai, Arabia Petræa, and Palestine, from the Red Sea to the Entering in of Hamath*, New York.

Rinaldi, Maura (1989) *Kraak Porcelain; A Moment in the History of Trade*, London.

Ritter, Carl (1848) *Allgemeine Erdkunde* Th. XIV: *Asien.* Band VIII. Zweite Abtheilung. Drittes Buch: *West-Asien.* Band VII. Fünfte Abtheilung: *Die westlichen Gliederungen von West-Asien. Das Gestadeland West-Asiens. Die Sinai-Halbinsel, Palästina und Syrien.* Erster Abschnitt: *Die Sinai-Halbinsel*, Berlin.

Ritter, Carl (1866) *The Comparative Geography of Palestine and the Sinaitic Peninsula, Translated and Adapted to the Use of Biblical Students by William L. Gage*, London.

Robert, Ulysse (1884) 'La *Chronique d'Arménie* de Jean Dardel, évêque de Tortiboli', *AOL* II, 1–15.

Roberts, David (1842–9) *The Holy Land, Syria, Idumea, Arabia, Egypt, & Nubia, from drawings made on the spot by D. Roberts [...] With historical descriptions by the Revd George Croly, [...] (Egypt and Nubia. With historical descriptions by William Brockedon.)*, London.

Roberts (1994) *Terra Santa Ieri e Oggi. Litografie di David Roberts*, testi di Fabio Bourbon, fotografie di Antonio Attini, Vercelli.

Roberts (2001) *The Sinai Portfolio. Ten Fine Lithographs by David Roberts, R.A.*, Cairo and New York.

Robinson, Edward (1867) *Biblical Researches in Palestine and the Adjacent Regions: A Journal of Travels in the Years 1838 & 1852. By Edward Robinson, Eli Smith, and Others*, volume I, London, third edition.

Rogers, Miss M.E. (1883) 'Mount Hor and the Cliffs of Edom' in Colonel Sir Charles W. Wilson, editor, *Picturesque Palestine; Sinai and Egypt*, London 1880–1884, volume III, 217–38.

Röhricht, Reinhold and Heinrich Meisner (1880) *Deutsche Pilgerreisen nach dem Heiligen Lande*, Berlin.

Ronen, A. (1971) 'Flint Implements from South Sinai. Preliminary Report', *PEQ* 102, 30–41.

Rooke, Henry (1783) *Travels to the Coast of Arabia Felix; and from Thence by the Red-Sea and Egypt, to Europe. Containing a Short Account of an Expedition Undertaken against the Cape of Good Hope. In a Series of Letters*, London.

Rosenthal, Renate and Renee Sivan (1978) *Ancient Lamps in the Schloessinger Collection, QEDEM* 8, Jerusalem.

Rosovsky, Nitza, editor (1996) *City of the Great King. Jerusalem from David to the Present*, Cambridge Massachusetts and London.

Rothenberg, Beno (1971) 'An Archaeological Survey of South Sinai. First Season 1967/1968. Preliminary Report', *PEQ* 102, 4–29, plates I–XI.

Rothenberg, Beno (1979a) 'Travellers, Painters, Surveyors and Scholars' in Rothenberg *et al.* 1979, 7–8.

Rothenberg, Beno (1979b) 'Badiet el Tih, the Desert of Wandering. Archaeology of Central Sinai' in Rothenberg *et al.* 1979, 109–27.

Rothenberg, Beno (1979c) 'Turquoise, Copper and Pilgrims. Archaeology of Southern Sinai' in Rothenberg *et al.* 1979, 137–72.

Rothenberg, Beno *et al.* (Avinoam Danin, Zvi Garfunkel, Paul Huber, Martin A. Klopfenstein, Eliezer D. Oren, Eitan Tchernov, Gerold Walser) (1979) *Sinai. Pharaohs, Miners, Pilgrims and Soldiers*, Washington and New York.

Rowley-Conwy, Peter *et al.* (John Rowley-Conwy and Deborah Rowley-Conwy) (1998) 'A Honeymoon in Egypt and the Sudan: Charlotte Rowley, 1835–1836' in Starkey & Starkey 1998, 108–17.

Rüppell, Eduard (1829) *Reisen in Nubien, Kordofan und dem peträischen Arabien vorzüglich in geographisch-statisticher Hinsicht*, Frankfurt.

Rüppell, Eduard (1838) *Reise in Abyssinien*, erster Band, Frankfurt am Main.

Russegger, Joseph (1847) *Reisen in Europa, Asien und Africa, mit besonderer Rücksicht auf die naturwissenschaftlichen Verhältnisse der betreffenden Länder, unternommen in den Jahren 1835 bis 1841*, dritter Band, *Reisen in Unter-Egypten, auf der Halbinsel des Sinai und im gelobten Lande, unternommen in den Jahren 1838 und 1839*, Stuttgart.

Russell, Kenneth W. (1985) 'The Earthquake Chronology of Palestine and Northwest Arabia from the 2nd through the Mid-8th Century A.D.', *BASOR* 260 (Fall/November), 37–59.

Saad El-Din, Morsi *et al.* (Gamal Mokhtar, Fouad Iskandar, Gawdat Gabra, Samir Sobhi and Ayman Taher) (1998) *Sinai the Site & the History*, photographs by Ayman Taher and Luciano Romano, New York and London.

Sachsen, Johann Georg Herzog zu (1912) *Das Katharinenkloster am Sinai*, Lepzig und Berlin.

Saint-Génois, Jules de (1846) *Les Voyageurs Belges du XIIIe au XVIIe siècle*, Bruxelles, second edition.

Sandys, George (1625) 'Relations of Africa, taken out of Master George Sandys his larger discourse observed in his Journey, begun Ann.

1610. Lib. 2' in Samuel Purchas, *His Pilgrimes. The Second Part. In Five Bookes.* The Sixth Booke: *Navigations, Voyages, and Land-Discoveries, with Other Historicall Relations of Afrike*, chapter VIII, 896–920.

Sargenton-Galichon, Adélaïde (1904) *Sinaï Ma'ân Pétra. Sur les traces d' Israël et chez les Nabatéens*, Paris.

Sartre, Maurice (1982) *Trois études sur l'Arabie romaine et byzantine*, Collection Latomus volume 178, Bruxelles.

Schaff, Philip (1878) *Through Bible Lands: Notes of Travel in Egypt, the Desert, and Palestine*, New York.

Scheicher, Elisabeth (1997) 'Kunstkammer: Katalog' in Kunsthistorisches Museum, Sammlungen Schloss Ambras, *Die Kunstkammer*, Innsbruck.

Scheuchzer, Jean-Jacques (1732) *Physique Sacrée, ou Histoire-Naturelle de la Bible [...] Enrichie de Figures en Taille-Douce, gravées par les soins de Jean-André Pfeffel*, tome second, Amsterdam.

Schienerl, Jutta (2000) *Der Weg in den Orient. Der Forscher Ulrich Jasper Seetzen: Von Jever in den Jemen (1802–1811)*, Oldenburg.

Schmidt, Carl and Bernhard Moritz (1926) 'Die Sinai-Expedition im Frühjahr 1914', *Sitzungsberichte der Preussischen Akademie der Wissenschaften. Philosophisch-historische Klasse* (VIII), 26–34.

Schubert, Gotthilf Heinrich von (1839) *Reise in das Morgenland in den Jahren 1836 und 1837*, zweiter Band, Erlangen.

Schubert, G.H. v. and J. Bernatz (1839) *Bilder aus dem Heiligen Lande. Vierzig Ausgewæhlte Original-Ansichten Biblisch-Wichtiger Orte, treu nach der Natur aufgenommen und gezeichnet von J.M. Bernatz*, Stuttgart.

Schubert, G.H. v. *et al.* (J. Roth and J.M. Bernatz) (1856) *Album des heiligen Landes. 50 Ausgewählte Original-Ansichten biblisch wichtiger Orte, treu nach der Natur gezeichnet von J.M. Bernatz*, Stuttgart and Leipzig.

Schubert, G.H. v. *et al.* (J. Roth, O. Fraas and J.M. Bernatz) (1868) *Palästina. Neues Album des heiligen Landes. 50 Ansichten biblisch wichtiger Orte. Natur-Aufnahmen von J.M. Bernatz, und anderen Künstlern*, Stuttgart.

Searight, Sarah and Malcolm Wagstaff, editors (2001) *Travellers in the Levant: Voyagers and Visionaries*, Durham.

Seetzen, Ulrich Jasper (1855) *Reisen durch Syrien, Palästina, Phönicien, die Transjordan-Länder, Arabia Petraea und Unter-Aegypten. Herausgegeben und commentirt von Fr. Kruse*, dritter Band, Berlin.

Seetzen (1995) *Ulrich Jasper Seetzen (1767–1811). Leben und Werk. Die arabischen Länder und die Nahostforschung im napoleonischen*

Zeitalter. Vorträge des Kolloquiums vom 23. und 24. September 1994 in der Forschungs- und Landesbibliothek Gotha Schloss Friedenstein, Gotha.

Ševčenko, Ihor (1966) 'The Early Period of the Sinai Monastery in the Light of its Inscriptions', *DOP* 20, 255–64, figures 1–18.

Severus (1845) 'Sulpicii Severi Dialogus I', *PL* XX, Parisiis, 185–202.

Shabetai, J.R. (1940) *Contribution to the Flora of Egypt*, Ministry of Agriculture, Egypt: Technical and Scientific Service Bulletin number 234, Cairo.

Shahîd, Irfan (1984a) *Rome and the Arabs: A Prolegomenon to the Study of Byzantium and the Arabs*, Washington, D.C.

Shahîd, Irfan (1984b) *Byzantium and the Arabs in the Fourth Century*, Washington, D.C.

Shahîd, Irfan (1989) *Byzantium and the Arabs in the Fifth Century*, Washington, D.C.

Shahîd, Irfan (1995) *Byzantium and the Arabs in the Sixth Century*, volume I, Part 2: *Ecclesiastical History*, Washington, D.C.

Shaw, Thomas (1738) *Travels, or Observations relating to Several Parts of Barbary and the Levant*, Oxford.

Sherman, A.J. (1997) *Mandate Days. British Lives in Palestine (1918–1948)*, London.

Shulsky, Linda S. (1998–9) 'Chinese Porcelain in Spanish Colonial Sites in the Southern Part of North America and the Caribbean', *Transactions of the Oriental Ceramic Society* 63, 83–98.

Sicard, Claude (1982) 'Voyage au Mont Sinai. Lettre du Père Sicard, Missionaire de la Compagnie de Jesus en Egypte. Au Père Fleuriau, de la même Compagnie' in *Œuvres II. Relations et Mémoires Imprimés*, edition critique de Maurice Martin, Le Caire, 126–38.

Sigoli, Simone (1843) *Viaggio al Monte Sinai di Simone Sigoli e in Terra Santa di Ser Mariano da Siena*, Parma.

Silvia (1887) *S. Hilarii Tractatus de Mysteriis et Hymni et S. Silviae Aquitanae Peregrinatio ad Loca Sancta*, quae inedita ex codice Arretino deprompsit Ioh. Franciscus Gamurrini, accedit *Petri Diaconi Liber de Locis Sanctis*, Biblioteca dell' Accademia Storico-Giuridica, volume quarto, Romae.

Silvia (1897) *The Pilgrimage of S. Silvia of Aquitania to the Holy Places (circ. 385 A.D.)*, translated, with introduction and notes by John H. Bernard, London 1896, in *The Library of the Palestine Pilgrims' Text Society*, volume I, London.

Skeat, T.C. (2000) 'The Last Chapter in the History of the Codex Sinaiticus', *Novum Testamentum* XLII, 4, 313–15.

Skrobucha, Heinz (1966) *Sinai*, with photographs by George W. Allan, translated by Geoffrey Hunt, London.

Sōphronios, Archimandritēs kai Skeuophylax Hieras Monēs Sina (1998) «Ἡμερολόγιον εὐρέσως τῶν νέων εὐρημάτων τοῦ Σινᾶ» in Ἱερὰ Μονὴ καὶ Ἀρχιεπισκοπὴ Σινᾶ, *Τὰ Νέα Εὐρήματα*, Athens.

Sōtēriou, Geōrgios and Maria Sōtēriou (1956) *Εἰκόνες τῆς Μονῆς Σινᾶ*, τόμος πρῶτος – *Εἰκόνες*, Collection de l'Institut Français d'Athènes 100, Athens.

Sōtēriou, Geōrgios and Maria Sōtēriou (1958) *Εἰκόνες τῆς Μονῆς Σινᾶ*, τόμος β΄ – *Κείμενον*, Collection de l'Institut Français d'Athènes 102, Athens.

Sozomen (1891) 'The Ecclesiastical History of Sozomen, comprising a History of the Church, from A.D. 323 to A.D. 425', translated from the Greek, revised by Chester D. Hartranft, in Henry Wace and Philip Schaff (supervisors), *A Select Library of Nicene and Post-Nicene Fathers of the Christian Church*, second series, translated into English with prolegomena and explanatory notes, volume II. Socrates, Sozomenus: Church Histories, Oxford and New York.

Sozomenus (1960) *Kirchengeschichte*, herausgeben im Auftrage der Kommission für Spätantike Religionsgeschichte der Deutschen Akademie der Wissenschaften zu Berlin von Joseph Bidez, eingeleitet, zum Druck Besorgt und mit Registern Versehen von Günther Christian Hansen, Berlin.

Stacquez, Le Docteur (1865) *L'Égypte, la Basse Nubie et le Sinaï. Relation d'après des notes tenues pendant le voyage que son Altesse Royale Monseigneur Le Duc de Brabant fit dans ces contrées, en 1862 et 1863*, Liége.

Stanley, Arthur Penrhyn (1887) *Sinai and Palestine in Connection with their History*, London, second edition.

Starkey, Janet and Okasha El Daly, editors (2000) *Desert Travellers from Herodotus to T.E. Lawrence*, Durham.

Starkey, Paul and Janet Starkey, editors (1998) *Travellers in Egypt*, London.

Stephens, John Lloyd (1837) *Incidents of Travel in Egypt, Arabia Petræa, and the Holy Land, by an American*, vol. I, New York.

Stephens, John Lloyd (1970) *Incidents of Travel in Egypt, Arabia Petræa, and the Holy Land, edited, and with an Introduction by Victor Wolfgang von Hagen*, Norman Oklahoma.

Stern, S.M. (1960) 'A Fāṭimid Decree of the Year 524 / 1130' in *BSOAS* 23, issue 3, 439–55.

Stern, S.M. (1964a) *Fāṭimid Decrees. Original Documents from the Fāṭimid Chancery*, London.

Stern, S.M. (1964b) 'Petitions from the Ayyūbid Period', *BSOAS* 27, issue 1, 1–32.

Stern, S.M. (1966) 'Petitions from the Mamlūk Period (Notes on the Mamlūk Documents from Sinai)', *BSOAS* 29, issue 2, 233–76.

Stochove, Vincent *et al.* (Gilles Fermanel and Robert Fauvel) (1975) *Voyage en Egypte. Vincent Stochove, Gilles Fermanel, Robert Fauvel 1631*, présentation et notes de Baudouin van de Walle, Le Caire.

Stone, Michael E., editor (1982a) *The Armenian Inscriptions from the Sinai. With Appendices on the Georgian and Latin Inscriptions by Michael van Esbroeck and William Adler*, Cambridge Massachusetts.

Stone, Michael E. (1982b) 'Sinai Armenian Inscriptions', *BiblArch* 45 number 1 (winter), 27–31.

Stone, Michael E., editor (1992a) *Rock Inscriptions and Graffiti Project: Catalogue of Inscriptions*, volume 1: *Inscriptions 1–3000*, Society of Biblical Literature. Resources for Biblical Study number 28, Atlanta.

Stone, Michael E., editor (1992b) *Rock Inscriptions and Graffiti Project: Catalogue of Inscriptions*, volume 2: *Inscriptions 3001–6000*, Society of Biblical Literature. Resources for Biblical Study number 29, Atlanta.

Strauss, Friedrich Adolph (1848) *Sinai und Golgatha. Reise in das Morgenland*, Berlin.

Strauss, Frederick Adolph (1849) *Sinai and Golgotha: A Journey in the East. With an Introduction by Henry Stebbing*, London.

Suchen, Ludolph von (1848) *Ueber ältere Pilgerfahrten nach Jerusalem, mit besonderer Rücksicht auf Ludolph's von Suchen Reisebuch des heiligen Landes. Eine historisch-litterarische Abhandlung, nach Handschriften und alten Drucken, von Ferdinand Deycks*, Münster.

Sudheim, Ludolphus de (1884) '*De Itinere Terre Sancte.* Introduction critique de G.A. Neumann', *AOL* II, Documents III. Voyages, 305–77.

Sudheim, Ludolf von (1937) *Ludolfs von Sudheim Reise ins Heilige Land nach der Hamburger Handschrift Herausgegeben*, akademische Abhandlung von Ivar v. Stapelmohr, Lund.

Sutton, Arthur W. (1913) *My Camel Ride from Suez to Mount Sinai*, London.

Swanson, Mark N. (2001) 'The Martyrdom of ᶜAbd al-Masīḥ, Superior of Mount Sinai (Qays al-Ghassānī)' in David Thomas, editor, *Syrian Christians under Islam. The First Thousand Years*, Leiden, 107–29.

Symeon Logothetes, cognomento Metaphrastes (1864a) 'Vita et conversatio et martyrium Ss. Martyrum Galactionis et Epistemes', *PG* CXVI, Parisiis, 93–108.

Symeon Logothetes, cognomento Metaphrastes (1864b) 'Martyrium Sanctæ et Magnæ Martyris Æcaterinæ', *PG* CXVI, Parisiis, 275–302.

Synaxarium (1902) 'Synaxarium Ecclesiae Constantinopolitanae e Codice Sirmondiano nunc Berolinensi adiectis Synaxariis Selectis', opera et studio Hippolyti Delehaye, *Acta Sanctorum* Novembris, Bruxellis.

Synaxis (1998) Σύναξις παντῶν τῶν Σιναϊτῶν Ἁγίων, εἰσαγωγὴ ὑπὸ Ἀρχιεπισκόπου Σινᾶ Δαμιανοῦ, Ἀκολουθίαι ὑπὸ Χαραλάμπους Μπούσια κ.ἄλ., Athens.

Tafur, Pero (1874) *Andanças é Viajes de Pero Tafur por diversas partes del mundo avidos (1435–1439)*, Coleccion de Libros Españoles, Raros ó Curiosos, tomo octavo, Madrid.

Tafur, Pero (1926) *Travels and Adventures 1435–1439, Translated and Edited with an Introduction by Malcolm Letts*, London.

Tafur (1934) *Andanças e Viajes de Pero Tafur por diversas Partes del Mundo Avidos (1435–1439), estudio preliminar, glosario e índice geografico por José María Ramos*, Madrid.

Taifel, Giovanni Christophoro (1598) *Il Viaggio del Molto Illvstre Signor. Giovanni Christophoro Taifel, Barone in Gunderstorff Austriaco, fatto di Constantinopoli verso Leuante*, Vienna.

Talbot, Alice-Mary (2008) 'Pilgrimage in the Eastern Mediterranean between the 7th and 15th centuries' in *Egeria* 2008, 37–46.

Tarnanidēs, Iōannēs (1988) *Τα ευρεθέντα το έτος 1975 Σλαβικά χειρόγραφα στη Μονή Αγ. Αικατερίνης του Σινά*, Thessaloniki.

Taylor, Jane (2001) *Petra and the Lost Kingdom of the Nabateans*, London and New York.

Tchernov, Eitan (1979) 'The Fauna. Meeting Point of Two Continents' in Rothenberg *et al.* 1979, 93–9.

Teodoreto (1986) *Storia dei monaci della Siria*, introduzione, traduzione e commento a cura di Salvatore di Meglio, Padova.

Tetsuo, Nishio (1992) *A Basic Vocabulary of the Bedouin Arabic Dialect of the Jbāli Tribe (Southern Sinai)*, Studia Sinaitica I, Tokyo.

Teufel, Hans Christoph (1972) 'Voyage de Hans Christoph Teufel 13 septembre–9 décembre 1588', traduit de l'italien par Nadine Sauneron, présentation et notes de Serge Sauneron, in *Voyages* 1972, 145–87.

Theodoret (1926) *Des Bischofs Theodoret von Cyrus Mönchsgeschichte*, aus dem Griechischen Übersetzt von Dr Konstantin Gutberlet, München.

Théodoret de Cyr (1977) *Histoire des moines de Syrie 'Histoire Philothée' I–XIII*, introduction, texte critique, traduction, notes par Pierre Canivet et Alice Leroy-Molinghen, Paris.

Theodoret of Cyrrhus (1985) *A History of the Monks of Syria*, translated with an introduction and notes by R.M. Price, Kalamazoo.

Theodosius (1965) 'Theodosii De Situ Terrae Sanctae', cura et studio P. Geyer, *CCSL* CLXXV (*Itineraria et alia Geographica*): II, Turnholti, 111–25.

Thevet, André (1984) *Voyages en Egypte 1549–1552*, présentation et notes de Frank Lestringant, Le Caire.

Thietmar, Magister (1936) *Een Pelgrimage naar den Sinaï Anno 1217 door Dr. Joh. de Groot en Dr. G.S. Overdiep*, Rotterdam.

Thietmarus, Magister (1857) *Peregrinatio. Ad fidem codicis Hamburgensis cum aliis libris manuscriptis collati edidit annotatione illustravit codicum recensum scripturae discrepantiam indicem rerum et verborum adiecit J.C.M. Laurent*, Hamburgi.

Thompson, Charles *et al.* (1977) *A View of the Holy Land, its Present Inhabitants, Their Manners and Customs, Polity and Religion. Antiquities and Natural History of Egypt, Asia, and Arabia; with a Curious Description of Jerusalem, as It Now Appears, and Other Parts of the World Mentioned in the Scriptures. Interspersed with Remarks, Notes, and References of Modern Travellers; Together with Historical, Geographical, and Miscellaneous Notes*, New York (reprint of the Wheeling 1850 edition).

Thompson, Thomas L. (1975) *The Settlement of Sinai and the Negev in the Bronze Age*, Beihefte zum Tübinger Atlas des Vorderen Orients Reihe B (Geisteswissenschaften) Nr 8, Wiesbaden.

Tilley, Christopher (1994) *A Phenomenology of Landscape. Places, Paths and Monuments*, Oxford / Providence.

Tischendorf, Constantinus (1846) *Monumenta sacra inedita sive reliquiae antiquissimae textus Novi Testamenti Graeci ex novem plus mille annorum codicibus per Europam dispersis*, Lipsiae.

Tischendorf, Constantinus (1862) *Bibliorum Codex Sinaiticus Petropolitanus [...] Ex tenebris protraxit, in Europam transtulit, ad iuvandas atque illustrandas sacras litteras edidit Constantinus Tischendorf*, Petropoli / Leipzig.

Tischendorf, Constantin (1863) *Die Anfechtungen der Sinai-Bibel*, Leipzig.

Tobler, Titus and Augustus Molinier, editors (1879) *Itinera Hierosolymitana et Descriptiones Terrae Sanctae Bellis Sacris Anteriora & Latina Lingua Exarata*, I, Genevae.

Tomadakes, Nikolaos V. (1990) «Ἱστορικὸ διάγραμμα» in Manaphēs 1990, 12–17.

Translatio (1903) Albertus Poncelet, 'Sanctae Catharinae Virginis et Martyris Translatio et Miracula Rotomagensia Saec. XI', *AB* 22, 423–38.

Tsafrir, Yoram, editor (1993a) *Ancient Churches Revealed*, Jerusalem.

Tsafrir, Yoram (1993b) 'The Development of Ecclesiastical Architecture in Palestine' in Tsafrir 1993a, 1–16.

Tsafrir, Yoram (1993c) 'Monks and Monasteries in Southern Sinai' in Tsafrir 1993a, 315–33.

Tshelebi, Evliya (1980) *Evliya Tshelebi's Travels in Palestine (1684–1650)*, translated from Turkish by St.H. Stephan, Jerusalem.

Turner, Victor and Edith Turner (1978) *Image and Pilgrimage in Christian Culture. Anthropological Perspectives*, New York.

Turner, William (1820) *Journal of a Tour in the Levant*, volume II, London.

Tyrwhitt, Reverend R. St. John (1864) 'Sinai' in Francis Galton, editor, *Vacation Tourists and Notes of Travel in 1862–3*, London and Cambridge, 327–56.

Usick, Patricia (1998) 'William John Bankes' Collection of Drawings of Egypt and Nubia' in Starkey & Starkey 1998, 51–60.

Vaczek, Louis and Gail Buckland (1981) *Travelers in Ancient Lands. A Portrait of the Middle East, 1839–1919*, Boston and New York.

Vaux, Roland de (1978a) *The Early History of Israel to the Exodus and Covenant of Sinai*, translated by David Smith, London.

Vaux, Roland de (1978b) *The Early History of Israel to the Period of the Judges*, translated by David Smith, London.

Venturi, Adolfo (1885) 'Zur Geschichte der Kunstsammlungen Kaiser Rudolf II', *Repertorium für Kunstwissenschaft* VIII, 1–23.

Vilnay, Zev (1963) *The Holy Land in Old Prints and Maps*, rendered from the Hebrew by Esther Vilnay in collaboration with Max Nurock, Jerusalem.

Vita Pauli (1892) 'Vita S. Pauli Iunioris in Monte Latro cum interpretatione Latina Iacobi Sirmondi S.I.', *AB* 11, 5–74.

Vives, José (1938) 'Andanças e Viajes de un hidalgo español (1436–1439) con una descripción de Roma', *Gesammelte Aufsätze zur Kulturgeschichte Spaniens* 7, 127–206.

Voyages (1972) H.-L. von Lichtenstein, S. Kiechel, H.-Chr. Teufel, G.-Chr. Fernberger, R. Lubenau, J. Miloïti, *Voyages en Egypte pendant les années 1587–1588*, récits traduits de l'allemand par Ursula Castel et traduits de l'italien par Nadine Sauneron, présentation, notes et index de Serge Sauneron, Le Caire.

Walser, Gerold (1979) 'Battlefields and Roads. From Romano-Byzantine Days to the Present' in Rothenberg *et al.* 1979, 221–36.

Walsh, Christine (2007) *The Cult of St Katherine of Alexandria in Early Medieval Europe*, Aldershot.

Warburton, Eliot (1845) *The Crescent and the Cross; or, Romance and Realities of Eastern Travel*, vol. I, London.

Watson, Oliver (2004) *Ceramics from Islamic Lands*, London.

Weeks, Emily M. (2001) 'John Frederick Lewis (1805–1876): mythology as biography, or dis-orienting the "languid Lotus-eater"' in Searight & Wagstaff 2001, 177–96.

Weill, Raymond (1904) *Recueil des Inscriptions Égyptiennes du Sinaï. Bibliographie, Texte, Traduction et Commentaire. Précédé de la Géographie, de l'Histoire et la Bibliographie des Établissements Égyptiens de la Péninsule*, Paris.

Weitzmann, Kurt (1966) 'Various Aspects of Byzantine Influence on the Latin Countries from the Sixth to the Twelfth Century', *DOP* 20, 1–24, figures 1–41.

Weitzmann, Kurt (1980) 'The Arts' in Galey 1980, 81–159.

Weitzmann, Kurt W. (1982a) *Studies in the Arts at Sinai*, Princeton.

Weitzmann, Kurt W. (1982b) 'The Mosaic in St. Catherine's Monastery on Mount Sinai' in Weitzmann 1982a, 5–18.

Weitzmann, Kurt W. (1982c) 'The Jephthah Panel in the Bema of the Church of St. Catherine's Monastery on Mount Sinai' in Weitzmann 1982a, 63–80.

Weitzmann, Kurt and George Galavaris (1990) *The Monastery of Saint Catherine at Mount Sinai: The Illuminated Greek Manuscripts*. volume One: *From the Ninth to the Twelfth Century*, Princeton.

Wellsted, Lieut. J.R. (1838) *Travels in Arabia*, volume II. *Sinai; Survey of the Gulf of Akabah; Coasts of Arabia and Nubia, &c., &c., &c.*, London.

Wellsted, J.R. (1842) *Reisen in Arabien. Deutsche Bearbeitung herausgeben mit berichtigenden und erläuternden Anmerkungen und einem Excurs über himjaritische Inschriften von Dr. E. Rödiger*, zweiter Band, Halle.

Wilken, Friedrich (1813) *Geschichte der Kreuzzüge nach morgennländischen und abendländischen Berichten*, zwenter Theil, Leipzig.

Wilken, Robert L. (1996) 'Christian Pilgrimage to the Holy Land' in Rosovsky 1996, 117–35.

Wilkinson, Sir Gardner (1843) *Modern Egypt and Thebes: Being a Description of Egypt; Including the Information Required for Travellers in that Country*, volume II, London.

Wilkinson, Sir Gardner (1847) *Hand-book for Travellers in Egypt; Including Descriptions of the Course of the Nile to the Second Cataract, Alexandria, Cairo, the Pyramids, and Thebes, the Overland Transit to India, the Peninsula of Mount Sinai, the Oases, &c. Being a New Edition, corrected and condensed, of 'Modern Egypt and Thebes'*, London.

Wilkinson, John (1977) *Jerusalem Pilgrims before the Crusades*, Warminster.

Williams, Caroline (1998) 'A Nineteenth-Century Photographer: Francis Frith' in Starkey & Starkey 1998, 168–78.

Wilson, C.W. and H.S. Palmer, under the direction of Henry James (1869) *Ordnance Survey of the Peninsula of Sinai*, in three parts, part I: *Account of the Survey (With Illustrations)*, part II: *Maps, Plans, and Sections*, part III: *Photographic Views* (I–III), Southampton.

Wolff, Anne (2000) 'Two Pilgrims to Saint Catherine's Monastery: Niccolò di Poggibonsi and Christopher Harant' in Starkey & El Daly 2000, 33–58.

Wolff, Anne (2003) *How Many Miles to Babylon? Travels and Adventures to Egypt and Beyond, 1300 to 1640*, Liverpool.

Wolff, Joseph (1824) *Missionary Journal and Memoir of the Rev. Joseph Wolf, Missionary to the Jews. Written by Himself. Revised and Edited by John Bayford*, London.

Wolff, Joseph (1827a) *The Promotion of Christianity amongst the Jews. The Substance of Two Speeches Delivered by the Rev. Joseph Wolff, at the Meetings of the Bath and Bristol Auxiliary Societies for Promoting Christianity amongst the Jews. In January, 1827. Being a General Outline of his Missionary Tour, through Palestine, Egypt, Arabia, Mesopotamia, Persia and Turkey*, Bristol-Bath-London.

Wolff, Joseph (1827b) *Sketch of the Life and Journal of the Rev. J. Wolff, Missionary to Palestine and Persia*, Norwich.

Wolff, Joseph (1860) *Travels and Adventures of the Rev. Joseph Wolff*, volume I, London, second edition.

Wolska, Wanda (1962) *La Topographie Chrétienne de Cosmas Indicopleustès: Théologie et Science au VIᵉ siècle*, Paris.

Yumiba Noritomo (1984) 'Fustat shutsudo no tōhen ichiranhyō' in Idemitsu Museum of Arts, *The Inter-Influence of Ceramic Art in East and West*, Tokyo.

Zachos, Agamemnōn (1937) Σινὰ καὶ Ἁγία Αἰκατερίνη. Ἐντυπώσεις καὶ μελέται (μετὰ πολλῶν πρωτοτύπων εἰκόνων), Athens.

Zafrir, H. *et al.* (J. Kronfeld, E. Mazor) (1991) 'The geochemical classification of southern Sinai waters' in G. Weinberger, editor, *Israel Geological Society Annual Meeting, 1991*, AKKO 22–25 April, 124.

Zimmermann, Heinrich (1905) 'Das Inventar der Prager Schatz- und Kunstkammer vom 6. Dezember 1621 nach Akten des K. und K. Reichsfinanzarchivs in Wien', *Jahrbuch der Kunsthistorischen Sammlungen des Allerhöchsten Kaiserhauses* XXV, Teil II, XIII–LXXV.

Index

For individual Sinaitic locations, see under 'place names'.
Page numbers in *italics* refer to illustrations